DINKY TOYS

DR. EDWARD FORCE

REVISED 4TH EDITION

4880 Lower Valley Road, Atglen, PA 19310 USA

#F344
Plymouth Belvedere $1.50
Length 4¼"

Dear Dinky Toy Enthusiast: *April, 1999*

Thank you for your interest in becoming a member of the international DINKY TOY CLUB of AMERICA (formerly the Highland Dinky Toy Club). Let us tell you about the Club:

WHO WE ARE: The Dinky Toy Club of America was founded by two individuals in the Spring of 1994 to further the collecting interest of Dinky Toys. We sought to continue and grow the interest of collecting Dinky Toys for the enjoyment of remembering what it was like collecting Dinkys as kids. To date, we have over 400 members throughout the United States, Canada, France, England, the Netherlands, New Zealand and Australia. This network of collectors has become the hub for some fascinating dialogue and trades of Dinkys among the members.

WHAT THE CLUB DOES: The Dinky Toy Club of America publishes and mails out to its members a Club Newsletter four (4) times a year - March, June, September, and December. The Newsletter contains sections such as "Dr. Dinky" - dealing with questions club members may have on history, identification numbers, paint, engineering specs, etc. relating to the toys; articles written by "Mr. Dinky" on historical perspectives of the Meccano era as well as other timely news; a *"Wanted/ 4 Sale"* section for members to seek, swap or sell pieces to other members; inclusion of periodic color, frame ready photos of selected Dinky pieces; a Technical Section that deals with tips on restoration, paints, parts, etc.; and news of annual meetings for members to get together to chat and see other members collections. This year we are in our 5th Annual Meet. We also sponsor a World Wide Web site for access to the internet for Dinky Collectors.

WHAT DOES IT COST? If you are interested in becoming a member of the Club, please write to the DTCA for membership dues or complete the attached Membership Application found on the following page and mail to: The DINKY TOY CLUB of AMERICA, P.O. Box 11, Highland, Maryland, 20777. We hope to see you as a member and look forward to chatting with you in the near future.

Sincerely,

Jerry

Jerry Fralick
Mr. Dinky (Mem # 1)

P.O. BOX 11, HIGHLAND, MARYLAND, 20777 -- TEL. & FAX: 301-854-2217
http://www.erols.com/dinkytoy

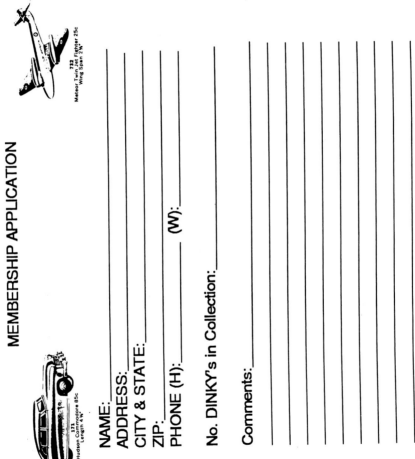

DINKY TOY CLUB OF AMERICA

MEMBERSHIP APPLICATION

171
Hudson Commodore 85c
Length 4¾"

732
Meteor Twin Jet Fighter 25c
Wing Span 2¾"

NAME: _____

ADDRESS: _____

CITY & STATE: _____

ZIP: _____

PHONE (H): _____ (W): _____

No. DINKY's in Collection: _____

Comments: _____
_____
_____
_____
_____
_____
_____
_____
_____
_____
_____

P.O. BOX 11, Highland, MD 20777
Tel. & Fax No.: 301-854-2217
http://www.erols.com/dinkytoy

Revised price guide: 1999
Copyright © 1996 & 1999 by Dr. Edward Force
Library of Congress Catalog Card Number: 99-62417

ISBN: 0-7643-0883-1
Printed in China

ACKNOWLEDGMENTS

I want to thank Jerry Fralick founder of the DINKY TOY CLUB of AMERICA (DTCA), for lending his assistance and knowledge of today's collectible market in revising the fourth edition of this price guide based on prices obtained from toy shows, auctions and internet sales. Again, many thanks go out to Peter Schiffer for encouraging me to revise this guide and for publishing it. To all the collectors who make this guide very special.

The terms "Dinky Toys", "Dinky Supertoys", "Modeled Miniatures", "Dublo Dinky Toys", "Speedwheels" and other terms used to refer to various special features of Dinky Toys have been the property of those firms that have owned the name of Dinky Toys. The names of real motor vehicles modeled in miniature by Dinky Toys, and of actual products named in logo designs, are copyrighted by the manufacturers of those vehicles and other products.

Published by Schiffer Publishing Ltd.
4880 Lower Valley Road
Atglen, PA 19310
Phone: (610) 593-1777; Fax: (610) 593-2002
E-mail: Schifferbk@aol.com
Please visit our web site catalog at **www.schifferbooks.com**

In Europe, Schiffer books are distributed by Bushwood Books
6 Marksbury Avenue Kew Gardens
Surrey TW9 4JF England
Phone: 44 (0)181 392-8585; Fax: 44 (0)181 392-9876
E-mail: Bushwd@aol.com

This book may be purchased from the publisher.
Include $3.95 for shipping. Please try your bookstore first.
We are interested in hearing from authors with book ideas on related subjects.
You may write for a free printed catalog.

Contents

Introduction

The purpose of this book is to offer the hobbyist a concise but thorough source of information on Dinky Toys products. The history of Dinky Toys has been told thoroughly in other books, especially in terms of the manufacturers and their corporate history; we shall confine ourselves here to those historical details which bear more or less directly on the models themselves.

The first Dinky Toys cars came on the market in December of 1933, but they were not called Dinky Toys until April of 1934. Until then they were Modelled Miniatures, sold under the name of their original manufacturers, the Frank Hornby firm best known for its electric trains. The Modelled Miniatures were, in fact, intended for use as accessories on model railroad platforms, and included figures of people and domestic animals, mailboxes, railroad signals, and even some non-motorized railroad rolling stock, in addition to the first of many motor vehicles. One of the most unusual early models was a signboard, carried by two painters with buckets and brushes, advertising Hall's Distemper—the whitewash-like stuff that painters apply, not what the vet gives shots for!

Production of Dinky Toys vehicles began more or less simultaneously in Liverpool and in Bobigny, France. British and French Dinky Toys were more or less closely related throughout their history, occasionally sharing models, but more often (and particularly in the early days) producing different though generically related series of models. More and more Dinky Toys were produced by both branches

through the late Thirties; then World War II brought production to a standstill for several years. By this time both branches had produced cars, trucks, buses, military vehicles, aircraft, ships and accessories of various kinds. Among the most popular models were the British branch's 38 series of sports cars and 39 series of American cars. All six of the 39 cars came out before the war, but only three of the 38 series did; one which did not, and in fact was never issued, was the legendary Triumph Dolomite; its place was taken by an Armstrong-Siddeley after the war.

It appears that remnants of prewar stocks were put on the market in time for the 1945 Christmas season, but no new production took place until 1946, when the last three 38 series sports cars joined the prewar trio. Numerous prewar models were now reissued, at first completely unchanged. One of the first notable changes occurred later in 1946: both branches had used plain cast wheel hubs and rubber tires until then; now British Dinky Toys began to appear with somewhat more realistic cast hubs with a raised central section, while a shortage of rubber compelled the French branch to produce one-piece all-metal wheels (including tires) for a time. The first entirely new postwar model, appropriately enough, a Jeep, appeared in 1946.

Since prewar dies and supplies had to be used for a while, there is no really clearcut dividing line between prewar and postwar production, but a number of changes (beginning with the wheel varieties already mentioned) took place during the Forties. In 1947 the first Dinky Supertoys were issued. These models of large vehicles had their own type of diecast wheel hubs, with a partly concave pattern, and treaded rubber tires. Until this point, all Dinky tires had been slick, but in the next few years a variety of treaded rubber tires came into being for cars and commercial vehicles alike.

Both branches expanded their production to include many interesting new models of various types, but they still used the original catalog numbering system of one, two or three digits followed in most cases by a letter. When a series (an excellent example is the 28 series of delivery vans) ran out of letters, it was continued on a three-digit (in this case 280) basis, and the first Dinky Supertoys were given three-digit 500-series numbers, a hint of what was to come in the Fifties: British Dinky Toys were changed to a three-digit numeral system in 1954, with some models not actually renumbered until a year or two later. French Dinky Toys changed to a similar all-numeral system during 1959. The 500 and 800 numbers were reserved for the French models, and the British system was prepared for this change a few years earlier, when the 500 series of Supertoys was renumbered with new 900 catalog numbers.

The British number change began at the start of 1954, and seems to have been finished by the start of 1956. Most numbers were changed as of January 1954; the 500 series moved to 900 numbers a year later, and some of them were shifted to 400 series numbers by the beginning of 1956. As is well known, the 1954 British Dinky catalog gave both numbers so everybody would know what was what.

French Dinky Toys, on the other hand, were renumbered during 1959. Thus any French model introduced early in 1959 had an old number briefly before the new system was introduced.

In the British system, one- and two-digit numbers were used for accessories, 100's for cars, 200 to 249 for racing and (later) sports cars, 250 to 299 for public service vehicles (buses, fire trucks, police cars, ambulances, road rollers, garbage trucks, etc.), 300's for agricultural vehicles (and much later for character cars), 400's for light and medium trucks, 600's for military vehicles, 700's for aircraft and accessories, and 900 numbers for Supertoys, including a few large aircraft. The French Dinky 500 numbers were used for cars and small trucks, with military vehicles, aircraft, Supertoys and accessories in the 800 series.

This era saw many changes in Dinky Toys. Bright two-tone color schemes for cars proliferated in 1956; a few, of course, had been used previously, including the last American issues of the 38 series. In that same year, Corgi Toys came on the market, equipped from the start with clear plastic windows, which appeared in Dinky Toys starting in 1958. Suspension was introduced in 1959, fingertip steering in 1960, and a wealth of moving and detailed parts in the Sixties. And in 1957 the first Dublo Dinky Toys appeared, intended (as the "Dublo" name implies) for use on OO gauge railroad platforms. Though a few small-scale models had been produced since the Thirties, most Dinky Toys had been built more or less to O gauge: 1/43 to 1/48 scale, with larger vehicles generally made to a slightly smaller scale so as not to look excessively big beside models of smaller vehicles. The Dublo series never really caught on and was withdrawn after a few years, leaving that field to Matchbox and other firms for the time being, while Dinky and Corgi competed for dominance in the O-gauge area.

In 1963 the British branch of Dinky Toys was bought by the Tri-Ang firm, and in the same year the first Dinky antique car, a Model T Ford, were issued. Dinky Toys' horizons were expanding in numerous ways, for in 1965 six models of American cars were made for Dinky in Hong Kong. Another Hong Kong range, the small-scale Mini-Dinky Toys, appeared in 1968, with each model sold in its own plastic garage. Most of the castings were completely of Hong Kong origin, though six pieces of heavy equipment originated with Mercury of Italy, were later produced by the unrelated US-Canadian firm of Mercury Industries, then by Gibbs of Ohio, and subsequently by

Universal of Hong Kong. Two racing cars in the series were made by Best Box (sometimes written "Bestbox") of The Netherlands; this firm, now called Efsi, Holland or Oto, is actually a government agency that hires handicapped workers.

During the Sixties both Dinky and Corgi began to make their models to a larger scale, approximately 1/35, instead of 1/43. While they had their reasons for doing so, many of us collectors wish they had not, for the newer models just don't fit in with the old ones—and they take up more shelf space too! Nevertheless, it happened.

Late in 1967 the diecast toy market was strongly influenced by the first Mattel Hot Wheels, making it necessary for numerous other firms, including Dinky Toys, to develop similar wheels. Dinky Speedwheels first appeared in 1969, and this change was paralleled by others that brought more realism, more gimmicks, more play value, and more character cars based on children's television shows and films. Speedwheels, usually with chromed hub patterns, appeared on a variety of vehicles, replacing to some extent the many realistic cast hubs that had begun to appear a few years before, and models of real cars and trucks were joined in growing numbers not only by motor vehicles for Lady Penelope, Parsley, Candy, Andy and the Bearandas and their ilk, but by a number of outer-space characters and vehicles as well, most notably those of the popular Star Trek program. This trend, which had begun with Santa Claus and the Dinky Beats, kept growing, to the dismay of those who prefer scale models of real road vehicles.

But all these modes were not enough to keep Dinky Toys solvent. French production ceased as of 1972, though the Spanish firm of Pilen manufactured some French Dinky Toys later in the Seventies, and Solido made an effort to do the same in 1981. The British branch struggled on until 1980, farming out some production to Polistil in Italy as well as to the Universal firm of Hong Kong.

Since then the name of Dinky Toys has changed hands at least two more times, and now and then Hong Kong products have appeared with the Dinky Toys name on their bubblepacks. In 1987 the Kenner-Parker firm, whose branches include Tonka Toys, sold the Dinky Toys name to Universal International of Hong Kong, already the owner of another time-honored and originally British trade name: Matchbox. Soon afterward, Kenner-Parker took over Polistil and acquired some of the last old Dinky Toys dies. Other dies had previously been sold to a firm in India, which markets them as Nicky Toys, and for a time some models were produced in South America as well.

Late in 1987 Universal brought the Dinky Toys name back to some semblance of life by applying it to new color variations of six Matchbox cars. The firm subsequently announced that the name would be used for a new series of cars of the Fifties. These cars are produced today under the Matchbox name operated by Tyco. Some new models were introduced in 1996 but were too late in production to be priced into this guide.

Row 1. 22g **Streamlined Tourer**, 22h **Streamlined Saloon**, 22f **Tank**, 22c **Motor Truck** (x2).

Row 2. 14a **Triporteur** (x2), 22e **Tractor**, 22s **Searchlight Lorry**, 26 French **Railcar**.

Row 3. 24d **French Vogue Saloon**, 24e **Super Streamlined Saloon**, 24h **2-Seat Sports Tourer**, 26 British **Railcar**.

Row 4. 24k **Peugeot 402**, 29a **Double Decker Bus**, 27 **Tramcar**, 24l **Peugeot 402 Taxi** (x2).

Row 1. 23a **Racing Car** (x3), 23m **Thunderbolt.**
Row 2. 23b **Hotchkiss** (x2), 23c **Mercedes-Benz** (x2).
Row 3. 23b **Renault**, 23d **Auto-Union** (x3).
Row 4. 23e **Speed of the Wind** (x3), 23p **Gardner's MG.**

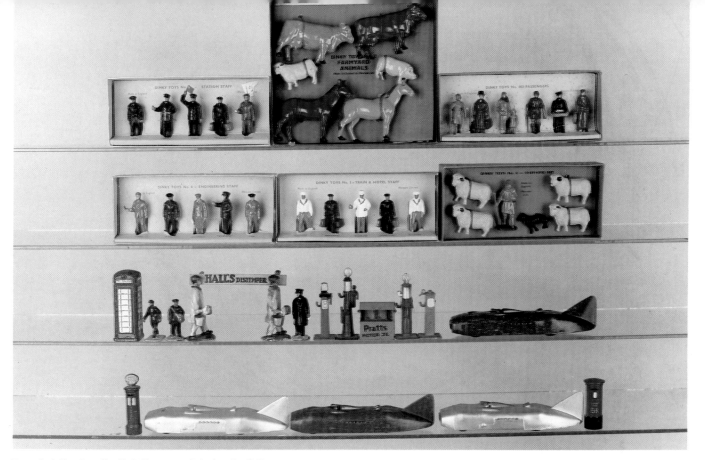

Row 1. 1 **Station Staff**, 2 **Farmyard Animals**, 3 **Passengers**.
Row 2. 4 **Engineering Staff**, 5 **Train & Hotel Staff**, 6 **Shepherd Set**.
Row 3. 12c **Telephone Box**, 12d **Telegraph Messenger**, 12e **Postman**, 13 **Hall's Distemper**, 13a **Cook's Man**, 49 **Petrol Pumps**, 23s **Streamlined Racing Car**.
Row 4. 12a **Pillar Box**, 23s **Streamlined Racing Car** (x3), 760 **Pillar Box**.

11

Row 1. 25e **Tipper** (x2), 25g **Trailer** (x2).
Row 2. 25h, 25k & 250 **Streamlined Fire Engine**, 25s **Six Wheel Wagon**.
Row 3. 28c **type 1, 2** and **3** (x2), and 280 **Delivery Vans**.
Row 4. 29b **Streamlined Bus** (x4) flanking 29c **Double Decker Bus**.

Row 1. 25a **Wagon** (2 French, 2 British).
Row 2. 25b **Covered Wagon** (2 French, 1 British), 25d **Tanker.**
Row 3. 25c **Flat Truck** (x2), 25f **Market Gardener's Van** (x2).
Row 4. 25d **Esso, Essolube, Petrol** and **Texaco Tankers.**

Row 1. 30a **Chrysler Airflow** (x2), 30g **Caravan** (x2).
Row 2. 30b **Rolls-Royce**, 30d **Vauxhall** (x3).
Row 3. 30c **Daimler** (x2), 30f **Ambulance** (x2).
Row 4. 30e **Breakdown Truck** (x2), 29d **Paris Bus** (x2).

Row 1. 33a **Mechanical Horse**, 33b **Flat**, 33c **Open**, 33d **Box**, 33e **Refuse** and 33f **Tank Trailers**.

Row 2. 33w/415 **Mechanical Horse and Trailer** (x4).

Row 3. 34a **Royal Air Mail Car**, 34b **Royal Mail Van** (x2), 35b/200 **Racer** (x3).

Row 4. 35a **Saloon Car** (x2), 35c **MG Sports Car** (x2), 35d **Austin 7** (x3), 35a **Simca 5**.

Row 1. 36a **Armstrong-Siddeley** (x2), 36b **Bentley** (x2).
Row 2. 36c **Humber** (x2), 36d **Rover** (x2).
Row 3. 36e **British Salmson 2-seat** (x2) and 36f **4-seat** (x2).
Row 4. 37a **Civilian Motorcyclist**, 37b **Police Motorcyclist**, 37c **Signal Corps Rider**, 36g **Taxi** (x2), 42b **Police Motorcycle Patrol**, 43b **RAC** and 44b **AA Motorcycle Patrols.**

Row 1. 38a **Frazer Nash-BMW** (x3), 38b **Sunbeam Talbot** (x2).
Row 2. 38c **Lagonda** (x2), 38d **Alvis** (x2).
Row 3. 38e **Armstrong-Siddeley** (x2), 38f **Jaguar** (x3).
Row 4. Front views of 36a **Armstrong-Siddeley**, 36b **Bentley**, 36d **Rover**, 25e **Tipper**, 38a, b, c, d, e & f (as above).

Row 1. 39a **Packard** (x3), 39b **Oldsmobile.**
Row 2. 39b **Oldsmobile** (x4).
Row 3. 39d **Buick** (x3), 39c **Lincoln Zephyr.**
Row 4. 39f **Studebaker** (x3), 39c **Lincoln Zephyr.**

Row 1. 151a **Medium Tank**, 151b **Covered Wagon**, 151c **Cooker Trailer**, 151d **Water Tank Trailer**, 60y **Fuel Tender**, 153 **Military Jeep**.
Row 2. 152a **Light Tank**, 152b **Reconnaissance Car**, 152c **Austin 7**, 162a **Light Dragon Tractor**, 162b **Trailer**, 162c **18-Pounder Gun**.
Row 3. 161a **Lorry Mounted Searchlight**, 161b **Anti Aircraft Gun**, 25j **Civilian Jeep** (x3).
Row 4. 39e **Chrysler** (x4).

Row 1. 501 **Foden Truck** (x2), 14a **BEV Electric Truck.**
Row 2. 502 **Foden Flat Truck** (x2), 14a **BEV Electric Truck.**
Row 3. 503 **Foden With Tailboard**, 504 **Foden Tanker**, 42a **Police Box** (x2).
Row 4. 25m/410 **Bedford Tipper** (x2), 25v/252 **Bedford Refuse Wagon** (x2).

Row 1. 521/921/409 **Bedford Articulated Truck**, 14c/401 **Fork Lift**, 25w/411 **Bedford Truck**.
Row 2. 511 **Guy 4-Ton Lorry** (x2), 551/951 **Trailer**.
Row 3. 512 **Guy Flat Truck** (x3).
Row 4. 513 **Guy With Tailboard** (x2), Type 1 & 2 **Guy** castings.

Row 1. 40e/153 **Standard Vanguard** (x3), 751/386 **Lawn Mower**, 105e/384 **Grass Cutter.**
Row 2. 40a/158 **Riley** (x2), 40b/151 **Triumph 1800** (x3).
Row 3. 40d/152 **Austin Devon** (x5).
Row 4. 105c/383 **Hand Truck** (x2) flanking 105a/381 **Garden Roller**, 105b/382 **Wheelbarrow**, 107a/385 **Sack Truck.**

Row 1. 27a/300 **Massey-Harris Tractor** (x2) pulling 27b/320 **Halesowen Trailer** and 27h/322 **Disc Harrow**, 27k/324 **Hay Rake.**
Row 2. 27c/321 **Spreader** (x2), 27n/301 **Field Marshal Tractor**, 27j/323 **Triple Gang Mower.**
Row 3. 27d/340 **Land Rover** and 27m/341 **Trailer** (x2), 27g/342 **Motocart.**
Row 4. 25p/251 **Road Roller**, 561/961 **Bulldozer**, 563/963 **Heavy Tractor**, 562/962 **Dump Truck.**

Row 1. 29d/570 **Paris Bus**, 29e **Isobloc Coach** (x2).
Row 2. 29e **Singledeck Bus** (x3), 27f/344 **Estate Car.**
Row 3. 29f/280 **Observation Coach** (x3), 29c **Double Decker Bus.**
Row 4. 29g/281 **Luxury Coach** (x2), 29c **Double Decker Bus** (with AEC, AEC Regent, Leyland and later AEC Regent front ends.

Row 1. 24n **Citroen 11bl** (x3), 47a, 47c/1 & 47c/2 **Traffic Signals.**
Row 2. 139b/171 **Hudson Commodore** (x4).
Row 3. 139a/170 **Ford Fordor** (x4).
Row 4. 139a/170 **Ford Fordor** (x2), 30h/253 **Daimler Ambulance** (x2).

Row 1. 25a **Ford Farm Truck**, 25h **Ford With Racks**, 25i **Ford Open Truck** (x2).
Row 2. 25j **Ford SNCF, Calberson & Grands Moulins de Paris Trucks**, 25m **Studebaker Dump Truck**.
Row 3. 25k **Studebaker Farm Truck**, 25l **Studebaker Covered Farm Truck**, 25m **Ford Dump Truck** (x2).
Row 4. 25o **Studebaker & Ford Milk Trucks**, 25p **Studebaker Open Truck**, 25s **Open** & 25t **Covered Trailers**.

Row 1. 30m/414 **Dodge Dump Truck** (x2), 30n/343 **Dodge Farm Truck** (x2).
Row 2. 25r/420 **Forward Control Truck** (x3), 30s/413 **Austin Covered Truck.**
Row 3. 30j/412 **Austin Truck** (x3), 30s/413 **Austin Covered Truck.**
Row 4. 25r **Studebaker Wrecker** (x2), 25u **Ford Esso Tanker**, 25v **Ford Garbage Truck.**

Row 1. 514 **Weetabix Van**, 571/971 **Coles Mobile Crane**, 514 **Slumberland Van**.
Row 2. 514/917 **Spratts Van**, 918 **Ever Ready Van**, 919 **Golden Shred Van**.
Row 3. 34c/492 **Loudspeaker Van** (x2), 531/417 **Leyland Comet** (x2).
Row 4. 532/418 **Leyland Comet** (x2), 533/419 **Leyland Cement Truck**.

Row 1. 25x/430 **Commer Wrecker** (x3), 30v/490-491 **Electric Dairy Van,** two logo types, front views.

Row 2. 30r/422 **Ford Thames** (x2), 30v/490-491 **Electric Dairy Van** (x2).

Row 3. 30p/440 **Studebaker Tanker** (2 Petrol, 2 Mobilgas).

Row 4. 441 **Castrol**, 442 **Esso** (x2) & 443 **National Benzole Tankers.**

Row 1. 40g/159 **Morris Oxford** (x5).
Row 2. 24q **Ford Vedette** (x3), 140b/156 **Rover 75.**
Row 3. 140b/156 **Rover 75** (x4).
Row 4. 40f/154 **Hillman Minx** (x5).

Row 1. 24r **Peugeot 203**, type 1 (x4).

Row 2. 24r **Peugeot 203**, type 2 (x2), 24t/535 **Citroen 2CV** (x3).

Row 3. 24s **Simca 8 Sports** (x3), 25y/405 **Universal Jeep** (x2).

Row 4. 24t/535 **Citroen 2CV**, rear view, 140a/106 **Austin Atlantic** (x3), 24s **Simca 8 Sports** with type 1 windshield.

Row 1. 31a/450 **Trojan Esso**, 31c/452 **Chivers**, 31b/451 **Dunlop**, 454 **Cydrax** & 455 **Brooke Bond Tea Vans**.
Row 2. 591 **AEC Shell Tanker**, 31d/453 **Trojan Oxo Van**, 991 **AEC Shell Tanker**.
Row 3. 32aj **Panhard Kodak Truck**, 30w/421 **Hindle Smart Helecs**, 31ab/575 **Panhard SNCF Truck**.
Row 4. 522/408 **Big Bedford** (x2) flanking 32c/576 **Panhard Esso Tanker**.

Row 1. 501/901 **Foden Open Truck**, 502/902 **Foden Flat Truck.**
Row 2. 503/903 **Foden Flat Truck With Tailboard** (x2).
Row 3. 505/905 **Foden Flat Truck With Chains** (x2).
Row 4. 504 **Foden Tank Truck**, 941 **Foden Mobilgas Tanker.**

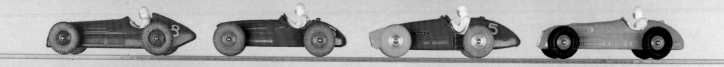

Row 1. 23f/232 **Alfa Romeo**, 23g/233 **Cooper-Bristol**, 23h/234 **Ferrari**, 23j/235 **HWM.**
Row 2. 23h **French** & 23k/230 **British Talbots**, 23j/511 **French Ferrari** showing patterned grille, 23n/231 **Maserati.**
Row 3. 24u **Simca Aronde** (x5, including type 1 & 2 grilles), 24ut **Simca Aronde Taxi.**
Row 4. 29h/282 **Duple Roadmaster Bus** (x4).

Row 1. 157 **Jaguar** (x4).
Row 2. 157 **Jaguar** (x2), 24x **Ford Vedette** (x2).
Row 3. 172 **Studebaker** (x4).
Row 4. 24v/538 **Buick** (x3), 271 **TS** & 272 **ANWB Motorcycles**.

Row 1. 582/982 **Pullmore Car Transporter**, 794/994 **Loading Ramp.**
Row 2. 980 & 581/981 **Horse Vans.**
Row 3. 979 **Race Horse Transporter**, 942 **Foden Regent Tanker.**
Row 4. 923 **Bedford Heinz Van (x2)**, 920 **Guy Heinz Van.**

Row 1. 470 **Austin Shell**, 471 **Nestle's** & 472 **Raleigh Vans**, 260 **Royal Mail Van**, 255 **Mersey Tunnel Van.**
Row 2. 480 **Bedford Kodak**, 481 **Ovaltine** & 482 **Dinky Toys Vans**, 25bv **Peugeot Mail** & 25bj **Mazda Vans.**
Row 3. 25c **Citroen Plain, Baroclem, Gervais (x2)** & **Cibie Vans.**
Row 4. 32d/899 **Delahaye Fire Truck**, 555/955 **Fire Engine**, 32e/583 **Berliet Fire Engine.**

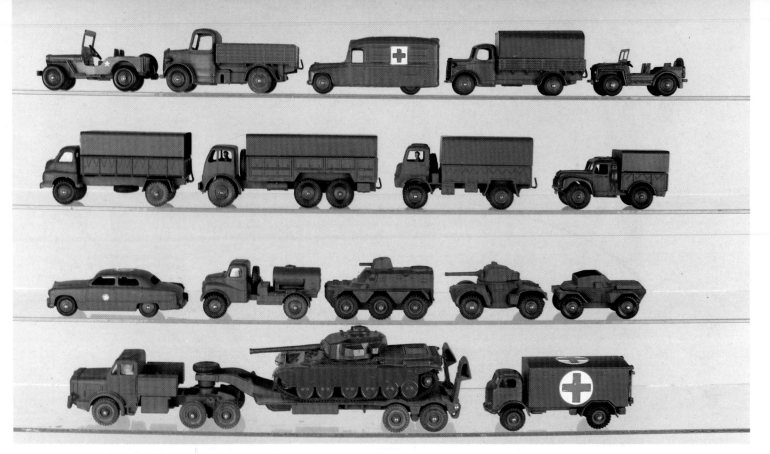

Row 1. 669 **Army Jeep**, 25wm **Bedford Army Truck**, 30hm/624 **Daimler Army Ambulance**, 30sm **Austin Army Truck**, 674 **Austin Champ.**

Row 2. 621 **Bedford**, 622 **Foden**, 623 **Bedford & 641 Humber Army Trucks.**

Row 3. 139am/675 **Ford Staff Car**, 643 **Water Tanker**, 676 **Personnel Carrier**, 670 **Armored Car**, 673 **Scout Car.**

Row 4. 660 **Tank Transporter**, 651 **Centurion Tank**, 626 **Army Ambulance.**

Row 1. 564/964 **Elevator Loader,** 752 **Goods Yard Crane.**
Row 2. 49d/592 **Esso Gas Pumps,** 965 **Euclid Dumper** (x2).
Row 3. 50/595 **Salev Crane,** 972 **Crane Truck.**

Row 1. 40j/161 **Austin Somerset** (x4), 109 **Austin-Healey.**
Row 2. 107 **Sunbeam Alpine** (x2), 108 **MG Midget** (x2), 109 **Austin-Healey.**
Row 3. 110 **Aston Martin** (x3), 111 **Triumph TR2** (x2).
Row 4. 133 **Cunningham** (x2), 132 **Packard** (x2).

Row 1. 131 **Cadillac Eldorado** (x2), 181 **Volkswagen** (x2).
Row 2. 24a/520 **Chrysler New Yorker** (x3), 181 **Volkswagen**.
Row 3. 162 **Ford Zephyr** (x3), 163 **Bristol**, 181 **Volkswagen**.
Row 4. 24y/540 **Studebaker Commander** (x4).

Row 1. 33c/579 **Simca Glass Truck (x2), 34b/581 Berliet Flat Truck With Container.**
Row 2. 33a **Simca Cargo Van, 33b/578 Simca Dump Truck, 33an Simca Bailly Van.**
Row 3. 35a/582 **Citroen Wrecker, 34a/580 Berliet Dump Truck, 465 Morris Capstan Van, 261 Telephone Van.**
Row 4. 283 **BOAC Coach, 29f/571 Chausson Bus, 70/810 Covered Trailer.**

Row 1. 688 **Artillery Tractor**, 687 **Gun Trailer**, 686 **Field Gun**, 692 **Medium Gun**, 693 **Howitzer**.
Row 2. 677 **Command Vehicle**, 642 **RAF Tanker**, 689 **Artillery Tractor**.
Row 3. 80d/818 **Berliet Army Truck**, 80e/819 **Howitzer**, 661 **Recovery Tractor**.
Row 4. 80a/815 **Panhard EBR**, 80c/817 **AMX Tank**, 80f/820 **Army Ambulance**, 80b/816 **Hotchkiss Jeep** (x2).

43

Row 1. 24c/522 **Citroen DS19** (x4).
Row 2. 236 **Connaught**, 190 **Caravan Trailer** (x2), 24xt **Ford Vedette Taxi.**
Row 3. 254 **Austin Taxi** (x4), 262 **VW Swiss Mail Car.**
Row 4. 24b/521 **Peugeot 403** (x2), 24z **Simca Versailles** (x2).

Row 1. 101 **Sunbeam Alpine** (x2), 102 **MG Midget** (x2), 129 **MG Midget**.
Row 2. 103 **Austin-Healey** (x2), 546 **Austin Healey**, 105 **Triumph TR2** (x2).
Row 3. 104 **Aston Martin** (x2), 506 **Aston Martin**, 238 **Jaguar D-type** (x2).
Row 4. 237 **Mercedes-Benz**, 182 **Porsche 356a** (x3), 22a/505 **Maserati**.

Row 1. 36a/897 **Willeme Log Truck**, 935 **Leyland Octopus With Chains**.
Row 2. 934 **Leyland Octopus** (x2).
Row 3. 943 **Leyland Esso Tanker**, 944 **Leyland Shell-BP Tanker**.
Row 4. 90/830 **Richier Road Roller**, 36b/896 **Willeme Semi-Trailer**.

Row 1. 062 **Singer**, 061 **Ford Prefect**, 063 **Commer Van**, 064 **Austin Lorry**, 065 **Morris Pickup**, 067 **Austin Taxi**, 068 **Royal Mail Van**.

Row 2. 066 **Bedford Flat Truck**, 069 **Tractor**, 070 **AEC Tanker**, 071 **VW Van**, 073 **Land Rover & Horse Trailer**.

Row 3. 072 **Bedford Articulated Truck** (x2), 076 **Lansing Bagnall Tractor & Trailer**, 24e/524 **Renault Dauphine**.

Row 4. 24e/524 **Renault Dauphine** (x5).

Row 1. 167 **AC Aceca** (x2), 164 **Vauxhall Velox** (x2), 239 **Vanwall.**
Row 2. 24d/523 **Plymouth Belvedere** (x3), 24f/525 **Peugeot 403 Break.**
Row 3. 169 **Studebaker Golden Hawk** (x2), 179 **Studebaker President** (x2).
Row 4. 173 **Nash Rambler** (x2), 174 **Hudson Hornet** (x2).

Row 1. 176 **Austin A105** (x4).
Row 2. 180 **Packard Clipper** (x2), 192 **De Soto Fireflite** (x2).
Row 3. 175 **Hillman Minx** (x2), 160 **Austin A30**, 166 **Sunbeam Rapier** (x2).
Row 4. 183 **Fiat 600** (x2), 160 **Austin A30**, 24h/526 **Mercedes-Benz 190SL** (x2).

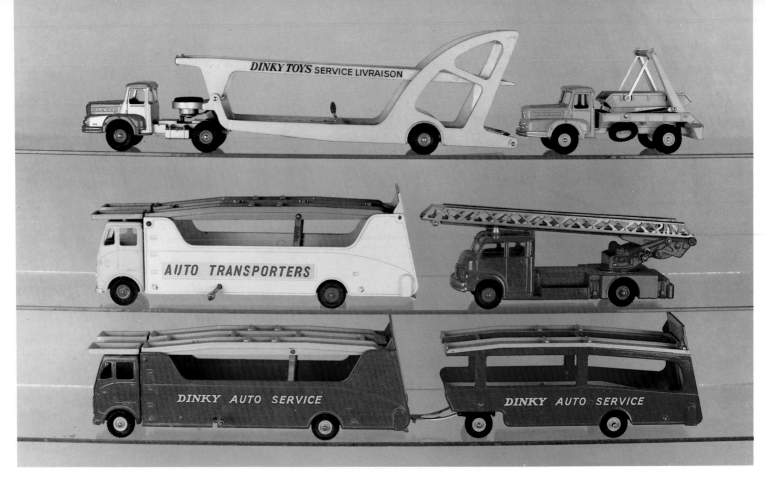

Row 1. **39a/894** Unic Auto Transporter, **38a/895** Unic Bucket Truck.
Row 2. **989** Car Carrier, **956** Fire Engine.
Row 3. **984** Car Carrier, **985** Car Carrier Trailer.

Row 1. 967 **BBC-TV Control Room**, 968 **Camera Truck**, 969 **Mast Truck**.
Row 2. 987 **ABC-TV Control Room**, 988 **TV Transmitter**, 665 **Missile Launcher**.
Row 3. 666 **Missile Erector**, 966 **Multibucket Truck**.

Row 1. 24u/544 **Simca Aronde** (x2), 24l/529 **Vespa**, 24n/531 **Fiat 1200** (x2).
Row 2. 24k/528 **Simca Chambord** (x2), 24zt **Simca Ariane Taxi**, 178 **Plymouth Plaza.**
Row 3. 191 **Dodge Royale,** 178 **Plymouth Plaza** (x2).
Row 4. 24j/527 **Alfa Romeo** 1900 (x2), 187 **VW Karmann-Ghia** (x2).

Row 1. 547 **Panhard PL17** (x2), 543 **Renault Floride** (x2).
Row 2. 168 **Singer Gazelle** (x2), 25d/562 **Citroen Fire Van**, 189 **Triumph Herald** (x2).
Row 3. 545 **De Soto Diplomat** (x2), 548 **Fiat 1800 Wagon** (x2).
Row 4. 165 **Humber Hawk** (x3), 256 **Humber Police Car**.

Row 1. 667 **Missile Servicing Platform**, 786 **Dunlop Tire Rack**, 977 **Servicing Platform Truck**.
Row 2. 986 **Mighty Antar**, 431 **Guy Open Truck**.
Row 3. 596 **LMV Street Sweeper**, 930 **Bedford Pallet-Jekta Van**, 432 **Guy Flat Truck**.
Row 4. 39b/893 **Unic Pipe Truck**, 960 **Cement Mixer**, 563 **Renault Estafette**.

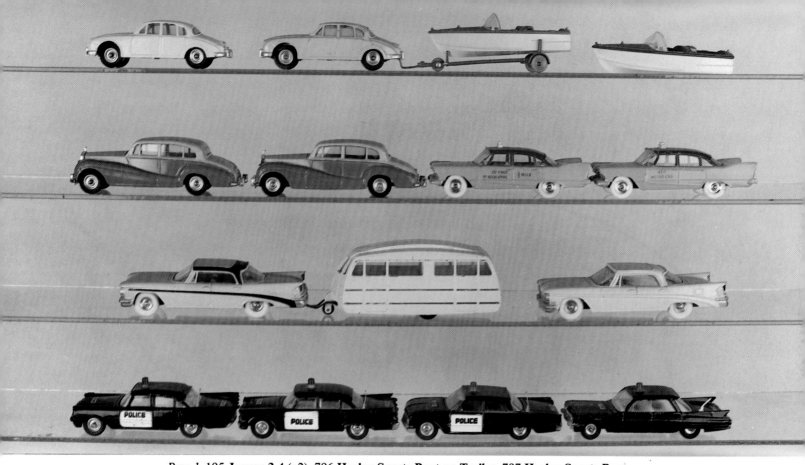

Row 1. 195 **Jaguar 3.4** (x2), 796 **Healey Sports Boat on Trailer**, 797 Healey Sports Boat.
Row 2. 150 & 551 **Rolls-Royce**, 265 & 266 **Plymouth Taxi**.
Row 3. 550 **Chrysler Saratoga** (x2), 811 **Caravan**.
Row 4. 258 **De Soto, Dodge, Ford & Cadillac Police Cars.**

Row 1. 886 **Richier Road Grader**, 785 **Service Station**.
Row 2. 884 **Brockway Bridgelayer**, 898 **Berliet Transformer Carrier**.
Row 3. 908 **Mighty Antar Transporter**, 888 **Berliet Saharien**.

Row 1. 948 **McLean Semi-Trailer**, 959 **Foden Dump Truck.**
Row 2. 448 **Chevrolet El Camino & Trailers**, 319 **Weeks Farm Trailer**, 295 **Standard Atlas.**
Row 3. 259 **Fire Engine**, 584 **Berliet GAK Covered Truck**, 585 **Berliet GAK Dump Truck.**
Row 4. 958 **Snow Plow Truck**, 586 **Citroen Milk Truck.**

Row 1. 194 **Bentley S2** (x2), 193 **Rambler Cross Country**, 257 **Rambler Fire Chief.**
Row 2. 549 **Borgward Isabella** (x2), 552 **Chevrolet Corvair** (x2).
Row 3. 185 **Alfa Romeo 1900** (x2), 184 **Volvo 122S** (x2).
Row 4. **155 Ford Anglia,** 555 **Ford Thunderbird** (x3).

Row 1. 112 **Austin-Healey Sprite,** 113 **MGB,** 120 **Jaguar E-type** (x2), 143 **Ford Capri.**
Row 2. 142 **Jaguar Mark X,** 197 **Morris Mini-Traveller** (x3), 119 **Austin Seven Countryman,** 145 **Singer Vogue.**
Row 3. 553 **Peugeot 404** (x2), 186 **Mercedes-Benz 220SE** (x2).
Row 4. 554 **Opel Rekord,** 188 **Caravan Trailer** (x2), 177 **Opel Kapitän.**

Row 1. 290 **Double Decker Bus** (x2), 291 **Exide Double Decker Bus**, 276 **Airport Fire Tender.**

Row 2. 292 (x2) & 293 **Leyland** (2 casting types) **Atlantean Buses.**

Row 3. 268 **Renault Dauphine Cab**, 263 & 277 **Superior Criterion Ambulance**, 269 **Jaguar 3.4 Police Car.**

Row 4. 949 **Wayne School Bus**, 953 **Continental Touring Coach.**

Row 1. 824 **Berliet Gazelle**, 883 **AMX Bridgelaying Tank**, 826 **Berliet Crane**.
Row 2. 821 **Mercedes-Benz Unimog**, 823 **Field Kitchen Trailer**, 825 **DUKW Amphibian**, 822 **M3 Halftrack**.
Row 3. 828 **Jeep with Missiles**, 890 **Berliet Transporter**, 829 **Jeep With Cannon**.
Row 4. 814 **Panhard AML**, 560 **Citroen Mail Truck** (x2), 562h **Citroen Wegenwacht**, 827 **Panhard EBR**.

Row 1. 147 **Cadillac 62**, 148 **Ford Fairlane** (x3).
Row 2. 512 **Go-Kart**, 557 **Citroen Ami-6** (x2), 559 **Ford Taunus 17M** (x2).
Row 3. 558 **Citroen 2CV**, 532 **Lincoln Premiere** (x3).
Row 4. 558 **Citroen 2CV**, 198 **Rolls-Royce Phantom** (x2), 556 **Citroen ID19 Ambulance**.

Row 1. 100 **Renault 4L**, 103 **Renault R8**, 104 **Simca 1000**, 105 **Citroen 2CV**, 106 **Opel Kadett**.
Row 2. 101 **Peugeot 404**, 102 **Panhard PL17**, 515 **Ferrari 250** (x2).
Row 3. 517 **Renault R8** (x2), 518 **Renault 4L** (x2), 138 **Hillman Imp**.
Row 4. 540 **Opel Kadett**, 519 **Simca 1000** (x2), 523 **Simca 1500**, 520 **Fiat 600D**.

Row 1. 538 **Ford Taunus 12M**, 196 **Holden Special** (x2), 146 **Daimler 2.5.**
Row 2. 534 **BMW 1500**, 539 **Citroen ID19**, 546 **Opel Rekord Taxi**, 533 **Mercedes-Benz 300.**
Row 3. 264 **Ford & Cadillac RCMP Cars**, 135 **Triumph 2000**, 117 **Caravan.**
Row 4. 144 **Volkswagen 1500**, 134 **Triumph Vitesse**, 118 **Triumph 2000 & Glider Trailer.**

Row 1. 240 **Cooper**, 241 **Lotus**, 141 **Vauxhall Victor Estate Car**, 242 **Ferrari**, 243 **BRM.**
Row 2. 114 **Triumph Spitfire** (x4), 140 **Morris 1100.**
Row 3. 137 **Plymouth Fury** (x2), 139 **Ford Cortina** (x2).
Row 4. 137 & 115 **Plymouth Fury**, 133 **Ford Cortina**, 130 **Ford Corsair.**

Row 1. 541 **Mercedes-Benz Bus**, 887 **Unic BP Tanker**.
Row 2. 437 **Muir-Hill Loader** (x3), 436 **Atlas Copco Compressor**.
Row 3. 425 **Bedford Coal Truck**, 434 **Bedford Wrecker**, 435 **Bedford Tipper**, 564 **Renault Estafette Glass Truck**.
Row 4. 424 **Commer Articulated Truck**, 936 **Leyland Test Chassis**, 492 **Election Minivan**.

Row 1. 970 **Bedford Jones Crane**, 975 **Bucyrus Excavator**.
Row 2. 275 **Brinks Armored Car** (x2), 914 **AEC British Road Services Semi-Trailer**.
Row 3. 925 **Leyland Dump Truck**, 885 **Saviem Pipe Truck**.
Row 4. 978 **Bedford Refuse Wagon** (x3).

Row 1. 952 **Vega Major Luxury Coach**, 475 **Model T Ford**, 289 **Routemaster Tern Shirts Bus.**
Row 2. 954 **Vega Major Luxury Coach**, 485 **Christmas Model T Ford**, 289 **Routemaster Schweppes Bus.**
Row 3. 961 **Swiss Mail Bus**, 476 **Morris Oxford**, 289 **Routemaster Esso Bus.**
Row 4. 486 **Dinky Beats Morris**, 289 **Routemaster Woolworth & Ever Ready Buses**, 477 **Parsley's Morris.**

Row 1. 279 **Aveling-Barford Roller** (x2), 803 **Unic SNCF Semi-Trailer.**
Row 2. 274 **AA Minivan,** 402 **Bedford Coca-Cola Truck,** 589a & 589 **Berliet Wreckers.**
Row 3. 273 **RAC Minivan,** 588 **Berliet Bottle Truck,** 577 **Berliet Cattle Truck,** 278 **Vauxhall Ambulance.**
Row 4. 274 **Mason Paints Minivan,** 280 **Mobile Bank,** 587 **Citroen Philips Van,** 289 **Routemaster Festival of London Stores** (right side of Schweppes bus in #60).

Row 1. 128 **Mercedes-Benz 600** (x2), 551 **Ford Taunus Police.**
Row 2. 127 **Rolls-Royce Silver Cloud** (x3).
Row 3. 516 **Mercedes-Benz 230SL**, 542 **Opel Rekord**, 530 **Citroen DS19** (x2).
Row 4. 524 **Panhard 24CT**, 136 **Vauxhall Viva** (x2), 525 **Peugeot 404 Break.**

Row 1. 001 **Buick Riviera**, 002 **Corvair Monza**, 161 **Ford Mustang** (x2).
Row 2. 171 **Austin 1800**, 003 **Chevrolet Impala** (x2), 151 **Vauxhall Victor.**
Row 3. 214 **Hillman Imp Rally**, 004 **Oldsmobile 88**, 005 **Ford Thunderbird**, 172 **Fiat 2300 Wagon.**
Row 4. 110 **Aston Martin DB5**, 006 **Rambler Classic Wagon**, 116 **Volvo 1800S** (x2).

Row 1. 528 **Peugeot 404 Cabriolet**, 183 **Morris Mini-Minor**, 152 **Rolls-Royce Phantom**, 536 **Peugeot 404** with 812 **Car Trailer.**
Row 2. 537 **Renault R16** (x2), 164 Ford Zodiac, 513 **Opel Admiral.**
Row 3. 262 VW Swiss Mail Car, 128 **Volkswagen 1200**, 163 **VW 1600TL**, 154 **Ford Taunus 17M.**
Row 4. 509 **Fiat 850**, 162 **Triumph 1300**, 156 **Saab 96**, 507 **Simca 1500 Break**, 508 **DAF.**

Row 1. 215 **Ford GT40** (x2), 281 **Fiat 2300 Camera Car**, 506 **Ferrari 275GTB.**
Row 2. 153 **Aston Martin DB6**, 212 **Ford Cortina Rally**, 501 **Citroen DS19 Police**, 282 **Austin 1800 Taxi.**
Row 3. 514 **Alfa Romeo Giulia TI**, 899 **Berliet Paris Bus**, 170 **Lincoln Continental.**
Row 4. 565 **Renault Estafette Camper**, 889u **Berliet City Bus**, 170 **Lincoln Continental.**

Row 1. 342 **Austin Minimoke** (x2), 601 **Austin Paramoke**, 305 **David Brown Tractor** (x2).

Row 2. 450 **Bedford Castrol Van**, 945 **AEC Esso Tanker**.

Row 3. 407 **Ford Kenwood Van**, 805 **Unic Bucket Truck**, 407 **Ford Hertz Van**.

Row 4. 567 **Unimog Snow Plow**, 570 **Peugeot J7 Van**, 569 **Berliet Dump Truck**.

Row 1. 100 **Lady Penelope's FAB-1**, 111 **Cinderella's Coach**, 106 **The Prisoner Minimoke**.
Row 2. 107 **Stripey the Magic Mini**, 101 & 106 **Thunderbird II**.
Row 3. 103 **Spectrum Patrol Car**, 104 **Spectrum Pursuit Vehicle**, 105 **Maximum Security Vehicle**.
Row 4. 108 **Sam's Car** (x4).

Row 1. 132 **Ford 40RV** (x2), 188 **Jensen FF**, 131 **Jaguar E-type**.
Row 2. 168 **Ford Escort** (x3), 173 **Pontiac Parisienne**.
Row 3. 169 **Ford Corsair**, 166 **Renault 16**, 159 **Ford Cortina II**, 157 **BMW 2000**.
Row 4. 158 **Rolls-Royce Silver Shadow** (x2), 160 **Mercedes-Benz 250SE**, 500 **Citroen 2CV**.

Row 1. 503 **Porsche Carrera**, 511 **Peugeot 204**, 1401 **Alfa Romeo Giulia Rally**, 1403 **Matra 530**, 1408 **Honda S-800**.

Row 2. 1407 **Simca 1100**, 1416 **Renault R6**, 1414 **Renault R8 Gordini**, 561 **Renault 4L Mail Car**, 1413 **Citroen Dyane 2CV**.

Row 3. 1415 **Peugeot 504**, 1402 **Ford Galaxie**, 1419 **Ford Thunderbird**, 1410 **Moskvitch 408**.

Row 4. 1400 **Peugeot 404 Taxi**, 1404 **Citroen Radio-TV Car**, 1429 **Peugeot 404 Police**, 1405 **Opel 1900**.

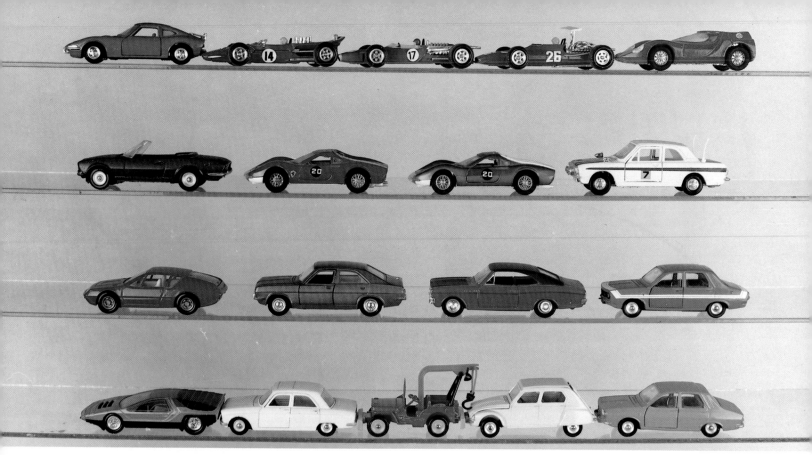

Row 1. 1421 **Opel GT**, 1433 **Surtees TS5**, 1417 **Matra Formula 1**, 1422 **Ferrari Formula 1**, 217 **Alfa Romeo OSI Scarabeo.**
Row 2. 1423 **Peugeot 504**, 216 **Ferrari Dino (x2)**, 205 **Lotus Cortina.**
Row 3. 1411 **Alpine A310**, 1409 **Chrysler 180**, 1420 **Opel Commodore**, 1424g **Renault 12 Gordini.**
Row 4. 1426 **Alfa Romeo Carabo**, 1428 **Peugeot 304**, 1412 **Jeep Wrecker**, 1413 **Citroen Dyane**, 1424 **Renault 12.**

Row 1. 187 **De Tomaso Mangusta**, 221 **Corvette Sting Ray** (x2), 1425 **Matra 630**.
Row 2. 189 **Lamborghini Marzal** (x4).
Row 3. 210 **Alfa Romeo 33** (x2), 190 **Monteverdi**, 174 **Mercury Cougar**.
Row 4. 165 **Ford Capri** (x2), 175 **Cadillac Eldorado**, 176 **NSU Ro-80**.

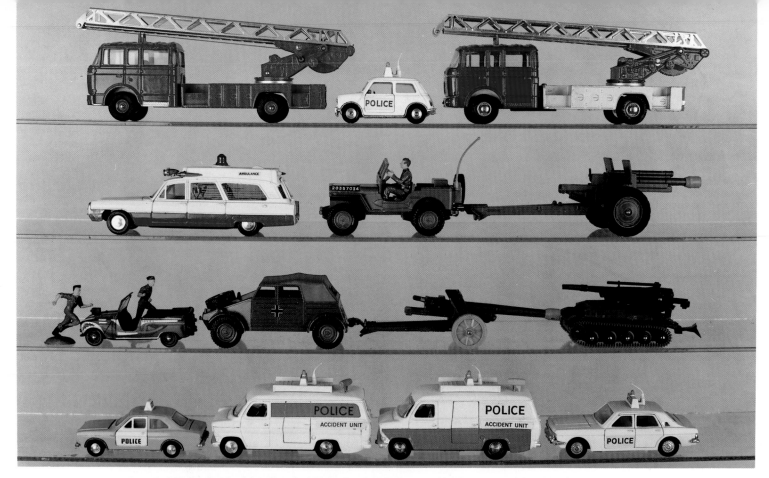

Row 1. 568 **Berliet Ladder Truck**, 250 **Police Mini-Copter**, 956 **Berliet Ladder Truck**.
Row 2. 267 **Cadillac Ambulance**, 615 **Army Jeep & Howitzer**.
Row 3. 1406 **Renault Sinpar**, 617 **VW & Antitank Gun**, 813 **Self-Propelled Gun**.
Row 4. 270 **Ford Panda Police Car**, 287 **Ford Transit Police Van (x2)**, 255 **Ford Zodiac Police Car**.

Row 1. 285 **Merryweather Fire Truck** (x2), 286 **Ford Transit Fire Van.**
Row 2. 570p **Peugeot Fire Van,** 809 **GMC Troop Transporter,** 572 **Berliet Dump Truck.**
Row 3. 290 **SR N6 Hovercraft** (x2), 252 **RCMP Patrol Car.**
Row 4. 344 **Land Rover Pickup** (x2), 566 **Citroen Police Van,** 564 **Armagnac Caravan.**

Row 1. 404 **Conveyancer Fork Lift** (x2), 571 **Saviem Race Horse Van.**
Row 2. 581 **Circus Animal Truck & Trailer.**
Row 3. 974 **AEC Hoynor Car Transporter**, 594 **Traffic Light.**

Row 1. 351 **Shado Interceptor**, 353 **Shado-2 Mobile**, 355 **Lunar Rover**.
Row 2. 352 **Ed Straker's Car**, 354 **Pink Panther**, type 1.
Row 3. 228 **Super-Sprinter**, 354 **Pink Panther**, type 2, 370 **Dragster**.
Row 4. 350 **Tiny's Minimoke**, 281 **Military Hovercraft**, 102 **Joe's Car**, 109 **Gabriel's Model T Ford**.

Row 1. 1430 & 202 **Fiat-Abarth 2000**, 149 **Citroen Dyane**, 218 **Lotus Europa** (x2).
Row 2. 1432 & 204 **Ferrari 312P**, 220 **Ferrari P5**, 223 **McLaren M8** (x2).
Row 3. 200 **Matra 630**, 213 **Ford Capri Rally** (x2), 179 **Opel Commodore**.
Row 4. 208 **VW-Porsche 914** (x2), 251 **Pontiac Police Car**, 224 **Mercedes-Benz C-111**.

Row 1. 225 **Lotus Formula 1** (x3).
Row 2. 226 **Ferrari 312B-2** (x2), 222 **Hesketh 308E.**
Row 3. 226 **Ferrari 312B-2** (x3)
Row 4. 192 **Range Rover**, 195 **Range Rover Fire Chief** (x2), 284 Austin London Taxi.

Row 1. 451 **Johnson Street Sweeper**, 973 **Eaton Yale Tractor Shovel**, 449 **Johnson Street Sweeper.**
Row 2. 254 **Police Range Rover** (x2), 296 **Viceroy 37 Coach** (x2).
Row 3. 283 **Red Arrow Bus** (x2), 308 **Leyland Tractor.**
Row 4. 288 **Superior Cadillac Ambulance** (x2), 308 **Leyland Tractor** (x2).

Row 1. 612 **Commando Jeep**, 808 **GMC Wrecker**, 620 **Berliet Missile Launcher**.

Row 2. 654 **155MM Mobile Gun**, 625 **Antitank Gun**, 683 **Chieftain Tank**.

Row 3. 680 **Ferret**, 682 **Alvis Stalwart**, 681 **DUKW Amphibian**, 609 **105MM Howitzer**.

Row 4. 800 **Renault Sinpar**, 810 **Dodge Command Car**, 807 **Renault Army Ambulance**, 676 **Daimler Armored Car**, 801 **AMX 13 Tank**.

87

Row 1. 410 **Royal Mail, Danish Mail, John Menzies, Dunlop, & Avis Vans.**
Row 2. 410 **MJ Hire, Portakabin, Opel, BBL Paints, & Esso Vans.**
Row 3. 410 **BOC, Parlophone, Jimmy Carter, Army & Hymo Vans.**
Row 4. 410 **AA Servce, Heron, Simpsons, Flash, & Olympus Vans.**

Row 1. **924 Aveling-Barford Dump Truck, 980 Coles Hydra Truck.**
Row 2. **967 Muir-Hill Loader-Trencher, 915 AEC Flat Semi-Trailer.**
Row 3. **410 Godfrey Davis, London Transport (x2), Findlaters, & National Vans.**
Row 4. **410 London, City, Metropolitan, Manchester, & Los Angeles Fire Vans.**

Row 1. 984 **Atlas Excavator**, 977 **Shovel Dozer.**
Row 2. 442 **Land Rover Wrecker** (x2), 282 **Land Rover Fire Truck** (x2).
Row 3. 412 **Bedford AA Van**, 295 **Yellow Pages Atlantean** (x2), 268 **Range Rover Ambulance.**
Row 4. 412 **Bedford Fire Van**, 291 **Kenning Atlantean** (x2), 293 **Viceroy Swiss Mail Bus.**

Row 1. 438 **Ford Dump Truck** (x2), 432 **Foden Dump Truck.**
Row 2. 438 and 440 **Ford Dump Trucks,** 439 **Ford Snowplow Truck.**
Row 3. 276 **Ford Transit Ambulance,** 416 **Ford Motorway Services Van,** 272 **Ford Transit Police Van.**
Row 4. 271 **Ford Transit Fire Van** (x2), 244 **Plymouth Police Car.**

Row 1. 622 **Bren Gun Carrier**, 656 **88MM Gun**, 691 **Antitank Striker**.
Row 2. 619 **Bren Gun Set**, 694 **Hanomag Tank Destroyer**.
Row 3. 692 **Leopard Tank**, 690 **Scorpion Tank**, 696 **Leopard AA Tank**.
Row 4. 667 **Armored Patrol Car**, 668 **Foden Army Truck**, 699 **Leopard Recovery Tank**.

Row 1. 672 **OSA Missile Boat**, 673 **Submarine Chaser**.
Row 2. 671 **Corvette**, 675 **Patrol Boat**.
Row 3. 678 **Rescue Launch**, 674 **Coast Guard Missile Launcher**, 604 **Bomb Disposal Land Rover**.
Row 4. 602 **Armored Command Car**, 870 **France**.

Row 1. 211 **Triumph TR7** (x2), 255 **Police Mini-Clubman**, 207 **Triumph TR7 Rally**, 112 **Purdey's Triumph TR7.**
Row 2. 518 **Renault 4L**, 227 **Beach Buggy**, 178 **Mini-Clubman** (x2), 530 **Citroen DS23.**
Row 3. 206 **Custom Corvette**, 124 **Rolls-Royce Phantom V**, 538 **Renault 16TX** (x2).
Row 4. 503/1405 **Alfa Romeo GTV**, 502/1404 **BMW 530**, 505/1306 **Peugeot 504**, 504/1402 **Citroen Visa.**

Row 1. 1454 **Matra Simca Bagheera**, 510 **Peugeot 204** (x2), 1453 **Renault 6**, 1450 **Simca 1100 Police**.
Row 2. 1539 **VW Scirocco**, 1541 **Ford Fiesta**, 500 **Citroen 2CV**, 1540 **Renault 14**.
Row 3. 1451 **Renault 17TS**, 1455 **Citroen CX Pallas**, 1452 **Peugeot 504**, 1543 **Opel Ascona**.
Row 4. 1424 **Renault 12**, 1407 **Simca 1100**, 1415 **Peugeot 504**, 1542 **Chrysler 1308 GT**.

Row 1. 300 **London Scene Set**, 284 **Austin London Taxi.**
Row 2. 267 **Paramedic Truck**, 976 **Michigan Tractor Dozer**, 428 **Trailer.**
Row 3. 917 **Mercedes-Benz Truck & Trailer.**

Row 1. 203 **Custom Range Rover**, 202 **Custom Land Rover**, 430 **Johnson Dump Truck**, 384 **Convoy Fire Rescue**.
Row 2. 382 **Convoy Dump Truck** (x2), 380 **Convoy Skip Dumper**, 381 **Convoy Farm Truck**.
Row 3. 385 **Convoy Royal Mail Truck**, 383 **Convoy National Carriers Truck**, 687 **Convoy Army Truck**, 385 **Convoy Los Angeles Fire Truck**.
Row 4. 274 **Ford Transit Ambulance**, 417 **Ford Transit Motorway Services Truck**, 269 **Ford Transit Police Van**.

Row 1. 963 **Road Grader**, 266 **ERF Fire Tender.**
Row 2. 945 **AEC Lucas Tanker**, 390 **Ford Transit Vampire Van.**
Row 3. 950 **Foden Burmah Tanker**, 263 **ERF Airport Fire Tender.**
Row 4. 940 **Mercedes-Benz Covered Truck**, 266 **ERF Fire Tender.**

Row 1. 278 **Plymouth Yellow Cab**, 201 **Plymouth Stock Car**, 219 **Jaguar Big Cat.**
Row 2. 122 **Volvo 265 Wagon** (x3).
Row 3. 180 **Rover 3500**, 115 **UB Taxi**, 120 **Happy Cab**, 241 **Silver Jubilee Taxi.**
Row 4. 123 **Princess** (x3).

Row 1. 616 **AEC Tank Transporter**, 745 **Bell Army Helicopter**.
Row 2. 618 **AEC Helicopter Transporter**, 744 **Sea King Army Helicopter**.
Row 3. 724 **Sea King Helicopter**, 736 **Sea King Bundesmarine Helicopter**.

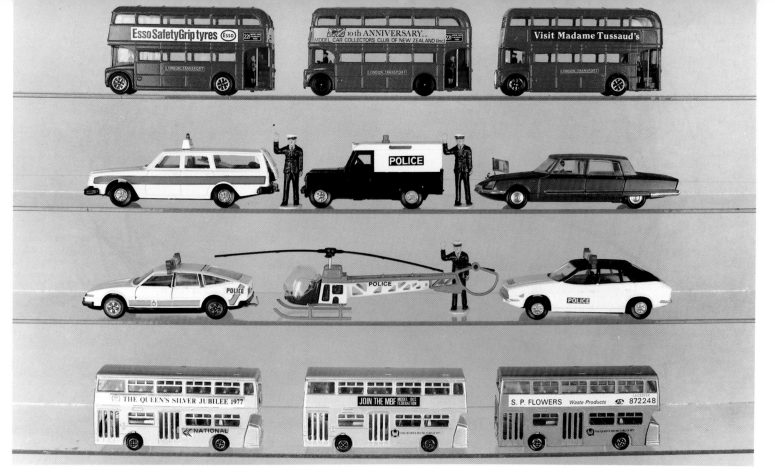

Row 1. 289 **Routemaster Esso, New Zealand Club & Madame Tussaud's Buses.**
Row 2. 243 **Volvo 265DL Police**, 277 **Police Land Rover**, 1435 **Citroen Presidentielle.**
Row 3. 264 **Rover 3500 Police**, 732 **Bell Police Helicopter**, 123p **Princess Police.**
Row 4. 297 **Silver Jubilee, Model Bus Federation & S. P. Flowers Buses.**

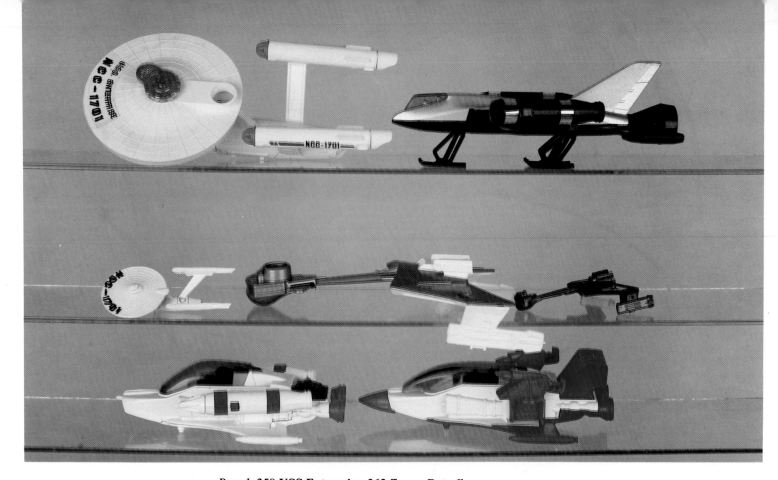

Row 1. 358 **USS Enterprise**, 363 **Zygon Patroller**.
Row 2. 803 **USS Enterprise**, 357 & 804 **Klingon Battle Cruisers**.
Row 3. 367 **Battle Cruiser**, 368 **Zygon Marauder**.

237 Dinky **Way Set.**

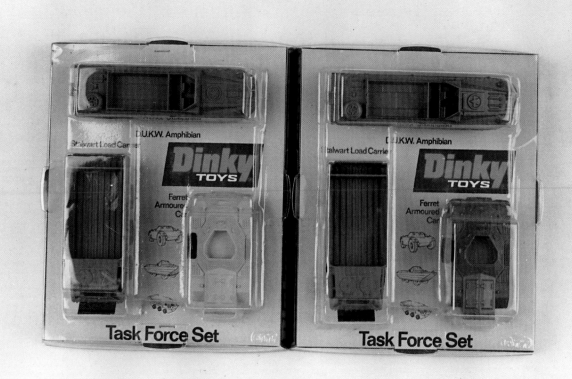

677 **Task Force Set** (x2).

Row 1. 366 **Space Shuttle**, 362 **Trident Starfighter**, 364 **NASA Space Shuttle**.
Row 2. 359 **Eagle Transport**, 360 **Eagle Freighter**.
Row 3. 361 **Galactic War Chariot** (x3).

Row 1. 294 **Police Vehicles Set.**
Row 2. 299 **Crash Squad Set.**

Row 1. 304 **Fire Rescue Set.**
Row 2. 303 **Commando Squad Set.**

Row 1. 60h **Singapore Flying Boat**, 60m **Four Engine Flying Boat.**
Row 2. 60a **Imperial Airways Liner**, 60r **Empire Flying Boat.**

Row 1. 60f **Cierva Autogiro**, 60g DH **Comet** (x2), 66f **Army Cooperation Autogiro.**
Row 2. 60d **Low Wing Monoplane**, 60c **Percival Gull** (x2), 60k **Light Tourer.**
Row 3. 60b **DH Leopard Moth**, 60e **General Monospar**, 60n **Fairey Battle**, 60s **Medium Bomber.**
Row 4. 60p **Gloucester Gladiator**, 62a **Spitfire**, 62h **Hawker Hurricane**, 62 **Single Seat Fighter.**

Row 1. 60w **Clipper III Flying Boat**, 62g **Flying Fortress.**
Row 2. 60t **Douglas DC3**, 60v **Whitley Bomber.**

Row 1. 64a **Amiot 370**, 64b **Bloch 220**, 64c **Potez 63**, 63b/700 **Mercury Seaplane.**
Row 2. 62k **The King's Envoy**, 62m **Airspeed Envoy**, 62b **Bristol Blenheim**, 62d **Camouflaged Blenheim.**
Row 3. 60b **Potez 58**, 60c **Henriot H180T**, 60d **Breguet Corsaire**, 60e **Dewoitine 500.**

Row 1. 62n **Junkers JU-90**, 62p **Ensign Class Airliner.**
Row 2. 62r DH **Albatross** (x2).

Row 1. 60a **Arc-en-ciel**, 61a **Dewoitine 338.**
Row 2. 64d **Potez 662**, 62t **Camouflaged Whitley.**

Row 1. 62y & 67a **Junkers JU-90.**
Row 2. 70a/704 **Avro York**, 62p **Armstrong Whitworth Airliner.**

Row 1. 702/999 **DH Comet** (x2).
Row 2. 70c/705 **Vickers Viking,** 804 **Nord Noratlas.**

Row 1. 891 & 997 **Caravelle.**
Row 2. 60e/706 & 708 **Vickers Viscount.**

Row 1. 701 **Shetland Flying Boat**, 715 **Bristol Helicopter.**
Row 2. 716 and 60d/802 **Sikorsky Helicopters.**

Row 1. **738 Sea Vixen, 801 Vautour, 735 Gloster Javelin.**
Row 2. **734 Supermarine Swift**, **737 Lightning**, **800 Mystere**, **736 Hawker Hunter.**
Row 3. **70b/730 Tempest**, **70d/731 Twin Engined Fighter**, **70e/732 Gloster Meteor**, **70f/733 Shooting Star.**

Row 1. 892 **Constellation**, 998 **Bristol Britannia.**
Row 2. 717 **Boeing 737 Lufthansa.**

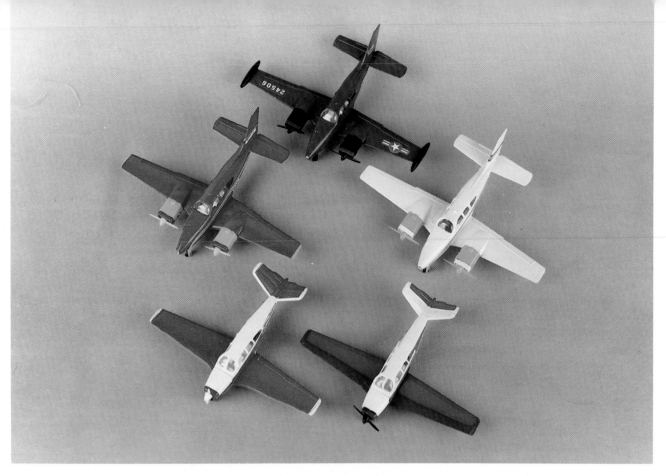

Row 1. 712 **U.S. Army T42A.**
Row 2. 715 **Beechcraft Baron** (x2).
Row 3. 710 **Beechcraft Bonanza** (x2).

Row 1. 721 **Junkers JU-87B Stuka**, 726 **Messerschmitt 109E.**
Row 2. 719 & 741 **Spitfire Mark II.**

Row 1. 739 **Mitsubishi Zero.**
Row 2. 728 **RAF Dominie,** 723 **Hawker Siddeley Executive Jet.**

722 Hawker Harrier, 731 **SEPECAT Jaguar.**

Row 1. 725 **Royal Navy Phantom II.**
Row 2. 730 **U.S. Navy** & 727 **USAF Phantom II.**

Dinky Builda Blazing Inferno & Space War Station.

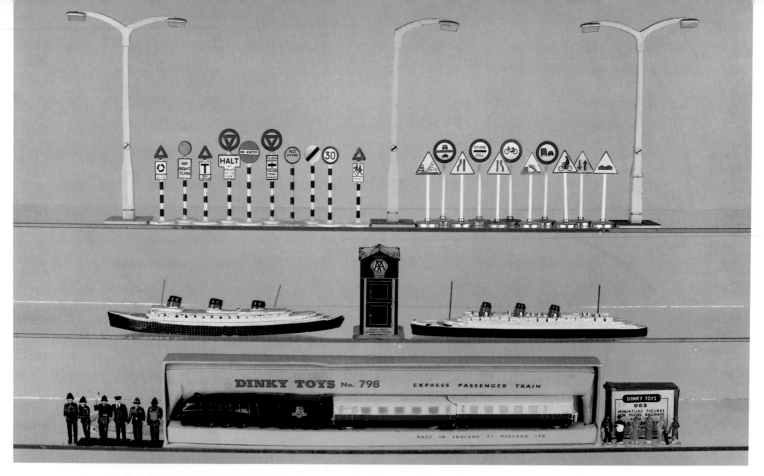

Row 1. 756 **Double Lamp Standard**, 768 & 769 **Road Signs**, 755 **Single Lamp Standard**, 595 **Road Signs**.
Row 2. 52c **Normandie**, 44a **AA Box**, 52 **Queen Mary**.
Row 3. 008 **Fire Station Personnel**, 798 **Express Train**, 053 **Passengers**.

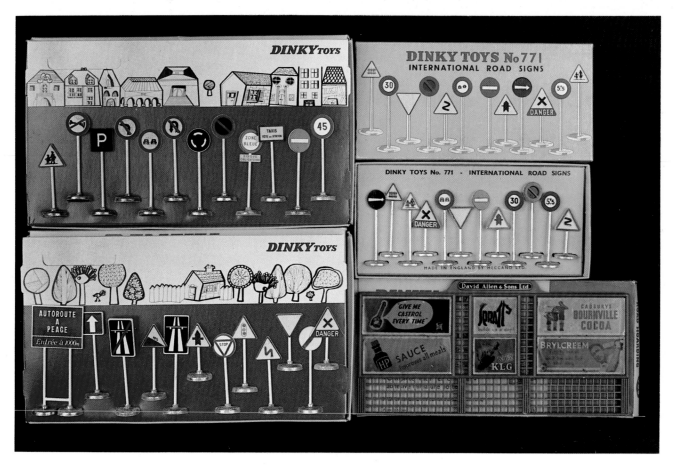

Left: 592 & 593 **Road Signs.**
Right: 771 **Road Signs**, 765 **Road Hoarding.**

A family of **Routemaster buses.**

A family of **Atlantean buses.**

Left: Mini-Dinky **12-Car Collector Case**, with its contents:
Row 1. 61 **Lotus**, 11 **Jaguar E-type.**
Row 2. 12 **Corvette Sting Ray**, 13 **Ferrari 250LM.**
Row 3. 19 **MGB**, 16 **Ford Mustang.**
Row 4. 10 **Ford Corsair**, 18 **Mercedes-Benz 230SL.**
Row 5. 20 **Cadillac**, 21 **Fiat 2300**, 14 **Chevy II**, 22 **Oldsmobile Toronado.**

Row 1. Mini-Dinky 10 **Ford Corsair** (x2), 11 **Jaguar E-type** (x2), 12 **Corvette Sting Ray** (x2).
Row 2. 13 **Ferrari 250LM** (x2), 14 **Chevy II** (x2), 22 **Oldsmobile Toronado.**
Row 3. 16 **Ford Mustang** (x3), 20 **Cadillac Coupe de Ville** (x2).
Row 4. 60 **Cooper**, 61 **Lotus**, 21 **Fiat 2300 Wagon** (x2), 18 **Mercedes-Benz 230SL**, 19 **MGB Roadster.**

Row 1. Matchbox/Dinky 7 **VW Golf**, 9 **Fiat Abarth**, 44 **Citroen 15CV**, 51 **Pontiac Firebird**, 60 **Toyota Supra**, 69 **1984 Corvette**.
Row 2. Mini-Dinky 94 **International Bulldozer**, 95 **International Skid Shovel**, 96 **Payloader Shovel**, 97 **Euclid Dumper**, Best Box 2519 **Cooper**.
Row 3. Mini-Dinky 98 **Michigan Scraper**, 99 **Caterpillar Grader**, Universal 8102 **Caterpillar Grader**, 8101 **Michigen Scraper**.
Row 4. Universal 8103 **International Bulldozer**, 8104 **International Skid Shovel**, 8105 **Payloader Shovel**, 8106 **Euclid Dumper**, **Best Box 2520 Lotus.**

Row 1. Hong Kong 101 **Corvette 1956**, 103 **Chevette**, 104 **Honda Accord**, 105 **Toyota Celica**, 106 **Datsun 280Z**, 107 **BMW Turbo.**
Row 2. 108 **Alfa Romeo**, 110 **Chevy Stepside**, 111 **Camper Pickup**, 113 **4x4 Pickup**, 114 **Pontiac Firebird**, 115 **Chevy Camaro.**
Row 3. 116 **Corvette 1963**, 117 **Corvette 1971**, 119 **Ford Van**, 120 **Jeep Renegade**, 121 **Chevy Estate Van**, 122 **Sun Van.**
Row 4. 129 **Ford Thunderbird**, 123 **Yamaha**, 124 **Honda**, 125 **Kawasaki**, 126 **Suzuki**, 130 **Chevrolet Convertible.**

Row 1. Pilen **Citroen 2CV, Citroen Dyane,** Pilen & Mira **Ford Fiesta,** Pilen **Matra Simca Bagheera.**
Row 2. Pilen **Renault 17TS,** Pilen & Mira **Chrysler 150,** Pilen **Citroen CX Pallas.**
Row 3. Pilen **Renault 14,** Mira & Pilen **VW Scirocco,** Pilen **Opel Ascona.**
Row 4. Sun Models **Studebaker Fire Truck,** Nutmeg Models **Studebaker Tanker & Pickup,** Sam Miller **Studebaker Fire Truck.**

Row 1. Hillco **Racing Car**, Metosul **Atlantean Bus** (x2), Minitoy **Racing Car.**
Row 2. Marusan 8507 **Service Car**, 8503 **Ambulance**, 8504 **Milk Truck**, 8505 **Observation Coach.**
Row 3. Marusan 8501 **Panhard Semi-Trailer**, 8502 **Royal Mail Van**, Lemeco ML71 **Austin Devon**, Nicky Toys 405 **Universal Jeep.**
Row 4. Jurgens **Cadillac Ambulance**, Nicky Toys 999 **DH Comet**, 693 **Howitzer.**

Row 1. Nicky Toys 054 **Standard Herald**, 113 **MGB**, 238 **Jaguar D-type**, 195 **Jaguar 3.4**, 134 **Triumph Vitesse**.
Row 2. 120 **Jaguar E-type**, 170 Lincoln Continental, 137 Plymouth Fury, 142 **Jaguar Mark X**.
Row 3. 239 **Vanwall**, 194 **Bentley S**, 186 **Mercedes-Benz 220SE**, 051 Mercedes-Benz Taxi.
Row 4. 735 **Gloster Javelin**, 295 **Standard Ambulance**, 962 Muir-Hill Dumper, 295 **Standard Atlas Bus**, 738 Sea Vixen.

Descriptions

I have tried to offer an adequately thorough description of every model and its major components, but space does not allow every single detail to be listed, nor have I tried to list every minor variation. Some collectors will want to go into the subject more deeply than this book does, while others will find this book too detailed for their interests, so I have tried to strike a happy medium by confining the listings to major variations: color and logo differences, noticeable casting changes, wheel types and the like.

One area I have not gone into very deeply is that of tires, simply because they are so easy to change. I have indicated whether a model was issued with black, white or gray tires, but have not generally tried to draw a dividing line between slick and treaded tires, or between rubber and plastic. As these changes are basically chronological in nature, it may well be that future research, which I hope this book will inspire, will bring out further information on the subject. On the other hand, there is no way of proving whether or not a a single specimen with an atypical type of tire was issued in that form or whether the tires were changed by a previous owner. In fact, I changed the tires on some of my Dinky Toys in my early days, before I became aware of the historical value of their authenticity.

I hope this book will inspire further research in other areas as well, for I see this book not as the last word on the subject, but as a beginning. I do not claim to list every variation that exists, or even

every major variation. If you have variations that are not listed here, please feel free to write. I am listing what I know or believe to exist, but I don't know everything there is to know about Dinky Toys and their variations, and I'll always be happy to receive additional information.

My main source of information has been my own collection, which includes nearly 1900 Dinky Toys collected over more than a quarter of a century. Other sources of data have been Cecil Gibson's "History of British Dinky Toys", Mike and Sue Richardson's "Dinky Toys & Modelled Miniatures", Jean-Michel Roulet's "Les Dinky Toys et Dinky Supertoys Français", Ed Symons' "Checklist of British Dinky Toys", and the "A2Z Dinky Specialised Book" compiled by Peter Harrington and Hugh Sutherland, as well as various other books and articles, plus numerous fellow collectors. Still in all, my data, as well as my time, money and energy, have their limitations. Perhaps in the future we can offer an edition with more nearly complete data; if so, it will be because people like you have contributed to it.

In describing the individual models, I have begun with the diecast metal parts: the BODY or main part of the vehicle's superstructure, or in some cases the CAB and REAR BODY of a truck as the two main pieces. Sometimes the cab is part of the CHASSIS-CAB to which the rear body is attached; in other cases a model may have a separate detailed CHASSIS that is more than a mere baseplate by virtue of including parts of the vehicle as well as lettering. Opening diecast parts can include DOORS, the HOOD, the TRUNK lid, a RAMP or TAILGATE, a removable TOP or COVER, as well as a swiveling FRONT AXLE MOUNT, a TOWBAR, the BLADE of a snowplow or bulldozer, a SHOVEL, BACK HOE or similar heavy eqipment parts, and the ARMS, BOOMS, etc. that hold and operate them. Non-moving metal parts may include a BUMPER, GRILLE, EXHAUST PIPE, MUFFLER, and many others, including a diecast DRIVER or STEERING WHEEL.

Most significant casting changes that apply to a series of models are easy to include in the listings, as the models to which they apply were numbered more or less consecutively. One change that applies to models in both the 200 and 400 series cannot be handled so easily: that of the three Ford Transit van castings. So let us state the most important differences here:

Type 1 (1966-1974): first type grille, sliding right front door, and a smaller casting (122 mm) than the other two.

Type 2 (1975-1978): a bigger casting (129 mm) of the same vehicle, with the same grille but without the sliding right front door.

Type 3 (1978-1980): the same size (129 mm) as Type 2, with a new grille and hood design, otherwise unchanged.

Finally we come to the wheels. If, as on some old Dinky Toys, the entire wheel, including the tire, is a single diecast piece, then it will be listed as a WHEEL; otherwise the term HUB will be used for a metal (or plastic) central section on which a rubber or plastic TIRE is mounted. Entire wheels can, of course, also be made of rubber, or more recently of plastic.

TIRES will be listed after wheels, generally with a notation of their color though not always of their material. Some wheel details will be listed; others can be inferred. Cast hubs were originally quite featureless; the type introduced in 1946 have a raised central area, and

Supertoy hubs have a partially concave pattern. PATTERNED cast hubs were used on numerous models in more recent years. Also made of metal, though not cast, are TURNED hubs (often called "spun" hubs), which were turned on a lathe rather than being cast in a mold, and almost always left unpainted (if painted, their color will be noted; otherwise they may be assumed to be the color of the unpainted metal.) Although British turned hubs can be understood not to have been cast, I have my doubts about some French types. For the sake of consistency I have referred to all the French Dinky metal hubs which M. Roulet describes as "concave" as "turned" to stress their concave profile. SPEEDWHEELS (Dinky Toys' registered name for their type of fast wheels) are made completely of plastic, often with chromed hub patterns. Along with wheels, the presence of SUSPENSION and STEERING will be noted.

Various sheet metal (also known as tinplate) parts have been used, notably the BASE of many an older model. The base sometimes holds a model together or holds the wheels and axles in place, and it often bears lettered information that identifies a model, sometimes including the catalog number. There are two basic baseplate types: the older type usually has lines around at least part of its edge, small lettering, and no catalog number. The newer type, introduced not too long before the 1954 numbering change, has no lines, large lettering, and often, though not always, a catalog number. If the same casting and base were used for several models (such as vans with different logo types), then they were deliberately made without numbers. Speaking of numbers, those which included letters have been printed with lower-case letters, while the letters actually used on baseplates have been capitalized, and the same system will be found in this book: upper-case letters in reference to what is seen on baseplates, otherwise lower-case letters. Other sheet metal parts can include a TOW HOOK, WINDSHIELD FRAME (as opposed to a transparent plastic or celluloid windshield itself), some types of STEERING

WHEEL, and various control pieces such as the tipping levers or blade-raising linkages that really work, or the control levers of bulldozers that just represent the real thing. The REAR COVER of many an older truck is also made of sheet metal and can be removed, while the TANK rear body of a tank truck is sometimes made of sheet metal but is not removable.

Many parts, including the body itself, can be made of plastic; these may be exterior parts such as a GRILLE, BUMPER, TOP, ANTENNA, TANK, LOAD, etc., interior items such as the INTERIOR itself (seats, inside floor, dashboard, etc.), DRIVER, STEERING WHEEL (not always listed, to save space), or ENGINE block, the transparent WINDOWS or WINDSHIELD (clear unless noted as tinted), and accessories such as figures (human or otherwise), luggage, signs, or the bullets or rockets of war vehicles.

Once the major parts of a model have been listed, we can turn to their finish and, if any, their logo. I have tried to give a good general idea of the colors of models and their parts without being excessively precise. I realize from reading other people's descriptions of models that we do not all draw the line between, for example, yellow and orange, or white and cream or ivory, in exactly the same place, and that some writers call unpainted metal parts silver. In this book UNPAINTED means bare metal, SILVER means painted silver, and CHROMED means plated in a silvery finish. I have tried to reserve the word WHITE for only a truly white finish, and to describe shades that are not quite white as off-white, ivory or cream. Of course, parts that were white when they were new may have aged in the interim to qualify for one of the not-quite-white terms. The major colors will be preceded by the adjective "light" or "dark" to indicate a shade notably lighter or darker than the medium shades indicated by an unmodified color name. At times when two shades of the same color appear on a model, adjectives such as "medium", "darker" or "lighter" will be used for clarification, with the latter two terms simply meaning a darker or lighter shade than the one previously mentioned. Other terms such as tan, charcoal gray, turquoise, aqua, navy blue and maroon will be used when my eyes advise me to, and I can assure you that MAROON models will be described as maroon and not merely as RED. (Warning: in some languages, maroon or a similar-looking term means a brown, tan or red-brown shade, but we use it here to mean a very dark red.)

The LOGO of a model includes the lettering, numbering, emblems or designs that appear on it. They can be painted (by hand or tampo-printed), applied as a DECAL (wet transfer) or an adhesive paper or plastic LABEL (dry transfer). Their major contents and colors will be noted. I have tried to note whether the logo is painted or applied with decals or labels, but I know I have not always succeeded.

The length of each model will be given in millimeters because the metric system is understood worldwide, exact, and a lot easier to print than fractions of an inch. If my measurements differ from yours by a millimeter or two, please don't be horrified; perhaps my ruler and my eyes are just less accurate than yours. As time did not allow me to measure every model in my collection, I have generally used dimensions listed in other published sources. In the case of Dinky airplanes, though, I wanted to include both length and wingspan (in that order) and so have measured all my airplanes myself.

The exact dating of Dinky Toys is not without its problems. The fact that some accessories were produced in the early Thirties is not a problem, but the events of the World War II era are sometimes debatable. I have found it convenient to end the prewar age as of 1940 and begin the postwar era as of 1946, though some production may have taken place in the interim. In general terms, the first year cited for a model is the year it was actually introduced or, lacking such precise information, the first year it was catalogued. The second year is the last year it was actually produced or catalogued—not the last year it was seen on the shelves of a toyshop! If only one year is stated, the item was produced for only that one year.

While some books have noted such details as the kinds of boxes the models have been sold in, or the presence or absence of the manufacturer's name on the model, this book does not. As noted above, data have had to be limited to some extent to keep the book from becoming too big and too expensive. The specialist can look for this information in other books on the subject, notably those books already cited.

This book includes information on all Dinky Toys, regardless of the nature of the item or its country of origin. I feel that the collector is likely to want information on French, Hong Kong and other non-British Dinky Toys, and may want to know about accessories as well as motor vehicles, not to mention aircraft (real and science-fiction types), ships and trains as well as cars and trucks. Thus I have tried to make the listings as complete as possible. What you as an individual hobbyist want to collect is for you to decide.

The photographs will be arranged in roughly chronological order, generally with models grouped in each picture in some more or less logical way. The models shown in the pictures are from my own collection. The listings are in numerical order, by catalog number. Perhaps some collectors would rather see all the cars listed together, all the emergency vehicles together, etc., but I feel that in a reference book of this type a numerical listing is the most practical system, with the photographs providing some sense of chronology. The Richardson and Roulet books in particular offer many photographs of British and French Dinky Toys respectively, many in color, and show some of the oldest and rarest Dinky Toys which I lack; you are urged to consult those books for additional visual data. Photographs in Dr. Gibson's book and drwings and descriptions in the A2Z book, as well as information in the Richardson and Roulet books, will come in handy for identifying such things as casting variations. And my book, "Miniature Emergency Vehicles", includes pictures and listings of all

Dinky Toys fire vehicles, ambulances and such—not to mention those of countless other manufacturers from all over the world.

The listings are divided into two sections, comprising the old and new numbering systems. True, some of the old 500 and 700 numbers seem to fit into the newer system, but I think it is less confusing to keep the two systems separate than to try to integrate them and end up with the old Dinky military models invading the 100 series of newer cars. British and French Dinky Toys will not be relegated to different sections of the book, though; there is no need to do so under the newer numbering system, and since there are fairly few cases of number duplication under the old system, other than the use of the same numbers for different British and French issues, it seems adequate to suffix the catalog numbers with a hyphen and the letter F (for France) and G (for Great Britain). Under the new system, the catalog numbers will also be suffixed with S for models made in Spain and with R for subsequent uses of the numbers. The suffix -H will also be used for models made in Hong Kong. Individual variations will be numbered consecutively with numerals. So the actual catalog number of any model will appear before the hyphen, with the letter and number after it indicating the basic model and the variation. In some cases, listings will include unnumbered subheadings to indicate casting or other substantial changes; these will not be numbered themselves, and the variations will be numbered consecutively for the entire model.

A price guide has been included to give you at least a vague idea of what models are worth. I am, frankly, not a believer in price guides, but my publishers and I know that books with price guides sell better than those without. I would urge you, though, not to expect the whole world to follow this price guide, but to obtain sales lists from a variety of dealers and see what models are actually selling for at toy shows.

As I have already said, the purpose of this book is to offer the collector as much concise, essential information as possible. The job is far from finished, as the many question marks in the listings make clear; sometimes I simply cannot verify a variation, sometimes only one or two details of it are known, while at other times only one or two details are lacking.

So I appeal to you; please feel free to send additional information you possess, such as variations not listed here and missing details of listed variations. During the next few years I'll gather all the data I can get and, I hope, produce an updated and much more nearly complete version of the book. I'll be very happy to receive any relevant data, though I must ask you not to quibble about measurements that differ by a millimeter from yours and not to add insignificant minor details for which we simply don't have room. For example, casting changes often include insignificant minor details as well as the big change that suffices to tell us what we want to know. More could be said of every model in the book—but then the book would be twice as big and cost twice as much. So let's limit ourselves to the more essential details that we need for identification of models and variations. My address, as stated at the end of this introduction, is not likely to change in the forseeable future, so please feel free to write.

And from here on, the subject is yours to do with as you like. I hope this book will be of use and interest to you, and that you will enjoy our hobby as much as I have. Whatever you choose to collect, happy hobbying to you all!

Dr. Edward Force
42 Warham Street
Windsor CT 06095

Ford Transit Vans: types 1, 2 and 3 front ends.

Variations

The Old System of Catalog Numbers

This system developed in the Thirties and remained in use until 1954 in Britain and 1959 in France. Some of the same numbers were used for different models in Britain and France; the suffix -F (for France) or -G (for Great Britain) will indicate the primary country of production of each model. Any later uses of the same number will be suffixed with R.

1-F   RAILROAD STATION STAFF   **1934-1940, 1946-1948**
Boxed set of six diecast (prewar) or five plastic (postwar) figures: 1a Chef de gare, 1b Portier, 1c Chef de train, 1d Sergent de ville, 1e Contrôleur.
  1. Six diecast figures, two porters (1934-1940).
  2. Five plastic figures, one porter (946-1948).

1-G   RAILROAD STATION STAFF   1931-1940, 1946-1953   _#001
Boxed set of six (prewar) or five (postwar) diecast figures: 1a Station Master, 1b Guard, 1c Ticket Collector, 1d Engine Driver, 1e Porter with bags, 1f Porter (prewar only).
  1. Six figures, more detailed painting (1931-1940).
  2. Five figures, less detailed painting (1946-1953).

1-H   FARMYARD EQUIPMENT SET   1952-1953   _#398
Boxed set of 27a Massey-Harris Tractor, 27b Halesowen Harvest Trailer, 27c Massey-Harris Manure Spreader, 27g Motocart and 27h Disc Harrow.
  1. Standard colors.

1-J   MILITARY GIFT SET   1955   _#699
Boxed set of 621, 641, 674 and 676 military vehicles. Note that the individual models had new numbers but the set was still numbered in the old system during 1955.
  1. Standard colors.

2-F   RAILROAD PASSENGERS   1934-1940, 1946-1948
Boxed set of six figures, two of them seated, and a bench: 2a Paysan normand, 2b Bécassine, 2c Jeune fille, 2d Boy-scout, 2e Garc,on assis, 2f Petite fille assis, 2g Banc.
  1. Various colors.

2-G   FARMYARD ANIMALS   1932-1940, 1946-1953   _#002
Boxed set of six diecast animals: two 2a Horse, two 2b Cow, one each 2c Pig, 2d Sheep.
  1. Various colors.

2-H   COMMERCIAL VEHICLES SET   1952-1953
Boxed set of 25m Bedford Tipper, 27b Halesowen Harvest Trailer, 30n Dodge Farm Wagon, 30P Petrol Tanker, 30s Austin Covered Wagon.
  1. Standard colors.

3-F   ANIMALS   1934-1940, 1946-1948
Boxed set of six diecast animals: one 3a pig, one 3b sheep, two 3c horse, two 3d cow.
  1. Some dark colors (1934-1940).
  2. All light colors)1946-1948).

3-G   PASSENGERS   1932-1940, 1946-1953   _#003
Six diecast figures: 3a Woman and child, 3b Businessman, 3c Male hiker, 3d Female hiker, 3e Newsboy, 3f Woman.
  1. Various colors.

3-H   PASSENGER CARS SET   1952-1954
Boxed set of 27f Estate Car, 30h Daimler Ambulance, 40E Standard Vanguard, 40g Morris Oxford, 40h Austin Taxi and 140b Rover 75.
  1. Standard colors.

4-F   RAILROAD EMPLOYEES   1934-1940, 1946-1948
Boxed set of six diecast figures: 4a Cuisinier, 4b Chauffeur, 4c Mécanicien, 4d Homme d'équipe, 4e Femme garde-barrière, 4f Porteur avec bagages.
  1. Various colors.

4-G   ENGINEERING STAFF   1932-1940, 1946-1953   _#004
Boxed set of diecast figures: 4a Electrician, 4b Fitter, 4c Storekeeper, 4d Greaser, 4e Engine Room Attendant. Each casting in this set is also used in another set.
  1. Various colors, 4b in blue & white (1932-1940).
  2. Various colors, 4b in tan & white (1946-1953).

4-H   RACING CARS SET   1953   _#249
Boxed set of 23f Alfa Romeo, 23g Cooper-Bristol, 23h Ferrari, 23j H. W. M. and 23n Maserati.
  1. Standard colors.

5-F   PASSENGERS   1934-1940, 1946-1948
Boxed set of six diecast figures: 5a woman and child, 5b Traveler, 5c Tourist, 5d Priest, 5e Newsboy, 5f Sportsman.
  1. Various colors.

5-G   TRAIN AND HOTEL STAFF   1932-1940, 1946-1953   _#005
Boxed set of four diecast figures: 5a Pullman car conductor, 5b Pullman car waiter, and two 5c Hotel porter.
  1. Various colors.

5-H   MILITARY VEHICLES SET   1953-1955
Boxed set of five military vehicles, for American market.
  1. 151a, 151b, 152b, 153a, 161b.
  2. 151a, 620, 671, 672, 690.

6-F   SHEPHERD SET   1934-1940, 1946-1948
Boxed set of 6a Shepherd, 6b Dog, and four 3b Sheep.
  1. Various colors.

6-G   SHEPHERD SET   1934-1940, 1946-1953   _#06
Boxed set of 6a Shepherd, 6b Dog, and four 2d Sheep.
  1. Shepherd in brown and black.
  2. Shepherd in brown and green.

10-F   ASSORTED FIGURES   1934-1940, 1946-1947
Combination of sets 1, 2 and 4.
  1. Standard colors.

12-G   POSTAL SET   1938-1940

Boxed set of 12a, 12b, 12c, 12d, 12e and 34b Royal Mail Van.
1. Standard colors.

12a-G GPO PILLAR BOX 50 mm high 1935-1940
Cast mailbox, painted red, with "Post Office" decals.
1. Oval sign on top of box.
2. No oval sign.

12b-G AIR MAIL PILLAR BOX 50 mm high 1935-1940
Cast mailbox, painted blue, with "Air Mail" decals. Same casting as 12a.
1. Oval sign on top of box.

12c-G TELEPHONE BOX 1936-1940, 1946-1948 #750
Cast box, originally 62 mm high, with silver trim.
1. Cream box, red window outlines (1936-1938).
2. Red box, black window outlines (1938-1940).
3. Red box, 58 mm high (1946-1948, reissued in 1954 as #750).

12d-G TELEGRAPH MESSENGER 1938-1940, 1946-1953 #011
Cast figure, 35 mm high.
1. Blue uniform, light brown pouch.

12e-G POSTMAN 1938-1940, 1946-1953 #012
Cast figure, 35 mm high, in blue uniform.
1. Red cuffs, dark brown bag.
2. Blue cuffs and bag.

13-G HALL'S DISTEMPER SIGN 1931-1941
Two cast men, 60 mm high, in white coats, with paint buckets and brushes, carrying cardboard sign with red "Hall's Distemper" lettering.
1. Red bucket tops and brushes.
2. Green bucket tops and brushes.
3. Blue bucket tops and brushes.

13a-G COOK'S MAN 1952-1953 #013
Cast figure of Thomas Cook travel guide, 40 mm high.
1. Dark blue coat.

14a-F TRIPORTEUR 70 mm 1935-1940, 1946-1952
Cast body, including driver, opening sheet metal box cover, cast hubs and rubber tires or cast wheels including tires. 1935: Prewar hubs, rubber tires, front bumper. 1935-1939: prewar hubs, rubber tires, no front bumper:
1. Red body, driver in yellow.
2. Yellow body, driver in blue.
3. Violet body, driver in gray.
4. Gray body, driver in brown. 1940-1949: Cast wheels, no bumper. 1950-1952: Cast yellow or green postwar hubs, rubber tires:
5. Red body, driver in green.
6. Light yellow body, driver in brown.
7. Dark yellow body, driver in brown.
8. Green body, driver in brown.
9. Green body, driver in gray.

14a-G B. E. V. ELECTRIC TRUCK 85 mm 1948-1953 #400
Cast body, tan driver and hubs, black tires, sheet metal tow hook.
1. Blue body.
2. Gray body.

14c-G COVENTRY CLIMAX FORK LIFT TRUCK 108 mm
1949-1953 #401
Cast orange body, green forks and hubs, black sheet metal lifting bars and base, operating crank.
1. No lettering.
2. Red "Coventry Climax" behind driver.

15-G RAILWAY SIGNALS 1937-1940
Boxed set of 15a/1, 15a/2, 15b, 15c/1 and 15c/2.
1. Standard colors.

15a/1-G SINGLE ARM SIGNAL: HOME 1937-1940

Cast sign, sheet metal arm.
1. Colors?

15a/2-G SINGLE ARM SIGNAL: DISTANT 1937-1940
Cast sign, sheet metal arm.
1. Colors?

15b-G DOUBLE ARM SIGNAL 1937-1940
Cast sign, sheet metal arm.
1. Colors?

15c/1-G JUNCTION SIGNAL: DISTANT 1937-1940
Cast sign, sheet metal arm.
1. Colors?

15c/2-G JUNCTION SIGNAL: HOME 1937-1940
Cast sign, sheet metal arm.
1. Colors?

16-G STREAMLINED PASSENGER TRAIN 1936-1940
1946-1953 #798
Cast interlocking locomotive-tender and two coaches, cast hubs, white or black tires, varying trim colors and lettering.
1. Silver Jubilee set, silver finish, open windows (1936-1940).
2. Dark blue, black and cream finish, closed windows, gold "LNER", number 2590, postwar hubs, black tires (1946-1952).
3. Black sheet metal base, line cast below coach windows, no number 2590, otherwise as type 2 (1953).

16a-F EXPRESS TRAIN 1935-1940
Cast interlocking bodies (2 identical end units plus central unit), cast hubs, white tires.
1. Cream upper, red lower body.
2. Cream upper, green lower body.
3. Blue-gray upper, dark blue lower body.
4. Gold upper, red lower body.
5. Gray upper, red lower body.
6. Gray upper, blue lower body.
7. May have been sold in 1940 minus central unit, as 16b.

17-F FREIGHT TRAIN 1935-1940
Cast 19a electric locomotive, 21c open car, 21b flat car with log, and 21d wrecker. See individual pieces for details.
1. Lattice wrecker boom.
2. Plain wrecker boom.

17-G PASSENGER TRAIN SET 1934-1940
Cast 17a locomotive, 17b tender, 20a coach, and 20b guard's van. See individual pieces for details.
1. Standard colors.

17a-G LOCOMOTIVE 1934-1940
Cast body and chassis.
1. Green, maroon and black.

17b-G TENDER 1934-1940
Cast body.
1. Gray and maroon.

18-F STEAM FREIGHT TRAIN 1934-1940
Cast 21a locomotive and three 21c wagons. See individual pieces for details.
1. Standard colors.

18-G TANK GOODS TRAIN SET 1934-1940
Cast 21a locomotive and three 21b wagons. See individual pieces for details.
1. Standard colors.

19-F PASSENGER TRAIN 1935-1940
Cast 19a electric locomotive and three 20a coaches. See individual pieces for details.
1. Standard colors.

19a-F ELECTRIC LOCOMOTIVE 1935-1940
Cast body, eight spoked wheels.

1. Light green body, red chassis.
2. Dark green body, black chassis.
3. Gold body, blue chassis.
4. Silver body, red chassis.

19-G MIXED GOODS TRAIN 1934-1940
Cast 21a locomotive, 21b wagon, 21c lumber wagon and 21d Shell petrol wagon. See individual pieces for details.
1. Standard colors.

20-F STEAM PASSENGER TRAIN 1935-1940
Cast 21a locomotive and three 20a coaches. See 21a for details of locomotive.
1. Standard colors.

20a-F PASSENGER CAR 1935-1940
Cast body, four small spoked wheels.
1. Red body, dark blue chassis.
2. Green body, dark blue chassis.

20-G TANK PASSENGER TRAIN 1934-1940
Cast 21a locomotive, two 20a coach, and 20b guard's van. See individual pieces for details.

20a-G COACH 1934-1940
Cast body and wheels.
1. Maroon body, white or cream roof, green chassis and wheels.
2. Tan body, white or cream roof, red chassis and windows.

20b-G GUARD'S VAN 1934-1940
Cast body, chassis and wheels.
1. Maroon body, cream roof, green chassis and wheels.
2. Tan body, cream roof, red chassis and wheels.

21-F MIXED FREIGHT TRAIN 1934-1940
Cast 21a steam locomotive, 21b flat car with log, 21c open wagon and 21d wrecker.
1. Lattice wrecker boom.
2. Plain wrecker boom.

21a-F STEAM LOCOMOTIVE 1934-1940
Cast main body, front body-chassis and six wheels.
1. Red body, blue chassis.
2. Green body, blue chassis.
3. Green body, black chassis.

21b-F FLAT CAR WITH LOG 1934-1940
Cast body, log and wheels.
1. Red body, green stakes, yellow log.

21c-F OPEN WAGON 1934-1940
Cast gondola body, chassis and wheels.
1. Green body and wheels.

21d-F WRECKER 1934-1940
Cast body, boom and wheels. 1934-1936: lattice pattern on boom; 1936-1940: plain boom. Combinations of:
1. Red, green or blue body, and
2. Red, yellow, green or blue boom.

21-G GOODS TRAIN SET 1932-1940
Cast 21a locomotive, 21b wagon, 21c crane, 21d Shell petrol tanker and 21e lumber wagon.
1. Standard colors.

21a-G LOCOMOTIVE 1932-1940
Cast body, chassis and wheels.
1. Red body, dark blue trim (1932-1934).
2. Green body, black roof, GWR logo (1934-1940).
3. Maroon body, black roof, LMS logo (1934-1940).

21b-G WAGON 1932-1940
Cast open body, chassis and wheels.
1. Red body, black chassis.

2. Green body, red chassis.

3. Green body, blue chassis.

4. Green body, black chassis.

21c-G CRANE   1932-1940
Cast body, boom and wheels.
1. Blue body, green lattice boom.
2. Blue body, green plain boom.

21d-G SHELL PETROL TANKER   1932-1940
Cast body, chassis and wheels, cast-in Shell logo on tank.
1. Red body, blue chassis.

21e-G LUMBER WAGON   1932-1940
Cast body, log and wheels.
1. Red body, green stakes, yellow log.

22-G MODELLED MINIATURES SET   1933-1935
Boxed set of 22a Sports Car, 22b Sports Coupe, 22c Motor Truck, 22d Delivery Van, 22e Farm Tractor and 22f Army Tank.
1. Standard colors.

22a-F SPORTS ROADSTER   85 mm 1933-1937
Open 2-seater with cast body, windshield-dash and wheels, body includes sloping shield grille.
1. Cream body, red fenders and folded top.
2. Green body, yellow fenders and folded top.
3. Blue body, yellow fenders and folded top.
4. Silver body, red fenders and folded top.
5. Gray body, blue fenders and folded top.

22a-G SPORTS CAR   82 mm 1933-1935
Open 2-seater with cast body, windshield-dash and wheels, sheet metal shell over vertical grid grille, no folded top.
1. Red body, cream fenders and seats.
2. Cream body, red fenders and seats.
3. Yellow body, green fenders and seats.
4. Blue body, yellow fenders and seats.

22a-H MASERATI 2000 SPORTS CAR   88 mm 1958 #505
Open sports-racing car with cast body, white driver and steering wheel, cast or turned hubs, white or black tires, plastic windshield, red interior, silver grille.
1. Red body, silver cast hubs.
2. Red body, unpainted turned hubs.

22b-F SPORTS COUPE   85 mm 1934-1937
Closed 2-seater with cast body and wheels, body includes sloping shield grille.
1. Red body, blue fenders.
2. Cream body, black fenders.
3. Green body, yellow fenders.
4. Blue body, red fenders.
5. Gray body, green fenders.

22b-G SPORTS COUPE   82 mm 1933-1935
Closed 2-seater with cast body and wheels, sheet metal shell over vertical grid grille.
1. Red body, cream fenders and top.
2. Cream body, green fenders and top.

22c-F SPORTS ROADSTER   85 mm 1934-1937
Open 2-seater with body and windshield casting (=22a-F), cast hubs, white tires.
1. Red body, red fenders and folded top.
2. Green body, yellow fenders and folded top.
3. Blue body, yellow fenders and folded top.
4. Silver body, red fenders and folded top.
5. Gray body, blue fenders and folded top.

22c-G MOTOR TRUCK   90 mm 1933-1935
Low-side open truck with cast chassis-cab, rear body and wheels, sheet metal shell over vertical grid grille, no rear window in cab.

---

1. Blue chassis-cab, red rear body.
2. Blue chassis-cab, tan rear body.

22c-H MOTOR TRUCK   84 mm 1935-1940, 1946-1950
Low-side open Bedford truck with cast body and hubs, black tires, open or closed rear window, no sheet metal radiator shell. Casting with open rear window (1935-1940):
1. Red body.
2. Green body.
3. Blue body. Casting with closed rear window (1946-1950):
4. Red body.
5. Green body.
6. Brown body.

22d-F SPORTS COUPE   85 mm 1934-1937
Closed 2-seater with cast body (=22b-F) and hubs, white tires, sloping shield grille.
1. Red body, blue fenders.
2. Cream body, black fenders.
3. Green body, yellow fenders,
4. Blue body, red fenders.
5. Gray body, green fenders.

22d-G DELIVERY VAN   83 mm 1933-1935
Closed van with cast chassis-cab, rear body and wheels, sheet metal shell over vertical grid grille, no logo.
1. Orange chassis-cab, blue rear body.
2. Blue chassis-cab, yellow rear body.
3. Gray chassis-cab, yellow rear body.

22d-H MECCANO DELIVERY VAN   83 mm 1934-1936 #28
Same castings and parts as 22d-G, with red "Meccano Engineering for Boys" logo.
1. Yellow chassis-cab and rear body.
2. Orange chassis-cab, blue rear body.
3. Yellow chassis-cab, blue rear body?

22e-G FARM TRACTOR   70 mm 1933-1940
Cast upper body, lower body-fenders, steering wheel and spoked front and rear wheels.
1. Red upper body and wheels, blue lower body.
2. Yellow upper body, blue lower body, red wheels.
3. Green upper body, yellow lower body, red wheels.
4. Blue upper body, white lower body, yellow wheels.

22f-G ARMY TANK   87 mm 1933-1940
Cast body and rotating turret, green or red rubber treads.
1. Orange body, ? turret.
2. Green body, orange turret.
3. Gray body and turret.

22g-G STREAMLINED TOURER   85 mm 1935-1940
Airflow-styled open 2-seater with cast body, windshield-dash-steering wheel and hubs, white tires.
1. Red body.
2. Cream body.
3. Green body.
4. Blue body.
5. Black body.

22h-G STREAMLINED SALOON   85 mm 1935-1940
Airflow-styled sedan with cast body and hubs, white tires. Somewhat similar to later Chrysler Airflow but smaller, less detailed.
1. Red body.
2. Cream body.

22s-G SEARCHLIGHT LORRY   84 mm 1939-1940
Cast body (=22c-H), adjustable searchlight, mount and hubs, black tires, silver lens, military finish.

---

1. Dull green body.

23-G RACING CAR SET   1936-1940
Boxed set of 23c Mercedes-Benz, 23d Auto-Union, 23e Speed of the Wind.
1. Standard colors.

23a-G RACING CAR   97 mm 1934-1938
MG Magnette-style cast body and hubs, white tires. Casting with 4 stub exhausts, no driver: 1934-1935:
1. Orange body, green trim.
2. Blue body, white trim. Casting with 6-branch exhaust pipe, driver's head, circle around racing number: 1935-1938:
3. Blue body and number, white trim and number disc.
4. Blue body and number, silver trim and number disc.

23a-H RACING CAR   94 mm 1938-1940, 1946-1953 #220
MG Magnette-style cast body and hubs, rubber tires, six-branch exhaust pipe, driver's head, no circle around number. Casting without transverse inner bulkhead: 1938-1940:
1. Red body, cream diamond-shaped trim.
2. Orange body, green diamond-shaped trim.
3. Cream body, green diamond-shaped trim.
4. White body, red diamond-shaped trim.
5. White body, blue diamond-shaped trim.
6. Brown body, cream diamond-shaped trim.
7. Red body, orange stripe trim.
8. Yellow body, blue nose and tail, #7.
9. Yellow body, blue diamond-shaped trim, #1.
10. Blue body, white nose and tail, #11.
11. Blue body, silver nose and tail, #11. Casting with transverse inner bulkhead: 1946-1953:
12. Silver body, red diamond-shaped trim, #4 (1946-1948).
13. Silver body, blue diamond-shaped trim?
14. Red body, silver trim, #4 in black circle (1952-1953).
15. Silver body, red trim, #4 in red circle (1953).

23b-F RENAULT RACING CAR   97 mm 1935-1940, 1946-1949
Nervasport-style closed single-seat cast body and wheels or hubs with white tires. Model with cast painted wheels (prewar):
1. Orange body, blue trim and wheels.
2. Yellow body, red trim and wheels.
3. Cream body, blue trim and wheels.
4. White body, green trim and wheels.
5. Blue body, red trim and wheels. Model with silver or black cast hubs and white tires (prewar):
6. Red body, green trim.
7. Orange body, blue trim.
8. Yellow body, red trim.
9. Cream body, blue trim.
10. White body, green trim.
11. Green body, white trim.
12. Green body, silver trim.
13. Blue body, red trim. Model with unpainted cast wheels (postwar):
14. Red body, green trim.
15. Orange body, green trim.
16. Orange body, blue trim.
17. Yellow body, red trim.
18. Cream body, blue trim.
19. White body, green trim.
20. Green body, white trim.
21. Green body, silver trim.
22. Blue body, red trim.

23. Blue body, white trim. Model with cream cast hubs, black tires (postwar):
24. Red body, silver trim, red number on cream disc.

23b-G HOTCHKISS RACING CAR   95 mm 1935-1940, 1946-1948
Closed single-seat cast body including headlight, cast hubs, white or black tires. Prewar types (numbers 4, 5 or 6, except type 1):
1. Blue body, white trim, no racing number.
2. Red body, silver trim.
3. Orange body, green trim.
4. Green body, yellow trim.
5. Blue body, red trim.
6. Blue body, white trim.
7. Blue body, darker blue trim. Prewar types sold in France from 1939 on:
9. Red body, silver trim, red number on cream disc, cast wheels.
10. Cast hubs, rubber tires, otherwise as type 9. Postwar types, "Hotchkiss" cast underneath:
11. Red body, silver trim, #5 in white or black circle.
12. Silver body, red trim, #5 in red circle.

23c-F MERCEDES-BENZ RACING CAR   92 mm 1949-1951
Open single-seat racer with cast body (=23c-G) and wheels or hubs with black tires, black or silver sheet metal base with French lettering, red trim and number disc, silver number 1 to 6, ivory driver.
1. Silver body, black or unpainted thick cast wheels.
2. Silver body, black thin cast wheels.
3. Silver body, red hubs, black tires.

23c-G MERCEDES-BENZ RACING CAR   92 mm 1936-1940, 1947-1950
Open single-seat racer with cast body (=23c-F) and hubs, black tires, sheet metal base (two types), white driver, silver grille, exhaust pipe and trim, number disc. Base with drive train detail but no lettering (prewar):
1. Red body, yellow number circle, red number 1 or 2.
2. Yellow body, blue number circle, yellow number 1 or 2.
3. Green body, yellow number circle, green number 1 or 2.
4. Blue body, yellow number circle, blue 1 or 2. Base with lettering including name, tan driver (postwar):
5. Blue body, black hubs and number circle.
6. Silver body, red hubs, number circle, grille and exhaust pipe.

23d-F AUTO-UNION RACING CAR   100 mm 1950-1952
Closed-cab racer with cast body (=23d-G), driver and hubs, black tires, sheet metal base with French lettering, silver grille, white driver, red number disc, number 1 to 6.
1. Light green body and number, red hubs.
2. Light green body and number, green hubs.

23d-G AUTO-UNION RACING CAR   100 mm 1936-1940, 1948-1950
Closed-cab racer with cast body (prewar) and hubs, black tires, sheet metal base (postwar), number disc with number 1, 2 or 3. Model with driver, no base (prewar):
1. Red body.
2. Green body.
3. Blue body.
4. Silver body. Model without driver, with base (postwar).
5. Red body, silver number circle.
6. Green body, blue number circle (see also 23d-F).
7. Blue body, yellow number circle.
8. Silver body, red number circle.

23e-G SPEED OF THE WIND RACING CAR   104 mm 1936-1940, 1946-1953 _#221
Open speed record car with cast body and hubs, black or gray tires, sheet metal base, white or tan driver, red or silver trim.
1. Silver body, detailed base, white number circle with 1, white driver, black hubs (prewar).

1. Yellow body.
2. Green body.
3. Blue body. Model with detailed base, tan driver, no number or disc (1946-1949):
4. Red body, silver hubs and trim, black tires.
5. Silver body, red hubs and trim, black tires. Model with plain base (lettering and 23E only), tan driver, red hubs, no number or disc (1949-1953):
6. Silver body, red hubs and air intakes, gray tires.

23f-G ALFA ROMEO RACING CAR   100 mm 1952-1953 _#232
Grand Prix racer with cast body and red hubs, black or gray tires, black sheet metal base with 23F, white driver and number 8, silver grille and exhaust pipes.
1. Red body.

23g-G COOPER-BRISTOL RACING CAR   89 mm 1953 _#233
Grand Prix racer with cast body and green hubs, black or gray tires, black sheet metal base with 23G, white driver and number 6, silver grille and exhaust pipes.
1. Green body.

23h-F TALBOT-LAGO RACING CAR   93 mm 1953-1959 _#510
Grand Prix racer with cast body (smaller than 23h-G) and hubs, black tires, black sheet metal base with 23H, white driver, silver grille and exhaust pipes.
1. Blue body and hubs, white tampo-printed number 1 to 6 (1953).
2. Blue body and hubs, yellow decal number 1 to 6 (1954-1958).
3. Blue body, chromed hubs, yellow decal number 22 to 27 (1954-1958).

23h-G FERRARI RACING CAR   101 mm 1953 _#234
Grand Prix racer with cast body and yellow hubs, black or gray tires, black sheet metal base with 23H, white driver, yellow number 5.
1. Dark blue body, yellow nose.

23j-F FERRARI RACING CAR   102 mm 1956-1959 _#511
Grand Prix racer, cast or turned hubs, black or gray tires, black sheet metal base with 23J, white driver, yellow number decal, stub exhausts (not same casting as 23h-G).
1. Red body, plain black grille, number 1 to 6, chromed cast hubs (1956).
2. Red body, black grid grille, number 1 to 6 or 33 to 38, chromed cast hubs (1957-1958).
3. Red body, black grid grille, unpainted turned hubs, number 22 to 27 (1958?).

23j-G H. W. M. RACING CAR   99 mm 1953 _#235
Grand Prix racer with cast body and green hubs, black or gray tires, black sheet metal base with 23J, white driver, yellow number 7.
1. Light green body.

23k-G TALBOT-LAGO RACING CAR   103 mm 1953 _#230
Grand Prix racer with cast body and blue hubs, black or gray tires, black sheet metal base with 23K, white driver, yellow number 4.
1. Blue body.

23m-G THUNDERBOLT SPEED CAR   126 mm 1938-1940
Enclosed, finned record car with cast body and hubs, black tires, black sheet metal base, silver grille and trim, Union Jack decals on fin. (See 23s for later use of casting.)
1. Light green body.
2. Silver body.

23n-G MASERATI RACING CAR   94 mm 1953 _#231
Grand Prix racer with cast body and red hubs, black or gray tires, black sheet metal base with 23N, white trim, driver and number 9.
1. Red body, white stripe.

23p-G GARDNER'S M.G. RECORD CAR 104 mm 1939-1940, 1946-1947
Speed record car with cast body and hubs, black tires, sheet metal base, white MG emblem.
1. Medium green body, Union Jack decals, white stripes on sides, white driver, gold base with "MG Magnette" (prewar).
2. Darker green body, Union Jack decals, no stripes, driver may or may not be painted white or silver, black base with "MG Record Car" (postwar).
3. Postwar version may exist with white stripes.

23s-G STREAMLINED RACING CAR   126 mm 1938-1940, 1948-1953 _#222
Speed record car with cast body (=23m-G) and hubs, black tires, black sheet metal base, no flag decals. Exhaust stubs and rear vents same color as grille (1938-1940):
1. Silver body, black grille.
2. Light green body, dark green grille.
3. Light blue body, dark blue grille. Cowling and three fins also same color as grille (1948-1953):
4. Light green body, dark green grille.
5. Blue body, dark blue grille.
6. Silver body, red grille.
7. Silver body, green grille.
8. Silver body, blue grille.

24-F CAR SET   1935-1940, 1946-1948
Boxed set of six cars: 24b, 24d, 24e, 24f, 24g, and 24h, in their standard versions, which vary as follows:
1. Chassis with raised X bars, lettering on center bar, well for spare wheel (24g and 24h have rear spare tire instead), plain cast hubs, white tires, grille without emblem, raised diamond on bumper, 24g and 24h have sheet metal windshield frame only (1935-1936).
2. Chassis with flat X bars, lettering on one of them, grille without emblem, bumper without diamond, solid sheet metal windshield, otherwise type 1 (1936-1938).
3. No spare wheel or well (24g and 24h have cast-in rear spare wheel cover), radiator has emblem at top, tires may be black, otherwise as type 2 (1938-1940).
4. Cast one-piece wheels, otherwise as type 3 (France only, 1940-1948).

24-G MOTOR CAR SET   1934-1940
Boxed set of eight models: 24a through 24h, standard versions as follows:
1. Chassis with raised X bars, lettering on center bar, well for spare wheel (24g and 24h have rear spare tire instead), plain cast hubs, white tires, grille without emblem, diamond on bumper, 24g and 24h have sheet metal windshield frame only (1934-1936).
2. Chassis with flat X bars, lettering on one of them, grille without emblem, bumper without diamond, solid sheet metal windshield, otherwise type 1 (1936-1938).
3. No spare wheel or well (24g and 24h have cast-in spare wheel cover), radiator has emblem at top, tires may be black, otherwise as type 2 (1938-1940).

24-H TOURING CAR SET   1955-1958
Boxed set of five cars, standard variations as follows:
1. Blue 24r Peugeot 203, gray 24t Citroen 2CV, olive 24u Simca Aronde, yellow & green 24v Buick, gray 24x Ford Vedette (1955).
2. Gray 24r Peugeot 203, red 24t Citroen 2CV, blue 24u Simca Aronde, orange & tan 24y Studebaker, yellow & black 24z Simca Versailles (1956).
3. Yellow & green 24a Chrysler, gray 24b Peugeot 403, red 24e Renault Dauphine, orange & cream 24y Studebaker, blue & ivory 24z Simca Versailles (1957).
4. Blue 24b Peugeot 403, green & white 24c Citroen DS19, gray & red 24d Plymouth, red 24e Renault Dauphine, blue & ivory 24z Simca Versailles (1958).

24a-F CHRYSLER NEW YORKER   112 mm 1956-1958 _#520
Convertible with cast body, cream steering wheel and chromed hubs, white tires, black sheet metal base (with or without "1955"), plastic interior and windshield, silver grille, bumpers, headlights and trim, +/-red taillights.
1. Dark red body, ivory interior.
2. Metallic silver blue body, ivory interior.
3. Yellow body, light green interior.
4. Mustard yellow body, light green interior.

24a-G AMBULANCE   102 mm 1934-1940
Cast body with open side windows, chassis, grille and hubs, white (or black?) tires, no spare, casting types as listed for 24-G. Castings 1 or 2 (raised X chassis, no grille emblem, 1934-1938):
1. Light gray body, red chassis.

The Old System of Catalog Numbers

2. Light gray body, dark gray chassis.
3. Cream body, red chassis.
4. Cream body, gray chassis.
5. Cream body, brown chassis. Casting 3 (flat X chassis, grille emblem, 1938-1940).
6. Cream body, red chassis.
7. Light gray body, red chassis.

24b-F   PEUGEOT 403 SEDAN   104 mm   1956-1959   _#521
Sedan with cast body, chromed cast or unpainted turned hubs, white tires, black sheet metal base with number 24B, +/-windows, silver grille, bumpers and headlights, red taillights.
1. Pale yellow body, cast hubs, no windows.
2. Dull blue body, cast hubs, no windows.
3. Gray body, cast hubs, no windows.
4. Pale yellow body, cast hubs, windows.
5. Pale yellow body, turned hubs, windows.
6. Gray body, cast hubs, windows.
7. Gray body, turned hubs, windows.

24b-G   LIMOUSINE   98 mm   1934-1940
Four-door sedan with cast body, chassis, grille and hubs, white or black tires, no spare, casting types as listed for 24-G. Casting 1 or 2 (raised X chassis, no grille emblem, 1934-1938):
1. Red body with horizontal hood louvers, red chassis? Casting 3 (flat X chassis, grille emblem, 1938-1940):
2. Light blue body with diagonal louvers, yellow chassis. Sold in France: casting 1 or 2 (1935-1936):
11. Yellow body, red chassis.
12. Yellow body, black chassis.
13. Green body, red chassis.
14. Green body, blue chassis.
15. Gray body, blue chassis. Sold in France: casting 3 (1938-1940):
16. Green body, red chassis.
17. Gray body, blue chassis. Sold in France: casting 4 (metal wheels, 1940-1948):
18. Red body, black chassis.
19. Yellow body, red chassis.
20. Green body, black chassis.
21. Yellow body, red chassis.
22. Gray body, red chassis.

24c-F   CITROEN DS19   112 mm   1956-1959   _#522
Sedan with cast body, chromed cast or unpainted turned hubs, white tires, black sheet metal base with number 24C, +/-windows, silver grille, bumper and headlights, red taillights.
1. Ivory body, black roof, cast hubs, no windows.
2. Green body, ivory roof, cast hubs, no windows.
3. Ivory body, black roof, cast hubs, windows.
4. Yellow body, blue-gray roof, cast hubs, windows.
5. Dark orange body, cream roof, cast hubs, windows.
6. Green body, gray roof, cast hubs, windows.
7. Turquoise body, gray roof, turned hubs, windows.
8. Tan body, gray roof, turned hubs, windows.

24c-G   TOWN SEDAN   97 mm   1934-1940
Open-cab town car with cast body, chassis, grille, windshield and hubs, white tires, with or without spare. Casting 1 or 2 (raised X chassis, spare, no grille emblem, 1934-1938):
1. Dark blue body and chassis.
2. Light green body, dark blue chassis. Casting 3 (flat X chassis, no spare, grille emblem, 1938-1940):
3. Dark blue body and chassis.
4. Light green body, red chassis.

24d-F   PLYMOUTH BELVEDERE   110 mm   1957-1959   _#523
Sedan with cast body, chromed cast or unpainted turned hubs, white tires, black sheet metal base with number 24D, silver grille, bumpers, headlights and trim, red taillights, no windows. Later issues have X-shaped reinforcement cast under roof.
1. Green body, black roof and lower sides, cast hubs, no X.
2. Gray body, red roof and lower sides, cast hubs, no X.
3. Green body, black roof and lower sides, cast hubs, X.
4. Gray body, red roof and lower sides, cast hubs, X.
5. Metallic brown body, tan roof and lower sides, cast hubs, X.
6. White body, light blue roof and lower sides, cast hubs, X.
7. Green body, black roof and lower sides, turned hubs, X.
8. Gray body, red roof and lower sides, turned hubs, X.
9. Metallic brown body, tan roof and lower sides, turned hubs, X.
10. White body, light blue roof and lower sides, turned hubs, X.

24d-G   VOGUE SALOON   107 mm   1934-1940
Two-door closed car with cast body, chassis, grille and hubs, white (or black?) tires, side spare. Casting 1 or 2 (raised X chassis, no grille emblem, 1934-1938):
1. Light blue body, dark blue chassis. Casting 3 (flat X chassis, grille emblem, 1938-1940):
2. Maroon body, light green chassis.
3. Pink body, green chassis. Sold in France: casting 1 or 2 (1935-1938):
11. Red body, black chassis.
12. Green body, red chassis.
13. Green body, yellow chassis.
14. Blue body, yellow chassis.
15. Blue body, black chassis. Sold in France: casting 3 (1938-1940):
16. Green body, red-brown chassis.
17. Gray body, black chassis. Sold in France, casting 4 (1940-1948):
18. Red body, black chassis.
19. Yellow body, red chassis.
20. Blue body, black chassis.
21. Gray body, red chassis.

24e-F   RENAULT DAUPHINE   92 mm   1957-1959   _#524
Sedan with cast body, chromed cast or unpainted turned hubs, black tires, black sheet metal base, silver bumpers, vents and headlights, red or orange taillights, +/-windows.
1. Ivory body, cast hubs, no windows.
2. Red body, cast hubs, no windows.
3. Brick red body, cast hubs, no windows.
4. Light green body, cast hubs, no windows.
5. Light olive green body, cast hubs, no windows.
6. Ivory body, cast hubs, windows.
7. Red body, cast hubs, windows.
8. Brick red body, cast hubs, windows.
9. Turquoise body, cast hubs, windows.
10. Tan body, cast hubs, windows.
11. Ivory body, turned hubs, windows.
12. Red body, turned hubs, windows.
13. Brick red body, turned hubs, windows.
14. Turquoise body, turned hubs, windows.
15. Tan body, turned hubs, windows.

24e-G   SUPER STREAMLINE SALOON   97 mm   1934-1940
Two-door fastback car with cast body, chassis, grille and hubs, no spare. Casting 1 or 2 (raised X chassis, no grille emblem, 1934-1938):
1. Red body, dark red chassis.
2. Red body, green chassis. Casting 3 (flat X chassis, grille emblem, 1938-1940):
3. Green body, blue chassis. Sold in France: casting 1 or 2 (1935-1938):
11. Green body, red chassis.
12. Green body, blue chassis.

13. Red body, yellow chassis.
14. Red body, black chassis.
15. Blue body, black chassis. Sold in France: casting 3 (1938-1940):
16. Red body, yellow chassis.
17. Red body, black chassis.
18. Blue body, black chassis. Sold in France: casting 4 (cast wheels, 1940-1948):
19. Red body, black chassis.
20. Yellow body, red chassis.
21. Green body, black chassis.

24f-F   PEUGEOT 403U FAMILIALE   107 mm   1959   _#525
Station wagon with cast body, chromed cast or unpainted turned hubs, black or white tires, black sheet metal base with number 24F, silver grille, bumpers and headlights, red taillights, no windows.
1. Light blue body, cast hubs, black tires.
2. Light blue body, turned hubs, black tires.
3. Light blue body, turned hubs, white tires.

24f-G   SPORTSMAN'S COUPE   100 mm   1934-1940
Coupe with cast body, chassis, grille and hubs, white or black tires, with or without spare wheel. Casting 1 or 2 (raised X chassis, spare, no grille emblem, 1934-1938):
1. Yellow body, brown chassis.
2. Dark blue body, blue chassis. Casting 3 (flat X chassis, no spare, grille emblem, 1938-1940):
3. Cream body, blue chassis. Sold in France: casting 1 or 2 (1935-1938):
11. Red body, black chassis.
12. Green body, yellow chassis.
13. Blue body, yellow chassis.
14. Blue body, black chassis. Sold in France: casting 3 (1938-1940):
15. Red body, black chassis.
16. Yellow body, red chassis.
17. Yellow body, black chassis.
18. Cream body, dark blue chassis.
19. Blue body, red-brown chassis. Sold in France: casting 4 (cast wheels, 1940-1948):
20. Red body, black chassis.
21. Yellow body, red chassis.
22. Green body, black chassis.
23. Blue body, black chassis.

24g-G   SPORTS TOURER (4-seater)   98 mm   1934-1940
Open 4-seater with cast body, chassis, grille and hubs, white or black tires, sheet metal windshield. Casting 1 or 2 (raised X chassis, windshield frame only, rear spare tire, no grille emblem, 1934-1938):
1. Blue body, brown chassis. Casting 3 (flat X chassis, solid windshield, cast-in rear spare cover, grille emblem, 1938-1940):
2. Cream body, green chassis.
3. Cream body, black chassis. Sold in France: casting 1 or 2 (1935-1938):
11. Yellow body, red chassis.
12. Green body, red chassis.
13. Blue body, red chassis.
14. Gray body, blue chassis. Sold in France: casting 3 (1938-1940):
15. Green body, red chassis.
16. Green body, red chassis. Sold in France: casting 4 (cast wheels, 1940-1948):
17. Red body, black chassis.
18. Yellow body, red chassis.
19. Gray body, red chassis.

24h-F   MERCEDES-BENZ 190SL COUPE   98 mm   1958-1959   _#526
Sports coupe with cast body, chromed cast or unpainted turned hubs, black tires, black sheet metal base with number 24H, black roof, silver grille, bumpers and headlights, red taillights, +/-windows.

1. Ivory body, cast hubs, no windows.
2. Silver body, cast hubs, no windows.
3. Ivory body, cast hubs, windows.
4. Silver body, cast hubs, windows.
5. Ivory body, turned hubs, windows.
6. Silver body, turned hubs, windows.

24h-G SPORTS TOURER (2-seater) 98 mm **1934-1940**

Open two-seater with cast body, chassis, grille and hubs, white or black tires, sheet metal windshield. Casting 1 or 2 (raised X chassis, windshield frame only, rear spare tire, no grille emblem, 1934-1938):
1. Red body, green chassis.
2. Yellow body, blue chassis. Casting 3 (flat X chassis, solid windshield, rear spare cover, grille emblem, 1938-1940):
3. Cream body, black chassis. Sold in France: casting 1 (1935-1938):
11. Red body, black chassis.
12. Yellow body, black chassis.
13. Green body, red chassis.
14. Green body, blue chassis.
15. Blue body, red chassis.
16. Black body, red chassis.
17. Black body, blue chassis. Sold in France: casting 3 (1938-1940):
18. Red body, black chassis.
19. Yellow body, black chassis.
20. Green body, red chassis. Sold in France: casting 4 (cast wheels, 1940-1948):
21. Red body, red chassis.
22. Yellow body, red chassis.
23. Cream body, red chassis.

24j-F ALFA ROMEO 1900 COUPE 102 mm **1959** #527

Sports coupe with cast body, chromed cast or unpainted turned hubs, black tires, black sheet metal base with number 24J, windows, silver grille, bumpers and headlights, red or orange taillights, windows.
1. Red body, cast hubs.
2. Blue body, cast hubs.
3. Red body, turned hubs.
4. Blue body, turned hubs.
5. Turquoise body, turned hubs.

24k-F PEUGEOT 402 **1939-1940, 1946-1949**

Sedan with cast body, wheels or hubs with white or black tires, sheet metal bumper, with or without sheet metal base. Model with unpainted cast wheels, no base (1939-40, 1946-48):
1. Red body.
2. Red-brown body.
3. Mustard yellow body.
4. Light blue body.
5. Bright blue body. Model with cast hubs, tires, no base (1939-1940):
6-10. Colors as above. Model with cast wheels, black base (1948-1949):
11-15. Colors as above.

24k-H SIMCA CHAMBORD 110 mm **1959** #528

Sedan with cast body, chromed cast hubs, white tires, black sheet metal base, windows, silver grille, bumpers and headlights, red taillights. Roof color is also on lower sides and fin panels.
1. Cream body, red sides and roof.
2. Light green body, dark green sides and roof.

24l-F PEUGEOT 402 TAXI 93 mm **1939-1940, 1946-1948**

Cast body (same as 24k-F), cast wheels or hubs with black or white tires, sheet metal bumper and taximeter, with or without sheet metal base. Model with unpainted cast

wheels, no base (1939-1940, 1946-1948):
1. Maroon body, cream sides.
2. Dark blue body, yellow sides.
3. Black body, yellow sides. Model with cast hubs, tires, no base (1939-1940):
4-6. Colors as before. Model with cast wheels, black base (1948-1949):
7-9. Colors as before.

24l-H VESPA 400 2CV 66 mm **1959** #529

Minicar with cast body and chromed hubs, black tires, black sheet metal base, windows, silver grille, bumpers and headlights, red taillights.
1. Blue body, gray roof panel.
2. Orange body, gray roof panel.

24m-F JEEP 80 mm **1946-1949**

Open Jeep with cast body and wheels, sheet metal windshield same color as body. Civilian types (1948-1949) have black wheels.
1. Olive body and wheels, white star in circle on hood (1946-1948).
2. Red body.
3. Orange body.
4. Yellow body.
5. Green body.
6. Blue body.
7. Tan body.
8. Gold body.
9. Silver body.

24m-H VOLKSWAGEN KARMANN-GHIA COUPE 95 mm **1959** #530

Coupe with cast body and chromed hubs, white tires, black sheet metal base, windows, silver bumpers and headlights.
1. Red body, black roof, body with wide nose.

(24mr ARMY JEEP AND TRAILER never issued)

24n-F CITROEN TRACTION AVANT 11BL 96 mm **1949-1958**

Sedan with cast body, headlights and wheels or painted or chrome hubs with black or white tires, black sheet metal base, silver trim. Casting with cast-in rear spare cover, sheet metal bumper (1949-1952):
1. Black body, cast wheels.
2. Navy blue body, cast wheels.
3. Metallic gray body, cast wheels.
4. Black body, yellow hubs, black tires.
5. Metallic gray body, red hubs, black tires.
6. Black body, cream hubs, black tires. Casting with cast-in bumper and trunk, new grille pattern (1953-1958):
7. Black body, cream hubs, black tires.
8. Light gray body, gray wheels, black or white tires.
9. Gray body, chrome hubs, white tires.

24n FIAT 1200 GRANDE VUE issued as 531)

24o-F STUDEBAKER STATE COMMANDER 100 mm **1949-1950**

Cast body (same as 39f-G) and wheels or hubs with black tires, black sheet metal base, silver trim.
1. Red body, cast wheels.
2. Cream body, cast wheels.
3. Metallic green body, cast wheels.
4. Cream body, yellow hubs.
5. Metallic green body, red hubs.

24p-F PACKARD SUPER EIGHT 105 mm **1949 only**

Cast body (same as 39a-G) and wheels or hubs with black tires, black sheet metal base, silver trim.
1. Bright blue body, cast wheels.
2. Turquoise body, black hubs.
3. Dark gold body, black hubs.

(24p LINCOLN PREMIERE issued as 532)

24q-F FORD VEDETTE 1949 105 mm **1950-1955**

Sedan with cast body and hubs, black tires, black sheet metal base (1950 type: small lettering; 1952 type: large lettering, two holes), silver trim.
1. Dark blue body, red hubs, 1950 base.
2. Metallic blue body, red hubs, 1950 base.
3. Metallic turquoise body, red hubs, 1950 base.
4. Gray body and hubs, 1950 base.
5. Metallic blue body, red hubs, 1952 base.
6. Turquoise body and hubs, 1952 base.
7. Grayish-tan body and hubs, 1952 base.

24r-F PEUGEOT 203 100 mm **1951-1959** #533

Sedan with cast body and hubs, black or white tires, black sheet metal base, no number, silver grille, bumpers and headlights. Casting with small rear wheel, gas filler on right rear fender, black tires:
1. Garnet red body, cream hubs.
2. Metallic turquoise blue body, cream hubs.
3. Metallic turquoise green body, cream hubs.
4. Metallic gold body, cream hubs.
5. Metallic gold body, red hubs.
6. Gray body and hubs. Casting with small rear window, no gas filler, black tires:
7. Garnet red body, cream hubs.
8. Metallic green body, cream hubs.
9. Gray-green body, gray hubs.
10. Gray body and hubs. Casting with small rear window, no gas filler, grid under roof, black tires:
11. Metallic green body, cream hubs.
12. Metallic blue body, cream hubs.
13. Metallic blue body and hubs.
14. Gray body and hubs.
15. Metallic blue body, chrome hubs.
16. Light gray body, chrome hubs.
17. Pale gray body, chrome hubs. Casting with large rear window, filler cap cover far back on right rear fender, grid under roof, chrome hubs, white tires:
18. Metallic blue body.
19. Light gray body.

24s-F SIMCA 8 CABRIOLET 95 mm **1952-1959** #534

Roadster with cast body (including interior and windshield frame), cream steering wheel, and hubs, white tires, black sheet metal base, no number, silver grille, bumpers and lights. Casting with thin windshield frame (top edge forms wide V):
1. Black body, tan interior, unpainted hubs.
2. Black body, red interior, unpainted hubs.
3. Black body, red interior, chrome hubs.
4. Gray body, red interior, unpainted hubs.
5. Gray body, red interior, chrome hubs. Casting with thick windshield frame (top edge is straight in back), red interior, chrome hubs:
6. Black body.
7. Gray body.
8. Bluish ivory body.
9. Blue-green body.

24t-F CITROEN 2CV 1950 87 mm **1952-1959** #535

Small car with cast, cast or turned hubs, black tires, black sheet metal base, no number, silver grille, headlights and sometimes bumpers, red or orange taillights, dark gray roof. Casting with one taillight, no grid under roof, cast hubs:
1. Metallic brownish gray body and hubs.
2. Medium gray body, cream hubs.
3. Dark gray body, cream hubs.
4. Dark gray body, tan hubs. Casting with one taillight, grid under roof, cast hubs.
5. Light gray body, cream hubs.

The Old System of Catalog Numbers

6. Dark gray body, cream hubs. Casting with three taillights, grid under roof (1957-1959):
7. Light garnet red body, cream cast hubs.
8. Dark garnet red body, cream cast hubs.
9. Grayish yellow body, cream cast hubs.
10. Dark oily blue body, cream cast hubs.
11. Light gray body, cream cast hubs.
12. Garnet red body, light gray turned hubs.
13. Oily blue body, dark blue roof, light gray turned hubs.
14. Grayish blue body, dark blue roof, light gray turned hubs.

24u-F SIMCA ARONDE 95 mm 1953-1959 #536
Sedan with cast body and hubs, white tires, black sheet metal base with number, silver grille, bumpers and headlights, red taillights. Casting with Simca 9 grille, no grid under roof, hubs match body;
1. Olive green body.
2. Very dark olive green body.
3. Gray body. Casting with Simca 9 grille, grid under roof, hubs match body:
4. Light olive green body.
5. Light gray body.
6. Medium gray body.
7. Greenish gray body. Casting with Elysee grille, new fender shape, grid under roof, chromed hubs (1956):
8. Light gray body.
9. Greenish gray body.
10. Sky blue body.
11. Sky blue body, ivory roof (1958).
12. Medium blue body, ivory roof (1958).
13. Light gray-green body, dark green roof (1958).

24ut-F SIMCA ARONDE TAXI 95 mm 1956-1959 #537
Cast body (= 24u), white Taxi sign with red letters, unpainted meter and hubs, white tires, black sheet metal base with number, silver Elysee grille, bumpers and headlights, maroon and silver trim.
1. Red body and hubs, blue roof.
2. Red body, blue roof, chromed hubs.

24v-F BUICK ROADMASTER 112 mm 1954-1959 #538
Sedan with cast body and unpainted or chromed hubs, white tires, black sheet metal base with number, silver grille, bumpers, headlights and trim, red taillights, no windows, +/- grid under roof.
1. Light yellow body, dark green roof.
2. Bright yellow body, green roof.
3. Blue body, black roof.
4. Blue body, ivory roof.
5. Orange body, black roof.
6. Ivory body, metallic light blue roof.

24x-F FORD VEDETTE 1953 105 mm 1954-1956
Sedan with cast body and hubs, white tires, black sheet metal base, silver trim.
1. Light gray body and hubs.
2. Navy blue body and hubs.
3. Navy blue body, chrome hubs.

24xt-F FORD VEDETTE TAXI 105 mm 1956-1959 #539
Cast body (= 24x), white Taxi sign with red letters, unpainted meter, and chromed hubs, white tires, black sheet metal base with number, silver grille, bumpers and headlights, red taillights.
1. Black body, cream roof (shade of roof varies).

24y-F STUDEBAKER COMMANDER 109 mm 1955-1959 #540
Coupe with cast body, chromed cast hubs, white tires, black sheet metal base with number, silver grille, bumpers and headlights, red taillights, grid under roof.
1. Ivory body, garnet red roof.

2. Dark orange body, dark cream to light tan roof.
3. Pale gray-green body, dark green roof.
4. Bright green body, dark green roof.
5. Ivory body, garnet red roof and side panels (1958).
6. Bright orange body, cream roof and side panels (1958).
7. Dark orange body, dark cream to light tan roof and side panels (1958).
(24z FORD COMETE COUPE never issued)

24z-F SIMCA VERSAILLES 105 mm 1956-1959 #541
Sedan with cast body and chromed hubs, white tires, black sheet metal base, silver trim, grid under roof.
1. Yellow body, black roof.
2. Light blue body, ivory roof.
(24zt SIMCA VERSAILLES TAXI never issued)

24zt-F SIMCA ARIANE TAXI 105 mm 1959 #542
Cast body (= 24z), white Taxi sign with red letters, unpainted meter and chromed hubs, white tires, black sheet metal base with number, windows, silver grille, bumpers and headlights, red taillights.
1. Black body, red roof.

25-F TRUCK SET 1935-1940, 1946-1948
Boxed set of 25a-F Wagon, 25b-F Covered Wagon, 25c-F Flat Truck, 25d-F Tanker, 25e-F Dump Truck and 25f-f Market Gardener's Van. Castings are different from British 25-f trucks in detail but similar in construction, with cast body, chassis (with three rounded triangular holes), grille with headlights, and wheels or hubs with rubber tires.
1. Set includes Standard tanker, all models with chromed or painted cast hubs, black or white tires (1935-1937).
2. Set includes Essolube tanker, models as before (1938-1939).
3. Set includes Essolube tanker, all models with cast wheels (1940, 1946-1948).

25-G COMMERCIAL MOTOR VEHICLES 1934-1940
Boxed set of six models, originally 25a-G Wagon, 25b-G Covered Wagon, 25c-G Flat Truck, 25d-G Petrol Tanker, 25e-G Tipper and 25f-G Market Gardener's Van; 25a and 25c replaced in 1937 by 25g-G Trailer and 25g-G Fire Engine. Casting types:
1. Black or green chassis with three rounded triangular holes, no bumper, short fenders, pointed rear with tow hook, sheet metal grille without headlights, body with long hood (1934-1935).
2. Similar chassis, cast grille with headlights, body with shorter hood (1936-1940).
3. Black chassis with one round hole, otherwise as type 2 (1946-1947).
4. Black chassis with cast-in drive train, front bumper, long fenders, square rear with longer tow hook, otherwise as types 2 and 3 (1947-1950). Note: 25a-b-c-d-e-f set can exist with casting 1 or 2, 25b-d-e-f-g-h set only with casting 2.

25a-F WAGON 110 mm 1935-1940, 1946-1949
Low-side open truck with cast body, chassis, grille and either cast hubs and rubber tires or cast one-piece wheels. Cast hubs with rubber tires (1935-1939):
1. Yellow body, tan chassis.
2. Yellow body, black chassis.
3. Green body, black chassis.
4. Blue body, black chassis. Cast one-piece wheels (1940, 1946-1949):
5. Red body, gray chassis.
6. Red body, black chassis.
7. Green body, black chassis.
8. Tan body, gray chassis.
9. Light gray body, black chassis.

25a-G WAGON 108/105/110 mm 1934-1940, 1946-1950
Low-side open truck with cast body, chassis and hubs, rubber tires, sheet metal or cast grille. All four casting types (see 25-G); type 1 and 2 chassis usually black, rarely green; type 3 and 4 chassis always black.
1. Red body, casting 1.
2. Blue body, casting 2.

3. Green body, casting 2.
4. Green body, casting 3.
5. Gray body, casting 3.
6. Gray body, casting 4.
7. Red body, casting 4.
8. Yellow body, casting 4.
9. Green body, casting 4.
10. Blue body, casting 4. Other color versions may also exist.

25a-H FORD LIVESTOCK TRUCK 94 mm 1950-1952
Stake truck with cast short chassis-cab, rear body and hubs, black tires, spare wheel, black sheet metal tow hook. One of a series of French Ford trucks.
1. Light metallic blue body, yellow hubs.
2. Metallic gray body, red hubs.
3. Bright yellow chassis-cab, red rear body and hubs (1952).

25b-F COVERED WAGON 110 mm 1935-1940, 1946-1949
Covered version of 25a-F with cast body, chassis, grille and either cast hubs and rubber tires or cast one-piece wheels, sheet metal rear cover. Cast hubs with rubber tires (1935-1939):
1. Red body, green cover, red-brown chassis.
2. Green body, tan cover, black chassis.
3. Blue body, tan cover, red chassis.
4. Blue body, tan cover, black chassis. Cast one-piece wheels (1940, 1946-1949):
5. Red body, cream cover, black chassis.
6. Red body, green cover, black chassis.
7. Red body, green cover, gray chassis.
8. Yellow body, green cover, red chassis.
9. Blue body, green cover, black chassis.
10. Brown body, gray cover with Primagaz logo, black chassis: I have this model but cannot swear to its authenticity.

25b-G COVERED WAGON 108/105/110 mm 1934-1940, 1946-1950
Covered version of 25a-G with cast body, chassis and hubs, rubber tires, sheet metal or cast grille, sheet metal rear cover. Chassis of casting 1 or 2 rarely green, otherwise all chassis are black.
1. Blue body, cream cover, casting 1.
2. Blue body, cream cover, casting 2.
3. Gray body and cover, casting 2.
4. Light green body, tan cover, Hornby Trains logo, casting 2.
5. Light green body, tan cover, Meccano Engineering logo, casting 2.
6. Light green body, green top, Carter Paterson Express Carriers logo, casting 2.
7. Light green body, tan cover, Carter Paterson Special Service logo, casting 2.
8. Green body and cover, casting 3.
9. Light blue body, black cover, casting 3.
10. Light gray body, dark gray top, casting 3.
11. Yellow body and cover, casting 4.

25b-H PEUGEOT D3A VAN 90 mm 1953-1954
Delivery van with cast body and hubs, black tires, black sheet metal base, silver trim.
1. Navy blue body, red hubs (1953).
2. Green upper body and hubs, yellow lower body, black "Lampe Mazda" logo on yellow panel (1953-1954).
(25bp PEUGEOT D3A FIRE VAN never issued)

25bv-H PEUGEOT D3A MAIL VAN
Casting and parts as 25b-H, cast or turned hubs, yellow stripe and "Postes" logo either tampo-printing or decal.
1. Dark green body and hubs, tampo-printed logo, plain surface under roof.
2. Grid cast under roof, otherwise as type 1.
3. Grid cast under roof, decal logo, otherwise as type 1.
4. Turned hubs, otherwise as type 3.

25c-F FLAT TRUCK 110 mm 1935-1940, 1946-1949

Flatbed truck with cast body, chassis, grille and either cast hubs and rubber tires or cast one-piece wheels. Cast hubs with rubber tires (1935-1939):
1. Red body, brown chassis.
2. Blue body, black chassis.
3. Turquoise body, black chassis.
4. Gray body, red chassis.
5. Gray body, black chassis. Cast one-piece wheels (1940, 1946-1949):
6. Cream body, red chassis.
7. Green body, black chassis.
8. Blue body, black chassis.
9. Gray body, red chassis.

25c-G   FLAT TRUCK   108/105/110 mm   1934-1940, 1946-1950
Flatbed truck with cast body, chassis and hubs, rubber tires, sheet metal or cast grille.
1. Dark blue body, casting 1.
2. Green body, casting 2.
3. Green body, casting 3.
4. Blue body, casting 3.
5. Orange body, casting 4.
6. Blue body, casting 4.
7. Gray body, casting 4. Other versions may also exist.

25c-H   CITROEN 1200KG VAN   90 mm   1954-1957
Delivery van with cast body, sliding door and hubs, black tires, black sheet metal, silver trim, no logo.
1. Metallic brownish-gray body, no grid under roof.
2. Metallic brownish-gray body, grid cast under roof.

25cg-F   CITROEN 1200KG VAN   90 mm   1957-1959   _#561
Castings and parts as 25c-H plus logo decals.
1. Cream body and hubs, green-blue-white-red Ch. Gervais logo (two similar types, 1957-1959).
2. Turquoise body, red hubs, Cibié logo (1959).

25d-F   TANK TRUCK   110 mm   1935-1940, 1946-1949
Gasoline tanker with cast body, chassis, grille and either cast hubs and rubber tires or cast one-piece wheels.
1. Red body, garnet red chassis, cast hubs, no logo (prewar).
2. Red body, black chassis, cast hubs, white tires, Standard logo on tank sides, Essolube on back (prewar).
3. Red body, black chassis, cast hubs, black tires, Essolube logo on tank sides, Esso in oval on back (prewar).
4. Garnet red chassis, black or white tires, otherwise as type 3 (prewar).
5. Cast one-piece wheels, otherwise as type 3 (1940).
6. Red-brown body, light gray chassis, otherwise as type 5 (1946).
7. Red body, black chassis, cast one-piece wheels, Esso logo on sides and back (postwar).
8. Gray chassis, otherwise as type 7 (postwar). Note: both British and French tankers are wider at front than other 25 series trucks and require wider grilles.

25d-G   PETROL TANK WAGON   105 to 110 mm   1934-1940, 1946-1950
Gasoline tanker with cast body, chassis and hubs, rubber tires, sheet metal or cast grille. Early chassis are rarely green, otherwise all chassis are black.
1. Red body, no logo, casting 1 (1934-1937).
2. Yellow body, Shell-BP logo, casting 1 (1934-1937).
3. Red body, Shell-BP logo, casting 1 (1937).
4. Red body, Shell-BP logo, casting 2 (1938-1940).
5. Green body, Power logo, casting 1 (1936-1937).
6. Green body, Power logo, casting 2 (1938-1940).
7. Green body, Esso logo, casting 2 (1939-1940).
8. Red body, Mobiloil logo, casting 2 (1939-1940).
9. Green body, Castrol logo, casting 1 (1934-1937).
10. Green body, Castrol logo, casting 2 (1938-1940).

11. Red body, Shell logo, casting 1 (1936-1937).
12. Red body, Texaco logo, casting 2 (1938-1940).
13. Dark blue body, Redline-Glico logo, casting 2 (1939-1940).
14. Gray body, white stamped Pool logo, casting 2 (1940).
15. Gray body with white front fenders, white stamped Pool logo, casting 2 (1940).
16. May exist with black stamped Pool logo.
17. Green body, white or black Petrol logo, casting 1 (1934-1937).
18. Green body, white or black Petrol logo, casting 2.
19. Red body, white or black Petrol logo, casting 1.
20. Red body, white or black Petrol logo, casting 2.
21. Red body, white or black Petrol logo, casting 3 (1946-1947).
22. Red body, white or black Petrol logo, casting 4 (1947-1950).
23. Orange body, white or black Petrol logo, casting 4 (1947-1950).
24. Green body, white or black Petrol logo, casting 4 (1947-1950).
25. Tan body, white or black Petrol logo, casting 4 (1947-1950).
26. Red body, Esso logo, casting 4 (postwar).

25d-H   CITROEN 2CV FIRE VAN   84 mm   1958-1959   _#562
Light box van with cast body, opening rear door and hubs, black tires, black sheet metal base with number, silver grille, bumper and headlights.
1. Red body and hubs, Pompiers de Paris decals.
2. Gray body, cream hubs, Club Dinky Toys de Lyon adhesive labels, promotional model (1959).

25e-F   DUMP TRUCK   110 mm   1935-1940, 1946-1949
Rear dumper with cast body, tipper, chassis, grille and either cast hubs and rubber tires or cast one-piece wheels. Cast hubs with rubber tires (1935-1939):
1. Green body, yellow tipper, tan chassis.
2. Green body, blue tipper, black chassis.
3. Blue body, yellow tipper, black chassis. Cast one-piece wheels (1940, 1946-1949):
4. Cream body, green tipper, red chassis.
5. Green body, yellow tipper, tan chassis.
6. Blue body, yellow tipper, black chassis.

25e-G   TIPPING WAGON   105 to 110 mm   1934-1940, 1946-1950
Rear dumper with cast body, tipper, chassis and hubs, rubber tires, sheet metal or cast grille. Chassis almost always black.
1. Maroon body, yellow tipper, casting 1.
2. Brown body, light blue tipper, casting 1.
3. Brown body and tipper, casting 1.
4. Gray body and tipper, casting 1.
5. Tan body and tipper, casting 2.
6. Gray body and tipper, casting 3.
7. Yellow body and tipper, casting 4.
8. Blue body, light red tipper, casting 4.
9. Red-brown body and tipper, casting 4.
10. Gray body and tipper, casting 4.
11. Gray body, red-brown tipper, casting 4.

25f-F   MARKET GARDENER'S VAN   110 mm   1935-1940, 1946-1949
High-side stake truck with cast body, chassis, grille and either cast hubs and rubber tires or cast one-piece wheels, sheet metal upper rear stake body same color as cast body. Cast hubs with rubber tires (1935-1939):
1. Cream body, black chassis.
2. Green body, red chassis.
3. Tan body, black chassis. Cast one-piece wheels (1940, 1946-1949):
4. Yellow body, red chassis.
5. Cream body, red chassis.
6. Aqua body, light gray chassis.
7. Turquoise body, black chassis.

25f-G   MARKET GARDENER'S VAN   105 to 110 mm   1934-1940

1946-1950
High-side stake truck with cast body, chassis and hubs, rubber tires, sheet metal or cast grille, and sheet metal upper rear stake body same color as cast body. Chassis almost always black.
1. Yellow cab, green chassis, casting 1.
2. Green body, black chassis, casting 1.
3. Yellow body, green chassis, casting 2.
4. Yellow body, black chassis, casting 2.
5. Green body, black chassis, casting 3.
6. Yellow body, black chassis, casting 4.

25f-F   FOUR WHEEL TRAILER   70 mm   1939-1940, 1946-1952
Flatbed truck trailer with cast body, front wheel mount and either cast hubs and black tires or cast one-piece wheels, sheet metal hitch and tow hook.
1. Red body, cast hubs, thick tires (1939-1947).
2. Green body, cast hubs, thick tires.
3. Blue body, cast hubs, thick tires.
4. Red body, cast wheels (1948).
5. Green body, cast wheels.
6. Turquoise body, cast wheels.
7. Red body, cast hubs, thin tires (1949-1950).
8. Green body, cast hubs, thin tires.
9. Red body, reinforced hitch, cast hubs, thin tires (1951-1952).

25g-G   TRAILER   69 mm   1935-1940, 1947-1953   _#429
Flatbed truck trailer with cast body, front axle mount (= body color) and hubs, black tires, sheet metal or wire hitch, sheet metal tow hook.
1. Green body, sheet metal hitch (prewar).
2. Dark blue body, sheet metal hitch.
3. Orange body black hubs, wire hitch (postwar).
4. Red body and hubs, wire hitch.
5. Green body, light green hubs, wire hitch.

25h-F   FORD FLAT TRUCK WITH RACKS   102 mm   1949-1950
Long-chassis flatbed truck with cast body and wheels or hubs with black tires, sheet metal rear rack, black front base and tow hook same color as body. All colors exist with either wheel type.
1. Red body.
2. Cream body.
3. Metallic green body.
4. Turquoise body.
5. Blue body.

25h-G   STREAMLINED FIRE ENGINE   102 mm   1936-1940, 1946-1953   _#250
Merryweather fire engine with cast body and hubs, rubber tires, sheet metal ladder, bell and black base, silver trim.
1. Red body and ladder (prewar, early postwar).
2. Red body, unpainted ladder (later postwar).

25i-F   FORD OPEN TRUCK   102 mm   1949-1952
Long-chassis low-side truck with cast body, wheels or hubs with black tires, black sheet metal front base, cast-in or sheet metal tow hook same color as body, spare wheel. Casting with large fuel tank, cast-in tow hook, cast black wheels or (rarely) cast hubs (body color) and black tires (1949-1950):
1. Red body.
2. Cream body.
3. Green body.
4. Blue body.
5. Chestnut brown body.
6. Metallic gray body.
7. Dark gray body. Casting with small fuel tank, sheet metal tow hook, cast hubs and black tires (1951-1952):

8. Dark red body and hubs.
9. Cream body and hubs.
10. Light blue body and hubs.

25j-F FORD COVERED TRUCK   102 mm 1949-1950
Covered long-chassis truck with cast body and one-piece wheels or hubs with black
tires, spare wheel, sheet metal cover and black front base, first long-chassis casting with
big fuel tank and cast-in tow hook. All 1949 issues had cast wheels, 1950 issues had
cast hubs with tires.
1. Red body, green cover.
2. Cream body, chestnut cover.
3. Light blue body, cream cover.
4. Dark blue body, chestnut cover.
5. Gold body, green cover.
6. Chestnut body, green cover.
7. Chestnut body and cover.

25jb-F FORD COVERED TRUCK: SNCF   102 mm 1949-1952
Casting and parts as 25j-F with yellow and black SNCF logo.
1. Medium blue body, navy blue cover, black metal wheels (1949).
2. Black hubs and tires, otherwise as type 1 (1950).
3. Second long-chassis casting (small fuel tank, sheet metal tow hook), otherwise as
   type 2 (1951-1952).

25j-F FORD COVERED TRUCK: CALBERSON   102 mm 1949-1952
Casting and parts as 25j-F with varying Calberson logo.
1. Brownish yellow body, black top, logo with letters of equal size, black cast wheels
   (1949-1950).
2. Golden yellow body, otherwise as type 1 (1950).
3. Golden yellow body, red hubs, black tires, otherwise as type 1 (1950).
4. Logo with truck coming out of letter O, otherwise as type 3 (1950).
5. Second long-chassis casting (small fuel tank, cast-in tow hook), otherwise as type
   4 (1950).
6. Logo with wider, closer letters, no truck coming from O, otherwise as type 5
   (1951).
7. Logo with less distinct lines, otherwise as type 5 (1952).
(25jr FORD COVERED TRUCK: ESSO never issued)

25jv-F FORD COVERED TRUCK: Grands Moulins De Paris 102 mm 1953
Second long-chassis casting, red cast body, black tires, red Grands Moulins de Paris
logo on white background.
1. Light gray body, black top. (This is the only regular issue; other prototypes also
   exist.)

25j-G JEEP   68 mm 1947-1948
Open Jeep with cast body and blue hubs, black tires, rear spare, sheet metal windshield
frame and steering wheel.
1. Red body and windshield frame.
2. Green body and windshield frame.

25k-F STUDEBAKER STAKE TRUCK   105 mm 1949-1952
High-side stake truck with cast chassis-cab, rear body and wheels or hubs with rubber
tires, spare wheel, sheet metal front base and tow hook. Casting with gap between front
fenders and bumper, somewhat rounded front windows; cast wheels in 1949, cast hubs
in 1950:
1. Red cab, yellow body, cast wheels or yellow hubs.
2 Red cab, blue body, cast wheels.
3. Red cab, turquoise body, red hubs.
4. Turquoise cab, red body, cast wheels.
5. Blue cab, red body, blue hubs.
6. Blue cab, turquoise cab, cast wheels or blue hubs. Casting with no gap between
   front fenders and bumper, squarish front windows, cast hubs (1951-1952):
7. Red cab, yellow body, red hubs.
8. Red cab, yellow body and hubs.

9. Blue cab, tan body, blue hubs.

25k-G STREAMLINED FIRE ENGINE (with firemen) 102 mm 1938-1940
Castings and parts as 25h-G plus six sheet metal firemen.
1. Red body and ladder.

25l-F STUDEBAKER STAKE TRUCK WITH COVER 105 mm 1949-1952
Casting and parts as 25k-F plus sheet metal rear cover. First casting (see 25k-F), cast
wheels in 1949, cast hubs with tires in 1950:
1. Red body, yellow cover and hubs.
2. Blue body, yellow cover, cast wheels.
3. Blue body, yellow cover, blue hubs.
4. Turquoise body, cream cover, metal wheels.
5. Turquoise body, cream cover, blue hubs. Second casting (see 25k-F), cast hubs with
   tires (1951-1952):
6. Red body, yellow cover and hubs.
7. Blue body, tan cover, red hubs.
8. Blue body, tan cover, blue hubs.

25m-F STUDEBAKER DUMP TRUCK   105 mm 1949-1954
Rear dumper with cast chassis-cab, tipper and wheels or hubs with black tires, spare
wheel, sheet metal front base and tow hook, tipping mechanism with crank. First
casting, cast wheels in 1949, cast hubs with tires in 1950:
1. Dark green cab, metallic gray body, cast wheels.
2. Dark green cab, metallic gray body, dark green cast hubs. Second casting, cast
   hubs with tires (1951-1954):
3. Dark green cab, metallic gray body, dark green hubs.
4. Khaki cab, silver body, cream wheels.

25m-G BEDFORD END TIPPER   98 mm 1948-1953 _#410
Dump truck with cast chassis-cab, tipper, opening tailgate, black and silver grille-
bumper-headlights, and hubs, black tires, black sheet metal base, tipping crank and
spiral, no windows.
1. Orange cab and tipper.
2. Medium green cab and tipper.
3. Dark green cab and tipper.
4. Tan cab and tipper.
5. Red cab, yellow tipper.

25m-H FORD DUMP TRUCK   94 mm 1950, 1954-1955
Short-chassis rear tipper with cast chassis-cab, tipper and hubs, black tires, sheet metal
front base and tow hook, tipping mechanism and crank.
1. Dark green cab, silver gray tipper, circular mold mark beside spare wheel (1950).
2. Dark green cab, metallic golden gray tipper, small mold marks under running
   boards, +/- grid under cab roof (1954-1955).

25n-F TRUCK SET   1949-1951
Boxed set of 25h Ford with tail rack, 25i Ford open truck, 25j Ford covered truck, 25k
Studebaker stake truck, 25l Studebaker covered stake truck, 25m Studebaker dump
truck.
1. Standard colors and castings.

25o-F STUDEBAKER MILK TRUCK   105 mm 1949-1954
Milk-can carrier with cast chassis-cab, rear body, ten milk cans, and either wheels or
hubs with tires, spare wheel, sheet metal front base, tow hook, Nestle logo decals or
tampo-print. All versions have light blue chassis-cab, white rear body, silver trim.
Casting with gap between front fenders and bumper, rounded front windows
(1949-1950):
1. Nestle decals, cast wheels (1949).
2. Nestle decals, blue hubs (1950).
3. No logo, blue hubs (1950). Casting with fenders meeting bumper, squarish
   windows (1951-1954):
4. Nestle decals, blue hubs (1951).
5. Nestle tampo-print, blue hubs (1953-1954).

25o-H FORD MILK TRUCK   94 mm 1950, 1954-1955

Cast rear body as 25o-F, short chassis-cab, ten milk cans, and hubs with tires, spare
wheel, sheet metal front base, tow hook, decal or tampo-print Nestle logo. All versions
have light blue chassis-cab and hubs, white rear body, silver trim. Earlier casting, no
grid under roof (1950):
1. Nestle decals with unoutlined letters. Later casting, with or without grid under
   roof (1954-1955).
2. Tampo-printed logo, no grid (1954).
3. Tampo-printed logo, grid (1954).
4. Decals with outlined letters, grid (1954-1955).

25p-F STUDEBAKER PICKUP TRUCK   105 mm 1949-1955
Open truck with cast chassis-cab, rear body-fenders, and wheels or hubs with tires,
spare wheel, sheet metal front base, tow hook, silver trim. All versions have yellow
chassis-cab and red rear body. Casting with gap between fenders and bumper, rounded
windows (1949-1950):
1. Cast wheels, lined rear bed (1949).
2. Red hubs, lined rear bed (1950). Casting with fenders meeting bumper, squarish
   windows (1951-1955):
3. Red hubs, unlined rear bed.

25p-G AVELING-BARFORD DIESEL ROLLER   110 mm 1948-1953
_#251
Cast body, 2-piece front roller and 2 rear rollers, black sheet metal base and tow hook.
Red roller sides, unpainted surfaces, tan driver.
1. Light green body.

25q-F STUDEBAKER COVERED PICKUP TRUCK 105 mm 1949-1952
Casting and parts as 25p-F plus sheet metal rear cover. Casting with gap between
fenders and bumper, rounded windows (1949-1950):
1. Green chassis-cab and cover, red rear body, cast wheels (1949).
2. Dark gray-green chassis-cab and cover, yellow-brown rear body, cast wheels
   (1949).
3. Green chassis-cab, cover and hubs, yellow rear body (1950). Casting with fenders
   meeting bumper, squarish windows (1951-1952):
4. Green chassis-cab, cover and hubs, yellow rear body.

25r-F STUDEBAKER WRECKER   120 mm 1949-1954
Tow truck with cast chassis-cab, rear body and wheels or hubs with tires, spare wheel,
black sheet metal boom and front base, silver trim. Chassis-cab and rear body are the
same color; logo (if any) is tampo-printed. Casting with gap between fenders and
bumper, rounded windows (1949-1950):
1. Dark red body, cast wheels, no logo (1949).
2. Dark red body, cast wheels, white "Dinky Service" (1949).
3. Bright red body and hubs, white "Dinky Service" (1950).
4. Bright red body and hubs, no logo (1950). Casting with fenders meeting bumper,
   squarish windows (1951-1954):
5. Bright red body and hubs, "Dinky Service".

25r-G FORWARD CONTROL LORRY   108 mm 1948-1953 _#420
Cab-over open truck with cast body and hubs, black tires, black sheet metal front base
and tow hook, silver grille, bumper and headlights, number 24R cast on bottom of
body.
1. Red body, green hubs.
2. Orange body, ? hubs.
3. Light green body, light yellow hubs.
4. Gray body, ? hubs.

25r-H FORD WRECKER   117 mm 1954-1955
Ford chassis-cab, other castings and parts as 25r-F, cast hubs with tires, silver trim,
with or without "Dinky Service" logo.
1. Red body and hubs, black tires, with logo (1954).
2. Red body, chrome hubs, white tires, no logo (1954-1955).

25s-F TRUCK SET   1948
Boxed set of French 25a-b-c-d-e-f trucks.

The Old System of Catalog Numbers

1. Cast wheels.

25s-G SIX-WHEELED WAGON   101 mm 1937-1940, 1946-1948

Cast body, dashboard with attached steering wheel, and six hubs, black tires, with or without sheet metal rear cover, silver grille.

1. Reddish-brown body, no rear cover (1937-1940).
2. Reddish-brown body, light gray cover (1946-1948).3. Green body, light gray cover (1946-1948).
3. Navy blue body, light gray cover (1946-1948).

25s-H OPEN TWO-WHEEL TRAILER   75 mm 1949-1952

Cast rear body of 25p-q-r, wheels or hubs with tires, black tow bar.

1. Red body, cast wheels, lined bed (1949).
2. Red body, cream hubs, lined bed (1950).
3. Yellow body, red hubs, plain bed (1951-1952).
4. Green body, yellow hubs, plain bed (1951-1952).

(25t COVERED MILITARY TRUCK never issued)
(Announced 1940: military version of French 25b.)

25t-F COVERED TWO-WHEEL TRAILER   75 mm 1949-1955

Cast rear body of 25p-q-r-s, wheels or hubs with black tires, black tow bar, sheet metal rear cover.

1. Yellow body, red-brown cover, cast wheels, lined bed (1949).
2. Red body, green cover, cast wheels, lined bed (1949).
3. Yellow body and hubs, red-brown cover, plain bed (1950).
4. Yellow body and hubs, red-brown cover, plain bed (1951-1955).
5. Red body, green cover and hubs, plain bed (1951-1955).

25t-G FLAT TRUCK AND TRAILER   ? mm 1948-1950

25c-G truck pulling 25g-G trailer.

1. Standard colors.

25u-F FORD TANK TRUCK   105 mm 1950-1952

Tanker with cast body and hubs, black tires, black sheet metal base, silver trim, Esso logo.

1. Red body and hubs, oval-design Esso decals on sides and rear, spare wheel, tow hook (1950).
2. Casting changed at rear, no spare wheel or tow hook, otherwise as type 1 (1951-1952).
3. Bright red body and hubs, plain Esso lettering on sides, otherwise as type 2 (1952).

25v-F FORD GARBAGE TRUCK   105 mm 1950-1955

Short-chassis refuse truck with cast chassis-cab, tipping rear body, tailgate and hubs, black tires, sheet metal front base and sliding rear covers, tipping crank and bar, silver trim.

1. Dark green body, light or bright green hubs, plain inside of tailgate and roof (1950-1951).
2. Dark green body and hubs, cast X inside tailgate (1952).
3. Grid cast under roof, otherwise as type 2 (1953).
4. Reinforced rear body, otherwise as type 3 (1954).

25v-G BEDFORD REFUSE WAGON   1948-1953 _#252

Garbage truck with cast chassis-cab, tipping rear body, opening tailgate, black and silver grille-bumper-headlights, and hubs, black tires, black sheet metal base, no number, sliding rear covers, tipping crank and spiral, no windows.

1. Tan body and hubs, green tailgate and covers, red hubs.

(25vs STUDEBAKER GARBAGE TRUCK never issued)

25w-G BEDFORD TRUCK   104 mm 1949-1953 _#411

Open truck with cast chassis-cab, rear body, grille with bumper and headlights and hubs (as 25m, 25v), black sheet metal base and body, black tires.

1. Green body and hubs, black fenders.
2. Green body (including fenders) and hubs.

25wm-G BEDFORD MILITARY TRUCK   104 mm 1952-1953 _#640

Castings and parts as 25w.

---

1. Olive body and hubs.

25x-G BREAKDOWN LORRY   123 mm 1950-1953 _#430

Wrecker with cast chassis-cab, rear body and red hubs, black tires, sheet metal boom (=rear body color) and black base, crank, line and hook, white tampo-printed "Dinky Service" logo, silver grille, bumper and headlights, no windows.

1. Dark gray chassis-cab, dark blue rear body.
2. Honey brown chassis-cab,, light green rear body.
3. Tan chassis-cab, rear blue body.

25y-G UNIVERSAL JEEP   83 mm 1952-1953 _#405

Jeep with cast body, black steering wheel and hubs, black tires and spare, black sheet metal windshield frame, front base and tow hook.

1. Red body and hubs.
2. Green body, light green hubs.

26-F RAILCAR   100 mm 1934-1940

Cast body, two rollers. First casting (1934) has no lower body lines, second casting (1935-1940) has two longitudinal lines just above and below axles. Two basic colors plus silver and other trim.

1. Red lower body, dark yellow upper body.
2. Red lower body, cream upper body.
3. Red lower body, brownish-green upper body.
4. Orange lower body, cream upper body.
5. Yellow lower body, cream upper body.
6. Green lower body, cream upper body.
7. Dark green lower body, dark yellow upper body.
8. Blue lower body, cream upper body.

26-G G.W.R. RAILCAR   106 mm 1934-1940

Cast body with pointed ends, two rollers. Roof almost always light cream.

1. Red body.
2. Yellow body.
3. Green body.
4. Blue body.
5. Brown body.

27-G TRAMCAR   77 mm 1934-1939

Cast body and four small wheels, Ovaltine or Lipton decals.

1. Red lower body, cream or white top.
2. Orange lower body, cream top.
3. Yellow lower body, cream top.
4. Green lower body, cream top.
5. Blue lower body, cream top.

27a-G MASSEY-HARRIS FARM TRACTOR   89 mm 1948-1953 _#300

Cast body, driver, muffler and wheels, black sheet metal seat, steering wheel, front axle mount and tow hook, yellow Massey-Harris logo.

1. Red body, tan driver, yellow hubs, unpainted treads.

27ac-G MASSEY-HARRIS TRACTOR AND SPREADER   203 mm 1950

27a Tractor and 27c Spreader. British models sold in France.

1. Red bodies, tan driver, yellow hubs.

27ak-G MASSEY-HARRIS TRACTOR AND HAY RAKE   157 mm 1953 _#310

27a Tractor and 27k Hay Rake.

1. Red bodies, yellow tractor hubs and rake wheels.

27b-G HALESOWEN HARVEST TRAILER   121 mm 1949-1953 _#320

Open trailer with cast body (including chassis), two removable racks, and wheels, small gray plastic hitch wheel, sheet metal tow hook.

1. Tan body, red racks and chassis, yellow hubs, unpainted treads.

27c-G MASSEY-HARRIS MANURE SPREADER   113 mm 1949-1953 _#321

Cast body, three silver rotors and two wheels, spring belt, two pulleys, yellow Massey-Harris logo.

---

1. Red body, yellow hubs, unpainted treads.

27d-G LAND ROVER   92 mm 1950-1953 _#340

Cast open body, tan driver, and hubs, black or gray tires, spare wheel, black sheet metal windshield frame, steering wheel, front base and tow hook.

1. Orange body, green interior, red hubs.
2. Light green body and hubs, tan interior.

27f-G ESTATE CAR   105 mm 1950-1953 _#344

Plymouth wagon with cast body and hubs, black tires, black sheet metal base, silver grille, bumper and headlights.

1. Tan body with brown panels, darker tan hubs, no number on base.
2. Number 27F on base, otherwise as type 1.

27g-G MOTOCART   110 mm 1949-1953 _#342

Open 3-wheel cart with cast chassis, tipping rear body, tan driver, one large front and two small rear wheels with red hubs and unpainted treads, black steering wheel.

1. Dark green chassis, dark tan rear body.
2. Light green chassis, otherwise as type 1.

27h-G DISC HARROW   86 mm 1951-1953 _#322

Cast frame and two sets of silver discs, black sheet metal tow hook and disc mount.

1. Red frame, yellow panels.

27j-G TRIPLE GANG MOWER   114 mm 1952-1953 _#323

Cast frame, three subframes, three yellow blades and six green wheels hitch at front, tow hook at rear of frame.

1. Red frame and subframes.

27k-G HAY RAKE   76 mm 1953 _#324

Cast frame and two spoked wheels, wire tines set in red sheet metal mount, black sheet metal lever, number 27K cast on frame.

1. Red frame, yellow wheels.

27m-G LAND ROVER TRAILER   78 mm 1953 _#341

Open trailer with cast body, including tow bar with black sheet metal spring, and two hubs, rubber tires.

1. Orange body, red hubs.
2. Light green body and hubs.

27n-G FIELD MARSHALL FARM TRACTOR   75 mm 1953 _#301

Cast body, tan driver, black stack and steering wheel, and wheels, black sheet metal base and tow hook, silver trim.

1. Orange body, green wheel hubs, unpainted treads.

28-G DELIVERY VAN   84/81/83 mm 1934-1940

Delivery van with many logo types. Three basic castings: Casting 1: as 22d: cast chassis-cab, rear body, wheels or hubs with rubber tires, sheet metal grille and clip, 84 mm; 1934-1935. Casting 2: cast Ford body with vertical grille pattern and five louvers, cast hubs, white tires, 81 mm; 1935-1938. Casting 3: cast Bedford body with mesh grille pattern and three louvers, open windows, cast hubs, rubber tires, 83 mm; 1939-1940. Promotional types:

1. Liverpool Echo logo, no other data; casting 1?
2. Green body, yellow sides, cream roof, green "Bentalls" decals, casting 2: 1936?
3. Red body, gold "Maison de Bonneterie" logo, casting 2, no other data.
4. Olive green body, casting 2, South African promo, no other data.

28/1-G DELIVERY VANS SET   1934-1938

Boxed set of six 28 series vans.

1. 28a Hornby, 28b Pickfords, 28c Manchester Guardian, 28d Oxo, 28e Ensign, 28f Palethorpe, casting 1 (1934-1935).
2. 28a Hornby, 28b Pickfords, 28c Manchester Guardian, 28e Firestone, 28f Palethorpe, 28n Atco, casting 2 (1935-1938).

28/2-G DELIVERY VANS SET   1934-1938

Boxed set of six 28 series vans.

1. 28g Kodak, 28h Sharps, 28j Crawfords, 28m Castrol, 28n Marsh & Baxter, 22d Meccano, casting 1 (1934-1935).
2. 28d Oxo, 28g Kodak, 28h Dunlop, 28k Marsh's Sausages, 28m Castrol, 28p

Crawfords, casting 2 (1935-1938).

28/3-G DELIVERY VANS SET 1936-1938
Boxed set of six 28 series vans:
1. 28r Swan, 28s Fry, 28t Ovaltine, 28w Osram, 28x Hovis, 28y Exide/Drydex, casting 2.

28a-G HORNBY TRAINS VAN 84/81 mm 1934-1936
Casting 1 or 2 with gold and black Hornby Trains logo.
1. Yellow body, casting 1.
2. Yellow body, casting 3.
3. Cream body, casting 3.

28a-H GOLDEN SHRED VAN 81/83 mm 1936-1940
Casting 2 or 3 with red and blue Golden Shred logo.
1. Yellow body, casting 2.
2. Yellow body, casting 3.
3. Cream body, casting 3. (A casting 1 variety may exist.)

28b/G PICKFORDS REMOVALS VAN 84/81 mm 1934-1935
Casting 1 or 2 with gold Pickfords logo.
1. Dark blue body, casting 1.
2. Dark blue body, casting 2.

28b-H SECCOTINE VAN 81/83 mm 1935-1940
Casting 2 or 3 with gold logo.
1. Light blue body, casting 2.
2. Light blue body, casting 3.

28c-G MANCHESTER GUARDIAN VAN 84/81/83 mm 1934-1940
Casting 1, 2 or 3, with gold logo.
1. Dark green chassis-cab, red rear body, casting 1.
2. Dark red body, casting 2.
3. Dark red body, casting 3.

28d-G OXO VAN 84/81/83 mm 1934-1940
Casting 1, 2 or 3, with gold logo, left: "Oxo, beef in brief"; right: "Oxo, beef at its best".
1. Light blue body, casting 1.
2. Light blue body, casting 2.
3. Dark blue body, casting 3.

28e-G ENSIGN CAMERAS VAN 84 mm 1934
Casting 1, with gold logo edged in black; left and right differ.
1. Red-orange body, casting 1.

28e-H FIRESTONE VAN 84/81/83 MM 1934-1940
Casting 1, 2 or 3, with red logo edged in black.
1. Dark blue body, casting 1?
2. White body, logo not red, casting 1.
3. Dark blue body, casting 2.
4. White body, casting 2.
5. Dark blue body, casting 3.
6. White body, casting 3.

28f-G PALETHORPE'S SAUSAGES VAN 84/81 mm 1934-1938
Casting 1 or 2, with gold logo edged in blue.
1. Light blue-green or gray-green body, casting 1.
2. Light gray-green body, casting 2.

28f-H VIROL VAN 81/83 mm 1938-1940
Casting 2 or 3, with black "Give your child a Virol constitution" logo.
1. Yellow body, casting 2.
2. Yellow body, casting 3.

28g-G KODAK CAMERAS VAN 1934-1940
Casting 1, 2 or 3, with red and black Kodak Film logo.
1. Yellow body, casting 1.
2. Yellow body, casting 2.
3. Yellow body, casting 3.

28h-G SHARPS TOFFEE VAN 84/81 mm 1934-1935
Casting 1 or 2 with gold and black "Sharps Toffee, Maidstone" logo.
1. Black chassis-cab, red rear body, casting 1.
2. Red body, casting 2.

28h-H DUNLOP TYRES VAN 81/83 mm 1935-1940
Casting 2 or 3, with gold "Dunlop Tyres" logo.
1. Red body, casting 2.
2. Red body, casting 3.

28k-G MARSH'S SAUSAGES VAN 84/81/83 mm 1934-1940
Casting 1, 2, or 3, with gold "Marsh's Sausages" logo.
1. Dark green body, casting 1.
2. Dark green body, casting 2.
3. Dark green body, casting 3.

28l-G CRAWFORD'S BISCUITS VAN 84/81/83 mm 1934-1940
Casting 1, 2 or 3, with gold logo edged in black.
1. Red body, casting 1.
2. Red body, casting 2.
3. Red body, casting 3.

28m-G WAKEFIELD CASTROL VAN 84/81/83 mm 1934-1940
Casting 1, 2 or 3, with red logo edged in black.
1. Green body, casting 1.
2. Green body, casting 2.
3. Green body, casting 3.

28n-G MARSH AND BAXTER'S VAN 84 mm 1934-1935
Casting 1, with ? logo.
1. Green body, casting 1.

28n-H MECCANO VAN 84/81 mm 1935
Casting 1 or 2, with red and black "Meccano Engineering for Boys" logo.
1. Yellow body, casting 1 (ex-22d).
2. Yellow body, casting 2.

28n-J ATCO MOWERS VAN 81/83 mm 1935-1940
Casting 2 or 3, with gold and red logo.
1. Green body, casting 2.
2. Green body, casting 3.

28p-G CRAWFORD'S BISCUITS VAN 81/83 mm 1935-1940
Casting 2 or 3, with gold "Crawford's Biscuits" logo.
1. Red body, casting 2.
2. Red body, casting 3.

28r-G SWAN PENS VAN 81/83 mm 1936-1940
Casting 2 or 3, with gold or silver "Swan Pens" logo.
1. Black body, casting 2.
2. Black body, casting 3.

28s-G FRY'S CHOCOLATE VAN 81/83 mm 1936-1940
Casting 2 or 3, with gold "Fry's Chocolate" logo.
1. Chocolate brown body, casting 2.
2. Chocolate brown body, casting 3.

28t-G OVALTINE VAN 81/83 mm 1936-1940
Casting 2 or 3, with gold and black "Drink Ovaltine for Health" logo.
1. Red body, casting 2.
2. Red body, casting 3.

28w-G OSRAM LAMPS VAN 81/83 mm 1936-1940
Casting 2 or 3, with gold and black logo.
1. Yellow body, casting 2.
2. Yellow body, casting 3.

28x-G HOVIS VAN 81/83 mm 1936-1940
Casting 2 or 3, with gold and black logo.
1. White body, casting 2.
2. White body, casting 3.

28y-G EXIDE/DRYDEX VAN 81/83 mm 1936-1940
Casting 2 or 3, with gold and black Drydex left and Exide right logo.
1. Red body, casting 2.
2. Red body, casting 3.

29/29a-G MOTOR BUS 69 mm 1934-1939
Cast body, base and four wheels, roof may be white, cream or silver. Logo: silver or red "Marmite", black "definitely does you good".
1. Yellow body.
2. Green body.
3. Blue body.
4. Maroon body.

29b-G STREAMLINE BUS 88 mm 1935-1940, 1948-1950
Cast body and hubs, rubber tires. Casting with open rear window, two grooves from window to end of body (1935-1940):
1. Red body, maroon trim.
2. Light green body, dark green trim.
3. Medium blue body, dark blue trim.
4. Gray body, dark blue trim.
5. Gray body, dark gray trim. Casting without window or grooves (1948-1950):
6. Cream and red body.
7. Light and dark green body.
8. Light and dark blue body.
9. Gray and red body.
10. Gray and blue body.

29c-G DOUBLE DECKER BUS 100 mm 1938-1940, 1946-1953 ⏤#290
Cast body, chassis-hood (originally including rear stairs) and hubs, rubber tires, cream upper body, roof sometimes gray, silver grille. Casting with AEC grille (big V at top, vertical center line running down from it), cutout fender edges, rear stairs, earlier issues with gray roof (1938-1940):
1. Red lower body.
2. Maroon lower body.
3. Orange lower body.
4. Green lower body.
5. Blue lower body. Casting without rear stairs, otherwise as before, front roof box, no decals (1946-1950):
6. Red lower body, cream upper body and roof.
7. Red lower body, gray upper body and roof.
8. Green lower body, cream upper body and roof.
9. Green lower body, gray upper body and roof. Casting with AEC Regent grille (small V and vertical line), straight fender edges, no rear stairs, "Dunlop, the world's master tyre" decals (1950-1953):
10. Red lower body, cream upper body and roof.
11. Green lower body, cream upper body and roof.

29d-F PARIS BUS 111 mm 1948-1951
Cast body and wheels or hubs and rubber tires, sheet metal top and base. Casting with small driver (1948-1949):
1. Green body, cream top, cast wheels.
2. Green body, cream top, cast hubs, rubber tires. Casting with large driver (1950-1951):
3. Lighter green body, cream top.
4. Lighter green body, white top.

29d-H SOMUA-PANHARD PARIS BUS 143 mm 1952-1959 ⏤#570
Cast body and hubs, black tires, black sheet metal base, silver trim.
1. Cream upper body, dark green lower body, no grid under roof.
2. Cream upper body, dark-green lower body, grid cast under roof.

29ds-F PARIS BUS 111 mm 1939-1940, 1946-1948
Cast body and wheels or hubs with rubber tires, sheet metal roof, sometimes sheet metal base, same model as 29d-F.
1. Dark green body, cream top, cast hubs, black tires, baseplate.

2. No baseplate, otherwise as type 1.
3. Dark green body, top varies from ivory to light tan, cast wheels, no baseplate.

29e-F ISOBLOC COACH   127 mm 1950-1955
Streamlined singledeck bus with cast body and hubs, sheet metal base and rear ladder to luggage rack cast into roof. Casting with plain luggage rack and fenders (1950):
1. Dark green body, light green roof and fenders.
2. Blue body, cream roof and fenders.
3. Blue body, silver roof and fenders. Casting with plain luggage rack, raised fenders (1951-1953):
4. Red body, silver roof and fenders.
5. Light blue body, silver roof and fenders. Casting with ridged luggage rack, raised fenders, -/+ grid cast under roof (1953-1955):
6. Red body, silver roof and fenders.
7. Light blue body, silver roof and fenders.

29e-G SINGLE DECK BUS   113 mm 1948-1952
Half-cab bus with cast body and hubs, black tires, black sheet metal base, silver grille and lights.
1. Cream body, light blue trim.
2. Green body, dark green trim.
3. Blue body, dark blue trim.

29f-F CHAUSSON BUS   154 mm 1956-1959 _#571
Singledeck bus with cast body and hubs, white tires, black sheet metal base, silver trim, emblem cast on sides.
1. Red lower body and hubs, cream upper body.
2. Navy blue lower body and hubs, ivory upper body.

29f-G OBSERVATION COACH   112 mm 1950-1953 _#280
Maudsley deck-and-a-half bus with cast body and hubs, black tires, silver grille and headlights.
1. Dark cream body and hubs, red trim.
2. Dark cream body, red trim and hubs.
3. Light gray body, red trim and hubs.
4. Gray body and hubs, red trim. (Note: shades of gray vary.)

29g-G LUXURY COACH   113 mm 1951-1953 _#281
Maudsley singledeck bus with cast body and hubs, black tires, black sheet metal base, silver grille and lights.
1. Maroon body, cream trim, red hubs.
2. Pale brown body, orange trim, cream hubs.
3. Green hubs, otherwise as type 2.
4. Blue body, cream trim and hubs.
5. Gray body, orange trim, light gray hubs.

29h-G DUPLE ROADMASTER COACH 119 mm 1952-1953 _#282
Leyland Royal Tiger bus with cast body and hubs, black tires, black sheet metal base, silver bumpers, grille bars and lights.
1. Cream upper body and hubs, dark green lower body.
2. Light green hubs, otherwise as type 1.
3. Dark blue body, silver stripes, light blue hubs.

30-G CAR SET   1935-1939
Boxed set of six models, including 30a Chrysler Airflow, 30b Rolls-Royce, 30c Daimler, 30d Vauxhall, 30e Breakdown Van. Standard colors and castings.
1. Sixth model is 30f Ambulance (1935-1937).
2. Sixth model is 30g Caravan (1937-1939).

30a-G CHRYSLER AIRFLOW   103 mm 1935-1940, 1946-1948
Cast body (formerly #32), chrome front bumper-grille-headlights and rear bumper, and black hubs, rubber tires (white prewar, black postwar).
1. Red body, white tires.
2. Maroon body, white tires.
3. Cream body, white tires.
4. Green body, white tires.

5. Turquoise body, white tires.
6. Blue body, white tires.
7. Red body, black tires.
8. Cream body, black tires.
9. Green body, black tires.
10. Blue body, black tires.

30b-G ROLLS-ROYCE   101 mm 1935-1940, 1946-1950
Cast body, black chassis (2 types), chrome grille-bumper-headlights and hubs, white (early prewar) or black tires. Casting with open chassis (three large holes; 1935-1940, early 1946):
1. Red body (prewar).
2. Cream body (prewar).
3. Green body (prewar).
4. Blue body (prewar).
5. Gray body (prewar).
6. Tan body (prewar and 1946).
7. Dark blue body (1946 only). Casting with solid chassis (one small hole, 1946-1950):
8. Tan body.
9. Dark blue body.

30c-G DAIMLER   98 mm 1935-1940, 1946-1950
Cast body, black chassis (2 types), chrome grille-bumper-headlights, and hubs, white (early prewar) or black tires. Casting with open chassis (1935-1940, early 1946):
1. Yellow body (prewar).
2. Cream body (prewar, 1946).
3. Pink body (prewar).
4. Turquoise body (prewar).
5. Green body (prewar, 1946).
6. Blue body (prewar, 1946).
7. Tan body (prewar, 1946). (Note: some prewar models have maroon chassis.) Casting with solid chassis (1946-1950):
8. Cream body.
9. Green body.
10. Tan body.
11. Gray body.

30d-G VAUXHALL   102 mm 1935-1940, 1946-1948
Cast body, chassis, chrome grille-bumper-headlights (two types) and hubs, white (early prewar) or black tires. Casting with first type (grid) grille, open chassis and spare wheel (1935-1938):
1. Yellow body, brown chassis.
2. Light green body, darker green chassis.
3. Blue body, ? chassis.
4. Light tan body, brown chassis.
5. Brown body, black chassis.
6. Gray body, ? chassis. Casting with second type (shield) grille, brown open chassis, with or without spare wheel (1938-1940):
7. Yellow body.
8. Green body.
9. Blue body.
10. Brown body.
11. Gray body. Casting with shield grille, black solid chassis, no spare (1946-1948):
12. Yellow body.
13. Green body.
14. Brown body.

30e-F TOW TRUCK   120 mm 1936-1940
25a-F truck plus cast boom in rear bed, with wire hook. Casting with open-lattice boom, cast hubs, tires (1936-1937):
1. Red body, black chassis, green boom.

2. Yellow body, maroon chassis, green boom.
3. Blue body, black chassis, green boom. Casting with solid boom, cast hubs, tires (1938-1939):
4. Red body and boom, black chassis.
5. Green body and boom, maroon chassis.
6. Blue body and boom, black chassis.
7. Blue body, black chassis, green boom. Casting with solid boom, cast wheels (1940):
8. Blue body and boom, black chassis.

30e-G BREAKDOWN VAN   92 mm 1935-1940, 1946-1948
Bedford tow truck with cast body, boom with spotlight, and chrome or black hubs, black tires, wire hook. Body based on 22c-G. Casting with open rear window (1935-1940):
1. Red body.
2. Yellow body.
3. Green body.
4. Brown body.
5. Gray body. (Note: early issues had black fenders.) Casting without rear window (1946-1948):
6. Red body.
7. Green body.
8. Gray body.

30f-G AMBULANCE   101/99 mm 1935-1940, 1946-1948
Cast body, chassis, Bentley grille-bumper-headlights, and hubs, rubber tires. Casting with open chassis, open side and rear windows (1935-1940):
1. Gray body, red chassis, grille without emblem (1935-1938).
2. Gray body, red chassis, grille with emblem (1938-1940). Casting with solid chassis, open side and rear windows (1946-1947):
3. Gray body, black chassis.
4. Cream body, black chassis. Casting with solid chassis, only cab windows open, 99 mm (1947-1948):
5. Cream body, black chassis.
6. Dull green body and chassis (for South African market).

30g-G CARAVAN   99 mm (with towbar) 1936-1940
House trailer with cast body and hubs, rubber tires, wire tow bar. Casting with or without roof light; lettering inside varies.
1. Cream upper body, blue lower body.
2. Cream upper body, light orange lower body.
3. Light green upper body, dark green lower body.
4. Tan upper body, chocolate brown lower body.
5. Gray upper body, red lower body.

30h-G DAIMLER AMBULANCE   96 mm 1950-1953 _#253
Cast squarish body and hubs, black tires, black sheet metal base, silver bumper and lights, red cast-in crosses.
1. Cream body, red crosses and hubs.

30hm-G DAIMLER MILITARY AMBULANCE   96 mm 1952?-1953 _#624
30h casting and parts in military finish.
1. Olive green body and hubs, red crosses on white panels.

30j-G AUSTIN WAGON   104 mm 1950-1953 _#412
Open truck with cast body, grille-headlights and hubs, black tires, black sheet metal base and tow hook.
1. Maroon body, dark red hubs.

30m-G REAR TIPPING WAGON   99 mm 1950-1953 _#414
Dodge dump truck with cast chassis-cab, tipper, opening tailgate, and hubs, black tires, black sheet metal front base, wire tipping lever, silver grille, bumper and headlights.
1. Orange chassis-cab, light green tipper and hubs.
2. Light blue chassis-cab and hubs, light gray tipper.

The Old System of Catalog Numbers

30n-G FARM PRODUCE WAGON 107 mm 1950-1953 _#343
Dodge stake truck with cast chassis-cab, low-side rear body and hubs, black tires, sheet metal rear stakes matching rear body, black front base and tow hook, silver grille, bumper and headlights.
1. Dark rose red chassis-cab, light blue rear body and hubs.
2. Yellow chassis-cab, green rear body and hubs.
3. Green chassis-cab, yellow rear body and hubs.

30p-G PETROL TANKER 112 mm 1950-1953 _#440
Studebaker tank truck with cast body and hubs, black tires, black sheet metal base, silver grille, bumper, headlights and filler caps.
1. Red body and hubs, black Petrol logo (1950-1952).
2. Green body and hubs, black Petrol logo (1950-1952).
3. Red body and hubs, white and blue Mobilgas logo on sides, red-white-blue Mobilgas shield emblem on rear (1952-1953).

30pa-G CASTROL TANKER 112 mm 1952-1953 _#441
Casting as 30p, red Castrol logo on white panel.
1. Light green body and hubs.

30pb-G ESSO TANKER 112 mm 1952-1953 _#442
Casting as 30p, red and dark blue "Esso Motor Oil/Petrol" logo on white tripe.
1. Red body and hubs.

30r-G FORDSON THAMES FLAT TRUCK 111 mm 1951-1953 _#422
Flat truck with cast body and hubs, black tires, black sheet metal front base and tow hook, silver grille bars, bumper and headlights, no number on bottom.
1. Red body and hubs.
2. Green body, light green hubs.

30s-G AUSTIN COVERED WAGON 104 mm 1950-1953 _#413
Cast body (as 30j), grille with headlights, and hubs, black tires, sheet metal rear cover, black sheet metal front base and tow hook.
1. Maroon body, tan cover and hubs.
2. Maroon body and hubs, tan cover.
3. Maroon body and hubs, cream cover.
4. Maroon body, red cover and hubs.
5. Dark blue body, light blue cover and hubs.
6. Brown body, tan cover.
7. Brown body, green cover, tan hubs.

30sm-G AUSTIN MILITARY TRUCK 104 mm 1952?-1953 _#625
Castings and parts as 30s, military finish.
1. Olive green body, cover and hubs.

30v-G BEV ELECTRIC DAIRY VAN 85 mm 1949-1953 _#490/491
Milk truck with cast body, chassis (including inner rear) and hubs, black tires, logo on front of truck, -/+ 30v on bottom.
1. Cream body, red chassis and hubs, NCB logo (1949-1953).
2. Light gray body, light blue chassis, red hubs, NCB logo (1949-1953).
3. Cream body, red chassis, blue hubs, Express Dairies logo (1951-1953).
4. Light gray body, light blue chassis and hubs, Express Dairies logo (1951-1953).

30w-G ELECTRIC ARTICULATED LORRY 135 MM 1953 _#421
Hindle Smart Helecs with cast cab, semi-trailer and hubs, black tires, black sheet metal cab base and hitch, maroon tow hook, silver headlight, cream and red British Railways decal on front of cab, number 30W on bottom.
1. Maroon cab, semi-trailer, red hubs.
2. Maroon cab, semi-trailer and hubs.

31-G HOLLAND COACHCRAFT VAN 88 mm 1935-1940
Streamlined van (same basic casting as 29b Streamline Bus, minus windows) with cast body and hubs, rubber tires, gold logo.
1. Red body.
2. Orange body.
3. Cream body.

4. Green body.
5. Blue body.
6. Dark blue body.

31a-G TROJAN ESSO VAN 86 mm 1951-1953 _#450
15 cwt. van with cast body and hubs, black tires, black sheet metal base, silver grille, bumper and headlights, red-white-blue Esso logo decals, white stripe.
1. Red body, maroon hubs.

31b-G TROJAN DUNLOP VAN 86 mm 1952-1953 _#451
Castings and parts as 31a, black and yellow Dunlop logo decals.
1. Red body, maroon hubs.

31c-G TROJAN CHIVERS VAN 86 mm 1953 _#452
Castings and parts as 31a, yellow-black-red-white Chivers Jellies logo decals.
1. Dark green body, lighter green hubs.

31d-G TROJAN OXO VAN 86 mm 1953 _#453
Castings and parts as 31a, silver and black Beefy Oxo logo decals.
1. Dark blue body, lighter blue hubs.

32-G AIRFLOW SALOON 103 mm 1935 _#30a
Identical to 30a; listed as 32 for only a few months.
1. Maroon body.

32a-F PANHARD COVERED SEMI-TRAILER 165 mm 1952
Cast cab, semi-trailer and hubs, black tires, sheet metal rear cover, no logo.
1. Navy blue cab, semi, cover and hubs.

32ab-F PANHARD S.N.C.F. SEMI-TRAILER 165 mm 1952, 1954-1959 _#575
Castings and parts as 32a, yellow-blue-red S.N.C.F. logo.
1. Navy blue cab, semi, cover and hubs, logo with locomotive (1952).
2. Logo with S.N.C.F. shield instead of locomotive, otherwise as type 1 (1954-1958).

32aj-F PANHARD KODAK SEMI-TRAILER 165 mm 1952-1954
Castings and parts as 32a, red and black Kodak logo.
1. Yellow cab, demi, cover and hubs.

32c-F PANHARD ESSO TANKER 165 mm 1954-1959 _#576
Tanker semi with cast cab, semi-trailer and hubs, black tires, black cab base, plated sheet metal ladder and catwalk, red-white-blue Esso logo.
1. Red cab, semi and hubs, white trim, Esso emblem with big wings, no grid under cab roof (1954-1955).
2. Medium emblem, grid under roof, otherwise as type 1 (1956-1958).
3. Small emblem: see #576.

32d-F DELAHAYE FIRE TRUCK 160 mm 1955-1959 _#899
Open-cab ladder truck with cast body and two-piece ladder mounts, red turned hubs, white tires, spare wheel, two-piece sheet metal aerial ladder, ladder rack and windshield frame, black base, white steering wheel, two operating cranks, silver running boards, deck, grille and headlights.
1. Red body and ladder mount.

32e-F BERLIET FIRE ENGINE 118 mm 1957-1959 _#583
Enclosed fire truck with cast body, silver ladder, two removable red and cream hose reels, and red hubs, white tires, black sheet metal base with number 32, hose racks, cream hose reel, silver grille, bumper, headlights, catwalks and rear fittings.
1. Red body, no decals (1957-1958).
2. Red body, Pompiers de Paris decals (1959).

33-G MECHANICAL HORSE AND TRAILERS
Boxed set of 33a Mechanical Horse and semi-trailers.
1. 33b, c, d, e and f trailers (1935-1937).
2. 33b, c, e and f trailers (1937-1940).

33a-F SIMCA CARGO VAN 133 mm 1955-1956
Cast chassis-cab, rear body, two opening rear doors and hubs, black tires, spare wheel, black sheet metal front base, silver trim, no logo.
1. Dark olive green chassis-cab, mustard yellow body.

2. Olive green chassis-cab, orange body.

33a-G MECHANICAL HORSE 65 mm 1935-1940
Cast body and three hubs, white tires, silver grille and lights.
1. Red body.
2. Yellow body.
3. Green body.
4. Blue body.
5. Gray body.

33an-F SIMCA CARGO VAN: BAILLY 133 mm 1956-1959 _#577
Castings and parts as 33a-F, yellow logo on black panel.
1. Yellow chassis-cab and rear body, white rear roof.

33b-F SIMCA CARGO DUMP TRUCK 127 mm 1955-1959 _#578
Cast chassis-cab, tipper, opening tailgate, and hubs, black tires, spare wheel, black sheet metal front base, silver grille, bumper and headlights.
1. Dark green chassis-cab and hubs, metallic gray tipper, plain rear bed (1955).
2. Grooved rear bed, otherwise as type 1.

33b-G FLAT TRAILER 64 mm 1935-1940
Mechanical horse trailer with cast body and hubs, white tires, sheet metal hitch same color as body.
1. Yellow body.
2. Green body.
3. Blue body.
4. Gray body.

33c-F SIMCA CARGO GLASS TRUCK 129 mm 1955-1959 _#579
Cast chassis-cab and flat rear body, cast or turned hubs, black tires, spare wheel, black sheet metal front base, sheet metal glass rack, plastic glass sheets, silver grille, bumper and headlights, red "Saint-Gobain" and "Miroitier" logo decals.
1. Gray chassis-cab, dark green body, gray cast hubs.
2. Light gray chassis-cab, bright green body, gray cast hubs.
3. Light gray chassis-cab, bright green body, turned hubs.
4. Light gray chassis-cab, dark green body, cream turned hubs.
5. Yellow-orange chassis-cab and cast hubs, bright green body (also sold in England).

33c-G OPEN TRAILER 64 mm 1935-1940
Low-side mechanical horse trailer with cast body and hubs, white tires, sheet metal hitch same color as body.
1. Green body.
2. Blue body.
3. Gray body.

33d-G BOX TRAILER 70 mm 1935-1940
Covered mechanical horse trailer with cast body and hubs, white tires, sheet metal cover and hitch same color as body.
1. Green body.
2. Gray body.
3. Blue body, gold and black Hornby Trains logo.
4. Green body, black and red Meccano Engineering for Boys logo.

33e-G REFUSE WAGON TRAILER 64 mm 1935-1940, 1946-1948?
Mechanical horse trailer with cast body and hubs, white (prewar) or black (postwar) tires, sheet metal hitch same color as body, and blue cover with opening hatch.
1. Yellow body.
2. Cream body.
3. Green body.
4. Dark blue body.
5. Gray body.

33f-G PETROL TANK TRAILER 61 mm 1935-1940
Mechanical horse trailer with cast body and hubs, white tires, sheet metal hitch same color as body, and tank.
1. Green body, red tank, no logo.

2. Green body, red tank, gold and black Esso logo (1937-1940).

3. Red body, green tank, red and black Wakefield Castrol logo (1937-1940).

33r-G RAILWAY MECHANICAL HORSE AND TRAILER   102 mm
1935-1940
Castings and parts as 33a-G mechanical horse and 33d-G box trailer.
1. Brown horse and trailer, black roofs, LMS logo.
2. Blue horse and trailer, black roofs, LNER logo.
3. Brown horse and trailer, cream roofs, GWR logo.
4. Green horse and trailer, white and/or black roofs, Southern Railway logo.

33w-G MECHANICAL HORSE & OPEN TRAILER   102 mm
1947-49, 1953   _#415
Castings and parts as 33a-G and 33c-G, with black tires.
1. Yellow cab, cream trailer.
2. Blue cab, cream trailer.
3. Tan cab, cream trailer.
4. Brown cab, cream trailer.
5. Red cab, tan trailer.

34a-F BERLIET DUMP TRUCK   128 mm 1955-1959   #580
Quarry dumper with cast chassis-cab and tipper, blue turned hubs, black tires, black sheet metal front base with number 34, crank to operate tipper, black front fenders with red lights, silver grille, bumpers and headlights.
1. Dark blue chassis-cab, orange tipper, no spare tire mount.
2. Spare tire mount but no tire, otherwise as type 1.

34a-G ROYAL AIR MAIL SERVICE CAR   83 mm 1935-1940?
Cast body and hubs, white tires, silver trim, gold emblem, white "Royal Air Mail Service" lettering.
1. Blue body and hubs.

34a-F BERLIET FLAT TRUCK WITH CONTAINER 125 mm 1956-1959
_#581
Cast chassis-cab (as 34a-F), flat rear body, container and sliding panel, cast or turned hubs, black tires, spare wheel, black sheet metal front base with number 34, light gray tow hook, black front fenders with red lights, silver grille, bumpers and headlights.
1. Red cab and cast hubs, black front fenders, light gray flatbed, dark gray container with plated eye on top.
2. Eye cast into container, otherwise as type 1.
3. Turned hubs, eye cast into container, otherwise as type 1.

34b-G ROYAL MAIL VAN   83 mm 1938-1940, 1948-1952
Cast body and black hubs, white (prewar) or black (postwar) tires, black sheet metal base, black "Royal Mail" and gold "GR" monogram, silver headlights. Casting with open rear windows (1938-1940).
1. Red body, black hood and fenders.
2. Red body and roof, black hood and fenders. Casting with closed rear windows (1948-1952).
3. Red body, black roof, hood and fenders.

34bn-F BERLIET BAILLY CONTAINER TRUCK 125 mm 1959   _#581n
Casting and parts as 34b-F.
1. Yellow chassis-cab and flatbed, black fenders, dark gray container, cast hubs.
2. Turned hubs, otherwise as type 1.

34c-G LOUDSPEAKER VAN   81 mm 1948-1953   #492
Cast body (as last 28 type), loudspeakers and hubs, black tires, silver trim. Loudspeakers are usually silver, rarely black.
1. Dark blue body, silver or blue hubs.
2. Green body and hubs.
3. Gray body, ? hubs.
4. Light brown body, black hubs and loudspeakers.
5. Brown body, black hubs.

35-G SMALL CARS SET   1936-1940

Boxed set of 35a saloon car, 35b racer, and 35c M.G. sports car.
1. Standard colors.

35a-F SIMCA 5   60 mm 1939-1940, 1946-1949
Bast body, black or white rubber tires (1939-1940), black cast wheels (1940, 1946-1948), or black rubber wheels (1948-1949).
1. Red body.
2. Garnet red body.
3. Maroon body.
4. Yellow body.
5. Cream body.
6. Light green body.   7. Green body.
8. Light blue body.
9. Blue body.
10. Blue-gray body.
11. Gray body.
12. Gold body.
13. Silver body.

35a-G SALOON CAR   51 mm 1936-1940, 1946-1948
Cast body, white (prewar) or black (postwar) rubber wheels, silver grille.
1. Blue body, darker blue spare wheel cover, white wheels.
2. Gray body, darker gray spare wheel cover, white wheels.
3. Blue body, white wheels.
4. Turquoise body, white wheels.
5. Gray body, white wheels.
6. Red body, black wheels.
7. Light blue body, black wheels.
8. Gray body, black wheels.

35a-H CITROEN U23 WRECKER   125 mm 1955-1959   #582
Tow truck with cast body, red cast or turned hubs, black tires, spare wheel, black sheet metal boom and base, winch with line and hook, silver bumper and headlights, yellow "Dinky Service" logo.
1. Red body, big rear boxes, gas tank closed at bottom (1955).
2. Red body, small rear boxes, gas tank open at bottom (1956-1959).

35b-G RACER   61 mm 1936-1940, 1946-1953   #200
R-type M.G. with cast body, white or black rubber wheels. Model with empty cockpit, white or black wheels (1936-1939):
1. Red body.
2. Silver body. Model with cast-in driver, white or black wheels (1939-1940):
3. Red body.
4. Yellow body?
5. Blue body.
6. Silver body. Model with cast-in driver, black wheels (1946-1953):
7. Red body.
8. Silver body.

35c-G M.G. SPORTS CAR   52 mm 1936-1940, 1946-1948
Cast open body, silver grille, white (prewar) or black (postwar) rubber wheels.
1. Red body, white wheels.
2. Maroon body, white wheels.
3. Green body, white wheels.
4. Dark blue body, white wheels.
5. Red body, black wheels.
6. Green body, black wheels.

35d-G AUSTIN 7 CAR   50 mm 1938-1940, 1946-1948
Cast open body, silver grille, white (prewar) or black (postwar) rubber wheels, with or without wire windshield frame. Some early models had the folded top painted a second color. Model with white wheels, windshield frame (1938-1940):
1. Yellow body.
2. Green body.

3. Blue body.
4. Greenish-gray body. Model with black wheels, windshield frame (1946):
5. Yellow body.
6. Blue body.
7. Tan body. Model with black wheels, no windshield frame (1947-1948):
8. Yellow body.
9. Tan body.

36-G MOTOR CARS SET   1937-1940
Set of six models: 36a, b, c, d, e and f; standard colors. Models use same basic bodies as 24 series but grilles are correct for makes of cars represented.
1. Prewar chassis and sheet metal figures.

36a-F WILLEME LOGGER SEMI-TRAILER 225 mm 1956-1959   #897
Truck with cast cab and semi-trailer, yellow turned hubs, black tires and spare, black sheet metal cab base, hitch and rest, unpainted metal rest wheel, wire bars, load of logs. Cab casting has straight bars flanking hitch.
1. Orange cab, yellow semi-trailer.

36a-G ARMSTRONG-SIDDELEY   97 mm 1937-1940, 1946-1948
Four-door sedan with cast body (as 24b-G), chassis with (prewar) or without (postwar) slits to attach sheet metal figures, grille and hubs, white or black tires. Casting with slits, figures, varying chassis colors, white tires (1937-1940):
1. Gray body.
2. Red-brown body. Casting without slits, no figures, black chassis and tires (1946-1948):
3. Maroon body.
4. Olive green body.
5. Blue body.
6. Gray body.

36b-F WILLEME SAVOYARDE COVERED SEMI-TRAILER   265 mm
1958-1959   _#581
Truck with cast cab, semi-trailer, and opening doors, orange cast and turned hubs, black tires, black sheet metal cab base and hitch, orange tow hook, two wheels on trailer rests, green plastic rear cover, silver grille, bumpers and headlights. Cab casting has straight bars flanking hitch.
1. Red cab, orange-yellow semi with red bars and chassis.

36b-G BENTLEY   100 mm 1937-1940, 1946-1948
Sports coupe with cast body (as 24f-G), chassis with (prewar) or without (postwar) slits to attach sheet metal figures, grille and hubs, white or black tires. Casting with slits, figures, varying chassis colors, white tires (1937-1940):
1. Yellow body.
2. Cream body.
3. Tan body. Casting without slits, no figures, black chassis and tires (1946-1948):
4. Tan body.
5. Green body.
6. Blue body.
7. Chocolate brown body.

36c-G HUMBER   91 mm 1937-1940, 1946-1948
Vogue saloon with cast body (as 24d-G), chassis with (prewar) or without (postwar) slits for sheet metal figures, grille and hubs, white or black tires. Casting with slits, figures, varying chassis colors, white tires (1937-1940):
1. Tan body.
2. Blue body. Casting without slits, no figures, black chassis and tires (1946-1948):
3. Blue body.
4. Red-brown body.
5. Gray body.

36d-G ROVER   94 mm 1937-1940, 1946-1948
Fastback coupe with cast body (as 24e-G), chassis with (prewar) or without (postwar) slits for sheet metal figure, grille and hubs, white or black tires. Casting with slits, figure, varying chassis colors, white tires (1937-1940):

The Old System of Catalog Numbers

1. Light green body.
2. Blue body. Casting without slits, no figure, black chassis and tires (1946-1948):
3. Light green body.
3. Darker green body.
3. Blue body.

36e-G BRITISH SALMSON (2-seat)   96 mm   1937-1940, 1946-1948
Open two-seater with cast body (as 24h-G), chassis with (prewar) or without (postwar) slits for sheet metal figure, grille and hubs, white or black tires. Casting with slits, figure, dark red chassis, white tires, +/- spare (1937-1940):
1. Dark blue body, spare tire.
2. Gray body, spare tire.
3. Gray body, no spare. Casting without slits, no figure, black chassis and tires, no spare (1946-1948):
4. Red body.
5. Light blue body.
6. Darker blue body.
7. Gray body.

36f-G BRITISH SALMSON (4-seat)   96 mm   1937-1940, 1946-1948
Open four-seater with cast body (as 24g-G), chassis with (prewar) or without (postwar) slits for sheet metal figure, grille and hubs, white or black tires. Casting with slits, figure, dark red chassis, white tires (1937-1940):
1. Red body. Casting without slits, no figure, black chassis and tires (1946-1948):
2. Green body.
3. Gray body.

36g-G TAXI   72 mm   1937-1940, 1946-1949
Taxi with cast body, chassis and hubs, black tires. Casting with open rear window, black chassis (1937-1940):
1. Maroon lower body.
2. Yellow lower body.
3. Green lower body.
4. Blue lower body.
5. Tan lower body. (Upper body, including roof, can be red, green, blue or black.) Casting usually without rear window, with black upper body/roof and chassis (1946-1949):
6. Brown lower body, open rear window (1946-1947).
7. Red lower body, no rear window (1947-1949).
8. Maroon lower body, no rear window (1947-1949).
9. Green lower body, no rear window (1947-1949).
10. Blue lower body, no rear window (1947-1949).

37a-G CIVILIAN MOTORCYCLIST   46 mm   1938-1940, 1946-1948
Motorcycle with cast black body including driver in varying colors, white (1937-1939) or black (1939ff) wheels.
1. Green driver, white wheels.
2. Blue driver, white wheels.
3. Brown driver, white wheels.
4. Black driver, white wheels.
5. Green driver, black wheels (1939-1940).
6. Blue driver, black wheels (1939-1940).
7. Brown driver, black wheels (1939-1940).
8. Black driver, black wheels (1939-1940).
9. Gray driver with brown helmet, black wheels (1946-1948).

37b-G POLICE MOTORCYCLIST   46 mm   1938-1940, 1946-1948
Cast black motorcycle including blue driver, white (1937-1939) or black (1939ff) wheels.
1. White wheels (1937-1939).
2. Black wheels, driver has painted-on chinstrap (1939-1940).
3. Black wheels, no chinstrap (1946-1948).

37c-G SIGNAL CORPS DESPATCH RIDER   46 mm   1938-1940
Same casting as 37b, green cycle, khaki driver, white or black wheels.

1. White wheels (1937-1939).
2. Black wheels (1939-1940).

38a-F UNIC MULTIBUCKET TRUCK   132 mm   1957-1959   #895
Cast body, bucket, two arms and hubs, spare wheel, sheet metal bucket arms and black base, plastic hydraulic cylinders.
1. Light gray and light yellow body.

38a-G FRAZER NASH-BMW SPORTS CAR   1940, 1946-1953   #100
Open two-seater with cast body, steering wheel and hubs, black tires, sheet metal base (unpainted prewar, black postwar), plastic windshield, silver grille and lights.
1. Blue body and hubs, gray seats.
2. Light gray body, red seats and hubs.
3. Light gray body, brown seats, black hubs.
4. Light gray body, blue seats and hubs. (Other combinations may exist. Color shades vary.)

38b-G SUNBEAM-TALBOT SPORTS CAR   1940, 1946-1953   #101
Open two-seater with cast body, steering wheel, headlights and hubs, black tires, sheet metal base (unpainted prewar, black postwar), plastic windshield, silver grille and lights.
1. Red body and hubs, maroon tonneau cover.
2. Maroon body, ? hubs, ? cover.
3. Yellow body and hubs, gray cover.
4. Yellow body, tan cover, black hubs.
5. Green body, ? hubs, ? cover.
6. Blue body, gray cover, black hubs.
7. Brown body, ? hubs, ? cover.
8. Gray body, ? hubs, ? cover.

38c-G LAGONDA SPORTS COUPE   1946-1953   #102
Open convertible with cast body, headlights, steering wheel and hubs, black tires, black sheet metal base, plastic windshield, silver grille and lights.
1. Maroon body, blue interior.
2. Green body, dark green interior.
3. Green body, gray interior.
4. Green body, black interior.
5. Gray body, maroon interior.
6. Gray body, dark gray interior.
7. Gray body, ? interior.

38d-G ALVIS SPORTS TOURER   1940, 1946-1953   #103
Open convertible with cast body, headlights, steering wheel and hubs, black tires, unpainted (prewar) or black (postwar) sheet metal base, plastic windshield, silver grille and lights.
1. Maroon body, black interior, red hubs, unpainted base.
2. Green body, brown interior, green hubs, unpainted base.
3. Green body, black interior, green hubs, unpainted base.
4. Blue body, ? interior, ? hubs, unpainted base.
5. Maroon body, various interior colors, black base.
6. Olive green body, various interior colors, black base. (Postwar interiors can be red, green, blue, brown, gray or black.)
(38e TRIUMPH DOLOMITE never issued)

38e-G ARMSTRONG-SIDDELEY COUPE   1946-1953   #104
Open convertible with cast body, steering wheel and hubs, black tires, black sheet metal base, plastic windshield, silver grille and lights.
1. Red body, ? interior, ? hubs.
2. Cream body, ? interior, ? hubs.
3. Light green body, light gray interior, green hubs.
4. Light gray body, green interior, ? hubs.
5. Light gray body, blue interior, gray hubs.

38f-G JAGUAR SPORTS CAR   80 mm   1946-1953   #105
Open two-seater with cast body, headlights, steering wheel and hubs, black tires, black

sheet metal base, silver grille and lights, two small plastic windshields.
1. Red body, maroon interior, red hubs.
2. Light blue body, ? interior, ? hubs.
3. Blue body, red interior, blue hubs.
4. Dark blue body, gray interior, black hubs.
5. Tan body, brown interior, black hubs.
6. Brown body, blue interior, black hubs.
7. Gray body, ? interior, ? hubs.

39-G U.S.A. SALOON CARS   1939-1940
Boxed set of six models: 39a, b, c, d, e and f.
1. Standard colors, clear lacquered bases.

39a-F UNIC AUTO TRANSPORTER   325 mm   1957-1959   #894
Cast cab, semi-trailer, upper deck and hubs, black tires, black sheet metal cab base, dark blue logo on upper deck.
1. Metallic silver gray cab and semi, orange trim.

39a-F/G PACKARD SUPER 8   107 mm   1939-1940, 1946-1950
Sedan with cast body and hubs with black tires or (French) cast one-piece wheels, clear lacquered (prewar) or black (postwar) sheet metal base. Model with clear lacquered base, black hubs (1939-1940):
1. Yellow body.
2. Green body.
3. Dark blue body.
4. Gray body.
5. Black body. Model with black base, cast hubs (usually black) and black tires (British issues, 1946-1953):
6. Green body.
7. Olive body.
8. Blue body.
9. Brown body. Model with black base, cast metal wheels (French issues, 1949):
10. Blue body.
11. Turquoise body.
12. Gold body.

39b-F UNIC SAHARIEN PIPE TRUCK   225 mm   1959   #899
Cast cab, semi-trailer and hubs, black tires, black sheet metal cab base, six black plastic pipes, white plastic equipment on cab roof.
1. Tan cab and semi, white parts.

39b-G OLDSMOBILE 6 SEDAN   100 mm   1939-1940, 1946-1952
Sedan with cast body and hubs, black tires, clear lacquered (prewar) or black (postwar) base, silver grille and lights. Models with clear lacquered base (1939-1940):
1. Green body.
2. Black body. Models with black base (1946-1950):
3. Cream body.
4. Green body.
5. Blue body.
6. Tan body.
7. Brown body.
8. Gray body. Models with two-tone finish, black base (sold in USA, 1952):
9. Cream body, tan fenders.
10. Light blue body, dark blue fenders.

39c-G LINCOLN ZEPHYR COUPE   106 mm   1939-1940, 1946-1952
Coupe with cast body and hubs, black tires, clear lacquered (prewar) or black (postwar) sheet metal base, silver grille and lights. Models with clear lacquered base (1939-1940):
1. Yellow body.
2. Green body.
3. Gray body. Models with black base (1946-1950):
4. Cream body.

5. Red body.
6. Brown body.
7. Gray body. Models with two-tone finish, black base (sold in USA, 1952):
8. Red body, maroon fenders.
9. Tan body, brown fenders.

39d-G   BUICK VICEROY   103 mm   1939-1940, 1946-1950
Sedan with cast body, headlights and hubs, black tires, clear lacquered (prewar) or black (postwar) sheet metal base, silver grille and lights. Models with clear lacquered base (1939-1940):
1. Maroon body.
2. Cream body.
3. Green body.
4. Blue body. Models with black base (1946-1950):
5. Maroon body.
6. Green body.
7. Gray body.

39e-G   CHRYSLER ROYAL   106 mm   1939-1940, 1946-1952
Sedan with cast body and hubs, black tires, clear lacquered (prewar) or black (postwar) sheet metal base, silver grille and lights. Models with clear lacquered base (1939-1940):
1. Cream body.
2. Green body.
3. Blue body.
4. Gray body. Models with black base (1946-1950)
5. Cream body.
6. Green body.
7. Blue body.
8. Tan body.
9. Gray body. Models with two-tone paint, black base (sold in USA, 1952):
10. Yellow body, tan fenders.
11. Green body, dark green fenders?

39f-F/G   STUDEBAKER STATE COMMANDER   1939-1940, 1946-1950
Coupe with cast body and hubs with black tires or (French) one-piece wheels, clear lacquered (prewar) or black (postwar) sheet metal base, silver grille and lights. Models with clear lacquered base (1939-1940):
1. Yellow body.
2. Green body.
3. Gray body. Models with black base (1946-1950)
4. Red body.
5. Cream body.
6. Green body.
7. Blue body.
8. Metallic blue body.
9. Brown body.
10. Gray body. Models with black French base, cast wheels (French issues, 1949):
11. Red body.
12. Cream body.
13. Metallic green body. Models with black French base, cast hubs, black tires (French issues, 1950):
14. Cream body, yellow hubs.
15. Metallic green body, red hubs.

40-F   CITY TRAFFIC SIGNS   1953-1959   #590
Set of six cast traffic signs.
1. Silver bases and poles, red-white-blue signs.

40a-G   RILEY SALOON   93 mm   1947-1953   #158
Sedan with cast body, headlights and hubs, black tires, black sheet metal base with small lettering and #40a, silver grille, bumper and headlights.
1. Cream body, green hubs.

2. Green body and hubs.
3. Dark blue body, ? hubs.
4. Gray body, ? hubs.

40b-G   TRIUMPH 1800 SALOON   91 mm   1948-1953   #151
Sedan with cast body, headlights and hubs, black tires, black sheet metal base with small lettering, no #, silver grille, bumpers and headlights. Casting with rear axle pillars (1948-1949):
1. Tan body, green hubs. Casting with axle tabs on baseplate (1949-1953):
2. Tan body, green hubs.
3. Gray body and hubs. (Models with blue body are #151.)
(40c JOWETT JAVELIN never issued)

40d-G   AUSTIN DEVON   86 mm   1949-1953   #152
Sedan with cast body and hubs, black tires, black sheet metal base with small lettering, silver grille and headlights.
1. Maroon body and hubs.
2. Light green body, cream hubs.
3. Dark green body, cream hubs.
4. Light blue body and hubs.
5. Dark blue body, light blue hubs.

40e-G   STANDARD VANGUARD   91 mm   1948-1953   #153
Sedan with cast body and hubs, black tires, black sheet metal base with small lettering, silver grille, bumpers and headlights. Casting has no horizontal line across trunk (see #153). Casting with open rear wheels (1948-1950):
1. Light brown body and hubs. Casting with covered rear wheels (1950-1953):
2. Light brown body and hubs.
3. Blue body, cream hubs. (Models with cream body are #153.)

40f-G   HILLMAN MINX   88 mm   1951-1953   #154
Sedan with cast body and hubs, black tires, black sheet metal base with small lettering, silver grille, bumpers and headlights.
1. Apple green body and hubs.
2. Dark green body, apple green hubs.
3. Dark tan body, dark cream hubs.
4. Lighter or darker tan or brown body?

40g-G   MORRIS OXFORD   93 mm   1950-1953   #159
Sedan with cast body and hubs, black tires, black sheet metal base with small lettering, silver grille, bumpers and headlights.
1. Medium green body, light green hubs.
2. Dark green body, light green hubs.
3. Gray-brown body, tan hubs.

40h-G   AUSTIN TAXI   1951-1953   #254
Taxi with cast body, black chassis-interior and hubs, black tires, white and black Taxi sign, silver grille, bumpers and headlights. Base +/- #40H at front.
1. Yellow body and hubs.
2. Dark blue body, light blue hubs. (Other body colors are #254.)

40j-G   AUSTIN SOMERSET   89 mm   1953   #161
Sedan with cast body and hubs, black tires, black sheet metal base, silver grille, bumpers and headlights.
1. Red body, brighter red hubs.
2. Light blue body, darker blue hubs.

41-F   ROAD TRAFFIC SIGNS   1953-1959   #591
Set of six cast traffic signs.
1. Silver bases and poles, red-cream-blue signs.

42-G   POLICE BOX, MOTORCYCLE AND POLICEMEN   1936-1940
Boxed set of 42a Police Box, 42b Motorcycle Patrol, 42c and 42d Policemen.
1. Standard colors.

42a-G   POLICE BOX   66 mm high   1936-1940, 1946-1953   #751
Single casting with silver windows and sign background, red light.
1. Dark blue box.

42b-G   POLICE MOTORCYCLE PATROL   47 mm   1936-1940, 1946-1953   #043
Motorcycle and sidecar with cast cycle and sidecar including figures, rubber wheels.
1. Blue cycle and figures, green sidecar, white wheels (1936-1940).
2. Black wheels, otherwise as type 1 (1946-1953).

42c-G   POINT DUTY POLICEMAN   42 mm high   1936-1940
Cast figure with blue helmet, trousers and boots. Right arm raised.
1. White coat and gloves.

42d-G   POINT DUTY POLICEMAN   40 mm high   1936-1940
Cast figure with white gloves. Left arm extended to side.
1. Blue uniform.

43-G   R.A.C. BOX, MOTORCYCLE AND GUIDES   1935-1940
Set of 43a Box, 43b Motorcycle Patrol, 43c and 43d Guides.
1. Standard colors.

43a-G   R. A. C. BOX   51 mm high   1935-1940
Sheet metal box with design and lettering.
1. Blue and white box.

43b-G   R.A.C. MOTORCYCLE PATROL   46 mm   1935-1940, 1946-1948
Motorcycle (with rider) and sidecar castings, rubber wheels.
1. Black and blue cycle and sidecar, more paint detail, white wheels (1935-1940).
2. Less paint detail (plain blue rider), black wheels (1946-1948).

43c-G   R.A.C. GUIDE DIRECTING TRAFFIC   37 mm high   1935-1940
Cast figure with white gloves, red sash, black boots.
1. Blue uniform.

43d-G   R.A.C. GUIDE SALUTING   36 mm   1935-1940
Cast figure with red sash, black boots.
1. Blue uniform.

44-G   A.A. BOX, MOTORCYCLE AND GUIDES   1935-1940
Set of 44a Box, 44b Motorcycle Patrol, and 44c and 44d Guides.
1. Standard colors.

44a-G   A. A. BOX   81 mm high   1935-1940
Sheet metal box with roof signs, design and lettering.
1. Yellow and dark blue box.

44b-G   A.A. MOTORCYCLE PATROL   45 mm   1935-1940, 1946-1953   #270
Cast motorcycle (with rider) and sidecar, rubber wheels.
1. Black and yellow cycle and sidecar, more paint detail, white wheels (1935-1940).
2. Less paint detail (plain rider), black wheels, otherwise as type 1 (1946-1953).

44c-G   A.A. GUIDE DIRECTING TRAFFIC   37 mm high   1935-1940
Cast figure with white gloves, black boots.
1. Yellow uniform.

44d-G   A.A. GUIDE SALUTING   36 mm   1935-1940
Cast figure with black boots.
1. Yellow uniform.

45-G   GARAGE   127 by 90 mm   1935-1940
Sheet metal garage with opening green doors, green windows and base.
1. Cream walls, red roof.

46-G   PAVEMENT SET   1937-1940
Cardboard pieces representing street surfaces.
1. Gray pieces.

46a-G   PAVEMENT SET   1948-1950
Reissue of 46. No differences.
1. Gray pieces.

47-G   ROAD SIGNS   1935-1940, 1946-1953   #770
Set of 12 black-white-red signs: 47e 30 Mile Limit, 47f End of Restriction, 47g School, 47h Steep Hill, 47k Bend, 47m Left Turn, 47n Right Turn, 47p Junction, 47q No Entry, 47r Main Road Ahead, 47s Crossing, no gates, 47t Traffic Circle.
1. Undersides of bases are white (1935-1940).

2. Undersides of bases are black (1946-1953).

47a-G   TRAFFIC SIGNAL 4-WAY   62 mm high   1935-1940
1946-1953   #773
Cast black and white signal with red-yellow-green lights on each of four sides.
1. Yellow globe on top, white underside of base.
2. Yellow globe on top, black underside of base.
3. Pointed top without globe, black underside.

47b-G   TRAFFIC SIGNAL 3-WAY   62 mm high   1935-1940
Cast black and white signal with red-yellow-green lights on each of three sides.
1. White underside of base.
2. Black underside of base.

47c-G   TRAFFIC SIGNAL 2-WAY   62 mm high   1935-1940
Cast black and white signal with red-yellow-green lights on each of two sides. Each type can have black or white underside.
1. Lights back to back (47c/1).
2. Lights at right angle (47c/2).

47d-G   BELISHA BEACON   51 mm   1935-1940, 1946-1953   #777
Cast yellow light on black and white pole.
1. No lettering on white underside of base.
2. Lettering on black underside of base.

47e through 47t: listed under 47 (see above).

48-G   PETROL STATION   145 by 45 mm   1935-1940
Sheet metal building with red-yellow and green signs, varicolored designs and lettering.
1. Yellow walls, red and green roof.

49-F   PETROL PUMPS   1935-1940, 1946-1953
Set of French 49a (two), 49b (one) and 49c (two). Standard colors.
1. With rubber hoses.
2. Without rubber hoses.

49-G   PETROL PUMP SET   1935-1940, 1948-1953   #780
Set of British 49a, b, c, d and e. Standard colors.
1. Rubber hoses (prewar).
2. Plastic hoses (postwar).

49a-F   COLUMN PUMP   60 mm   1935-1940, 1946-1953
Cast pump with pointed top, with rubber hose except 1946-1949.
1. Red pump.
2. Yellow pump.
3. Cream pump.
4. Green pump.
5. Blue pump.
6. Dark blue pump.
7. White pump.
8. Gold pump.

49a-G   BOWSER PETROL PUMP   46 mm high   1935-1940, 1946-1953
Cast pump with hose.
1. Green pump, rubber hose (prewar).
2. Green pump with plastic hose (postwar).

49b-F   MOBILE PUMP   47 mm   1935-1940, 1946-1953
Short pump on wheels, with hose except 1946-1949.
1. Red pump.
2. Yellow pump.
3. Cream pump.
4. Green pump.
5. Blue pump.
6. Dark blue pump.
7. White pump.
8. Gold pump.

49b-G   WAYNE PETROL PUMP   39 mm high   1935-1940, 1946-1953

Cast pump with hose.
1. Light blue pump, rubber hose (prewar).
2. Light blue pump with plastic hose (postwar).

49c-F   DOUBLE PUMP   55 mm high   1935-1940, 1946-1953
Cast pump with square top, two rubber hoses except 1946-1949.
1. Red pump.
2. Yellow pump.
3. Cream pump.
4. Green pump.
5. Blue pump.
6. Dark blue pump.
7. White pump.
8. Gold pump.

49c-G   THEO PETROL PUMP   58 mm high   1935-1940, 1946-1953
Cast pump with hose.
1. Blue pump, rubber hose (prewar).
2. Blue pump, plastic hose (postwar).

49d-F   ESSO GAS PUMPS   90 by 92 mm   1954-1959   #592
Cast silver gray base, two pumps, and red-white-blue Esso sign on pole.
1. Red/white and blue/white pumps.

49d-G   SHELL PETROL PUMP   53 mm high   1935-1940, 1946-1953
Cast pump with hose.
1. Red pump, rubber hose (prewar).
2. Red pump, plastic hose (postwar).

49e-G   PRATTS OIL BIN   43 mm high   1935-1940, 1946-1953
Cast box and opening cover, red and silver interior.
1. Yellow box with "Pratts Motor Oil" lettering (prewar).
2. Yellow box without lettering (postwar).

50-F   SALEV MOBILE CRANE   89 by 156 mm   1957-1959   #595
Cast body, chassis, blue driver, white or cream steering wheel, and red hubs, black tires, red sheet metal boom and mount, two cranks, line and hook, black stripes.
1. Light gray body, yellow chassis, red lower body, rivet holding boom mount to body is inside casting.
2. Rivet head outside casting, otherwise as type 1.

50-G   SHIPS OF THE BRITISH NAVY   1934-1940
Set of fourteen 1/1800 scale ships: 50a Hood, 50b Nelson and Rodney, 50c Effingham, 50d York, 50e Delhi, 50f Destroyers (three), 50g Submarine, 50h Destroyers (three), 50k Submarine. Also sold in France.
1. Standard colors.

50a-G   CRUISER "HOOD"   146 mm   1934-1940
Cast hull with four rotating turrets, two masts.
1. Gray ship, "HMS Hood" cast underneath.
2. Gray ship, name not cast underneath (1940).

50b-G   BATTLESHIP "NELSON"   119 mm   1934-1940
Cast hull with three rotating turrets, rear mast.
1. Gray ship, "HMS Nelson" cast underneath.
2. Gray ship, "HMS Rodney" cast underneath.
3. Gray ship, no name cast underneath (1940).

50c-G   CRUISER "EFFINGHAM"   102 mm   1934-1940
Cast hull with two funnels, two masts.
1. Gray ship, "HMS Effingham" cast underneath.
2. Gray ship, name not cast underneath (1940).

50d-G   CRUISER "YORK"   99 mm   1934-1940
Cast hull with two funnels, two masts, covered side deck areas.
1. Gray ship, "HMS York" cast underneath.
2. Gray ship, name not cast underneath (1940).

50e-G   CRUISER "DELHI"   81 mm   1934-1940
Cast hull with two small funnels, forward mast.

1. Gray ship, "HMS Delhi" cast underneath.
2. Gray ship, name not cast underneath (1940).

50f-G   DESTROYER "BROKE" CLASS   58 mm   1934-1940
Cast hull with two funnels, forward mast.
1. Gray ship.

50g-G   K-CLASS SUBMARINE   57 mm   1934-1940
Cast hull with one mast near front of long superstructure.
1. Gray ship.

50h-G   DESTROYER "AMAZON" CLASS   52 mm   1934-1940
Cast hull with two funnels, one mast, less superstructure than 50f.
1. Gray ship.

50k-G   X-CLASS SUBMARINE   66 mm   1934-1940
Cast hull with one mast, shorter superstructure than 50g.
1. Gray ship.

51-G   FAMOUS LINERS   1934-1940
Set of six 1/1800 scale models: 51b Europa, 51c Rex, 51d Empress of Britain, 51e Strathaird, 51f Queen of Bermuda, 51g Britannic.
1. Standard colors.

51a-G   UNITED STATES LINER   ? mm   1936-1938
Cast hull with red and black funnels.
1. White hull and superstructure.

51b-G   NORDDEUTSCHER LLOYD "EUROPA"   165 mm   1934-1940
Cast hull with two light brown funnels, two masts.
1. Black hull, white superstructure.

51c-G   ITALIA LINE "REX"   152 mm   1934-1940
Cast hull with two red-green-white funnels, two masts.
1. Black hull, white superstructure.

51d-G   CANADIAN PACIFIC "EMPRESS OF BRITAIN"   130 mm   1934-1940
Cast hull with three cream funnels, brown masts and hatches.
1. White hull and superstructure.

51e-G   PENINSULAR & ORIENT "STRATHAIRD"   114 mm   1934-1940
Cast hull with three cream funnels, brown masts and bridge.
1. White hull and superstructure.

51f-G   FURNESS "QUEEN OF BERMUDA"   99 mm   1934-1940
Cast hull with three red and black funnels, brown lifeboats, two masts.
1. Light gray hull, white superstructure.

51g-G   CUNARD WHITE STAR "BRITANNIC"   115 mm   1934-1940
Cast hull with two light brown and black funnels, light brown upper deck, two masts.
1. Black hull, white superstructure.

52-G   CUNARD WHITE STAR "QUEEN MARY"   175 mm   1934-1940
1947-1949
Cast black hull, white superstructure, three red and black funnels, two masts, blue swimming pool, with or without rollers.
1. #52: "No. 534" on underside and box (1934).
2. #52: "No. 534" and "Queen Mary" on underside (1934).
3. #52: "Queen Mary" on underside (1934-1935).
4. #52b: identical to type 3 (1935-1936).
5. #52m: identical to types 3 and 4 (1936-1940).
6. #52a: with rollers, otherwise as #52 (1937-1940, 1947-1949).

52c-F   "NORMANDIE"   175 mm   1937-1940, 1946-1948
Cast hull with three black and red funnels, two masts, no rollers.
1. Black hull, white superstructure.

52d-F   "NORMANDIE"   175 mm   1937-1940, 1946-1948
Cast hull with details as 52c plus rollers.
1. Black hull, white superstructure.
(52e "QUEEN ELIZABETH" never issued)

53a-F   "DUNKERQUE"   120 mm   1937-1940

The Old System of Catalog Numbers

Cast hull with two turrets, funnel, mast, airplane launcher, no rollers. Sold in Britain as 53az, 1938-1939.

1. Gray ship.

53b-F "DUNKERQUE"   **120 mm**   **1937-1940**

Cast hull with details as 53a plus rollers.

1. Gray ship.

60-F AIRPLANES   **1934-1940**

Set of six French planes: 60a Arc-en-ciel, 60b Potez 58, 60c Henriot H180T, 60d Breguet-Corsaire, 60e Dewoitine 500, 60f Cierva Autogiro.

1. Standard colors.

60-G AEROPLANES SET   **1934-1940**

Set of six British planes: 60a Imperial Airways Liner, 60b Leopard Moth, 60c Percival Gull, 60d Low Wing Monoplane, 60e Cierva Monospar, 60f Cierva Autogiro.

1. Standard colors.

60-H AIRPLANE SET   **1957**

Set of four French planes: 60a Mystere IV, 60b Vautour, 60d Sikorsky, 60e Vickers Viscount.

1. Standard colors. Note: two dimensions, first the length, then the wingspan, will be given for all airplanes which I have been able to measure. All propellers and rotors are made of sheet metal; almost all are red.

60a-F DEWOITINE "ARC-EN-CIEL"   **100 by 135 mm**   **1935-1940**

Trimotor plane with cast fuselage including wings, three propellers.

1. Gold with red trim.
2. Gold with blue trim.
3. Silver with red trim.
4. Cream with red trim.
5. Cream with green trim.

60a-G IMPERIAL AIRWAYS LINER   **109 by 127 mm**   **1934-1940**

Armstrong-Whitworth Atalanta with cast fuselage, four engines attached to wing, and two wheels, sheet metal wing and propellers.

1. Red with cream trim.
2. Yellow with blue wing tips.
3. Gold with blue trim.
4. Gold, no trim, #G-ABTI.
5. Silver, no trim, #G-ABTI.
6. "Imperial Airways" stamped under wing, otherwise as type 4.
7. "Imperial Airways" stamped under wing, otherwise as type 5.

60a-H MYSTERE IV A   **68 by 59 mm**   **1957-1959**   _#800_

French jet fighter with cast body and three wheels.

1. Metallic silver gray, blue trim, red-white-blue roundel decals.

60b-F POTEZ 58   **54 by 75 mm**   **1935-1940**

High-wing monoplane with cast fuselage including engine, two wheels, sheet metal wing and propeller.

1. Red and silver.
2. Yellow and gray.

60b-G LEOPARD MOTH   **54 by 76 mm**   **1934-1940**

High-wing De Havilland monoplane with cast fuselage including engine, two wheels, sheet metal wing and propeller.

1. Green with yellow trim.
2. Dark blue with orange trim.
3. Red, no trim, #G-ACPT.
4. Green, no trim, #G-ACPT.
5. Gold, no trim, #G-ACPT.
6. Silver, no trim, #G-ACPT.
7-10. "DH Leopard Moth" stamped under wing, otherwise as types 3 through 6.
11-14. Window not open, otherwise as types 7-10.

60b-H VAUTOUR   **92 by 80 mm**   **1957-1959**   _#801_

French twin-jet plane with cast body and wheels.

1. Metallic silver gray body, blue trim, red-white-blue roundel decals.

60c-F HENRIOT H 180 T   **52 by 80 mm**   **1935-1940**

High wing monoplane with cast fuselage including engine, two wheels, sheet metal wing and propeller.

1. Red with silver trim.
2. Green with white trim.
3. Blue with white trim.

60c-G PERCIVAL GULL   **55 by 76 mm**   **1934-1940**

Low wing monoplane with cast fuselage including engine, two wheels, sheet metal wing and propeller.

1. White with blue trim.
2. Cream with red trim.
3. White, no trim, #G-ADZO.
4. Red, no trim, #G-ADZO.
5. Yellow, no trim, #G-ADZO.
6. Light blue, no trim, #G-ADZO.
7-10. Windows not open, "Percival Gull" stamped under wing, otherwise as types 3 to 6.

60c-H LOCKHEED SUPER CONSTELLATION   **182 by 199 mm**   **1956-1959**   _#892_

Airliner with cats body and wheels, four propellers, Air France logo.

1. Metallic silver gray body, logo and window decals.

60d-F BREGUET "CORSAIRE"   **49 by 78 mm**   **1935-1940**

Low wing monoplane with cast fuselage and two wheels, sheet metal wing and propeller.

1. Red and yellow.
2. Red and green.
3. Silver and red.

60d-G LOW WING MONOPLANE   **55 by 77 mm**   **1934-1940**

Vickers plane with cast fuselage including engine, two wheels, sheet metal wing and propeller. Casting without pilot until mid-1936.

1. Red with cream trim, no pilot.
2. Orange with cream trim, no pilot.
3. Gold with blue trim, no pilot.
4. Red, #G-AVYP, pilot cast in.
5. Orange, #G-AVYP, pilot cast in.
6. Silver, #G-AVYP, pilot cast in.

60d-H SIKORSKY S58 HELICOPTER   **76 mm**   **1957-1959**   _#802_

Cast body and wheels, two black rotors, Sabena logo.

1. White and silver gray body, light blue stripe.

60e-F DEWOITINE 500   **53 by 80 mm**   **1935-1940**

Low wing monoplane with cast fuselage, two wheels, sheet metal wing and propeller.

1. Cream with red trim.

60e-G GENERAL MONOSPAR   **53 by 83 mm**   **1934-1940**

Twin-engine plane with cast fuselage, wings, engines and wheels, two propellers.

1. Gold with red trim.
2. Silver with blue trim.
3. Gold, #G-ABVP.
4. Silver, #G-ABVP.
5. Gold, #G-ABVP, "General Monospar" stamped under wing.
6. Silver, #G-AVYP, "General Monospar" stamped under wing.

60e-H VICKERS VISCOUNT   **130 by 150 mm**   **1957-1959**   _#803_

Airliner with cast upper fuselage and lower fuselage-wings, six small wheels, four propellers, blue nose cowling, F-BGNX registration, Air France logo decals.

1. Metallic silver gray, with white upper fuselage.

60f-F CIERVA AUTOGIRO   **74 mm**   **1935-1940**

Cast fuselage and two wheels, sheet metal rotor and propeller. Existed simultaneously with and without cast-in pilot.

1. Red, cream rotor.
2. Cream, red rotor.
3. Cream, blue rotor.
4. Gold, red rotor.
5. Silver, red rotor.
6. Silver, blue rotor.

60f-G CIERVA AUTOGIRO   **52 mm**   **1934-1940**

Cast fuselage and two wheels, sheet metal rotor and propeller.

1. Gold with blue trim and rotor, no pilot.
2. Gold with blue trim and rotor, pilot cast in.

60f-H SE 210 CARAVELLE   **172 by 180 mm**   **1959**   _#891_

Twin-engine jet airliner with cast upper fuselage, lower fuselage-wings, engines, opening stair ramp and wheels, blue nose cowling, silver cockpit windows, F-BGNY registration, Air France logo and window decals.

1. Metallic silver gray, with white upper fuselage.

60g-G DE HAVILLAND COMET   **59 by 87 mm**   **1935-1940, 1946-1940**

Low wing monoplane with cast body, two wheels, two propellers.

1. Red with gold trim.
2. Gold with blue trim.
3. Silver with blue trim.
4. Red, no trim, #G-ACSR.
5. Gold, no trim, #G-ACSR.
6. Silver, no trim, #G-ACSR.
7-9. "DH Comet" cast under wing, otherwise as types 4 to 6.
10. Red, #G-RACE, "Light Racer" under wing.
11. Gold, #G-RACE, "Light Racer" under wing.
12. Silver, #G-RACE, "Light Racer" under wing.

60h-G SINGAPORE FLYING BOAT   **89 by 126 mm**   **1936-1940**

Cast fuselage, two fore-and-aft engines and floats, sheet metal wings and propellers. With or without rollers or gliding hook hole.

1. Silver, red-silver-blue painted roundels.
2. Silver, casting cut away at nose (1940).
3. Light gray, red-white-blue roundel decals, casting cut away at nose (1940).

60k-G PERCIVAL GULL   **55 by 76 mm**   **1936-1940, 1946-1949**

Same castings and parts as 60g.

1. Light blue fuselage, silver wings and tail, blue G-ADZO: Amy Mollison's plane (1936-1939).
2. Black G-ADZO, otherwise as type 1: H. L. Brook's plane.
3. Closed side windows, name under wing, otherwise as type 1 (1939-1940). Casting with "Light Tourer" cast under wing (1946-1949):
4. Red plane.
5. Light green plane.
6. Dark green plane.

60m-G FOUR ENGINE FLYING BOAT   **89 by 126 mm**   **1936-1940**

Same castings and parts as 60h, name under wing, roller.

1. Red plane, black G-EVCU.
2. Light green plane, black G-EXGF or G-EYCE.
3. Dark blue plane, black G-EYCE.
4. Silver plane, black G-EUTG.

60n-G FAIREY BATTLE BOMBER   **59 by 75 mm**   **1937-1940**

Low wing plane with cast body and two wheels, red propeller.

1. Silver with light blue cockpit cover, painted roundels.
2. Name under wing, otherwise as type 1 (1938).
3. Roundel decals, otherwise as type 2 (1939).
4. Light gray, no wheels or mounts (1940).

60p-G GLOSTER GLADIATOR   **38 by 44 mm**   **1937-1940**

Biplane with cast fuselage-lower wing, two wheels, sheet metal upper wing, struts and propeller.

1. Silver with painted roundels, no name under wing.
2. Name under wing, otherwise as type 1 (1938).
3. Silver with roundel decals, name under wing (1939).
4. Light gray with roundel decals, name under wing (1940).

60-r-G   EMPIRE FLYING BOAT   128 by 157 mm   1937-1940, 1946-1949
Four-engine plane with cast fuselage, wing with four nacelles, two floats, four propellers, roller. At least fifteen different versions exist, all with black names on the nose and registration letters (not all different) on the wings.

1. Silver plane, original nose shape.
2. Silver plane, changed nose (1940).
3. Silver plane, G-ADUV, brass roller (1946-1949).

60s-G   CAMOUFLAGED MEDIUM BOMBER   59 by 75 mm   1938-1940
Same castings and parts as 60n. Green and brown camouflage finish on top, black below, silver cockpit.

1. One painted roundel with yellow rim.
2. Two painted roundels with yellow rim.
3. Two darker roundels.

60t-G   DOUGLAS DC-3   92 by 133 mm   1938-1940
Two-engine airliner with cast body, two wheels, two propellers.

1. Silver plane, black PH-ALI.

60v-G   ARMSTRONG WHITLEY BOMBER   97 by 117 mm   1937-1940
Two-engine bomber with cast body and two wheels, two propellers, red-white-blue roundel decals.

1. Silver plane.

60w-G   CLIPPER III FLYING BOAT 94 by 164 mm   1938-1940, 1946-1949
Four-engine plane with cast fuselage, wings with four nacelles, two floats, four propellers.

1. Silver plane, USA and NC 16736 lettering, full name cast under wing (prewar).
2. Silver plane, no lettering, only "Flying Boat" under wing (postwar).
3. Dark green plane, otherwise as type 2.
4. Light blue plane, otherwise as type 2.

60x-G   ATLANTIC FLYING BOAT   128 by 157 mm   1937-1940
Four-engine plane with casting and parts as 60r, with roller.

1. Light blue fuselage, cream wings, black G-AZBP.

60y-G   THOMPSON FUEL TENDER   84 by 120 mm   1938-1940
Three-wheel vehicle with cast body and wheels, gold "Shell Aviation Services" logo.

1. Red body, black fenders.

61-F   AIRPLANES   1937-1940, 1946?
Set of six planes: 61a Dewoitine D338, 61b Potez 56, 61c Farman 360, 61d Potez 58, 61e Henriot H180M, 61f Dewoitine Chasseur.

1. Standard colors.

61-G   RAF AEROPLANES SET   1937-1941
Set of 60h, two 60n and two 60p.

1. Standard colors.

61a-F   DEWOITINE D338   104 by 134 mm   1938-1940
Same casting as 30a, two wheels, sheet metal nacelle caps and propellers.

1. Red with gold trim.
2. Green with silver trim.

61b-F   POTEZ 56   54 by 75 mm   1938-1940
Same fuselage as 60c, two wheels, wings with two nacelles, two propellers. Silver upper fuselage and fin.

1. Red plane.
2. Yellow plane.
3. Blue plane.

61c-F   FARMAN F360   49 by 78 mm   1938-1940
Same casting and parts as 60d.

1. Silver and red.
2. Silver and yellow.

61d-F   POTEZ 58   54 by 75 mm   1938-1940
Same castings and parts as 60b, red crosses on wings.

1. Silver and red.
2. Silver and yellow.

61e-F   Henriot H 180 M   52 by 80 mm   1938-1940
Same castings and parts as 60c. Roundels on wings.

1. Silver plane.

1f-F   DEWOITINE CHASSEUR   53 by 80 mm   1938-1940
Same castings and parts as 60e. Roundels on wings.

1. Silver plane.

62-F   ASSORTED AIRPLANES   1938-1940
Set of three French and three British airplanes. French: 64a Amiot 370, 64c Potez 63, 64d Potez 662. British: 60R Empire Flying Boat, 60w Clipper, 62n Junkers JU90.

1. Standard colors.

62a-G   SUPERMARINE SPITFIRE   43 by 51 mm   1940, 1946-1949
Small fighter with cast body, red propeller, roundels.

1. Silver plane, wing roundels only (prewar).
2. Silver plane, longer nose, wing and side roundels (postwar).

62b-G   BRISTOL BLENHEIM   59 by 79 mm   1940, 1946-1949
Two-engine bomber with cast body, two red propellers, roundels.

1. Silver plane, "Blenheim Bomber" cast under wing (prewar).
2. Silver plane, "Medium Bomber" cast under wing (postwar).

62d-G   CAMOUFLAGED BLENHEIM   59 by 79 mm   1940
Casting and parts as 62b, roundels, "Blenheim Bomber" under wing.

1. Camouflage finish.

62e-G   CAMOUFLAGED SPITFIRE   43 by 51 mm   1940
Casting and parts as 62a, roundels.

1. Camouflage finish.

(62f DE HAVILLAND FLAMINGO never issued)

62g-G   BOEING FLYING FORTRESS   94 by 145 mm   1939-1940   1946-1948
Four-engine bomber with cast upper fuselage-tail, lower fuselage-wings and two wheels, four red propellers, red-white-blue star roundels and tail stripes.

1. Silver plane, "Boeing Flying Fortress" cast under wing (prewar).
2. Silver plane, "Long Range Bomber" cast under wing (postwar).
3. Blue-gray nose, otherwise as type 2.

62h-G   CAMOUFLAGED HURRICANE   38 by 51 mm   1939-1940
Small fighter with cast body, red propeller, roundels.

1. Camouflage finish.

62k-G   THE KING'S AIRSPEED ENVOY   60 by 91 mm   1938-1940
Two-engine passenger plane with cast body, two wheels, two propellers, blue G-AEXX, silver windows.

1. Silver wings, red and blue fuselage, fin and nacelles.

62m-G   AIRSPEED ENVOY   60 by 91 mm   1938-1940, 1946-1949
Same castings and parts as 62k. Casting with "Airspeed Envoy" under wing, five different registrations (prewar):

1. Red plane.
2. Green plane.
3. Blue plane.
4. Silver plane. Casting with "Light Transport" under wing, G-ATMH registration (postwar):
5. Red plane.
6. Blue plane.
7. Silver plane.

62-G   JUNKERS JU-90   121 by 164 mm   1938-1940
Four-engine airliner with cast body and two wheels, four red propellers, blue

windows, four different registrations.

1. Silver plane, black lettering.

62p-G   ARMSTRONG WHITWORTH ENSIGN   ? by 174 mm   1938-1940   1945-1949
Four-engine airliner with cast fuselage, wings and two wheels, four red propellers. Casting with "Ensign Class Airliner" under wing:

1. Silver plane, six different registrations. Casting with "Armstrong Whitworth Airliner" under wing (postwar):
2. Silver plane.
3. Green and silver.
4. Blue and silver.
5. Gray and green.

62r-G   DE HAVILLAND ALBATROSS   97 by 146 mm   1939-1940   1946-1949
Four-engine airliner with cast upper fuselage-tail, lower fuselage-wings and two wheels, four red propellers. Casting with "DH Albatross" under wing (prewar):

1. Silver plane, G-AEVB registration. Casting with "Four Engined Liner" under wing (postwar):
2. Silver with red elevators.
3. Light blue with red elevators.
4. Gray with red elevators.
5. Blue plane, G-ATPV.
6. Tan plane, G-ATPV.
7. Gray plane, G-ATPV.
8. Silver plane, G-ATPV.

62s-G   HAWKER HURRICANE   38 by 51 mm   1939-1940, 1946-1949
Same castings and parts as 62h, roundels.

1. Silver plane with wheels, red-white-blue roundels, two-bladed propeller (prewar).
2. Silver plane without wheels or mounts, red-blue wing and red-white-blue side roundels, two-bladed propeller (1940).
3. Silver plane without wheels or mounts, three-bladed propeller (postwar).

62t-G   CAMOUFLAGED WHITLEY BOMBER 97 by 117 mm   1939-1940
Castings and parts as 60v, green and brown camouflage finish on top, black finish below.

1. Yellow-rimmed red-white-blue roundels (1939).
2. Unrimmed red-blue roundels (1940).

62w-G   IMPERIAL AIRWAYS FROBISHER AIRLINER   97 by 146 mm   1939-1940
Castings and parts as 62r, four red propellers, "Frobisher Class Airliner" cast under wing.

1. Silver plane, G-AFDI Frobisher lettering.
2. Silver plane, G-AFDJ Falcon lettering.
3. Silver plane, G-AFDK Fortuna lettering.

62x-G   BRITISH 40 SEATER AIRLINER   ? by 174 mm   1939-1940
Same castings and parts as 62p, "British 40 Seater Airliner" cast under wing, silver propellers, G-AZCA registration.

1. Red with maroon trim.
2. Yellow with maroon trim.
3. Light green with dark green trim.
4. Light blue with dark blue trim.

62y-G   GIANT HIGH SPEED MONOPLANE   121 by 164 mm   1939-1940   1946-1949
Same castings and parts as 62n, "Giant High Speed Monoplane" cast under wing. Model with D-AZBK registration.

1. Light green with dark green trim.
2. Light blue with dark blue trim.
3. Blue with brown trim. Model with G-ATBK registration (postwar):

The Old System of Catalog Numbers

4. Light green with dark green trim.
5. Medium green with dark green trim.
6. Gray with dark green trim.
7. Silver plane.

63-G   MAIA COMPOSITE AIRCRAFT   128 by 157 mm   1939-1940
Combination of 63a Maia Flying Boat and 63b Mercury Seaplane, which attaches to the top of the Flying Boat by sheet metal clips.
1. Silver planes.

63a-G   MAIA FLYING BOAT   128 by 157 mm   1939-1940
Same castings and parts as 60r plus sheet metal clip, G-ADHK registration.
1. Silver plane, original nose casting.
2. Silver plane, cutaway nose casting.

63b-G   MERCURY SEAPLANE   70 by 102 mm   1939-1940   1946-1953 #700
Four-engine seaplane with cast body and two floats, four red propellers. Model with G-ADHJ registration, "Mercury Seaplane" cast under wing, sheet metal clip (prewar):
1. Silver plane, "Mercury" on nose. Model with G-AVKW registration, only "Seaplane" cast under wing, no clip (postwar):
2. Silver plane, only G-AVKW lettering.

64-G   AEROPLANE SET   1939-1940
Set of 60g, 62h, 62k, 62m, 62s and 63b.
1. Standard colors.

64a-F   AMIOT 370   62 by 104 mm   1939-1940, 1946-1948
Two-engine plane with cast body and two wheels, two red propellers, roundels.
1. Red body.
2. Rose red body.
3. Blue body.
4. Tan body.
5. Silver body.
(64ac AMIOT 370 OBSERVATION, camouflage colors never issued)

64b-F   BLOCH 220   89 by 105 mm   1939-1940, 1946-1948
Two-engine airliner with cast body and two wheels, two red propellers, F-AOHJ registration.
1. Garnet red body.
2. Pale green body.
3. Ivory body.
4. Silver body.

64c-F   POTEZ 63   60 by 91 mm   1939-1940, 1946-1948
Two-engine plane with cast body and two wheels, two red propellers, roundels.
1. Red body.
2. Blue body.
3. Tan body.
4. Silver body.
(64cc POTEZ 63 RECONNAISSANCE, camouflage colors never issued)

64d-F   POTEZ 662   76 by 103 mm   1939-1940
Four-engine airliner with cast body and two wheels, four red propellers, F-ARAY registration.
1. Red body.
2. Yellow body.
3. Light blue body.
4. Silver body.
(64d POTEZ 662 AIRLINER (1946) never issued)
(64dc POTEZ 662 BOMBER, camouflage colors never issued)
(64e POTEZ 161 never issued)
(64f LEO 47 never issued)
(64g LEO 246 never issued)

64/o-F   DEWOITINE D338   104 by 134 mm   1939-1940, 1946-1948
Same model as later type 61a, sold under both numbers.

1. Light green body.
2. Silver body, F-ADBF.

65-G   AEROPLANE SET   1939-1940
Set of 60r, 60t, 60v, 60w, 62n, 62p, 62v, 62w.
1. Standard colors.

66-G   CAMOUFLAGED AEROPLANE SET   1939-1940
Set of 66a, b, c, d and e.
1. Camouflage colors.

66a-G   HEAVY BOMBER   109 by 127 mm   1940
Same castings and parts as 60a, with red-blue roundels.
1. Green and brown camouflage above, black below.

66b-G   DIVE BOMBER FIGHTER   54 by 76 mm   1940
Same castings and parts as 60b, with red-blue roundels.
1. Green and brown camouflage above, black below.

66c-G   TWO SEATER FIGHTER   55 by 76 mm   1940
Same castings and parts as 60c, red-blue roundels.
1. Green and brown camouflage above, black below.

66d-G   TORPEDO DIVE BOMBER   55 by 77 mm   1940
Same castings and parts as 60d, red-blue roundels.
1. Green and brown camouflage above, black below.

66e-G   MEDIUM BOMBER   53 by 83 mm   1940
Same castings and parts as 60e, red-blue roundels.
1. Green and brown camouflage above, black below.

66f-G   ARMY CO-OPERATION AUTOGIRO   52 mm   1940
Same castings and parts as 60f, casting with pilot, roundels.
1. Silver gray body, silver rotor.

67a-G   JUNKERS JU-80 HEAVY BOMBER   121 by 164 mm   1940
Same castings and parts as 62n and 62y, black and white German roundels.
1. Black above, light blue below.

68-G   AIRCRAFT IN SERVICE CAMOUFLAGE   1940
Two each of 60s, 62d, three each of 62e, 62h, one each of 62t, 68a, 68b.
1. Camouflage colors.

68a-G   ARMSTRONG WHITWORTH ENSIGN LINER? by 174 mm   1940
Same castings and parts as 62p and 62x, red-blue wing and red-white-blue side roundels.
1. Green and brown camouflage above, black below.

68b-G   FROBISHER LINER   97 by 146 mm   1940
Same castings and parts as 62r and 62w, red-blue wing and red-white-blue side roundels.
1. Green and brown camouflage above, black below.
(70 MODERN LOCOMOTION SET (1939) never issued) (Was to have included 23b Renault, 26 Railcar, 60a Arc-en-ciel, 52b Normandie, 53 Dunkerque.)

70-F   4-WHEEL COVERED TRAILER   111 mm   1957-1959 #810
Truck trailer with cast body, front axle mount and hubs, black tires, green sheet metal cover and tow hook, wire tow bar.
1. Red body.
2. Yellow body.

70a-G   AVRO YORK AIRLINER   124 by 160 mm   1946-1953 #704
Four-engine airliner with cast fuselage-tail, wings with four nacelles, and two wheels, silver sheet metal fuselage base, four red propellers, black G-AGJC, blue cockpit window.
1. Silver body, thin tail fin (1946-1949).
2. Silver body, thick tail fin (1952-1953).

70b-G   HAWKER TEMPEST II FIGHTER   54 by 64 mm   1946-1953 #730
Single engine fighter with cast body, red propeller, roundels.
1. Silver body, yellow-rimmed side roundels (1946-1949).
2. Silver body, unrimmed side roundels (1952-1953).

70c-G   VICKERS VIKING AIRLINER   98 by 140 mm   1947-1953 #705
Two-engine airliner with cast upper fuselage-tail and lower fuselage-wings, two red propellers, black G-AGOL.
1. Light gray body, silver windows (1947-1949).
2. Silver body, blue windows (1950-1953).

70d-G   TWIN ENGINED FIGHTER   48 by 76 mm   1946-1953 #731
Small two-engine plane with cast body, two red propellers.
1. Silver body, lettering on underside correct.
2. Silver body, letter N of Meccano backward.

70e-G   GLOSTER METEOR FIGHTER   64 by 67 mm   1946-1953 #732
Twin-jet fighter with cast body, roundels.
1. Silver body, yellow-rimmed side roundels (1946-1949).
2. Silver body, unrimmed side roundels (1950-1953).

70f-G   LOCKHEED SHOOTING STAR   56 by 61 mm   1947-1953 #733
Twin-jet fighter with cast body and wing tanks, blue and white star roundels, black nose trim.
1. Silver body, blue cockpit, "Made in England by Meccano" cast underneath (1947-1949).
2. Silver body including cockpit, word "by" deleted (1952-1953).
(70g AVRO TUDOR never issued)

80a-F   PANHARD E B R   103 mm   1958-1959 #815
Army tank with cast body, turning turret, gun barrel, four wheels, four turned hubs, black tires, black sheet metal base, silver headlights, red taillights.
1. Olive body, turret, wheels and hubs.

80b-F   HOTCHKISS-WILLYS JEEP   60 mm   1958-1959 #816
Jeep with cast body, steering wheel and hubs, black tires and spare, olive sheet metal windshield frame, silver headlights, red taillights, +/- driver.
1. Olive body and hubs, no driver or mounting hole (1958).
2. Olive body and hubs, plastic driver, hole in seat (1959).

80c-F   AMX 13 ARMORED CAR   108 mm   1958-1959 #817
Army tank with cast body, turning turret, gun barrel, front and rear hubs, olive plastic inner hubs, black rubber treads, black sheet metal base, silver headlights, decals.
1. Olive body and hubs.

80d-F   BERLIET 6x6 ARMY TRUCK   146 mm   1958-1959 #818
Covered truck with cast chassis-cab, body and six hubs, black tires and spares, olive sheet metal rear cover, black base and tow hook, silver grille and headlights, flag decals.
1. Olive body, cover and hubs.

80e-F   155 ABS HOWITZER   146 mm   1958-1959 #819
Four-wheel howitzer with cast two-part chassis, barrel, swiveling mount and olive hubs, black tires, wire parts.
1. Olive barrel, mount and chassis.

80f-F   RENAULT ARMY AMBULANCE   85 mm   1959 #820
Van-type ambulance with cast body and opening rear door, olive turned hubs, black tires, black sheet metal base, windows, red cast-in crosses on white panels, silver headlights, flag decals.

90-F   RICHIER ROAD ROLLER   112 mm   1958-1959 #830
Roller with cast body, chassis, roof, rollers, front roller mount and blue driver, metal roof pillars and exhaust stack, black sheet metal base and tow hook, cream steering wheel, silver grilles, red trim.
1. Dark yellow body and roller sides.

100?-G   DOLLY VARDEN DOLL HOUSE   1936-1940
Collapsible leatherboard house with brick lower and half-timbered upper walls, tile roofs, brick chimney, packed in container which forms its yard. May not have been numbered.
1. As above.

101-F   DINING ROOM SET   1936-1940

Set of 101a Table, 101b Sideboard, two 101c Armchairs, four 101d Chairs.
1. Light brown.
2. Dark brown.

101-G   DOLLY VARDEN DINING ROOM SET   1936-1940
Set of 101a Table, 101b Sideboard, two 101c Carver Chairs, four 101d Chairs.
1. Walnut finish.

102-F   BEDROOM SET   1936-1940
Set of 102a Bed, 102b Wardrobe, 102c Vanity, 102d Bureau, 102e Bench, 102f Chair.
1. Light brown.
2. Dark brown.

102-G   DOLLY VARDEN BEDROOM SET   1936-1940
Set of 102a Bed, 102b Wardrobe, 102c Dressing Table, 102d Chest, 102e Stool.
1. Light and dark green.
2. Mauve and gold.

103-F   KITCHEN SET   1936-1940
Set of 103a Refrigerator, 103b Kitchen Cabinet, 103c Stove, 103d Table, 103e Chair.
1. Green and ivory.
2. Blue and ivory.

103-G   DOLLY VARDEN KITCHEN SET   1936-1940
Set of 103a Refrigerator, 103b Kitchen Cabinet, 103c Electric Stove, 103d Table, 103e Chair.
1. Light green and cream.
2. Tan green and cream.

104-F   BATHROOM SET   1936-1940
Set of 104a Bathtub, 104b Bath Mat, 104c Sink with Mirror, 104d Bench, 104e Hamper, 104f Toilet.
1. Pink.
2. Green?

104-G   DOLLY VARDEN BATHROOM SET   1936-1940
Set of 104a Bathtub, 104b Bath Mat, 104c Wash Basin, 104d Toilet, 104e Hamper.
1. Pink and white.
2. Light green and white.

105a-G   GARDEN ROLLER   67 mm   1948-1953   #381
Cast handle and two roller halves, mounted on axle; roller surface unpainted.
1. Red roller sides, green handle.

105b-G   WHEELBARROW   82 mm   1949-1953   #382
Cast body and unpainted wheel.
1. Tan exterior, red interior.

105c-G   HAND TRUCK   126 mm   1949-1953   #383
Cast body, swiveling front axle mount, handle and hubs, black tires, sheet metal tow hook (body color).
1. Green body and mount, yellow handle and hubs.
2. Blue body, maroon and handle, yellow hubs.

105e-G   GRASS CUTTER   73 mm   1949-1953   #384
Cast frame/handle, blade unit and two wheels, all linked by axle.
1. Yellow frame, red blades, green wheels.

107a-G   SACK TRUCK   65 mm   1949-1953   #385
Cast body and two black wheels.
1. Blue body.

(125a MILITARY SEARCHLIGHT TRUCK (1940) never issued)
(125b MILITARY ANTI-AIRCRAFT GUN TRUCK (1940) never issued)
(125c MILITARY TANK TRUCK (1940) never issued)
(All based on French 25 series trucks, announced in 1940.)

139a-G   FORD FORDOR SEDAN   102 mm   1949-1953   #170
Sedan with cast body and hubs, black tires, black sheet metal base with small lettering, no number, silver grille, bumpers and headlights.
1. Red body and hubs.
2. Yellow body and hubs.

3. Green body and hubs.
4. Light brown body, red hubs.

139am-G   FORD U.S. ARMY STAFF CAR   102 mm   195?-1953   #675
Same castings and parts as 139a, silver headlights, white circled star decal on roof, white star decals on roof.
1. Olive body and hubs.

139b-G   HUDSON COMMODORE   111 mm   1949-1953   #171
Sedan with cast body and hubs, black tires, black sheet metal base with small lettering, no number, silver bumpers, grille and lights.
1. Cream body, maroon roof and hubs.
2. Blue body, tan roof and hubs.

140a-G   AUSTIN A90 ATLANTIC   1951-1953   #106
Roadster with cast body, tan steering wheel, dashboard and hubs, black or white tires, black sheet metal base with small lettering, no number, silver bumpers, lights and trim.
1. Dark pink body, tan steering wheel, yellow hubs, black tires.
2. Pale blue body, red interior and wheels, black tires.
3. Black body, red interior and wheels, white tires.

140b-G   ROVER 75   101 mm   1951-1953   #156
Sedan with cast body and hubs, black tires, black sheet metal base with big letters, no number, silver grille ornament, bumpers and headlights.
1. Maroon body and hubs.
2. Pale yellow body, yellow hubs.
3. Light yellow body, blue hubs.

150-G   ROYAL TANK CORPS SET   1938-1940
Set of 150a, two 150b, two 150c, one 150e. Later sold in USA as #600.
1. Standard colors.

150a-G   ROYAL TANK CORPS OFFICER   1938-1940
Cast figure holding binoculars. Black beret.
1. Khaki uniform.

150b-G   ROYAL TANK CORPS PRIVATE (sitting)   1938-1940
Cast seated figure with arms folded. Later sold in USA as #604.
1. Black uniform and beret.

150c-G   ROYAL TANK CORPS PRIVATE (standing)   1938-1940
Cast figure with arms behind back.
1. Black uniform and beret.

150d-G   ROYAL TANK CORPS DRIVER   1938-1940
Cast seated figure with arms reaching out.
1. Black uniform.

150e-G   ROYAL TANK CORPS N. C. O.   1938-1940
Cast marching figure.
1. Black uniform and beret.

151-G   ROYAL TANK CORPS MEDIUM TANK UNIT   1938-1940
Set of 151a, b, c and d, 150d.
1. Standard colors.

151a-G   MEDIUM TANK   92 mm   1937-1940
Tank with cast body and turret, black sheet metal base, chain treads on toothed hubs, antenna, white markings.
1. Green body and turret.

151b-G   COVERED TRANSPORT WAGON 99 mm   1938-1940, 1946-1948
Six-wheel covered truck with cast body, dashboard and hubs, spare wheel, sheet metal rear cover and rear seats.
1. Green body and cover.

151c-G   FIELD KITCHEN TRAILER   60 mm   1938-1940, 1946-1948
Two-wheel trailer with cast body and hubs, black tires.
1. Green body.

151d-G   WATER TANK TRAILER   52 mm   1938-1940, 1946-1948
Two-wheel trailer with cast body and hubs, black tires.
1. Green body.

152-G   ROYAL TANK CORPS LIGHT TANK UNIT   1938-1940
Set of 152a, b, c and 150d.
1. Standard colors.

152a-G   LIGHT TANK   68 mm   1937-1940
Tank with cast body and turret, chain treads on toothed hubs, antenna, white markings.
1. Gloss green body and turret, silver treads (prewar).
2. Matt green body and turret, black treads (postwar).

152b-G   RECONNAISSANCE CAR   89 mm   1938-1940, 1946-1948
Six-wheel car with cast body and hubs, black tires, black or green sheet metal base. Later sold in USA as #671.
1. Gloss green body (prewar).
2. Matt green body (postwar).
3. Olive brown body (postwar).

152c-G   AUSTIN 7 STAFF CAR   51 mm   1938-1940
Same casting and parts as 35d, with wire windshield frame, black rubber wheels, hole in seat.
1. Gloss green body.

153a-G   JEEP   69 mm   1946-1948
Same castings and parts as 25j, in military colors. Later sold in USA as #672.
1. Matt green body, white star on hood. (Numbers planned but never used because numbering system was changed: 153b-673 Scout Car, 153c-623 Army Wagon, 153d-670 Armored Car, 153e-674 Austin Champ, 153f-641 Cargo Truck.)

156-G   MECHANIZED ARMY SET   1939-1940
Combined 151, 152, 161 and 162 sets, total of 12 pieces.
1. Standard colors.

160-G   ROYAL ARTILLERY PERSONNEL   1939-1940
Set of 160a, b, c and two 160d.
1. Standard colors.

160a-G   ROYAL ARTILLERY N. C. O.   1939-1940
Cast figure with steel helmet and binoculars.
1. Khaki uniform.

160b-G   ROYAL ARTILLERY GUNNER (seated)   1939-1940
Cast seated figure with steel helmet. Later sold in USA as #608.
1. Khaki uniform.

160c-G   ROYAL ARTILLERY GUN LAYER   1939-1940
Cast seated figure with steel helmet and arms reaching out.
1. Khaki uniform.

160d-G   ROYAL ARTILLERY GUNNER (standing)   1939-1940
Cast figure with steel helmet, arms at sides.
1. Khaki uniform.

161-G   MOBILE ANTI-AIRCRAFT SET   1939-1940
Set of 161a and 161b.
1. Standard colors.

161a-G   LORRY MOUNTED SEARCHLIGHT   99 mm   1939-1940
Open truck with cast body (same as 151a truck), dashboard, searchlight and hubs, black tires, sheet metal searchlight mount.
1. Gloss green.

161b-G   ANTI-AIRCRAFT GUN ON TRAILER   115 mm   1939-1940, 1946-1948
Cast trailer, elevating gun, control and hubs, black tires, sheet metal folding panels, holes for crew. Later sold in USA as #690.
1. Gloss green (prewar).
2. Matt green (postwar).
3. Olive brown (postwar).

162-G   18 POUNDER FIELD GUN UNIT   1939-1940, 1946-1948?
Set of 162a, b and c. Later sold in USA as #691.
1. Standard prewar colors.

The Old System of Catalog Numbers

2. Standard postwar colors.

162a-G LIGHT DRAGON TRACTOR   89 mm 1939-1940, 1946-1948
Cast body, usually with chain treads on toothed hubs. With or without holes in seats.
1. Gloss green body, holes in seats, chain treads (prewar).
2. Green body, black rubber wheels, holes in seats (prewar).
3. Green body, no holes in seats, chain treads (postwar).

162b-G TRAILER   54 mm 1939-1940, 1946-1948
Two-wheel ammunition trailer with cast body and hubs, black tires.
1. Gloss green body.

162c-G 18-POUNDER GUN   78 mm 1939-1940, 1946-1948
Cast one-piece body, including gun, and two hubs, black tires.

280-G DELIVERY VANS   1937-1940
Set of six type 2 or 3 280-series vans: 280a Viyella, 280b Lyons or Hartleys, 280c Shredded Wheat, 280d Bisto, 280e Ekco or Yorkshire Evening Post, and 280f Mackintosh's.
1. Type 2 castings, standard colors (1937-1939).
2. Type 3 castings, standard colors (1939-1940).

280-H DELIVERY VAN   83 mm 1948-1954
Third type van casting, cast hubs, black tires. no logo, silver grille and bumper.
1. Red body.
2. Blue body.

280a-G VIYELLA VAN   81/83 mm 1937-1940
Type 2 or 3 casting with white and black "Viyella for the Nursery" logo, silver grille.
1. Light blue body, type 2 casting (1937-1939).
2. Light blue body, type 3 casting (1939-1940).

280b-G LYONS VAN   81 mm 1937-1938
Type 2 van with orange-red and white Lyons Tea logo, silver grille.
1. Dark blue body.

280b-H HARTLEY'S VAN   81 mm 1938-1940
Type 2 or 3 van with red and green "Hartley's is Real Jam" logo, silver grille.
1. Cream body, type 2 casting (1938-1939).
2. Cream body, type 3 casting (1939-1940).

280c-G SHREDDED WHEAT VAN   81/83 mm 1937-1940
Type 2 or 3 van with black and red Shredded Wheat logo, silver grille.
1. Cream body, type 2 casting (1937-1939).
2. Cream body, type 3 casting (1939-1940).

280d-G BISTO VAN   81/83 mm 1937-1940
Type 2 or 3 van with Bisto logo, silver grille.
1. Yellow body, type 2 casting, "Ah, Bisto!" logo (1937-1938).
2. Yellow body, type 2 casting, "Bisto" and design (1938-1939).
3. Yellow body, type 3 casting, "Bisto" and design (1939-1940).

280e-G EKCO VAN   81 mm 1938
Type 2 van with gold Ekco logo, silver grille.
1. Green body.

280e-H YORKSHIRE EVENING POST VAN   81/83 mm 1938-1940
Type 2 or 3 van with black and gold Yorkshire Evening Post logo, silver grille.
1. Cream body, type 2 casting (1938-1939).
2. Cream body, type 3 casting (1939-1940).

280f-G MACKINTOSH'S VAN   81/83 mm 1938-1940
Type 2 or 3 van with gold Mackintosh's Toffee logo, silver grille.
1. Red body, type 2 casting (1938-1939).
2. Red body, type 3 casting (1939-1940).

280?-G KNORR VAN   8 mm 1939?
Casting, color and other data unknown, Knorr decals.
1. Existence unconfirmed

500 series Foden 8-wheel trucks have two casting types:
Type 1: high narrow grille with rounded top and straight vertical sides, Foden lettering: 1947-1952.
Type 2: Grille with narrow raised V-shaped central section and horizontal bars to

each side: 1953-1954. Trucks may or may not have tow hooks; cabs have trim in the color of the rear body or hubs, as well as silver grille, bumper and headlights.

501-G FODEN DIESEL 8-WHEEL TRUCK   188 mm 1947-1954 _#901
Open truck with cast chassis-cab, rear body and eight Supertoy hubs, black or gray tires, spare wheel, black sheet metal cab base, tow hook, silver grille, bumper and headlights. Casting with type 1 grille:
1. Rust red cab and hubs, black chassis, tan body.
2. Rust red cab, rear body and hubs, black chassis.
3. Blue cab, rear body and hubs, black chassis.
Casting with type 2 grille:
4. Green chassis-cab, orange rear body, ? hubs.
5. Orange chassis-cab, gray-brown rear body, green hubs.

502-G FODEN DIESEL FLAT TRUCK   188 mm 1947-1954 _#902
Flatbed truck with cast chassis-cab, rear body and eight Supertoy hubs, black or gray tires, spare wheel, black sheet metal cab base, tow hook, silver grille, bumper and headlights. Casting with type 1 grille:
1. Red chassis-cab, blue rear body, ? hubs.
2. Orange cab, light green rear body and hubs.
3. Dark green cab, rear body and hubs, black chassis.
4. Gray chassis-cab and rear body, blue hubs.
Casting with type 2 grille:
5. Green chassis-cab, orange rear body, ? hubs.
6. Red chassis-cab and hubs, light green rear body.
7. Orange chassis-cab and hubs, light green rear body.
8. Orange chassis-cab, light green rear body and hubs.
9. Yellow chassis-cab and hubs, light green rear body.

503-G FODEN DIESEL FLAT TRUCK WITH TAILBOARD   188 mm 1947-1954 _#903
Cast chassis-cab, rear body with tailboard, and eight Supertoy hubs, black or gray tires, spare wheel, black sheet metal front base, tow hook, silver grille, bumper and headlights. Casting with type 1 grille:
1. Red chassis-cab, blue rear body, ? hubs.
2. Dark blue chassis-cab, orange rear body, light blue hubs.
Casting with type 2 grille:
3. Dark purplish-blue chassis-cab, orange rear body, light blue hubs.
4. Light blue chassis-cab and hubs, tan rear body.

504-G FODEN DIESEL TANKER   188 mm 1948-1954 _#941
Tanker with cast chassis-cab and eight Supertoy hubs, black or gray tires, spare wheel, sheet metal tank, catwalk, ladder, front base and tow hook, silver grille, bumper and headlights. Casting with type 1 grille:
1. Dark blue chassis-cab, light blue tank and hubs.
2. Red chassis-cab, tan tank and hubs.
Casting with type 2 grille:
3. Dark blue chassis-cab, light blue tank, red hubs.
4. Red chassis-cab and hubs, tan tank.
5. Red chassis-cab, tank and hubs, red-white-blue Mobilgas logo.

505-G FODEN DIESEL FLAT TRUCK WITH CHAINS   188 mm 1952-1954 _#905
Cast chassis-cab, flat rear body, six stakes, and Supertoy hubs, black or gray tires, spare wheel, chain through eyes of stakes, black sheet metal front base, tow hook, silver grille, bumper and headlights. Casting with type 1 grille:
1. Green chassis-cab and rear body, light green hubs.
Casting with type 2 grille:
2. Green chassis-cab and rear body, light green hubs.
3. Maroon chassis-cab and rear body, red hubs.
4. Red chassis-cab and hubs, light gray rear body.

510 series Guy Otter trucks have two casting types:
Type 1: thin vertical-line brackets beside front license plate.
Type 2: triangular brackets beside front license plate. All models have a tow hook, silver grille, bumper and headlights. Early issues have regular cast hubs, later

issues have Supertoy hubs.

511-G GUY OTTER TRUCK   133 mm 1947-1954 _#911 _#431
Open truck with cast chassis-cab, rear body and hubs, black tires, spare wheel, black sheet metal cab base. Casting with type 1 brackets:
1. Tan cab and rear body, red chassis and fenders, ? hubs.
2. Brick red cab and rear body, black chassis and fenders, red hubs.
3. Dark green chassis-cab, light green rear body and hubs.
4. Dark blue chassis-cab, light blue rear body and hubs.
Casting with type 2 brackets:
5. Dark blue chassis-cab, light blue rear body and hubs.
6. Dark green chassis-cab, light green rear body and hubs?

512-G GUY OTTER FLAT TRUCK   133 mm 1947-1954 _#912 _#432
Flatbed truck with cast chassis-cab, rear body and hubs, black tires, spare wheel, black sheet metal cab base. Casting with type 1 brackets:
1. Dark brown cab and rear body, black chassis and fenders, ? hubs.
2. Maroon cab and rear body, black chassis and fenders?, ? hubs.
3. Red chassis-cab, blue rear body, ? hubs.
4. Orange chassis-cab, light green rear body and hubs.
5. Blue chassis-cab and hubs, light green rear body.
6. Blue chassis-cab, orange rear body, ? hubs.
7. Blue chassis-cab, yellow rear body, ? hubs.
Casting with type 2 brackets:
8. Red chassis-cab, light blue rear body and hubs.
9. Light blue chassis-cab and hubs, red rear body.

513-G GUY OTTER FLAT TRUCK WITH TAILBOARD   133 mm 1947-1954 _#913 _#433
Cast chassis-cab, rear body with tailboard, and hubs, black tires, spare wheel, black sheet metal cab base. Casting with type 1 brackets:
1. Yellow cab and rear body, blue-black chassis, fenders and hubs.
2. Dark green chassis-cab, light green rear body and hubs.
Casting with type 2 brackets:
3. Purplish-blue chassis-cab, orange rear body, light blue hubs.
4. Purplish-blue chassis-cab, red rear body, ? hubs.

514-G GUY OTTER VAN   133 mm 1949-1954 _#917
Box van with cast chassis-cab, rear body, two opening rear doors, and Supertoy hubs, black tires, spare wheel, black sheet metal bases, silver grille and headlights. Casting with type 1 brackets:
1. Red chassis-cab, body, doors and hubs, gold and black Slumberland logo (1949-1952).
2. Dark blue chassis-cab, body and doors, light blue hubs, gold Lyons Swiss Rolls logo (1951-1954).
Casting with type 2 brackets:
3. Dark blue chassis-cab, body and doors, light blue hubs, gold Lyons Swiss Rolls' logo. (I assume both casting types exist.)
4. Dark blue chassis-cab, body, doors and hubs, maroon and black Weetabix logo (1952-1953 or 1954).
5. Pale red chassis-cab, dark cream body and doors, bright red hubs, black and brown Spratts logo, pale red stripe (1953-1954).

521-G BEDFORD ARTICULATED TRUCK   165 mm 1948-1954 _#921 _#409
Open semi with cast body, grille, semi-trailer, hitch and six hubs, black tires, spare tire, black sheet metal cab base, tow hook, black grille. Hitch casting includes upper surface of cab rear, spare tire mount and fenders.
1. Dark yellow cab and semi, black fenders and hitch, red hubs.
2. Red cab, dark yellow semi, black fenders, ? other details.
3. Maroon cab, tan semi, ? other details.

522-G BIG BEDFORD TRUCK   146 mm 1952-1954 _#922 _#408
Open truck with cast chassis-cab, rear body and Supertoy hubs, gray or black tires, black sheet metal cab base, tow hook, silver trim.
1. Dark blue chassis-cab, light orange rear body, dark yellow hubs.

2. Maroon chassis-cab, tan rear body and hubs.

531-G LEYLAND COMET TRUCK 140 mm 1949-1954 ⊿#931 ⊿#417
Stake truck with cast chassis-cab, and Supertoy hubs, gray tires, spare wheel, sheet metal rear stake body, black cab base, tow hook, silver trim.
1. Dark blue chassis-cab, yellow-orange rear body, red hubs.
2. Dark blue chassis-cab, light blue rear body, ? hubs.
3. Red chassis-cab, yellow rear body, ? hubs.

532-G LEYLAND COMET TRUCK WITH TAILBOARD 143 mm 1952-1954 ⊿#931 ⊿#408 ⊿#932 ⊿#418
Open truck with cast chassis-cab, opening tailboard and four hubs, gray tires, spare wheel, black sheet metal cab base, silver trim.
1. Green chassis-cab and hubs, orange rear body.
2. Dark blue chassis-cab, light blue rear body, cream hubs.

533-G LEYLAND COMET CEMENT TRUCK 143 mm 1953-1954 ⊿#419
Flat truck with cast chassis-cab, rear body and Supertoy hubs, gray tires, spare wheel, black sheet metal cab base, silver trim, blue "Portland Blue Circle Cement" decals on doors, blue-black and white lettering on sides and rear of body.
1. Yellow chassis-cab, rear body and hubs.

551-G TRUCK TRAILER 105 mm 1948-1954 ⊿#951 ⊿#428
Open 4-wheel trailer with cast body, black axle mount, and red hubs, gray or black tires, wire tow bar, sheet metal tow hook.
1. Light gray body, ridged hubs.
2. Light gray body, Supertoy hubs.

555-G COMMER FIRE ENGINE 140 mm 1952-1954 ⊿#955
Enclosed fire engine with cast body, two-piece ladder and Supertoy hubs, two bells on roof, black sheet metal ladder mount, tow hook and base, silver grille, bumpers,

headlights and rear panels, gray hose reels, no windows.
1. Red body, brown ladder.
2. Red body, silver ladder.

561-G BLAW-KNOX BULLDOZER 143 mm 1949-1954 ⊿#961
Heavy tractor with cast body, bulldozer blade, tan driver, black arms, stacks and hubs, gray rubber treads, black sheet metal levers and parts, black hydraulic cylinders.
1. Red body and blade.

562-G MUIR-HILL DUMP TRUCK 106 mm 1948-1954 ⊿#962
Quarry dumper with cast chassis-cab, tipper, wheels with red hubs, black steering wheel and swiveling seat, tan driver, black sheet metal base, front axle mount and tow hook, silver ornament and headlights.
1. Yellow chassis-cab and tipper.

563-G BLAW-KNOX HEAVY TRACTOR 118 mm 1948-1954 ⊿#963
Same body casting as #561, tan driver, black stacks, light green hubs, green rubber treads, black sheet metal base, tow hook and levers.
1. Red body.
2. Orange body.

564-G ELEVATOR LOADER 156 mm 1952-1954 ⊿#964
Cast frame, chute, hopper, rollers, gears, and light blue Supertoy hubs, gray tires, rubber belt, sheet metal parts, wire towbar and crank, no number cast on hopper.
1. Yellow frame, blue chute and hopper.

571-G COLES MOBILE CRANE 160 mm 1949-1954 ⊿#971
Cast body, black chassis, blue driver, and yellow Supertoy hubs, gray tires, yellow sheet metal crane boom, black base, two cranks, line and hook, "Coles" and stripe decals. Also sold in France in 1951.
1. Dark yellow body.

581-G HORSE BOX 175 mm 1953-954 ⊿#981

Long van with cast body, chassis, opening rear and side ramp doors, and hubs, black tires, +/- red and cream British Railways logo.
1. Maroon body, chassis and ramps, red hubs, logo (British issue).
2. No logo, otherwise as type 1 (U.S. issue).

583-G PULLMORE CAR TRANSPORTER 248 mm 1953-1954 ⊿#982
Cast cab, hitch, semi-trailer body, chassis, opening ramp, blue ridged and Supertoy hubs, black tires, spare wheel, black and silver grille-headlights, black sheet metal base, dark blue "Dinky Toys Delivery Service" logo on semi sides and ramp.
1. Light blue cab and entire semi.
2. Light blue cab and semi with tan decks.
3. Medium blue cab, light blue entire semi.

591-G A.E.C. TANKER 153 mm 1952-1954 ⊿#991
Tank truck with cast body and yellow Supertoy hubs, gray or black tires, black sheet metal base, silver grille and headlights, yellow "Shell Chemicals Limited" lettering on sides, red and yellow Shell emblem on rear.
1. Red cab and rear body, orange-yellow tank.

701-G SHETLAND FLYING BOAT 170 by 237 mm 1947-1949
Cast fuselage-tail, hull, wings with nacelles, and floats, four black 4-blade sheet metal propellers, G-AGUD registration.
1. Silver body.

751-G LAWN MOWER 140 mm 1949-1953 ⊿#386
Cast frame-handles, grass catcher, blade and rollers.
1. Green frame and catcher exterior, red blades and catcher interior.

752-G GOODS YARD CRANE 195 mm 1953 ⊿#973
Cast base, swiveling mount and crane boom, two cranks, line and hook, black lettering.
1. Dark yellow crane and mount, blue base.

The New System of Catalog Numbers

The newer Dinky Toys catalog numbering system was introduced in 1954 in Britain, though it had its origins earlier. The older system included three-digit series such as the 280 vans and 500 heavy trucks; some of these numbers were in use when the new system was introduced; some fit into the new system, while others were changed to fit in. A year later additional changes were made in the British system, with all the 500 series vehicles changed to 900 numbers. Apparently it was already known that the 500 numbers would be used by the French branch of Dinky Toys, though this did not come to pass until 1959, when all French Dinky Toys were changed to 500 and 800 numbers, completing the change to the new system. Whereas the British change took place at the beginning of 1954, the French change was made during 1959, so that models introduced early in the year still had old-style catalog numbers for a short time.

We must note, though, that the Mini-Dinky Toys made in Hong Kong in the Sixties had two-digit numbers, and the last French-Spanish Dinky Toys had four-digit 1400 and 1500 numbers. More recently, another Hong Kong series has used three-digit numbers, and the newest Dinky Toys (pending the appearance of newer ones from Matchbox) have no numbers except those they had when they were part of the Matchbox Series! All of the recent Hong Kong and Macau products will be listed at the end of this section, but as we begin with number 001, we still find ourselves at least partly in Hong Kong. All the Hong Kong models will be suffixed with the letter H, all those made in Spain with the letter S.

The New System of Catalog Numbers

001-G STATION STAFF #1_1954-1955
Same figures as set #1.
1. Less detailed painting than formerly.
001-H BUICK RIVIERA 122 mm 1965-1967
Hardtop with cast body, opening hood and trunk lid, and black base, unpainted circle-pattern metal tires, black plastic tires, red interior, silver bumpers, silver and red engine block, red taillights, #57/001 on base; 1/42 scale.
1. Pale blue body, cream hardtop.
001-J BLAZING INFERNO 1979
Dinky Builda folding cardboard kit.
1. Burning building.
002-G FARMYARD ANIMALS #2_1954-1955
Same figures as set #2.
1. Painted as before.
002-H CHEVROLET CORVAIR MONZA 105 mm 1965-1967
Rear-engine sedan with cast body, opening front and rear hoods and black base, unpainted metal wheels, black tires, plastic windows, white interior, silver engine, headlights and bumpers, yellow taillights, #57/002 on base; 1/42 scale.
1. Red body, black top.
002-J SPACE WAR STATION 1979
Dinky Builda folding cardboard kit.
1. Spacecraft station.
003-G PASSENGERS #3_1954-1955
Same figures as set #3.
1. Painted as before.
003-H CHEVROLET IMPALA 125 mm 1965-1967
Sedan with cast body, opening hood and trunk, and black base, unpainted metal hubs, black tires, plastic windows, red interior, red and silver engine, silver grille and bumpers, red taillights, #57/003 on base; 1/42 scale.
1. Yellow body, cream top.
2. Brighter yellow body including top.
004-G ENGINEERING STAFF #4_1954-1955
Same figures as set #4 minus 4c.
1. Painted as before.
004-H OLDSMOBILE DYNAMIC 88 129 mm 1965-1967
Hardtop with cast body, opening hood and trunk, and black base, unpainted metal hubs, black tires, plastic windows, red interior, silver engine, grille and bumpers, red taillights, #57/004 on base; 1/42 scale. Originally announced as a Dodge and may actually represent a Dodge, but identified on the base as an Oldsmobile.
1. White body, light blue hardtop.
005-G TRAIN AND HOTEL STAFF #5_1954-1955
Same figures as set #5.
1. Painted as before.
005-H FORD THUNDERBIRD 122 mm 1965-1967
Coupe with cast body, opening sdoors, and black base, unpainted metal wheels, black tires, plastic windows, red interior, silver grille, bumpers and headlights, red taillights, #57/005 on base; 1/42 scale.
1. Light blue body, white top.
006-G SHEPHERD SET #6_1954-1955
Same figures as set #6.
1. Painted as before.
006-H RAMBLER CLASSIC 119 mm 1965-1967
Station wagon with cast body, opening hood and tailgate, and black base, unpainted metal hubs, black tires, plastic windows, cream interior, silver grille, bumpers and lights, #57/006 on base; 1/42 scale.
1. Dull green body, silver roof rack.
007-G PETROL PUMP ATTENDANTS 1960-1967
Plastic figures of man and woman.

1. White coats.
008-G FIRE STATION PERSONNEL 1961-1967
Five plastic firemen figures, one of which clips onto ladder, plus fire hose.
1. Dark blue uniforms.
009-G SERVICE STATION PERSONNEL 1962-1966
Eight plastic figures: four mechanics, woman pump attendant, three male motorists, all different.
1. Variety of colors.
010-G ROAD MAINTENANCE PERSONNEL 1962-1966
Six plastic figures of workmen, hut, barrier, lanterns and air compressor hose.
1. Variety of colors.
011-G TELEGRAPH MESSENGER #12d_1954-1956
Cast figure, same as 12d.
1. Blue uniform.
012-G POSTMAN #12e_1954-1956
Cast figure, same as 12e.
1. Blue uniform.
013-G COOK'S MAN #13a_1954-1956
Cast figure, same as 13a.
1. Blue coat.
ACCESSORIES available at various times:
013 Battery, 1.5 volt, for models 276 and 277 1962.
020 Tires, 16 mm black: 1969-1976.
021 Tires, 20 mm black: 1970-1976.
022 Tires, 16 mm black: 1971-1976.
023 Tires, 16 mm black: 1971-1976.
024 Tires, 23 mm black, 1971-1976.
025 Tires, details and dates unknown.
026 Tires, 20 mm black, for racing cars: dates unknown.
027 Tires, 27 mm black, 1976.
028 Tires, details and dates unknown.
029 Treads, 260 mm black, for tanks, dates unknown.
030 Treads, black, for #104: 1969-1976.
031 Treads, black, for tanks: 1976.
032 Treads, black, for #353: 1973-1976.
033 Treads, black, for #654, 683: 1973-1976.
034 Battery, 1.5 volt, for #102 and others: 1971-1973.
035 Battery, 1.5 volt, for #719, 1042: 1970-1977.
036 Battery, 1.5 volt, for #102 and others: 1962-1977.
037 Light bulb, red, for 276, 277: 1962-1971.
038 Light bulb, blue (listed as orange), for #276: 1962-1969.
039 Light bulb for #160, 952: 1966-1975.
040 Light bulb for #157, 176: 1969-1977.
042 Light bulb for #102: 1970-1977.
080 Tires, 38 mm black: 1976.
081 Tires, 14 mm white: 1964-1976.
082 Tires, 20 mm black, for antique cars: 1964-1973.
083 Tires, 20 mm gray, for Supertoys: 1964-1967.
084 Tires, 18 mm black: 1966-1976.
085 Tires, 15 mm white: 1964-1970.
086 Tires, 16 mm black: 1966-1976.
087 Tires, 35 mm white: 1963; black-1976.
088 Tires, 25 mm black: 1969-1976.
089 Tires, 19 mm black: 1963-1976.
090 Tires, 14 mm black: 1962-1976.
091 Tires, 13 mm black: 1960-1976.
092 Tires, 15 mm black: 1958-1976.
093 Tires, 27 mm black: 1956-1971.

094 Tires, 20 mm black: 1954-1973.
095 Tires, 18 mm black: 1956-1976.
096 Tires, 24 mm black: 1954-1973.
097/1 Tires, 32 mm black: 1954-1973.
097/2 Wheels, 10 mm, dates unknown.
098/1 Tires, 17 mm black: 1970-1977.
098/2 Wheels, 12 mm, dates unknown.
099 Tires, 20 mm black: 1954-1976.
041-G CIVILIAN MOTORCYCLIST #37a_195?
Model 37a renumbered for export.
1. As before.
042-G POLICE MOTORCYCLIST #37b_195?
Model 37b renumbered for export.
1. As before.
043-G POLICE MOTORCYCLE AND SIDECAR #42b_195?
Model 42b renumbered for export.
1. As before.
045-G AA MOTORCYCLE AND SIDECAR #44b_195?_#270
Model 44b renumbered for export, later #270.
1. As before.
Note: the #37c Despatch Motorcyclist may also have been renumbered for export; the number is not known, though 044 would be logical.
050-G RAILWAY STAFF 1961-1969
Plastic figures, OO scale.
1. Twelve figures.
051-G STATION STAFF #1001_1954-1959
HO scale version of #001, #1001 1952-1953.
1. Six figures.
052-G RAILWAY PASSENGERS 1961-1969
Plastic figures and seat, OO scale.
1. Twelve-piece set.
053-G PASSENGERS #1003_1954-1959
HO scale version of #003, #1003 1952-1953.
1. Six figures.
054-G STATION PERSONNEL 1961-1969
Plastic figures and accessories, OO scale.
1. Details not known.

DUBLO DINKY TOYS: the following models were made to OO scale:
061-G FORD PREFECT 59 mm 1958-1960
Sedan with cast body, black sheet metal base, gray plastic wheels, silver grille, bumpers and headlights.
1. Tan body.
2. Gray body.
062-G SINGER ROADSTER 51 mm 1958-1960
Roadster with cast body, gray plastic wheels, red interior, silver grille, bumpers and headlights.
1. Orange body.
2. Tan body.
063-G COMMER VAN 54 mm 1958-1960
Light van with cast body, black sheet metal base, gray plastic wheels, silver grille, bumper and headlights.
1. Blue body.
064-G AUSTIN LORRY 64 mm 1957-1962
Open truck with cast body, black or gray plastic wheels, silver grille, bumper and headlights.
1. Green body, gray wheels.
2. Green body, black wheels.

The New System of Catalog Numbers

065-G MORRIS PICKUP TRUCK   54 mm   1957-1960
Pickup with cast body, gray plastic wheels, silver grille, bumper and headlights.
1. Red body.

066-G BEDFORD FLAT TRUCK   108 mm   1957-1960
Flatbed truck with cast body, gray plastic wheels, silver grille, bumper and headlights.
1. Gray body.

067-G AUSTIN TAXI   59 mm   1959-1967
Taxi with cast body and base-driver-seat, gray plastic wheels, black and cream Taxi sign, silver grille, bumpers and headlights.
1. Cream upper body, blue lower body, black base.

068-G ROYAL MAIL VAN   47 mm   1959-1964
Light van with cast body, black sheet metal base, gray plastic wheels, silver grille, bumper and headlights.
1. Red body, yellow Royal Mail logo.

069-G MASSEY-FERGUSON TRACTOR   36 mm   1959-1964
Farm tractor with cast body, gray plastic wheels, silver grille, black sheet metal tow hook.
1. Dark blue body.

070-G A.E.C. MERCURY TANKER   90 mm   1959-1964
Tank truck with cast body, black sheet metal base, black plastic wheels, windows, black grille, silver bumper and headlights, orange taillights.
1. Green cab, red tank, Shell-BP decals.

071-G VW DELIVERY VAN   54 mm   1960-1964
Light van with cast body, black sheet metal base, black plastic wheels, silver VW emblem, bumpers and headlights.
1. Light orange body, red Hornby Dublo logo.

072-G BEDFORD ARTICULATED FLAT TRUCK   117 mm   1959-1964
Flat semi with cast cab and semi-trailer, gray or black plastic wheels, windows, silver grille, bumper and headlights.
1. Light orange cab, red semi, treadless gray wheels.
2. Light orange cab, red semi with shallow grooves in flatbed, treaded black wheels.

073-G LAND ROVER AND HORSE TRAILER   105 mm   1960-1964
Cast Land Rover body, trailer body and tailgate, black sheet metal baseplates and tow hook, gray plastic wheels and spare, tan horse, windows, silver grille, bumper and headlights.
1. Green Land Rover and tailgate, orange trailer body.
(074 LAND ROVER not sold separately)
(075 HORSE TRAILER not sold separately)

076-H LANSING BAGNALL TRACTOR AND TRAILER   75 mm
1960-1964
Cast tractor, seat with driver, and flat trailer, black plastic wheels, sheet metal tow hook and front axle mount, wire towbar.
1. Maroon tractor and trailer, dark blue seat and driver.
(077 A.E.C. BULK CEMENT TRANSPORTER never issued)

078-G LANSING BAGNALL TRAILER   1960-1964
Trailer of #076 sold separately.
1. Maroon trailer.

100-F RENAULT 4L   84 mm   1962-1968
Small car with cast body, turned hubs, black tires, black sheet metal base, silver grille, bumpers and lights. Junior series.
1. Pale green body.

100-G FRAZER NASH-BMW   #38a_1954-1955
Renumbering of #38a for U.S. market. Details as 38a.
1. Colors as 38a.

100-H LADY PENELOPE'S FAB 1   147 mm   1966-1976
Limousine with cast body, unpainted chassis and opening grille, six 6-spoke hubs, black tires, suspension, gold interior, figures of Lady Penelope and Parker, clear plastic windshield and sliding roof, jewel headlights, concealed weapons.

1. Pink body, two pink stripes on roof.
2. Pink body, no stripes on roof.

101-F PEUGEOT 404   101 mm   1962-1969
Sedan with cast body, turned hubs, black tires, black sheet metal base, silver grille, bumpers and lights. Junior series.
1. Brick red body.
2. Bright red-orange body.

101-G SUNBEAM TALBOT   92 mm   #38b_1954-1955
Renumbering of #38b for U.S. market. Details as 38b.
1. Colors as 38b.

101-H SUNBEAM ALPINE   94 mm   1957-1960
Sports car with cast body, cream steering wheel, driver in brownish-gray suit, and hubs, black tires, black sheet metal base, big lettering, no number, plastic windshield, silver grille, bumpers and headlights, red or orange taillights.
1. Dark blue body, dark cream interior and hubs, orange taillights.
2. Turquoise body, blue interior and hubs, red taillights.

101-J THUNDERBIRDS 2 & 4   143 mm   1967-1973
Spacecraft with cast upper and lower body, removable upper and lower pod and ramp, yellow plastic Thunderbird 4 with black numbers, red jets and folding legs, two red and clear plastic jets, red intakes, pale blue windows, green and white labels, black and silver louver label, black pod rollers.
1. Gloss green body and pod.
2. Metallic green body and pod.

102-F PANHARD PL17   106 mm   1963-1968
Sedan with cast body, turned hubs, black tires, black sheet metal base, silver bumpers and lights. Junior series.
1. Dull light gray-blue body.
2. Bright light blue body.

102-G LAGONDA   102 mm   #38c_1954-1955
Renumbering of #38c for U.S. market. Details as 38c.
1. Colors as 38c.

102-H MG MIDGET   83 mm   1957-1960
C-type MG with cast body, black steering wheel and driver in brownish-gray suit, cast or turned hubs, black tires, black sheet metal base, big lettering, no number, plastic windshield, silver grille, bumpers and headlights, red taillights.
1. Orange body, red interior and cast hubs.
2. Orange body, red interior, unpainted turned hubs.
3. Light green body, cream interior and cast hubs.
4. Light green body, cream interior, unpainted turned hubs.

102-J JOE'S CAR   139 mm   1969-1975
Fantasy car with cast body parts, wings and wheel mounts, turned hubs, black tires, white plastic interior, clear windows, red driver, dark red jet, chrome ducts, jewel headlights.
1. Metallic greenish-blue body and wings, white trim.

103-F RENAULT R8   91 mm   1963-1968
Sedan with cast body, turned hubs, black tires, black sheet metal base, silver bumpers and two or four headlights. Junior series.
1. Dark red body, two headlights.
2. Red body, four headlights: R8 Gordini.

103-G ALVIS SPORTS TOURER   95 mm   #38d_1954-1955
Renumbering of #38d for U.S. market. Details as 38d.
1. Colors as 38d.

103-H AUSTIN-HEALEY 100   86 mm   1957-1960
Sports car with cast body, tan steering wheel, driver in brownish-gray suit, and hubs, black tires, black sheet metal base, big lettering, no number, clear windshield, silver grille, bumpers and headlights, red or orange taillights.
1. Red body, light gray interior and hubs, orange taillights.
2. Light yellow body, red interior, hubs and taillights.

103-J SPECTRUM PATROL CAR   121 mm   1968-1975
Fantasy car with cast body and base, patterned hubs, black tires, yellow or cream plastic interior, clear and frosted windows, white antenna, sound apparatus, silver lights.
1. Red body, yellow base and interior.
2. Metallic red body, cream base and interior (1974-1975).
3. Metallic dark gold body, yellow base and interior.

104-F SIMCA 1000   87 mm   1964-1968
Sedan with cast body, turned hubs, black tires, black sheet metal base, silver bumpers and headlights.
1. Lime green body.

104-G ARMSTRONG-SIDDELEY   96 mm   #38e_1954-1955
Renumbering of #38e for U.S. market. Details as 38e.
1. Colors as 38e.

104-H ASTON MARTIN DB3S   87 mm   1957-1960
Sports-racing car with cast body, tan steering wheel, driver in brownish-gray suit, and hubs, black tires, black sheet metal base, big lettering, no number, silver grille and headlights, red taillights.
1. Salmon body, red interior and hubs.
2. Pale blue body, dark blue interior, medium blue hubs.

104-J SPECTRUM PURSUIT VEHICLE   160 mm   1968-1977
Fantasy car with cast body, chassis, two hatches and tread assembly, ten patterned hubs, black tires and treads, cream plastic nose, red hatch parts, black antennas, red and white rockets, red and cream trim, SVP and emblem labels.
1. Metallic light blue body and chassis.

105-F CITROEN 2CV   87 mm   1964-1968
Light car with cast body, light gray turned hubs, black tires, black sheet metal base, silver grille, bumpers and headlights. Junior series.
1. Gray body.

105-G JAGUAR SS   80 mm   #38f_1954-1955
Renumbering of #38f for U.S. market. Details as 38f.
1. Colors as 38f.

105-H TRIUMPH TR2   84 mm   1957-1960
Sports car with cast body, tan steering wheel, driver in grayish-brown suit, cast or turned hubs, black tires, black sheet metal base, big lettering, no number, clear plastic windshield, silver grille, bumpers and headlights, red taillights.
1. Yellow body, light green interior and cast hubs.
2. Yellow body, light green interior, unpainted turned hubs.
3. Light gray body, red interior and cast hubs.
4. Light gray body, red interior, unpainted turned hubs.

105-J MAXIMUM SECURITY VEHICLE   137 mm   1968-1975
Fantasy vehicle with cast body, two gullwing doors and red chassis, plastic interior and ramps, cream plastic case with "Radioactive" label, trim and emblem labels.
1. Light cream body, red trim, interior and ramps, patterned metal hubs with black tires.
2. Light cream body, pale blue interior and ramps, black plastic wheels.

106-F OPEL KADETT   89 mm   1965-1969
Sedan with cast body, turned hubs, black tires, black sheet metal base, silver bumpers and headlights.
1. Light yellow body.

106-G AUSTIN ATLANTIC   95 mm   #140a_1954-1958
Roadster with cast body, dashboard, tan steering wheel, and hubs, black or white tires, black sheet metal base, silver bumpers, lights and trim. Identical to 140a.
1. Dark pink body, light tan interior, yellow hubs, black tires.
2. Pale blue body, red interior and hubs, black tires.
3. Black body, red interior and hubs, white tires.

106-H "THE PRISONER" MINIMOKE   73 mm   1968-1970
Minimoke with cast body, turned hubs, black tires, white plastic hood, top, spare

wheel cover and antenna, brown engine, bicycle emblem, taxi sign and red-white stripe labels.
  1. White body.

106-J THUNDERBIRDS 2 & 4 153 mm 1974-1979
Castings and parts similar to but larger than #101; lower body and ramp are now black plastic, legs are yellow or red, rollers are unpainted metal.
  1. Metallic blue upper body and pod, yellow legs.
  2. Metallic blue upper body and pod, red legs.

107-G SUNBEAM ALPINE 94 mm 1955-1959
Same casting as 101 but with driver in white racing helmet and coveralls, black-on-white racing number decals, +/- number on base.
  1. Raspberry red body, light gray interior, light tan hubs, racing number 34.
  2. Dark red body, cream or light tan interior and hubs, number ?
  3. Pale blue body, dark cream interior, tan hubs, number 26.
  4. Blue hubs, otherwise as type 3.

107-H STRIPEY THE MAGIC MINI 75 mm 1967-1969
Mini with cast body, opening doors and silver base-grille-bumpers, turned hubs, black tires, red plastic interior, windows, red-yellow-blue diagonal stripe decals, jewel headlights, four plastic figures: Candy, Andy and the Bearandas.
  1. White body and doors.

108-G MG MIDGET 83 mm 1955-1959
Same casting as 102 but with driver in white racing helmet and coveralls, black-on-white racing number decals, +/- number on base.
  1. Red body and hubs, tan interior, racing number 24.
  2. Cream body, maroon interior, red hubs, number 28.
  3. Yellow or cream? hubs, otherwise as type 2.

108-H SAM'S CAR 111 mm 1969-1975
Fantasy open body and base, five-spoke hubs, black tires, yellow plastic interior, red or silver grilles. Badge in box.
  1. White body, ? base, ? grilles (1969-1971).
  2. Chrome body, charcoal base, red grilles (1972-1973).
  3. Dark gold body, ? base, ? grilles (1973-1974).
  4. Metallic red body, charcoal base, silver grilles (1974-1975).
  5. Metallic dark red body, almost black base, silver grilles (1974-1975).
  6. Pale blue body, charcoal base, red grille (dates?).

109-G AUSTIN-HEALEY 100 86 mm 1955-1959
Same casting as 103 but with driver in white racing helmet and coveralls, black-on-white racing number decals, +/- number on base.
  1. Cream body, red interior and hubs, racing number 23.
  2. Orange body, blue interior and hubs, number 21.

109-H GABRIEL'S MODEL T FORD 83 mm 1969-1971
Model T casting and parts as #475, with driver in black and black-on-yellow "Gabriel" labels.
  1. Yellow open cab and spoked wheels, rest of body and interior black.

110-G ASTON MARTIN DB3S 87 mm 1956-1959
Same casting as #104 but with driver in white racing helmet and coveralls, black-on-white racing number decals, +/- number on base.
  1. Light green body, red interior and hubs, racing number 22.
  2. Medium green body, red interior and hubs, number 22.
  3. Light gray body, blue interior and hubs, number 20.

110-H ASTON MARTIN DB5 111 mm 1966-1970
Open sports car with cast body, opening hood and doors, and black base, spoked hubs, black tires, suspension, black or cream plastic interior, clear windshield and door windows, chrome bumpers, grille and engine, inner door and dash labels.
  1. Metallic red body, black interior.

111-G TRIUMPH TR2 86 mm 1956-1959
Same casting as #105 but with driver in white racing helmet and coveralls, black-on-

white racing number decals, number on base.
  1. Salmon body, blue interior and hubs, racing number 29.
  2. Turquoise body, red interior and hubs, number 25.

111-H CINDERELLA'S COACH 242 mm 1976-1977
Cast or plastic body, chassis and front axle mount, plastic wheels, suspension, seats, figures, roof, decorations, horses, hitches and plinth.
  1. Gold cast coach, white and gold horses, pink figures, brown suspension, hitches and plinth.
  2. Gold plastic coach, gray plinth, otherwise as type 1?

112-G AUSTIN-HEALEY SPRITE II 79 mm 1961-1966
Open sports car with cast body, turned hubs, black tires, suspension, black sheet metal base with number, dark cream plastic interior, clear windshield, silver grille, bumpers and headlights.
  1. Red body. South African issues:
  2. Turquoise body.
  3. Light blue body.
  4. Dark blue body.

112-H PURDEY'S TRIUMPH TR7 98 mm 1978-1980
Sports coupe with cast body and opening doors, chrome-hub black Speedwheels, black plastic base-bumpers-interior, red taillights, monogram and stripe decals.
  1. Yellow body, black P monogram decal.
  2. Yellow body, silver P monogram decal.
  3. Yellow body, Purdey name decal?

113-G MGB SPORTS CAR 86 mm 1962-1968
Open sports car with cast body and opening doors, turned hubs, black tires, black sheet metal base, driver in gray, clear windshield, silver grille, bumpers and headlights, red taillights.
  1. Ivory body, red interior. South African issue:
  2. Red body.

(**113 JOHN STEED'S "AVENGERS" JAGUAR XJC** never issued)

114-G TRIUMPH SPITFIRE 89 mm 1963-1970
Open sports car with cast body, opening hood and base, turned hubs, black tires, driver in blue dress, clear windshield, silver or jewel headlights, silver grille and bumpers, red or orange taillights.
  1. Metallic silver gray body, red interior and taillights, silver cast-in headlights, black base and engine (1963-1965).
  2. Red body, dark cream interior, light gray base, silver engine, orange taillights (dates?).
  3. Metallic gold body, red interior and taillights, charcoal base, black engine, jewel headlights, "I've got a (tiger) in my tank" decal (1966-1969).
  4. Metallic purple body including engine and taillights, gold interior, unpainted base, jewel headlights (1970).

115-G PLYMOUTH FURY 122 mm 1965-1969
Open convertible with cast body and opening hood, patterned hubs, black tires, suspension, black sheet metal base, no number, plastic driver and passenger, clear windshield, white antennas, silver engine, grille and bumpers, jewel headlights, red interior and taillights.
  1. Ivory body.

115-H U. B. TAXI 86 mm 1978-1980
Oldtime taxi with cast body, chassis, gold grille and windshield, yellow plastic hubs, black tires, black plastic top, yellow-black-white logo and design labels.
  1. Dark blue body, yellow chassis.

116-G VOLVO P1800S 105 mm 1966-1971
Coupe with cast body, opening doors, trunk and hood, and cream base, spoked hubs, black tires, suspension, cream plastic interior, clear windows, chrome engine, grille and bumpers, jewel headlights, orange taillights.
  1. Red body, no trim.
  2. Metallic dark red body, silver trim.

117-G FOUR BERTH CARAVAN 132 mm 1963-1970
Modified #188 body casting with clear plastic roof and windows, tan interior and door, red tabletop, turned hubs, black tires, gray plastic front wheel, black sheet metal base, no number, unpainted tow hook.
  1. Cream upper body, pale blue lower body.
  2. Yellow entire body.

118-G GLIDER SET 289 mm 1967-1969
Set of #135 Triumph 2000, cream plastic trailer with clear top, turned hubs, black tires, number on bottom, clear top, red and yellow plastic glider.
  1. Car with white body, blue roof.

120-G JAGUAR E-TYPE 91 mm 1962-1967
Hardtop sports coupe with cast upper and lower body, turned hubs, black tires, removable black plastic hardtop with clear windows, clear windshield, cream interior, silver bumpers and headlights.
  1. Red body.
  2. Metallic silver blue body.

120-H HAPPY CAB 86 mm 1978-1979
Same castings and parts as #115, gold cast grille and windshield, gold plastic hubs, black tires, blue plastic roof, multicolored "Happy Cab", flower and face labels.
  1. White body, yellow chassis.

121-G GOODWOOD RACING SET 1963-1966
Boxed set of 009 Service Station Personnel, 112 Austin-Healey Sprite, 113 MGB, 120 Jaguar E-type and 182 Porsche 356A.
  1. Standard colors.

122-G TOURING CARS GIFT SET 1963-1965
Set of 188 Caravan, 193 Rambler, 195 Jaguar, 270 AA Patrol, 295 Standard Atlas and 796 Healey Sports Boat on Trailer.
  1. Standard colors.

122-H VOLVO 265DL ESTATE CAR 1977-1980
Station wagon with cast body and opening hatch, black Speedwheels, black plastic base-grille-bumpers, light brown interior, windows.
  1. Metallic blue body, solid 6-spoke silver hubs (1977).
  2. Metallic light blue body, pierced 12-spoke chrome hubs (1978).
  3. Cream body, six-bolt hubs (1979).
  4. Orange body, wheels as on type 2; made in Italy by Polistil (1980).

123-G MAYFAIR GIFT SET 1963-1964
Set of four cars from 009, 142 Jaguar X, 150 Rolls-Royce Silver Wraith, 186 Mercedes-Benz 220SE, 194 Bentley S2, 198 Rolls-Royce Phantom V, and 199 Austin 7 Countryman.
  1. Standard colors.

123-H AUSTIN PRINCESS 2200HL 128 mm 1977-1980
Sedan with cast body, black Speedwheels, black plastic base and interior, windows, silver or black bumpers, grille and headlights.
  1. White body, black bumpers and grille, solid 6-spoke silver hubs.
  2. White main body, black top, silver bumpers and grille, 6-spoke silver hubs.
  3. Copper-bronze body, black area around rear window, silver bumpers and grille, 12-spoke pierced chrome hubs.
  4. All bronze body, or bronze with black roof?

123p-G AUSTIN PRINCESS POLICE CAR 128 mm year?
Same casting and parts as 123, Speedwheels with six-bolt hubs, red-white-blue roof bar, blue and white Police labels.
  1. White body, black roof.

124-G HOLIDAY GIFT SET 1964-1967
Set of 137 Plymouth Fury, 142 Jaguar X, 796 Healey Sports Boat on Trailer, and 952 Vega Luxury Coach.
  1. Standard colors.

124-H ROLLS-ROYCE PHANTOM V 141 mm 1977-1979
Limousine with cast body, opening front doors and trunk, and black base with #152

The New System of Catalog Numbers

(model is a revised #152), 6-spoke hubs, black tires, suspension, plastic interior, windows, chauffeur figure (two sizes, in blue or black), chrome grille and bumpers.
1. Metallic blue body, cream interior.
2. Metallic blue body, black interior.

125-G FUN AHOY GIFT SET   1964-1969
Set of 130 Ford Corsair and 796 Healey Sports Boat on Trailer.
1. Standard colors.

126-G MOTOR SHOW SET   1967-1969
Set of 127 Rolls-Royce Silver Cloud, 151 Triumph 1800, 171 Austin 1800 and a Ford Cortina; standard colors. Fourth car is:
1. 133 Ford Cortina Mark IA.
2. 159 Ford Cortina Mark II.

127-G ROLLS-ROYCE SILVER CLOUD III   125 mm   1964-1972
Limousine with cast body, opening doors and two-piece hood, and black base with number, patterned hubs, black tires, cream or orange plastic interior, windows, chrome grille and bumpers, jewel headlights, red or orange taillights, silver engine.
1. Metallic dark red body, cream interior, orange taillights.
2. Metallic silver blue body, orange interior, red taillights.
3. Metallic gold body, orange interior, red taillights.
(128 AUSTIN-HEALEY 100: numbered for U.S. market?)

128-G MERCEDES-BENZ 600   145 mm   1964-1979
Limousine with cast body, opening hood, trunk and four doors, and black base, patterned hubs, black tires, suspension, plastic interior with chauffeur, clear windows and headlights, chromed grille, bumpers and engine, silver trim, silver engine decal.
1. Metallic dark red body, pale blue interior, concentric hub pattern, two passengers, luggage in truck, orange taillights (1964-1973).
2. Metallic dark blue body including taillights, orange interior, solid 6-spoke hubs, no passengers or luggage (1974-1979).

129-G MG MIDGET   83 mm   1955-1956
Same castings and parts as 102, without driver, renumbered for U.S. market.
1. Red body and hubs, tan interior.
2. White body, red interior and hubs.

129-H VOLKSWAGEN 1300 SEDAN DE LUXE   100 mm   1965-1976
Sedan with cast body, opening doors and hoods, and unpainted base-bumpers, turned hubs and black tires, with suspension, or speedwheels, cream plastic interior, windows, jewel headlights, silver trim, silver engine.
1. Metallic blue body, turned hubs, black tires (1965-1970).
2. Metallic blue body, speedwheels (1971-1976).

130-G FORD CONSUL CORTINA   108 mm   1963-1969
Sedan with cast body, opening hood and black or charcoal base with number, turned hubs, black tires, suspension, steering, cream plastic interior, windows (door windows slide), jewel headlights, painted taillights, silver grille, bumpers and engine.
1. Metallic red body, orange taillights (1963-1967).
2. Green or blue-green body?
3. Light blue body (1967-1969).

131-G CADILLAC ELDORADO   119 mm   1956-1962
Convertible with cast body, tan steering wheel, driver in brownish-gray, cast or turned hubs, black tires, black metal base with big lettering and number, plastic windshield, silver grille, bumper and headlights, red taillights.
1. Yellow body, red interior.
2. Yellow body, red interior, turned hubs.
3. Salmon body, gray interior, tan hubs.
4. Salmon body, gray interior, turned hubs.

131-H JAGUAR E-TYPE 4.2 2+2   112 mm   1968-1978
Sports coupe with cast body, opening doors, hood and hatch, and black base, spoked wheels with black tires and suspension or Speedwheels, plastic interior, windows and headlights, chromed grille, bumpers and engine, silver mirrors, engine and bumpers, white antenna.
1. White body, red interior, spoked wheels (1968-1970).

---

2. Bronze body, pale blue interior, spoked hubs (1970-1971?)
3. Bronze body, pale blue interior, Speedwheels (1971-?).
4. Mauve body, white interior, Speedwheels (dates?).

132-G PACKARD CONVERTIBLE   114 mm   1955-1960
Convertible with cast body dashboard, tan steering wheel, driver in brownish-gray, and cast or turned hubs, black tires, black sheet metal base with big letters and number, plastic interior, silver grille, bumpers and headlights, red taillights.
1. Light green body, red cast hubs.
2. Tan body, red cast hubs.
3. Light green body, turned hubs.
4. Tan body, turned hubs.

132-H FORD 40RV GT40 LE MANS   100 mm   1967-1974
Sports-racing coupe with cast body, opening front and rear hoods, removable front panel and black or charcoal base, spoked hubs, black tires, silver or silver and black engine, windows.
1. Silver body, red interior and lights, silver mirrors, charcoal base, red and white "Ford" and stripe labels.
2. Blue body, other details not known.
3. Metallic green body, other details not known.
4. Dayglow red body, yellow rear hood, front panel and interior, black base, no mirrors, red and silver "Ford" and stripe labels.

133-G CUNNINGHAM C5R   102 mm   1955-1960
Sports-racing car with cast body, driver in light blue helmet and coveralls, black steering wheel and hubs, black tires, black sheet metal base with big lettering and number, plastic windshield, blue stripes and number 31, black grille, silver headlights.
1. White body, tan interior, medium blue hubs.
2. Ivory body, light blue interior and hubs, red taillights.

133-H FORD CORTINA MARK 1A   102 mm   1965-1969
Sedan with cast body and opening doors, turned hubs, black tires, suspension, steering, black sheet metal base, red plastic interior, windows, jewel lights, silver grille and bumpers.
1. Metallic golden yellow body, white roof.
2. Gold body?

134-G TRIUMPH VITESSE   87 mm   1963-1966
Light car with cast body, turned hubs, black tires, suspension, black sheet metal base with number, red plastic interior, windows, white stripes, silver grille, bumpers and headlights, red taillights.
1. Metallic blue body.
2. Metallic green body.

135-G TRIUMPH 2000   107 mm   1963-1969
Sedan with cast body, opening hood and trunk, and gray base with number, turned hubs, black tires, suspension, steering, red plastic interior, windows, silver grille, bumpers, engine and headlights, red taillights, brown luggage.
1. Metallic blue body, white roof.
2. Turquoise body, white roof.
3. White body, blue roof (only in #118).

136-G VAUXHALL VIVA   94 mm   1964-1973
Sedan with cast body, opening hood and trunk, and base with number, turned hubs, black tires, suspension, steering, red plastic interior, windows, silver engine, grille, bumpers and headlights, red taillights.
1. White body, black base.
2. Pale blue body, ? base.
3. Metallic blue body, unpainted base.

137-G PLYMOUTH FURY CONVERTIBLE   122 mm   1963-1966
Hardtop convertible with cast body and opening hood, turned or patterned hubs, black tires, suspension, black sheet metal base, no number, removable plastic hardtop, windshield, silver engine, grille, bumpers and headlights, red taillights, white or dark green cast-in folded top. Same basic model as #115, which has no hardtop.

---

1. Metallic gray body, ? interior, ? hardtop, turned hubs.
2. Metallic pale green body, white interior, dark green hardtop, turned hubs.
3. Metallic pale green body, cream interior, ivory hardtop, turned hubs.
4. Dark purplish-blue body, red interior, turned hubs, ? hardtop.
5. Pale pink body, magenta interior, patterned hubs, ? hardtop.

138-G HILLMAN IMP   86 mm   1963-1973
Light car with cast body, opening hood and trunk, and base with number, turned hubs, black tires, suspension, steering, plastic interior, windows, silver rear engine, bumpers and emblem, silver or jewel headlights, red taillights.
1. Metallic green body, red interior, cast-in headlights.
2. Metallic green body, cream interior, ? headlights.
3. Metallic red body, red interior, ? headlights.

139-G FORD CORTINA MARK I   102 mm   1963-1964
Sedan with cast body and opening doors, turned hubs, black tires, suspension, steering, black sheet metal base with number, tan plastic interior, windows, silver grille, bumpers and headlights, red taillights.
1. Metallic dark blue body.
2. Light blue body.

140-G MORRIS 1100   87 mm   1963-1969
Sedan with cast body and opening doors, turned hubs, black tires, suspension, black sheet metal base with number, red plastic interior, windows, silver engine, grille, bumpers and headlights, red taillights.
1. Light blue body.
2. Dark blue body.
3. White and blue (South African issue).

141-G VAUXHALL VICTOR ESTATE CAR   87 mm   1963-1967
Station wagon with cast body and opening hatch, turned hubs, black tires, suspension, steering, black sheet metal base with number, blue plastic interior, windows, silver grille, bumpers and headlights, red taillights.
1. Yellow body.
2. Pinkish-orange body (South African issue).

142-G JAGUAR MARK X   107 mm   1962-1969
Sedan with cast body, opening hood, and light gray base with number, turned hubs, black tires, suspension, steering, red plastic interior, windows, brown luggage, silver grille, bumpers and headlights, red taillights.
1. Metallic silver blue body.
2. Color unknown (South African issue).

143-G FORD CAPRI   90 mm   1962-1967
Coupe with cast body, turned hubs, black tires, suspension, steering, black sheet metal base with number, red plastic interior, windows, silver grille, bumpers and headlights, red taillights.
1. Turquoise body, white roof.

144-G VOLKSWAGEN 1500   93 mm   1963-1966
Two-door with cast body and opening front hood, turned hubs, black tires, suspension, steering, black sheet metal base with number, red plastic interior, windows, brown luggage, silver bumpers and headlights, red taillights.
1. Ivory body.

145-G SINGER VOGUE   94 mm   1962-1967
Sedan with cast body, turned hubs, black tires, suspension, steering, black sheet metal base with number, red plastic interior, windows, silver grille, bumpers and headlights, red taillights.
1. Metallic pale green body.

146-G DAIMLER 2.5 LITRE   97 mm   1963-1967
Sedan with cast body (modified #195 Jaguar), turned hubs, black tires, suspension, steering, black sheet metal base, no number, red plastic interior, windows, silver bumpers, headlights and panel on trunk lid, red taillights.
1. Metallic greenish-blue body.

147-G CADILLAC 62   113 mm   1962-1969

Sedan with cast body, turned hubs, black tires, suspension, steering, black sheet metal base +/- number, red plastic interior, windows, silver grille, bumpers and headlights, red taillights.
1. Metallic blue body.
2. Metallic dark green body.

148-G FORD FAIRLANE   **111 mm   1962-1966**
Sedan with cast body, turned hubs, black tires, suspension, steering, black sheet metal base +/- number, light tan plastic interior, silver grille, bumpers and headlights, red taillights.
1. Metallic bright green body.
2. Light apple green body.
3. Metallic silver green body.
4. Bright blue body (South African issue).

149-G SPORTS CAR GIFT SET   **1958-1959**
Set of 107 Sunbeam Alpine, 108 MG Midget, 109 Austin-Healey, 110 Aston Martin, 111 Triumph TR2.
1. Standard colors.

149-H CITROEN DYANE   **91 mm   1971-1974**
Light car with cast body (same as French #1413) and opening hood, Speedwheels with 8-spoke hubs, suspension, spare wheel, black plastic roof and base, plastic interior, windows, silver engine, grille, bumpers and headlights, "Made in England" on base.
1. Metallic bronze body, black interior.
2. Metallic bronze body, brown interior.
3. Metallic bronze body, red interior.

150-G ROLLS-ROYCE SILVER WRAITH   **121 mm   1959-1962**
Limousine with cast body, turned hubs, black tires, suspension, black sheet metal base with number, windows, chrome grille, bumpers and headlights, red taillights.
1. Light gray upper, dark gray lower body.

151-G TRIUMPH RENOWN 1800   **92 mm   #40b_1954-1960**
Sedan with cast body, headlights and hubs, black tires, black sheet metal base with axle tabs, silver grille, bumpers and headlights. Identical to 40b until 1958, when a new sheet metal base with big lettering was introduced. Model with old type base, as 40b (1954-1957):
1. Blue body and hubs.
2. Blue body, tan hubs.
3. Tan body, green hubs.
4. Gray body and hubs. Model with new type base (1957-1960):
5. Blue body and hubs.
6. Blue body, tan hubs.
7. Tan body, green hubs.
8. Gray body and hubs.

151-H VAUXHALL VICTOR 101   **105 mm   1966-1968**
Sedan with cast body, opening hood and trunk, and black base, turned hubs, black tires, suspension, steering, plastic interior, windows, chrome frames, jewel headlights, silver engine, grille and bumpers.
1. Metallic maroon body, tan interior, orange taillights.
2. Yellow body.
3. Lime green body.
4. Green body.

152-G AUSTIN DEVON A40   **86 mm   #40d_1954-1960**
Sedan with cast body and hubs, black tires, black sheet metal base, silver grille, bumpers and headlights. Identical to 40d until 1958, when a new base with big lettering was introduced. Model with old type base as 40d (1954-1957):
1. Maroon body and hubs.
2. Dark green body, cream hubs.
3. Olive green body and hubs.
4. Dark blue body, light blue hubs. Model with new type base (1958-1960):
5. Dark green body, cream hubs.

6. Dark blue body, light blue hubs.
7. Rose lower, olive green upper body, cream hubs.
8. Orange lower, light blue upper body and hubs.

152-H ROLLS-ROYCE PHANTOM V   **141 mm   1965-1976**
Limousine with cast body, four opening doors, two-piece opening hood, and base, patterned hubs, black tires, suspension, steering, cream plastic interior, windows, chauffeur, +/- two passengers and mirrors, silver engine, chrome grille and bumpers, jewel headlights, red taillights.
1. Blue-black body, brick red taillights, silver mirrors, dark cream interior, two passengers, concentric patterned hubs, charcoal base.
2. Black body, red taillights, no mirrors or passengers, light cream interior, 16-spoke hubs, black base.

153-G STANDARD VANGUARD   **91 mm   #40e_1954-1960**
Sedan with cast body and hubs, black tires, black sheet metal base with rear axle tabs and big lettering, silver grille, bumpers and headlights. Identical to later 40e. Casting now has horizontal line across trunk as well as covered rear wheels.
1. Dark cream body and hubs.
2. Cream body, dark cream hubs.
3. Blue body, cream hubs.
4. Blue body, tan hubs.
5. Light brown body and hubs.

153-H ASTON MARTIN DB6   **111 mm   1966-1971**
Fastback with cast body, opening hood, trunk and doors, and black base, no number, spoked hubs, black tires, suspension, steering, red or white plastic interior, clear headlights and windows, chrome engine, grille and bumpers.
1. Metallic silver blue body, red interior (1966-1969).
2. Blue-gray (or blue-green?) body, white interior (1971).

154-G HILLMAN MINX   **88 mm   #40f_1954-1958**
Sedan with cast body, black tires, black sheet metal base, silver grille, bumpers and headlights. Identical to 40f until 1958, when a new base with big lettering was introduced. Model with old type base, as 40f (1954-1957):
1. Apple green body and hubs.
2. Dark green body, apple green hubs.
3. Dark tan body, dark cream hubs.
4. Rose upper, light blue lower body, blue hubs.
5. Yellow upper, dark lime green lower body, yellow hubs. Model with new type base (1958):
6. Rose upper, light blue lower body, blue hubs.
7. Yellow upper, dark lime green lower body, yellow hubs.

154-H FORD TAUNUS 17M   **110 mm   1966-1968**
Sedan with cast body, opening hood, trunk and doors, and black base with number, plain hubs, whitewalls, black tires, suspension, steering, red plastic interior, windows, chrome grille, bumpers and headlights, silver engine, red taillights.
1. Yellow body, white roof.
(155 AUSTIN WESTMINSTER COUNTRYMAN never issued)

155-G FORD ANGLIA   **81 mm   1961-1966**
Small sedan with cast body, turned hubs, black tires, suspension, steering, black metal base with number, red plastic interior, windpows, silver grille, bumpers and headlights, red taillights.
1. Turquoise green body.
2. Light blue body.
3. White body (South African issue).

156-G ROVER 75   **102 mm   #140b _1954-1960**
Sedan with cast body and hubs, black tires, black sheet metal base, silver grille ornament, bumpers and headlights. Identical to 140b. "Rover 75" cast under roof from 1956 on.
1. Pale yellow body, yellow hubs.
2. Light yellow body, blue hubs.

3. Maroon body and hubs.
4. Light green upper, medium green lower body and hubs.
5. Light blue upper, light yellow lower body and hubs.
6. Dark purplish-blue upper, light yellow lower body and hubs.

156-H SAAB 96   **98 mm   1966-1971**
Small sedan with cast body, opening doors, and charcoal base, turned hubs, black tires, suspension, cream plastic interior, windows, chrome grille and bumpers and headlights.
1. Metallic maroon body, orange taillights.
2. Metallic blue body, red? taillights.

157-G JAGUAR XK120   **98 mm   1954-1962**
Sports coupe with cast body, cast or turned hubs, black tires, black sheet metal base with big lettering and number, silver grille, bumpers and headlights, red or orange taillights (if any).
1. Red body and hubs, orange taillights.
2. Red body, turned hubs, orange taillights.
3. Light orange body, yellow-orange hubs.
4. Dark green body, turned hubs, red taillights.
5. Light cream body, tan hubs.
6. Light green body, turned hubs, red taillights.
7. Magenta upper, turquoise lower body, magenta hubs.
8. Light gray upper, light orange lower body, light gray hubs.

157-H BMW 2000 TILUX   **121 mm   1968-1973**
Sedan with cast upper and lower body, patterned 16-spoke hubs, black tires, suspension, steering, red plastic interior, windows, silver grille, bumpers and headlights, red taillights, battery mount in bottom of car to operate directional lights.
1. Off-white upper, metallic dark blue lower body.
2. Plain disc hubs, otherwise as type 1?

158-G RILEY SALOON   **92 mm   #40a_1954-1960**
Sedan with cast body, headlights and hubs, black tires, black sheet metal base with big letters and number 40A, silver grille, bumpers and headlights. Same castings as 40a.
1. Light yellow body, green hubs.
2. Light green body, green hubs.
3. Gray body, ? hubs.

158-H ROLLS-ROYCE SILVER SHADOW   **125 mm   1967-1973**
Limousine with cast body, opening hood and four doors, silver engine, bumpers and grille, and base with number, patterned hubs, black tires, suspension, steering, cream plastic interior, windows.
1. Metallic dark red body, charcoal base, concentric hubs.
2. Metallic dark blue body, light blue base, 16-spoke hubs.

159-G MORRIS OXFORD   **93 mm   #40g_1954-1960**
Sedan with cast body and hubs, black tires, black sheet metal base, silver grille, bumpers and headlights. Identical to 40g until 1958 when new base with big lettering was introduced. Model with old type base, as 40g (1954-1957):
1. Medium green body, light green gubs.
2. Dark green body, light green hubs.
3. Gray-brown body, tan hubs. Model with new type base (1958-1960):
4. Ivory upper, magenta lower body, cream hubs.
5. Light green upper, dark cream lower body, light green hubs.

159-H FORD CORTINA MARK II   **105 mm   1967-1970**
Sedan with cast body, opening hood, trunk and doors, and unpainted base-grille-lights-bumpers, concentric patterned hubs, black tires, suspension, steering, red plastic interior, windows.
1. White body.

160-G AUSTIN A30   **78 mm   1958-1962**
Small sedan with cast body, gray plastic wheels (2 types), black sheet metal base with number, silver grille, and headlights, red taillights.
1. Turquoise body, smooth wheels.
2. Turquoise body, treaded wheels.

3. Tan body, smooth wheels.
4. Tan body, treaded wheels.

160-H MERCEDES-BENZ 250SE 117 mm 1968-1972
Sedan with cast body and unpainted base-grille-bumpers with number, turned hubs, black tires, suspension, steering, cream plastic interior, clear windows and headlights, red taillights, battery mount in bottom of car to operate lights.
1. Metallic dark blue body.

161-G AUSTIN SOMERSET 90 mm #40j 1954-1960
Sedan with cast body and hubs, black tires, black sheet metal base, silver grille, bumpers and headlights. Identical to 40j.
1. Red body, brighter red hubs.
2. Light blue body, darker blue hubs.
3. Dark yellow upper, red lower body and hubs.
4. Cream upper, black lower body, cream hubs.

161-H FORD MUSTANG 2=2 111 mm 1965-1973
Sports coupe with cast body, opening hood, trunk and doors, and base, 6-spoke hubs, black tires, suspension, steering, plastic interior, clear windows and headlights, red taillights, chrome engine and bumpers, black and silver grille label, Mustang decal.
1. White body, red interior, charcoal base (1967-1970).
2. Yellow body, tan interior, ? base (1970).
3. Light orange body, pale blue interior, unpainted base (1971-1973).

162-G FORD ZEPHYR 97 mm 1956-1960
Sedan with cast body and hubs, black tires, black sheet metal base with number, silver grille, bumpers and headlights, +/- red taillights.
1. Cream upper, lime green lower body, darker cream hubs, red taillights.
2. Dark green lower body, otherwise as type 1.
3. Light blue upper, medium blue lower body, light gray hubs, no red taillights.

162-H TRIUMPH 1300 92 mm 1967-1969
Light car with cast body, opening hood and trunk, and charcoal base with number, turned hubs, black tires, suspension, steering, red plastic interior, windows, jewel headlights, silver grille and bumpers, red taillights.
1. Pale blue body.

163-G BRISTOL 450 100 mm 1956-1960
Sports-racing car with cast body and hubs, black tires, black sheet metal base with number, black-on-white #27 decals.
1. Green body, light green hubs.

163-H VW 1600TL FASTBACK 102 mm 1966-1971
Fastback with cast body, opening front and rear hoods and doors, and unpainted base-bumpers, 8-spoke hubs with black tires or Speedwheels, suspension, cream plastic interior, windows, jewel headlights, orange taillights.
1. Red body, 6-spoke hubs, black tires.
2. Metallic blue body, Speedwheels.

164-G VAUXHALL CRESTA 97 mm 1957-1960
Sedan with cast body and hubs, black tires, black sheet metal base with number, silver trim, grille, bumpers and headlights, red or orange taillights.
1. Dark cream upper body and hubs, maroon lower body, orange taillights.
2. Light gray upper body and hubs, green lower body, red taillights.

164-H FORD ZODIAC IV 114 mm 1966-1971
Sedan with cast body, opening hood, trunk and four doors, and base, 16-spoke hubs, black tires, suspension, steering, red plastic interior, windows, chrome engine, grille and bumpers, jewel head- and taillights.
1. Metallic silver body, charcoal base.
2. Metallic blue body, ? base.
3. Metallic bronze body, ? base.

165-G HUMBER HAWK 102 mm 1959-1963
Sedan with cast body, cast or turned hubs, black (or rarely white) tires, suspension, black sheet metal base, usually with number, windows, silver grille and headlights, red taillights. Without or (later) with license plate under front bumper.

1. Dark cream upper body, maroon lower body and roof, ? hubs, no front license plate. (Cast hubs are rare.)
2. Turned hubs, otherwise as type 1.
3. Light green upper body, black lower body and roof, ? hubs, no front license plate. (Cast hubs are rare.)
4. Turned hubs, otherwise as type 3.
5. Front license plate, otherwise as type 2.
6. Front license plate, otherwise as type 4.
7. Light green body, front license plate, otherwise as type 4.
8. Light green body, black roof, no license plate, turned hubs—may be a factory error.

165-H FORD CAPRI MARK IA 102 mm 1969-1974
Coupe with cast body, opening doors, and unpainted base-grille-bumpers, no number, 5-spoke hubs with black tires and suspension or 4-spoke Speedwheels, yellow-orange plastic interior, clear windows and headlights, silver frames of door windows, red taillights.
1. Metallic purple body, 5-spoke hubs.
2. Metallic greenish-blue body, Speedwheels.
3. Yellow body?
4. Cherry red body?

166-G SUNBEAM RAPIER 90 mm 1958-1963
Sedan with cast body, cast or turned hubs, black tires, black sheet metal base with number, windows, silver grille, bumpers and headlights, red taillights.
1. Yellow upper, orange lower body, tan hubs.
2. Turned hubs, otherwise as type 1.
3. Turquoise upper, blue lower body, light blue hubs.
4. Turned hubs, otherwise as type 3.

166-H RENAULT R16 98 mm 1967-1970
Sedan with cast body, opening hood and hatch, and charcoal base, no number, turned hubs, black tires, suspension, steering, red plastic interior, clear windows and headlights, red taillights, silver grille and bumpers, black engine and spare details. Same casting as French #537.
1. Blue body.

167-G A.C. ACECA 89 mm 1958-1963
Sports coupe with cast body, cast or turned hubs, black tires, black sheet metal base with number, silver grille, bumpers and headlights, red taillights.
1. Light gray body, red top and hubs.
2. Turned hubs, otherwise as type 1.
3. Light yellow body, brown top, tan hubs.
4. Turned hubs, otherwise as type 3.

168-G SINGER GAZELLE 94 mm 1959-1963
Sedan with cast body, turned hubs, black tires, black sheet metal base with number, windows, silver grille, bumpers and headlights, red taillights.
1. Yellow upper, green lower body.
2. Light gray upper, green lower body.

168-H FORD ESCORT 97 mm 1968-1977
Sedan with cast body, opening hood, trunk and doors, and unpainted base-bumpers with number, patterned hubs with black tires and suspension or 8-spoke Speedwheels, plastic interior, silver engine, grille and headlights.
1. Metallic dark red body, cream interior, yellow taillights, 5-spoke hubs.
2. Pale blue body, red interior and taillights, concentric hubs.
3. Metallic dark blue body, cream interior, no taillights, 8-spoke Speedwheels.

169-G STUDEBAKER GOLDEN HAWK 108 mm 1958-1963
Sports coupe with cast body and hubs, white tires, black sheet metal base with number, windows, silver grille, bumpers, headlights and trim, red taillights.
1. Light green body, dark cream rear and hubs.
2. Tan body, red rear and hubs.

169-H FORD CORSAIR 2000E 108 mm 1967-1969

Sedan with cast body, opening hood, and charcoal base with number, 16-spoke hubs, black tires, suspension, steering, red plastic interior, windows, green engine, jewel headlights, red taillights.
1. Metallic silver body, black textured top.

170-G FORD FORDOR 102 mm #139a 1954-1959
Sedan with cast body and hubs, black tires, black sheet metal base, silver grille, bumpers and headlights. Identical to 139a until 1956, when new base with big lettering and number was introduced. Model with old type base (=139a, 1954-1955):
1. Red body and hubs.
2. Yellow body and hubs.
3. Green body and hubs.
4. Light brown body, red hubs. Model with new type base with number 170, body color to just below windows (1956-1957):
5. Pale yellow upper, red lower body and hubs.
6. Pink upper, blue lower body and hubs. Model with new type base with number 170, upper color to front wheel arch (1958-1959):
7. Pale yellow upper, red lower body and hubs.
8. Pink upper, blue lower body and hubs.

170-H LINCOLN CONTINENTAL 129 mm 1964-1970
Sedan with cast body, opening hood and trunk, and charcoal base, no number, concentric hubs, black tires, suspension, steering, blue plastic interior, windows, chromed engine, grille and bumpers, jewel headlights, red taillights.
1. Metallic burnt orange body, white roof (1964-1966).
2. Light blue body, white roof (1967-1970).

(170 FORD GRANADA GHIA 128 mm never issued) (A few samples were made, 1978-1980).

171-G HUDSON COMMODORE 111 mm #139b 1954-1959
Sedan with cast body, cast or turned hubs, black tires, black sheet metal base, silver grille, bumpers and headlights. Identical to 139b until 1954, when new type base with big lettering was introduced. Model with old type base (=139b, 1954):
1. Cream body, maroon roof and hubs.
2. Blue body, tan roof and hubs. Model with new type base (1954-1959):
3. Cream body, maroon roof and hubs (1954-1955).
4. Blue body, tan roof and hubs (1954-1955).
5. Red upper body and hubs, turquoise lower body (1956-1959).
6. Blue upper body and hubs, light gray lower body (1956-1959).
7. Red upper body, turquoise lower body, turned hubs (1959).
8. Blue upper body, light gray lower body, turned hubs (1959).

171-H AUSTIN 1800 101 mm 1965-1968
Sedan with cast body, opening hood and trunk, and charcoal base with number, turned hubs, black tires, suspension, steering, red plastic interior, clear windows and headlights, red taillights, silver window frames, engine, grille and bumpers.
1. Metallic blue body.

172-G STUDEBAKER LAND CRUISER 108 mm 1954-1959
Sedan with cast body, cast or turned hubs, black tires, black sheet metal base with big lettering and numbers, silver grille, bumpers and headlights, sometimes red taillights.
1. Light green body, medium green hubs.
2. Blue body, tan hubs.
3. Magenta upper body (to just below windows, above door handles), light cream lower body, dark cream hubs.
4. Tan upper body (to just below windows, above door handles), dark cream lower body and hubs.
5. Same colors as type 3, but magenta to just below door handles.
6. Same colors as type 5, but tan to just below door handles.
7. Turned hubs, otherwise as type 5.
8. Turned hubs, otherwise as type 6.

172-H FIAT 2300 STATION WAGON 108 mm 1965-1969
Wagon with cast body, opening hood and tailgate, and charcoal base with number,

The New System of Catalog Numbers

turned hubs, black tires, suspension, steering, red plastic interior, white opening rear hatch, windows, adjustable rear seat back, jewel headlights, red taillights, silver engine, grille and bumpers.
1. Off-white body, blue roof.
2. Light blue body, blue roof?

173-G NASH RAMBLER   102 mm 1958-1962
Station wagon with cast body, cast or turned hubs, white tires, black sheet metal base, windows, silver grille, bumpers and headlights, red taillights.
1. Pink body, blue trim, cream hubs, bright red taillights.
2. Turned hubs, otherwise as type 1.
3. Turquoise body, maroon trim and taillights, turned hubs.
4. Green body, cherry red trim?
5. Blue body, pink trim?

173-H PONTIAC PARISIENNE   132 mm 1968-1973
Sedan with cast body and unpainted base-grille-bumpers-lights, no number, 6-spoke hubs with black tires and suspension or Speedwheels, yellow plastic interior, windows, antennas, red taillights.
1. Blue body, 6-spoke hubs (1968-1970?).
2. Metallic maroon body, 6-spoke hubs.
3. Speedwheels, otherwise as type 2?

174-G HUDSON HORNET   111 mm 1958-1963
Sedan with cast body, cast or turned hubs, white tires, black sheet metal base with number, windows, silver grille, bumpers, headlights and rear emblem, red or orange taillights.
1. Red body, dark cream roof, trim and hubs.
2. Turned hubs, otherwise as type 1.
3. Yellow body, gray roof and trim, light gray hubs.
4. Turned hubs, otherwise as type 3.

174-H MERCURY COUGAR   122 mm 1969-1973
Sedan with cast body, opening doors and silver base-grille-bumpers with number, patterned hubs with black tires and suspension or Speedwheels, plastic interior, windows, retracting antenna.
1. Red body, gray interior.
2. Red body, brown interior.
3. Blue body, brown interior.
4. Blue body, gray interior.
5. Metallic dark blue body, orange interior.
6. Speedwheels, otherwise as type 5?

175-G HILLMAN MINX   90 mm 1958-1961
Sedan with cast body, cast or turned hubs, black tires, black sheet metal base with number, windows, silver grille, bumpers and headlights, red taillights.
1. Light green upper, tan lower body, dark cream hubs.
2. Turned hubs, otherwise as type 1.
3. Blue upper, light gray lower body, blue hubs.
4. Turned hubs, otherwise as type 3.

175-H CADILLAC ELDORADO   133 mm 1969-1973
Sedan with cast body with textured top, opening doors, and silver base-rear bumper with number, patterned hubs with black tires and suspension or Speedwheels, plastic interior, windows, chrome grille-lights-front bumper, red taillights.
1. Gold body, ? interior (1969).
2. Metallic purple body, black top, orange interior (1970).
3. Blue body, ? interior (1971).
4. ? body, ? interior, Speedwheels (date?).

176-G AUSTIN A105   102 mm 1958-1963
Sedan with cast body, cast or turned hubs, black or white tires, black sheet metal base with number, windows, silver grille, bumpers and headlights.
1. Cream body and hubs, dark blue trim, black tires.
2. Cream body and hubs, lighter blue roof and trim, white tires.

3. Turned hubs, otherwise as type 2.
4. Light gray body, red trim and hubs, black tires.
5. Light gray body and hubs, red trim and roof, white tires.
6. Turned hubs, otherwise as type 5.

176-H N.S.U. RO-80   114 mm 1969-1974
Sedan with cast body and unpainted base-grille-bumpers, no number, turned hubs, black tires, suspension, plastic interior, clear windows and lights, battery mount in bottom to operate lights.
1. Blue body, white interior.
2. Metallic maroon body, light tan interior.
3. Green body?

(177 STANDARD VANGUARD III never issued)

177-G OPEL KAPITAN   100 mm 1961-1966
Sedan with cast body, black sheet metal base, no number, turned hubs, black tires, suspension, steering, red plastic interior, windows, silver grille, bumpers and headlights, red taillights.
1. Pale blue body.

178-G PLYMOUTH PLAZA   110 mm 1959-1963
Sedan with cast body, cast or turned hubs, white tires, black sheet metal base, no number, windows, silver grille, bumpers and headlights, red taillights. Cast hubs are rare.
1. Salmon body, light green top and trim, ? hubs.
2. Turned hubs, otherwise as type 1.
3. Light blue body, dark blue top and trim, ? hubs.
4. Turned hubs, otherwise as type 3.
5. Light blue body, white top and trim, turned hubs.

178-H MINI CLUBMAN   82 mm 1975-1980
Mini with cast body, opening doors and unpainted base-rear bumper, no number, Speedwheels +/- chromed hubs, black plastic interior, windows, jewel or cast-in headlights.
1. Bronze body, red taillights, jewel headlights, chromed hubs.
2. Bronze body, red taillights, cast-in headlights, black hubs.
3. Red body including taillights, cast-in headlights, black hubs.

179-G STUDEBAKER PRESIDENT   110 mm 1958-1963
Sedan with cast body, cast or turned hubs, white tires, black sheet metal base with number, windows, silver grille, bumpers and headlights, red taillights.
1. Yellow body, blue trim and hubs.
2. Turned hubs, otherwise as type 1.
3. Pale blue body, dark blue trim, tan hubs.
4. Turned hubs, otherwise as type 3.

179-H OPEL COMMODORE   107 mm 1971-1974
Hardtop with cast body including black textured top, opening hood and doors, Speedwheels with chrome hubs, black plastic base, no number, plastic interior, windows, silver vent window frames, chrome engine, grille, bumpers and headlights.
1. Metallic dark blue body, pale blue interior.
2. Metallic turquoise body, black interior.

180-G PACKARD CLIPPER   13 mm 1958-1963
Sedan with cast body, cast or turned hubs, white tires, black sheet metal base with number, windows, silver grille, bumpers and headlights, red taillights.
1. Light tan body and hubs, rose roof and trunk lid.
2. Turned hubs, otherwise as type 1.
3. Orange body, gray roof, trunk lid and hubs.
4. Turned hubs, otherwise as type 3.

180-H ROVER 3500   131 mm 1979-1980
Sedan with cast body, opening front doors and hatch, Speedwheels with 5-spoke chromed hubs, black plastic base-bumpers-interior, clear windows and headlights, red taillights, orange directionals, unpainted sheet metal tow hook. Made in Hong Kong.
1. White body.

181-G VOLKSWAGEN   90 mm 1956-1970
Beetle with cast body, cast or turned hubs, black tires, black sheet metal base +/- number or unpainted base without number, silver bumpers and headlights, red taillights.
1. Dark lime green body, green hubs, black base, number.
2. Gray body, blue hubs, black base, ? #.
3. Dull gray-blue body, turned hubs, black base, no number.
4. Pale blue body, turned hubs, unpainted base, no number. Issued in South Africa:
5. White body.
6. Lime green body.
7. Light blue body.

182-G PORSCHE 356A   89 mm 1958-1966
Sports coupe with cast body, cast or turned hubs, black tires, black sheet metal base with number, windows, silver bumpers, grille and headlights, red or orange taillights.
1. Maroon body, orange taillights, ? hubs.
2. Turned hubs, otherwise as type 1.
3. Cream body, red taillights, blue hubs.
4. Turned hubs, otherwise as type 3.
5. Light blue body, red taillights, cream hubs.
6. Turned hubs, otherwise as type 5.

183-G FIAT 600   71 mm 1958-1960
Minicar with cast body, gray plastic wheels, black sheet metal base with number, silver grille, bumpers and headlights, red or orange taillights.
1. Dark red body, orange taillights, smooth wheels.
2. Treaded wheels, otherwise as type 1.
3. Light green body, red taillights, smooth wheels.
4. Treaded wheels, othwerwise as type 3.

183-H MORRIS MINI MINOR   75 mm 1966-1975
Mini with cast body, opening hood and doors, and unpainted base-grille-bumpers, disc hubs and black tires or Speedwheels, plastic interior, windows, silver engine, jewel headlights, red or orange taillights.
1. Red body, black roof, orange taillights, disc hubs.
2. White body, black roof, ? wheels.
3. Blue body, black roof, ? wheels.
4. Blue body, red roof, ? wheels.

184-G VOLVO 122S AMAZON   97 mm 1961-1965
Sedan with cast body, turned hubs, black tires, suspension, steering, black sheet metal base with number, cream plastic interior, windows, silver grille, bumpers and headlights, red or orange taillights.
1. Red body, orange taillights.
2. White body, red taillights.

(185 RENAULT FREGATE never issued)

185-G ALFA ROMEO 1900   102 mm 1961-1963
Sports coupe with cast body, turned hubs, black tires, suspension, steering, black sheet metal base, plastic interior, windows, silver grille, bumpers and headlights, red or orange taillights.
1. Red body, cream interior, orange taillights.
2. Yellow body, red interior and taillights.

186-G MERCEDES-BENZ 220SE   102 mm 1961-1967
Sedan with cast body, turned hubs, black tires, suspension, steering, black sheet metal base with number, cream plastic interior, windows, chromed grille, bumpers and headlights, red taillights.
1. Dull gray-blue body.
2. Light blue body.
3. Color? South African issue.

187-G VW KARMANN-GHIA   97 mm 1959-1964
Coupe with cast body, turned hubs, white tires, suspension, black sheet metal base, no number, windows, silver bumpers, vents, trim and headlights, red or orange taillights.

1. Red body, black top.
2. Apple green body, light yellow top.
3. Light yellow body, green top.

187-H DE TOMASO MANGUSTA 5000   102 mm 1968-1977
Sports coupe with cast body, chassis with number, front hood and two opening rear panels, 5-spoke hubs, black tires, plastic interior, windows, gold engine and mufflers, black grille, silver headlights.
1. Dayglow red main body, ivory hood, rear panels and chassis, black interior, left hand drive.
2. Cream interior, right hand drive, otherwise as type 1.

188-G FOUR BERTH CARAVAN   133 mm 1961-1963
House trailer with cast body, turned hubs, black tires, gray plastic front wheel, black sheet metal base with number, unpainted tow bar, tan plastic door and interior, clear windows including small square window in center of roof.
1. Dark cream upper, light green lower body.
2. Dark cream upper, light blue lower body.

188-H JENSEN FF   121 mm 1968-1974
Sports coupe with cast body, opening hood and doors, and unpainted base-bumpers-grille-engine with number, 5-spoke hubs, black tires, suspension, steering, plastic interior, windows, jewel headlights, red taillights.
1. Yellow body, red interior.
2. Yellow body, black interior.
3. Turquoise green body, red interior.
4. Turquoise green body, black interior.

189-G TRIUMPH HERALD   86 mm 1959-1964
Light car with cast body, turned hubs, black tires, suspension, black sheet metal base with number, windows, silver grille, front bumper uprights and headlights, red taillights.
1. Green top and lower body, light cream upper body.
2. Pale blue top and lower body, light cream upper body.

189-H LAMBORGHINI MARZAL   137 mm 1968-1978
Modernistic coupe with cast body, opening front and rear hoods, white cast or black plastic base, 5-spoke hubs and black tires or Speedwheels with chrome hubs, plastic interior and engine, windows.
1. Dayglow red body, white hoods and base, black rear window, black interior, chrome engine, 5-spoke hubs.
2. Yellow body, otherwise as type 1.
3. Bright apple green body, red interior, otherwise as type 1.
4. Speedwheels, otherwise as type 3.
5. Metallic peacock blue body, white hoods and rear window, black plastic base, red interior and engine, Speedwheels.

190-G CARAVAN   121 mm 1956-1964
Trailer with cast body and hubs, black or white tires, black sheet metal base, unpainted tow bar, gray plastic or black cast front wheel.
1. Cream upper, orange lower body, black front wheel.
2. Gray front wheel, otherwise as type 1.
3. Cream upper, blue lower body, black front wheel.
4. Gray front wheel, otherwise as type 3.
5. Cream upper, red lower body, ? wheel.

190-H MONTEVERDI 375L   116 mm 1970-1974
Sports coupe with cast body, opening hood, trunk and doors, and unpainted base-bumpers-grille with number, 16-spoke patterned hubs with black tires and suspension or Speedwheels, cream plastic interior, windows, chrome engine, silver vents, jewel headlights.
1. Metallic maroon body, patterned hubs.
2. Metallic maroon body, Speedwheels.

191-G DODGE ROYAL   113 mm 1959-1964
Sedan with cast body, turned hubs, white tires, black sheet metal base with number,

silver trim, grille, bumpers and headlights, red taillights.
1. Dark cream body, light brown tailfin trim.
2. Dark cream body, blue tailfin trim.
3. Light greenbody, black tailfin trim.

192-G DE SOTO FIREFLITE   116 mm 1958-1963
Sedan with cast body, turned hubs, white tires, black sheet metal base, no number, windows, silver grille, bumpers and headlights, red taillights.
1. Light gray body, red roof panel and trim.
2. Aqua green body, tan roof panel and trim.
3. Blue body, tan roof panel and trim.

192-H RANGE ROVER   109 mm 1970-1980
4WD car with cast body, opening hood, doors, tailgate and hatch, and unpainted base-grille-bumper, no number, 5-bolt patterned hubs with black tires or Speedwheels, plastic interior, windows, jewel or cast-in headlights, chrome engine.
1. Metallic bronze body, light blue interior, jewel headlights, 5-bolt hubs.
2. White interior, otherwise as type 1.
3. Yellow body, blue-gray interior, cast-in headlights, Speedwheels.

193-G RAMBLER CROSS COUNTRY   102 mm 1961-1969
Station wagon with cast body, turned hubs, white tires, black sheet metal base with number, red plastic interior, windows, black roof rack, chrome grille, bumpers and headlights, red taillights.
1. Yellow body, white roof.
2. Blue body, yellow roof?
3. Cream body, lavender roof?
4. Lavender body?
5. Lime green body?
6. Gray-green body, South African issue.

194-G BENTLEY S2   113 mm 1961-1967
Convertible with cast body, cream steering wheel, driver in brownish-gray, turned hubs, black tires, suspension, black sheet metal base with number, plastic windshield, chrome grille, bumpers and headlights, red taillights, tan or cream folded top.
1. Light gray body, maroon interior, tan folded top.
2. Bronze body, maroon interior?, blue folded top.
3. Cream body, red interior, dark cream folded top, South African issue.
4. Lime green body, red interior, ? folded top, South African issue.

(195 JAGUAR XK150 never issued)

195-G JAGUAR 3.4 MARK II   97 mm 1960-1966
Sedan with cast body, turned hubs, black tires, suspension, steering, black sheet metal base with number, red plastic interior, windows, silver grille, bumpers and headlights, red taillights.
1. Light yellow body.
2. Light gray body.
3. Red body.
4. ? body, South African issue.

195-H FIRE CHIEF'S RANGE ROVER   109 mm 1971-1978
Same castings and parts as #192 plus blue dome light and red-background Fire Service labels.
1. Metallic dark red body, pale blue interior, 5-bolt hubs, black tires, jewel headlights.
2. Bright red body, white interior, 12-spoke chrome-hub Speedwheels, jewel headlights.
3. Cast-in headlights, ? interior, otherwise as type 2.

(196 Morris Oxford, Vauxhall Cresta, Austin 7 Mini Pickup were planned at various times but never issued)

196-G HOLDEN SPECIAL SEDAN   108 mm 1963-1970
Sedan with cast body, opening hood and trunk, and light gray base with number, turned hubs, black tires, suspension, plastic interior, windows, tan luggage,

silver engine, grille and bumpers, jewel headlights and taillights.
1. Metallic bronze body, off-white roof, pale greenish interior (1963-1966).
2. Turquoise body, white roof, red interior (1967-1970).

197-G MORRIS MINI-TRAVELLER   73 mm 1961-1970
Mini wagon with cast body, turned hubs, black tires, suspension, steering, black sheet metal base with number, plastic interior, windows, tan woodwork, silver grille, bumpers and headlights, red taillights.
1. Cream body, red interior.
2. Cream body, yellow interior.
3. ? body, white interior.
4. ? body, brown interior.

(198 ROVER 105R never issued)

198-G ROLLS-ROYCE PHANTOM V   125 mm 1962-1969
Limousine with cast body, turned hubs, black tires, suspension, steering, black sheet metal base with number, red plastic interior, sliding windows, chauffeur in blue, chromed grille, bumpers and headlights, red taillights.
1. Metallic silver green body, cream sides.
2. Ivory body, light gray sides.
3. ? colors, otherwise as type 1.

199-G AUSTIN 7 COUNTRYMAN   73 mm 1961-1970
Mini wagon with cast body, turned hubs, black tires, suspension, steering, black sheet metal base with number, red plastic interior, windows, tan woodwork, silver grille, bumpers and headlights, red taillights. Casting almost identical to 197.
1. Pale blue body.
2. Red body?

200-G MIDGET RACING CAR   57 mm #35b 1954-1957
Cast body including driver, black rubber wheels. Identical to last 35b.
1. Red body.
2. Silver body.

200-H MATRA 630 LE MANS   105 mm 1971-1974
Sports-racing car with cast body, chassis, opening rear hood and removable front panel, Speedwheels with spoked chromed hubs, black plastic interior, chromed radiator, engine, filler cap and windshield wiper, clear headlights, black-on-white racing number.
1. Light blue body and chassis, number 5.
2. Light blue body and chassis, number 36.

201-G RACING CAR SET   1965-1969
Boxed set of figures plus 240 Cooper, 241 Lotus, 242 Ferrari, and 243 BRM.
1. Standard colors.

201-H PLYMOUTH STOCK CAR   135 mm 1979-1980
Stock car with cast body, 5-star hubs, wide black tires, black plastic base, bumpers, grille and headlights, red interior, windows, blue and white number 34, "426 c.i." and other decals.
1. Dark blue body.

202-G FIAT-ABARTH 2000   88 mm 1971-9174
Sports-racing car with cast body, chassis and opening rear hood, Speedwheels with spoked chrome hubs, plastic interior, window, chrome engine, black louvers, black stripe labels.
1. Red body and chassis, white interior, front grille?
2. Tangerine body, white hood and chassis, black interior, front grille.
3. No front grille, open slot at nose?

202-H CUSTOMIZED LAND-ROVER   108 mm 1979-1980
Closed Land Rover with cast body, opening hood and doors, and black base, cast 5-star hubs, wide black tires, white plastic rear rack and chassis-guard-exhaust pipes, red interior, black stripe labels.
1. Yellow body.

203-G CUSTOM RANGE ROVER   115 mm 1979-1980
Range Rover with cast body, opening hood, doors, tailgate, hatch and black base, cast

The New System of Catalog Numbers

5-star hubs, wide black tires, white plastic chassis-guard-exhaust pipes (as on 202), red interior, windows, silver engine, yellow-orange-red stripe labels.
1. Black body.

204-G   FERRARI 312P   102 mm   1971-1975
Sports-racing car with cast body, air intake and opening doors, Speedwheels with spoked chromed hubs, black plastic base-interior, clear windshield and headlights, chromed mirror, black-on-white racing number label.
1. Red body and doors?, number 60 (1971-1972).
2. Red body, white doors, number 24 (1973-1975).

205-G   TALBOT-LAGO   102 mm   1962-1964
Same model as 230, sold in bubblepack, for export.
1. Blue body, yellow plastic hubs.

205-H   LOTUS CORTINA MARK II RALLY   105 mm   1968-1971
Rally car with cast body, opening hood, trunk and doors, and unpainted base-bumpers-grille-headlights, 5-spoke patterned hubs, black tires, suspension, steering, pale blue plastic interior, windows, silver engine, white antennas, chromed mirrors, yellow taillights, red stripe labels, Rallye Monte Carlo emblems with black number 7.
1. White body, red hood and trunk, spare wheel.
2. No spare wheel, otherwise as type 1.

206-G   MASERATI   92 mm   1962-1964
Same model as 231, sold in bubblepack, for export.
1. Red body, white trim, yellow plastic hubs.

206-H   CUSTOMIZED CORVETTE STING RAY   113 mm   1977-1980
Sports coupe with cast body (same as 221) and opening doors, wide Speedwheels with 6-star chromed hubs, windows, plastic base-bumpers-grille-headlights-mufflers, red-yellow-white flame labels.
1. Red body, chrome base, orange interior.
2. Red body, black base, light brown interior?

207-G   ALFA ROMEO 158   102 mm   1962-1964
Same model as 232, sold in bubblepack, for export.
1. Red body, red plastic hubs.

207-H   TRIUMPH TR7 RALLY   98 mm   1977-1980
Sports coupe with cast body (same as 112 and 211) and opening doors, Speedwheels with spoked chromed hubs, black plastic base-bumpers-interior, windows, red and blue trim, blue Leyland and number 8 decals.
1. White body.
2. Red body?

208-G   COOPER-BRISTOL   98 mm   1962-1964
Same model as 233, sold in bubblepack, for export.
1. Green body, red plastic hubs.

208-H   VW-PORSCHE 914   89 mm   1971-1979
Coupe with cast body, opening hood and doors, and black base-bumpers, plastic interior.
1. Gray-blue body, red interior, white hood, patterned hubs, black tires, chromed lights and bumper strips.
2. Yellow body and hood, black interior, otherwise as type 1.
3. Metallic silver blue body, black hood, red interior, black plastic lights and bumper strips, Speedwheels with chromed spoked hubs.

209-G   FERRARI   101 mm   1962-1964
Same model as 234, sold in bubblepack, for export.
1. Blue body, yellow nose, yellow plastic hubs.

210-G   VANWALL   1962-1964
Same model as 239, sold in bubblepack, for export.
1. Green body, yellow plastic hubs.

210-H   ALFA ROMEO 33 LE MANS   107 mm   1971-1973
Sports-racing coupe with cast body, opening doors and rear hood, and white base with number, cast 5-star hubs, black tires, suspension, plastic interior, chromed engine and mirrors, clear windows and headlights, black number 36 on white disc labels.

1. Metallic dark blue body, black front hood, red interior.
2. Dayglow red body, black front hood and doors, cream interior.

211-G   TRIUMPH TR7   98 mm   1975-1979
Sports coupe with cast body (same as 112 and 207) and opening doors, Speedwheels with spoked chromed hubs, plastic black base, windows, interior and bumpers.
1. Metallic blue body, gray interior and bumpers (1975).
2. Red body, gray interior and bumpers.
3. Red body, black interior and bumpers.
4. Yellow body, black interior and bumpers (1979).

212-G   FORD CORTINA MARK 1A RALLY   102 mm   1967-1969
Rally car with cast body and opening doors, turned hubs, black tires, suspension, steering, black sheet metal base, no number, red plastic interior, windows, chromed front and roof lights, jewel head- and taillights, silver grille and bumpers, number 8, East African Safari and other labels. Modified 133 casting.
1. White body, black hood.

213-G   FORD CAPRI RALLY   102 mm   1971-1974
Rally car with cast body, (same as 165) opening doors and unpainted base-bumpers, no number, cast 5-star hubs with black tires and suspension or Speedwheels with spoked chromed hubs, orange plastic interior, clear windows and headlights, door window frames, chrome or black front lights and mirrors, chrome vents, black hood, black number 20 on white disc labels.
1. Metallic dark red body, cast hubs, black tires, chromed window frames, lights and mirrors.
2. Speedwheels, otherwise as type 1.
3. Metallic bronze body, speedwheels, light gray window frames, black front lights and mirrors.

214-G   HILLMAN IMP RALLY   86 mm   1966-1969
Rally car with cast body (same as 138), opening hood and trunk, and silver base and engine, no number, turned hubs, black tires, suspension, steering, red plastic interior, windows, chromed front lights, jewel headlights, red taillights, white stripes, number 35 and Monte Carlo Rally labels.
1. Dark blue body.

215-G   FORD GT   96 mm   1966-1974
Sports-racing coupe with cast body, opening front and rear hoods, and black base, no number, turned or spoked hubs, black tires, red plastic interior, clear windows and headlights, black number 7 and blue stripe decals, red taillights if any.
1. White body, gold engine and front suspension, turned hubs, red taillights.
2. Spoked hubs, otherwise as type 1.
3. Metallic green body, silver engine and front suspension, spoked hubs.
4. No number 7 decals, otherwise as type 3.

216-G   FERRARI DINO   98 mm   1967-1974
Sports coupe with cast body, opening doors and hatch, and white base with number, spoked hubs, black tires, plastic interior, clear windows and nose, cast-in spare wheel hub with black tire, unpainted engine, white number 20 on black disc labels, silver rear grille.
1. Red body, pale blue interior, red air intakes, orange taillights, doors have window frames.
2. No window frames, otherwise as type 1.
3. Blue body, orange interior, silver taillights.
4. White hatch, otherwise as type 3.

217-G   ALFA ROMEO OSI SCARABEO   90 mm   1968-1974
Modernistic car with cast body, opening rear hatch and unpainted base with number, spoked hubs with black tires and suspension or Speedwheels, yellow or white plastic interior, clear windows and headlights, chromed engine, orange taillights, green and white four-leaf clover emblem decals.
1. Dayglow red body, yellow interior, spoked hubs.
2. Speedwheels, otherwise as type 1.
3. Green body, ? interior, Speedwheels.

4. Orange body, ? interior, Speedwheels.

218-G   LOTUS EUROPA   96 mm   1970-1975
Sports coupe with cast body, opening doors and hatch, and base, no number, cast 5-spoke hubs with black tires and suspension or Speedwheels with spoked chromed hubs, black plastic interior, gold engine, windows, jewel headlights, red taillights, orange-red-black stripe label.
1. Yellow body, blue roof and rear side panels, cast hubs, red-white-black checkered flag labels.
2. Speedwheels, no checkered flag labels, otherwise as type 1.
3. Yellow body, black roof and rear side panels, Speedwheels, no checkered flag labels.

219-G   JAGUAR XJ 5.3C BIG CAT   137 mm   1977-1980
Sports coupe with cast body, chromed hubs, black tires, black plastic base and interior, windows, silver grille and headlights. Made in Hong Kong. Not always boxed.
1. White body, number 2 and Leyland labels.
2. White body, red-white-black cat and trim labels.

220-G   RACING CAR   95 mm   #23a_1954-1955
MG racer with cast body and red hubs, black tires. Same casting as last type 23a, without inner transverse bulkhead.
1. Silver body, red trim, silver number 4 in red disc.

220-H   FERRARI P5   96 mm   1970-1975
Sports car with cast body, opening gullwing doors, and cream base with number, cast 5-spoke hubs with black tires and suspension or Speedwheels, orange plastic interior, clear windows and nose, silver engine and rear end.
1. Metallic dark red body, cast hubs.
2. Speedwheels, otherwise as type 1.

221-G   SPEED OF THE WIND   105 mm   #23e_1954-1957
Record car with cast body and hubs, black tires, black sheet metal base. Identical to last 23e.
1. Silver body.

221-H   CORVETTE STING RAY   113 mm   1969-1978
Sports coupe with cast body, opening hood and doors, unpainted swiveling headlights with lever, unpainted cast or black plastic base-grille-bumpers, cast spoked hubs with black tires and suspension or Speedwheels, plastic interior, windows.
1. Metallic bronze body, black interior, unpainted base, spoked hubs, silver engine.
2. Red body and interior, ? other details.
3. White body and engine, black base, red interior, Speedwheels.

222-G   STREAMLINED RACING CAR   127 mm   #23s_1954-1957
Record car with cast body and hubs, black tires, black sheet metal base. Identical to last 23s.
1. Silver body, red trim.
2. Silver body, green trim.
3. Silver body, blue trim.

222-H   HESKETH 308E   132 mm   1978-1980
Grand Prix car with cast body and wing, unpainted 5-star hubs, wide black tires, black plastic engine and base, chromed chassis and exhaust pipes, yellow racing number and Olympus labels.
1. Dark blue body, number 24.
2. Dark blue body, number 2.
3. Bronze body, number 24.
4. Bronze body, number 2.

223-G   McLAREN M8 CAN-AM   94 mm   1970-1978
Sports-racing car with cast body, opening rear hood, unpainted cast or black plastic base, cast 5-star hubs with black tires and suspension or Speedwheels, red interior, windows, chrome or black engine, black racing number on white disc labels.
1. White body, blue rear hood, chromed engine and mirrors, wire roll bar, unpainted base, gold rear grilles, number 5, cast hubs (1970-1974).
2. Metallic green body, hood and grilles, black base and engine, no mirrors or roll

bar, Speedwheels with spoked chromed hubs, number 7 (1976-1978).
3. Number 5, otherwise as type 2.

224-G MERCEDES-BENZ C-111   102 mm   1970-1974
Sports coupe with cast body, opening gullwing doors and rear hood, and black base-bumper-rear grille with number, 16-spoke hubs with black tires and suspension or Speedwheels, cream plastic interior and vents, clear windows and headlights, gold engine, silver louvers.
1. Metallic dark red body, 16-spoke hubs.
2. Metallic dark red body, Speedwheels.

225-G LOTUS FORMULA 1   127 mm   1970-1978
Grand Prix car with cast body, flat or ridged wing, cast or black plastic base and engine, cast 4-spoke hubs, black tires (2 types), chromed steering wheel, mirrors, suspension, exhaust pipes and roll bar, clear windshield, white driver with black helmet, black number on white disc label.
1. Metallic dark red body, yellow wing, blue metal engine, cream metal base, narrow tires, number 7 (1971-1973).
2. Unpainted engine, otherwise as type 1 (1971-1973).
3. Metallic lime green body and wing, unpainted engine, white metal base, wide tires, number 7.
4. Metallic blue body and wing, black plastic engine and base, number 7.
5. Number 2, otherwise as type 4.
6. Unpainted ridged wing, otherwise as type 4.

226-G FERRARI 312B   121 mm   1972-1980
Grand Prix car with cast body, cast or plastic base, cast 5-star hubs, wide black tires, plastic fin-wing, windshield, engine, dashboard-steering wheel, white driver with black helmet, chrome mirrors, exhaust pipes and suspension, black number 2 on white disc labels.
1. Metallic dark red body, black metal base, white fin-wing with checkered flag labels, black dash-steering wheel, chrome engine (1972-1975).
2. Metallic gold body, black plastic base, fin-wing, engine and dash-steering wheel.
3. Metallic bronze body, otherwise as type 2.
4. Metallic bronze body, red dash, otherwise as type 2.
5. Metallic bronze body, red dash, white plastic base, fin-wing and engine.
6. Yellow plastic base, fin-wing and engine, otherwise as type 5.

227-G BEACH BUGGY   105 mm   1974-1979
Dune buggy with cast body and silver base, cast 5-star hubs, black tires, plastic top, interior and windows, silver headlights, red taillights, red and black stripe label.
1. Green body, white interior, ? top.
2. Pink body, black interior and top.
3. Orange-yellow body, red interior, light gray top.

228-G SUPER SPRINTER   113 mm   1970-1972
Dragster with cast body, unpainted engine, white exhaust pipes and orange cab, spoked front and 5-spoke rear hubs, black tires, blue roll bar and air intake, black driver with white helmet, windshield.
1. Metallic blue body.

229-G MOTORWAY SERVICES GIFT SET   1970-1972
Boxed set of 257 Rambler Fire Chief, 269 Jaguar Police Car, 276 Airport Fire Tender, 434 Bedford Crash Truck, and one other model:
1. 263 Superior Ambulance.
2. 277 Superior Ambulance.

230-G TALBOT-LAGO   102 mm   #23k_1954-1964
Grand Prix car, same casting as 23k, with #230 on base. Blue body, white driver, yellow number 4, black or gray tires.
1. Blue cast hubs.
2. Unpainted turned hubs.
3. Yellow plastic hubs (=205).

231-G MASERATI   92 mm   #23n_1954-1964
Grand Prix car, same casting as 23n, with #231 on base. Red body, white stripe, driver

and number 9, black or gray tires. (Note: though sometimes called the 4CLT-48 Formula I car, this is actually the two-liter 1952 Formula Two car, quite similar to the 4CLT.)
1. Red metal hubs.
2. Unpainted turned hubs.
3. Yellow plastic hubs (=206).

232-G ALFA ROMEO   102 mm   #23p_1954-1964
Grand Prix car, same casting as 23p, with #232 on base. Red body, white driver and number 8, black or gray tires.
1. Red cast hubs.
2. Turned hubs.
3. Red plastic hubs (=207).

233-G COOPER-BRISTOL   89 mm   #23g_1954-1964
Grand Prix car, same casting as 23g, with #233 on base. Green body, white driver and number 6, black or gray tires.
1. Green cast hubs.
2. Unpainted turned hubs.
3. Red plastic hubs.

234-G FERRARI   102 mm   #23h_1954-1964
Grand Prix car, same casting as 23h, with #234 on base. Blue body, white driver, yellow nose and number 5, black or gray tires.
1. Yellow cast hubs, entire nose cone is yellow.
2. Unpainted turned hubs, yellow triangle on nose.
3. Yellow plastic hubs, yellow triangle on nose.
Note: types 2 and 3 may exist with yellow nose cone.

235-G H.W.M.   98 mm   #23j_1954-1960
Grand Prix car, same casting as 23j, with 235 on base. Light green body, white driver, yellow number 7, black or gray tires.
1. Green metal hubs.

236-G CONNAUGHT   97 mm   1956-1959
Grand Prix car with cast fully streamlined body, cast green hubs, black tires, black sheet metal base with number, white driver, black air intake, black number 32 on white disc decals.
1. Green body.

237-G MERCEDES-BENZ   98 mm   1957-1969
Grand Prix car with cast fully streamlined body and driver, turned or plastic hubs, black tires, black sheet metal base with number, black steering wheel, red cockpit and number 30, silver grille.
1. White body, pale blue driver, turned hubs.
2. White body, pale blue driver, red plastic hubs.
3. White body, yellow driver, red plastic hubs.

237-H DINKY WAY GIFT SET   1978-1979?
Boxed set of 178 Mini-Clubman, 211 Triumph TR7, 382 Convoy Dump Truck, 412 Bedford AA Van (without logo), and roadway. For export only; see #240 for British version.
1. No logo on #412, otherwise standard colors.

238-G JAGUAR D-TYPE   87 mm   1957-1965
Sports-racing car with cast body and driver, turned or blue plastic hubs, black tires, black sheet metal base with number, black plastic steering wheel.
1. Aqua body, white driver, dark blue cockpit, blue cast hubs.
2. Unpainted turned hubs, otherwise as type 1.
3. Aqua body, yellow driver, white cockpit, blue plastic hubs.
4. Yellow plastic hubs, otherwise as type 3.
Note: one Jaguar shown in the photo has number discs that were sold (no catalog number) from 1957 on for use on racing and sports cars.

239-G VANWALL   95 mm   1958-1965
Grand Prix car with cast body, white driver, cast or plastic hubs, black tires, black sheet metal base with number, black plastic steering wheel, silver exhaust pipe, black

number 35 on white disc decals, white Vanwall lettering decals.
1. Green body, lighter green cast hubs.
2. Green body, yellow plastic hubs (=210).

240-G COOPER RACING CAR   83 mm   1963-1970
Grand Prix car with cast upper and lower body, turned hubs, black tires, suspension, blue plastic removable engine cover, white driver with yellow helmet, windshield, black number 20 on white disc decals.
1. Light blue body and base, two white stripes.

240-H DINKY WAY GIFT SET   1978-1980
Boxed set of 211 Triumph TR7, 255 Mini-Clubman Police Car, 382 Convoy Dump Truck, 412 Bedford AA Van, and cardboard roadway.
1. Standard colors.

241-G LOTUS RACING CAR   83 mm   1963-1970
Grand Prix car with cast upper and lower body, turned hubs, black tires, suspension, green plastic removable engine cover, white driver with red helmet, windshield, black number 24 on white disc decals.
1. Green body.

241-H SILVER JUBILEE AUSTIN TAXI   112 mm   1977
Cast body, opening back doors and unpainted base-bumpers-grille, no number, Speedwheels with 12-spoke chromed hubs, light gray plastic interior, driver, windows, Union Jack label on trunk, black crest and lettering labels, red taillights. Modified 284 casting.
1. Metallic silver body.

242-G FERRARI RACING CAR   89 mm   1963-1971
Grand Prix car with cast upper and lower body with number, turned hubs, black tires, suspension, red plastic removable engine cover, white driver with silver helmet, windshield, silver air intakes and exhaust pipes, Ferrari emblems and black number 36 on white disc decals.
1. Red body.

243-G B.R.M. RACING CAR   83 mm   1964-1971
Grand Prix car with cast upper and lower body, turned hubs, black tires, suspension, yellow plastic removable engine cover, white driver with silver helmet, windshield, silver exhaust pipes, black number 70 on white disc decals.
1. Metallic green body.

243-H VOLVO 245DL POLICE CAR   141 mm   1978-1980
Station wagon with cast body (same as #116) and opening hatch, Speedwheels with 6-spoke silver or 12-spoke chromed hubs, black plastic base-bumpers-grille, red or tan interior, clear windows and headlights, white roof sign with blue light, accessories, red and blue stripes and white and blue police labels.
1. White body, red interior, 6-spoke hubs.
2. White body, tan interior, 6-spoke hubs.
3. White body, ? interior, 12-spoke hubs.

244-G PLYMOUTH POLICE CAR   161 mm   1977-1980
Sedan with cast body (same as #201), Speedwheels with 5-spoke or chromed 12-spoke hubs, black plastic base, no number, red interior, gray radar gun, antenna and roof bar with red lights, windows, silver grille, bumpers and headlights, red taillights, white-on-black Police labels.
1. Black body with white roof, hood and trunk areas, 5-spoke hubs.
2. 12-spoke hubs, otherwise as type 1.

245-G SUPERFAST GIFT SET   1968-1973
Boxed set of 131 Jaguar E-type, 153 Aston Martin DB6 and 188 Jensen FF.
1. Standard colors.

246-G INTERNATIONAL G.T. GIFT SET   1968-1973
Boxed set of 187 De Tomaso Mangusta, 215 Ford GT and 216 Ferrari Dino.
1. Standard colors.

(248 CONTINENTAL TOURING COACH never issued)

249-G RACING CAR GIFT SET   1955-1958
Formerly set #4, including five or six models, four of which are 231 Maserati, 232 Alfa

Romeo, 233 Cooper-Bristol and 234 Ferrari.
1. "Racing Car Gift Set" also includes 235 H.W.M. (1955-1958).
2. "World Famous Racing Cars" set also includes 230 Talbot and 239 Vanwall (1958).

250-G FIRE ENGINE   #25h_1954-1962
Same castings and parts as 25h, red hubs, black tires, black sheet metal base with number, unpainted sheet metal ladder, bell, silver grille and rear panel.
1. Red body.

250-H MINI-COOPER S POLICE CAR   75 mm 1968-1974
Cast body, opening hood and doors, roof sign, and unpainted base-grille-bumpers, no number, turned hubs, black tires, red plastic interior, white antenna, blue dome light, windows, jewel headlights, red and yellow taillights, silver engine, blue and white Police labels, Austin Cooper S trunk decal.
1. White body and roof sign.

251-G AVELING BARFORD ROAD ROLLER 111 mm #25p_1954-1963
Roller with cast body including driver, roof, two-piece front roller and mount, and two rear rollers, black sheet metal base and tow hook, wire roof supports. Model unchanged from 25p.
1. Green body, roof and mount, red roller sides, unpainted surfaces.

251-H PONTIAC PARISIENNE POLICE CAR   132 mm 1971
Sedan with cast body (modified from 173), unpainted siren and base-grille-bumpers-lights, 6-spoke cast hubs, black tires, white plastic interior, windows, driver, red dome light, chrome mirrors, white retracting antennas and levers, black-on-white Police labels.
1. White body, black roof.

252-G BEDFORD REFUSE WAGON   108 mm #25v_1954-1964
Garbage truck with cast chassis-cab, tipping rear body, opening tailgate, black and silver grille-bumper-headlights, and hubs, black tires, black sheet metal base, no number, sliding rear covers, tipping crank and spiral, +/- windows. Same castings as 25v.
1. Tan chassis-cab and rear body, green tailgate and sliding covers, red hubs, no windows.
2. Olive green chassis-cab and rear body, black tailgate and covers, cream hubs, windows.
3. Orange and gray body, green tailgate and covers, ? other details.
4. Silver and orange body?

252-H R.C.M.P. POLICE CAR   132 mm 1969-1974
Sedan with cast #173 Pontiac Parisienne body and unpainted base-grille-bumpers-lights, 6-spoke cast hubs, black tires, suspension, cream plastic interior, red-coated driver, windows, red dome light and taillights, coat of arms labels on doors.
1. Dark blue body.
Note: the 1969 and 1970 catalogs call this model a Chevrolet, but the picture is identical to that of the Pontiac shown later.

253-G DAIMLER AMBULANCE   96 mm #30h_1954-1964
Ambulance with cast body and red hubs, black tires, black sheet metal base without, later with number, red crosses cast on sides of body, silver grille, bumpers and headlights.
1. Cream body, no number on base (=30h, 1954-1959).
2. White body, number on base (1960-1962).
3. Windows, otherwise as type 2 (1963-1964).

254-G AUSTIN TAXI   94 mm #40h_1954-1962
Taxi with cast body and chassis-interior with driver, cast or turned hubs, black tires, white-on-black Taxi sign, silver grille, bumpers and headlights. Same casting and parts as 40h.
1. Light blue body, ? other details.
2. Dark blue body, light blue hubs, black chassis.
3. Dark yellow body and hubs, black chassis.
4. Brown chassis, otherwise as type 3.

5. Dark yellow upper body and hubs, green lower body, black chassis with #254.
6. Black body, gray chassis with #254, turned hubs.

254-H RANGE ROVER POLICE CAR   109 mm 1972-1980
Range Rover with cast body (=192, 195), 5-bolt pasterned hubs, black tires (or Speedwheels?), police sign, unpainted hatch and base-grille-bumper, plastic interior, blue dome light, white antenna, jewel headlights, white-on-blue Police labels.
1. Off-white body and roof sign, pale blue interior, red and blue stripe type 1.
2. All-red stripe labels, otherwise as type 1.
3. White interior?
4. Red interior?
5. Speedwheels?
6. Cast-in headlights?

255-G MERSEY TUNNEL POLICE LAND-ROVER   73 mm 1955-1961
Short-chassis Land-Rover with cast body and red hubs, black tires, black sheet metal base with number and tow hook, silver grille, bumper and headlights, yellow "Mersey Tunnel" and yellow-on-black "Police" lettering.
1. Matt red body, slick tires.
2. Gloss red body, treaded tires.

255-H FORD ZODIAC MARK IV POLICE CAR   114 mm 1967-1972
Cast modified #164 body, police sign, charcoal base, red plastic interior, driver, blue dome light, jewel head- and taillights, cast 16-finned hubs, blue and white Police labels, other details as 164.
1. Off-white body and roof sign.

255-J MINI CLUBMAN POLICE CAR   82 mm 1977-1979
Cast modified #178 body, police sign, white opening doors, and unpainted base-bumper, Speedwheels with spoked chromed hubs, black plastic interior, light blue dome light, blue and white Police labels, other details as 178.
1. Pale blue body and roof sign.

256-G HUMBER HAWK POLICE CAR   102 mm 1960-1964
Cast modified #165 body, turned hubs, black tires, cream plastic interior, driver, gray antenna, black Police sign with white lettering, other details as 165.
1. Black body.

257-H NASH RAMBLER FIRE CHIEF   102 mm 1961-1968
Cast body (=173), turned hubs, black tires, red plastic dome light, yellow "Fire Chief" decals, other details as 173.
1. Red body.
2. Red body, suspension, steering.

258-G POLICE CAR   1960-1968
Model uses modified 192 De Soto, 191 Dodge, 148 Ford or 147 Cadillac castings with antenna, white door panels, and Police decals or labels.
1. De Soto Fireflite casting, black body, white painted door panels, Police decals, 114 mm (1960-1961).
2. Dodge Royal casting, black body, white door panels, Police decals, 116 mm (1961-1962).
3. Ford Fairlane casting, black body, white door panels, red interior, Police decals, 111 mm (1962-1963).
4. White interior, otherwise as type 3.
5. Cadillac casting, black body, white door labels instead of painted panels, 111 mm (1967-1968).

259-G FIRE ENGINE   117 mm 1962-1969
Enclosed Bedford Miles fire truck with cast body, turned or red plastic hubs, black tires, suspension, steering, black sheet metal base +/- number, unpainted ladder and bell on roof, windows, pale gray hose reels, silver grille, bumper and headlights, Fire Brigade emblem decals.
1. Red body, turned hubs, number on base.
2. Red body, red plastic hubs, no number on base.

260-G ROYAL MAIL VAN   78 mm 1955-1961
Morris van with cast body and red hubs, black tires, black sheet metal base with

number, silver grille, bumpers and headlights, gold "Royal Mail" and royal monogram logo.
1. Gloss red body, black roof panel.
2. Slightly darker red body, black roof panel.

260-H BUNDESPOST VOLKSWAGEN   100 mm 1971-1976
Modified 129 casting; details not known. For German market.
1. Yellow body.

261-G TELEPHONE SERVICE VAN   73 mm 1956-1961
Morris van with cast body and olive green hubs, black tires, black sheet metal base with number, unpainted ladder on cast-in roof rack, black grille, silver headlights, white lettering on doors, crown decals.
1. Dark green body, black roof panel.

261-H FORD TAUNUS POLICE CAR   110 mm 1967-1968
Modified 154 casting, blue dome light, red interior, other details not known. For German market.
1. White body, green doors, hood and trunk.

262-G VOLKSWAGEN PTT CAR   90 mm 195?-195?
Modified 181 casting, turned hubs, black tires, Swiss flag and PTT decals on doors, other details as 181. For Swiss market.
1. Dark yellow body, black fenders.

262-H VOLKSWAGEN PTT CAR   100 mm 1966-1975
Modified 129 casting, black base-bumpers, turned hubs, black tires, white interior, Swiss flag and PTT decals on doors.
1. Dark yellow body, black fenders.
2. Does it exist with more modern hubs?

263-G SUPERIOR CRITERION AMBULANCE   127 mm 1962-1968
Ambulance with cast body and number, turned hubs, black tires, suspension, steering, black sheet metal base, light green plastic interior, removable stretcher with patient, driver and attendant, windows, white siren, red dome light, silver grille, bumpers and headlights, red taillights, top lights and stripes, "Ambulance" and stripes on windows.
1. Light cream body.

263-H AIRPORT RESCUE TENDER   177 mm 1978-1980
Cast modified 266 body, roof panels, hose reels and spotlight, yellow plastic hubs, black tires, white plastic base, interior and ladder, blue dome lights, windows, silver grille, bumper, headlights and rear body panels, 'white and red "Airport" and "Rescue" labels, emblem labels.
1. Yellow body.

264-G R.C.M.P. PATROL CAR   111 mm 1962-1968
Modified 148 Ford Fairlane, later 147 Cadillac casting with turned hubs, black tires, cream plastic interior, two red-coated figures, red dome light, gray antenna, emblem decals or labels on white door panels, other details as 148 and 147.
1. Modified 148 Ford Fairlane casting, dark blue body, white painted door panels (1962-1965).
2. Modified 147 Cadillac casting, dark blue body, white door panel labels (1966-1968).

264-H ROVER 3500 POLICE CAR   131 mm 1979-1980
Cast modified 180 body, opening doors and hatch, Speedwheels with 5-spoke chromed hubs, black plastic base-bumpers-interior, clear windows and headlights, orange directionals, red taillights, red roof bar with blue and white label, yellow and blue stripe labels with blue Police lettering and emblem. Made in Hong Kong.
1. White body, black window posts.

265-G PLYMOUTH PLAZA TAXI   110 mm 1959-1966
Cast modified 178 body, turned hubs, white tires, suspension, cream plastic interior and roof sign, red lettering stating rates, other details as 178.
1. Orange body, red roof and window posts.

266-G PLYMOUTH PLAZA TAXI   110 mm 1965-1967
Same casting, parts and details as 265, but lettering on doors says "450 Metro Cab".

Canadian version.

1. Orange body, red roof and window posts.

266-H ERF FIRE TENDER   223 mm 1976-1980

Fire truck with cast body, unpainted roof panels, hose reels and spotlight, and fire escape ladder, plastic ladder wheels and extension, red plastic hubs, black tires, plastic interior, base, windows, blue dome lights, silver grille, bumper, headlights and rear panels, white-on-red "Fire Service" labels with coat of arms.

1. Red body, white interior, hose reels and base, unpainted fire escape ladder with gray extension and wheels.
2. Red body, yellow interior, hose reels and base, white fire escape ladder, extension and wheels.
3. Red body with Falck labels, other details not known.
4. Metallic red body, otherwise as type 1 or 2

267-G SUPERIOR CADILLAC AMBULANCE   152 mm 1967-1971

Ambulance with cast body, opening rear door, unpainted siren and roof light mounts, and black base, concentric hubs, black tires, suspension, steering, light green plastic interior, removable stretcher with patient, red lights including working dome light, battery mount in bottom of model, green tinted windows, unpainted grille, bumpers and headlights, orange taillights.

1. White upper, red lower body.

267-H EMERGENCY PARAMEDIC TRUCK   119 mm 1979-1980

Light truck with cast body, speedwheels with 6-spoke silver hubs, black plastic base, yellow interior, windows, silver grille, bumpers, headlights and roof bar, yellow-on-red labels.

1. Red body.

268-G RENAULT DAUPHINE MINICAB   92 mm 1962-1966

French 524 body casting, turned hubs, black sheet metal base with number, silver air intakes, bumpers and headlights, orange taillights, various advertising decals.

1. Red body, no interior, Kenwood decals.
2. Red body, no interior, Meccano decals.
3. Red body, cream interior, ? decals.

268-H RANGE ROVER AMBULANCE   109 mm 1974-1978

Range Rover with cast body, opening hood, doors, tailgate and hatch, roof bar and unpainted base-grille-bumper, Speedwheels with 5-bolt hubs, blue plastic interior, windows, blue dome lights, removable stretcher with patient, silver engine, jewel headlights, red taillights, red and blue Ambulance labels.

1. White body.

269-G JAGUAR MOTORWAY POLICE CAR   95 mm 1962-1966

Modified 195 body, black tires, suspension, steering, red plastic interior, two figures, blue dome light, gray antenna, white-on-black Police decal, other details as 195.

1. White body.

269-H FORD TRANSIT POLICE VAN   129 mm 1978-1980

Van with cast type 3 body, opening side and rear doors, roof bar and charcoal base, 16-fin hubs, black tires, suspension, red plastic interior, windows, blue roof lights, silver grille, bumpers and headlights, Police labels on sides and roof bar, red and blue stripe labels, policeman figure, signs and cones.

1. White body and roof bar.

270-G AA MOTORCYCLE PATROL   47 mm #44b_045 _1959-1964

Cast cycle and sidecar (as before), black rubber or plastic wheels, tan driver, silver headlight and handlebars, tan uniform, black AA emblem on sidecar.

1. Black cycle and sidecar fender, yellow sidecar body, rubber wheels.
2. Plastic wheels, otherwise as type 1.

270-H FORD ESCORT PANDA POLICE CAR   97 mm 1969-1977

Modified 168 body, unpainted base-bumpers, concentric hubs and black tires or Speedwheels with spoked chromed hubs, white plastic roof sign, blue and white Police labels, other details as 168.

1. Light turquoise body, white doors and roof sign, cast hubs.

2. Speedwheels, otherwise as type 1.

271-G TOURING SECOURS MOTORCYCLE   47 mm 1959-1962?

Cast cycle and sidecar (=270), blue and yellow TS emblem, other details as 270. For Belgian market.

1. Black cycle and sidecar fender, yellow sidecar body.

271-H FORD TRANSIT FIRE SERVICE VAN   129 mm 1975-1977

Van with cast type 2 body, opening side and rear doors, unpainted ladder and bells on roof, and black base, cast 5-bolt hubs, black tires, suspension, plastic interior, windows, pump with hose, yellow roof rack, antenna, silver grille and bumpers, jewel or cast-in headlights, yellow taillights, white-on-red labels.

1. Red body, gray interior, jewel headlights, black antenna, Fire Service labels with coat of arms.
2. White interior and antenna, cast-in silver headlights, otherwise as type 1?
3. Red body, white interior and antenna, cast-in silver headlights, Falck Zonen labels.

272-G A.N.W.B. MOTORCYCLE   47 mm 1959-1962?

Cast cycle and sidecar (=270), black ANWB emblem on sidecar, other details as 270.

1. Black cycle and sidecar fender, yellow sidecar box.

272-H FORD TRANSIT POLICE VAN   129 mm 1975-1978

Van with cast type 2 body, opening side and rear doors, roof rack and black base, 5-bolt cast hubs, black tires, suspension, gray plastic interior, rack and device on roof, windows, silver grille, bumpers and headlights, red taillights, blue dome light, Police and Accident Unit labels, two signs and four cones carried inside.

1. White body.
2. Did it originally have jewel headlights?

273-G MINI-MINOR R.A.C. VAN   78 mm 1966-1970

Minivan with cast body and charcoal base, turned hubs, black tires, suspension, steering, red plastic interior, blue roof sign and opening rear doors, windows, silver grille, bumers and headlights, red taillights, white and blue RAC Road Service decals.

1. Blue body, white roof.

274-G MINI-MINOR A.A. VAN   78 mm 1965-1973

Same casting as 273, black base, blue plastic interior, yellow plastic roof sign and opening rear doors, black and yellow AA emblems and lettering, other details as 273.

1. Dark yellow body.

274p-G MASON'S PAINTS MINI-VAN   78 mm 1970

Same casting as 273/274, charcoal base, red plastic interior, maroon roof sign and opening rear doors, maroon and white Joseph Mason Paints decals, other details as 273 and 274.

1. Maroon body.

274-H FORD TRANSIT AMBULANCE   129 mm 1978-1980

Van with cast type 3 body, opening side and rear doors, roof bar and brown base, 16-fin hubs, black tires, suspension, red plastic interior, windows, removable stretcher with patient, silver grille and bumpers, silver headlights, red taillights, blue roof lights, red cross and Ambulance labels, black window labels.

1. White body.

275-G BRINKS ARMORED CAR   120 mm 1964-1979

Van with cast body, blue chassis-grid-running boards, and hubs, black tires, plastic interior, windows, doors, mirrors, decals or labels.

1. Off-white body and doors, green interior with two figures and two bullion cases, cream hubs, suspension, cream-blue-black Brinks decals (1964-1969).
2. Light gray body and doors, white roof, colorless interior, no figures or cases, unpainted hubs, no suspension, black and blue Brinks labels (1976-1979).
3. Dark gray body and doors, black base, "Protection Luis R. Picaso Manriques (Mexico)"_labels, other details not known (1976 promotional).

276-G AIRPORT FIRE TENDER   117 mm 1962-1970

Modified 259 casting, turned hubs, black tires, suspension, black sheet metal base, gray plastic foam gun on roof, amber dome light, windows, bell, silver grille, bumpers and headlights, light gray hose reel, rear axle cam and battery to operate dome light, decals.

1. Red body, white "Airport Fire Control" decals.
2. Red body, same "Fire Brigade" decals as 259.

276-H FORD TRANSIT AMBULANCE   129 mm 1976-1978

Van with cast type 2 body, opening side and rear doors, roof bar and black base, 5-bolt cast hubs, black tires, suspension, red plastic interior, removable stretcher with patient, windows, silver grille, bumpers and headlights, red taillights, blue dome lights, red cross and Ambulance labels, black window labels.

1. White body.

277-G SUPERIOR CRITERION AMBULANCE   129 mm 1962-1969

Ambulance with cast body (=263) and opening rear door, turned hubs, white tires, suspension, steering, black sheet metal base, faintly greenish front and dark green rear interior, clear front and green tinted rear windows, red dome light operated by battery and rear axle cam, white plastic siren and figures, silver grille, bumpers and headlights, red top lights and taillights.

1. Metallic silver body, cream roof, window posts and rear door.

277-H POLICE LAND-ROVER   110 mm 1979-1980

Closed Land-Rover with cast body, opening hood and doors, and black base-bumper, cast 6-spoke hubs, black tires, white plastic rear cover, blue dome light, red interior, windows, silver grille and headlights, Police labels, policeman figure.

1. Blue-black body, white rear cover.

278-G VAUXHALL VICTOR AMBULANCE   87 mm 1964-1970

Modified 141 casting with opening rear door, turned hubs, black tires, suspension, steering, black sheet metal base, green plastic interior, windows, white removable stretcher with patient and red blanket, driver, off-white raised roof section with blue dome light, silver grille, bumpers and headlights, red taillights, red cross decals.

1. Off-white body.

278-H PLYMOUTH YELLOW CAB   133 mm 1978-1980

Cast body (=202, 244) and roof sign, speedwheels with 6-spoke or chromed 12-spoke hubs, black plastic base and interior, windows, gray antenna, silver grille, bumpers and headlights, red taillights, Yellow Cab Co. labels.

1. Yellow body, 6-spoke hubs.
2. Yellow body, 12-spoke hubs.

279-G AVELING BARFORD DIESEL ROLLER   116 mm 1965-1980

Roller with cast body, cab, 2-piece roller mount, two-piece front and two one-piece side rollers, plastic windows (side windows slide), driver in blue, orange cab roof and base with number, plastic engine doors, Master Pavior decals on sides, emblem decal on nose.

1. Orange body, gray engine doors, green roller sides, unpainted surfaces.
2. Yellow cab with black roof, silver entire rollers, otherwise as type 1.
3. Yellow engine doors, ? other details.
4. Gray plastic roof and base?
5. Gray rollers?
6. Black rollers?

280-G OBSERVATION COACH   124 mm #29f_1954-1960

Casting and parts in 29f, deck-and-a-half body has raised cast-in stripes and wheel covers painted trim color.

1. Dark cream body and hubs, red trim.
2. Dark cream body, red trim and hubs.
3. Light gray body, red trim and hubs.
4. Medium gray body and hubs, red trim.
5. Blue body, red trim?
6. Green body, red trim?

280-H MOBILE BANK   124 mm 1966-1968

Cast body and charcoal base with number, turned hubs, black tires, suspension, orange-brown interior, blue curtains, clear windows, roof and dome light, figure, blue stripe around body with cream "Midland Bank Limited" lettering, gold and tan emblems.

1. Cream upper body, silver lower body, grille, bumpers and headlights.

The New System of Catalog Numbers

281-G LUXURY COACH 114 mm #29g_1954-1960
Same casting and parts as 29g, singledeck body has raised cast-in stripes and wheel covers painted trim color.
1. Maroon body, cream trim, red hubs.
2. Pale brown body, orange trim, cream hubs.
3. Pale brown body, cream trim, light green hubs.
4. Cream body and hubs, red trim.
5. Blue body, cream trim and hubs.

281-H FIAT 2300 NEWS CAMERA CAR 108 mm 1967-1970
Modified 172 casting with silver base, unpainted roof rack, 16-fin plastic hubs, black tires, suspension, steering, red plastic interior, gray camera, yellow tripod and base, cameraman figure, Pathe News labels, other details as 172.
1. Black body.

281-J SRN6 ARMY HOVERCRAFT 139 mm 1973-1976
Cast body (=290), wings, white engine, unpainted revolving screen, and black base with number 290, black plastic skirt, door and turret, blue propeller, olive antenna, white interior, windows, cast 6-spoke hubs, black tires, "Army XV 614" and Union Jack labels.
1. Olive body and wings.

282-G DUPLE ROADMASTER COACH 121 mm #29h_1954-1960
Same casting and parts as 29h, body with raised cast-in stripes sometimes painted silver.
1. Cream upper body and hubs, dark green lower body.
2. Cream upper body, dark green lower body, light green hubs.
3. Dark red body, silver stripes, red hubs.
4. Yellow-orange body, red stripes and hubs.
5. Dark blue body, silver stripes, light blue hubs.

282-H AUSTIN 1800 TAXI 101 mm 1966-1968
Modified 171 casting with silver base, turned hubs, black tires, red interior, white roof sign, red-on-white Taxi decals, other details as 171.
1. Blue body, white hood, trunk and roof sign.

282-J LAND-ROVER FIRE APPLIANCE 119 mm 1974-1980
Cast main and rear bodies, opening hood and doors, and unpainted ladder, hose reels, spotlight and base-bumper, speedwheels with 5-bolt or chromed 12-spoke hubs, plastic interior, windows, blue dome lights, silver gray equipment and ladder rack, jewel or cast-in headlights, silver grille and engine, red-background labels.
1. Red body, black interior, 5-bolt hubs, jewel headlights, Fire Service labels.
2. White interior, chrome 12-spoke hubs, otherwise as type 1.
3. White interior, chrome 12-spoke hubs, cast-in headlights, otherwise as type 1.
4. Red body, white interior, chrome 12-spoke hubs, jewel headlights, Falck labels.

283-G B.O.A.C. COACH 121 mm 1956-1963
Singledeck bus with cast body and hubs, black tires, black sheet metal base with number, silver grille, bumpers and headlights, blue lettering along edge of roof, orange B.O.A.C. lettering and emblem below windows.
1. Navy blue body, white hubs.
2. I have one with white tires—are they original?

283-H RED ARROW SINGLE DECK BUS 167 mm 1971-1977
Bus with cast body, two pairs of opening doors, and cast 5-bolt hubs, black tires, pale blue plastic interior, windows, levers to operate doors and bell, silver grille and headlights, white stripe labels with Red Arrow logo.
1. Bright red body, white doors, cream base.
2. Metallic dark red body and doors, cream base.
3. Black base, ? other details.

284-G AUSTIN TAXI 112 mm 1972-1979
London taxi with cast body, opening rear doors and unpainted base-grille-bumpers, Speedwheels with 6-spoke hubs or 12-spoke chrome hubs, suspension, red and black cast-in roof sign, plastic interior, windows, driver, jewel or cast-in headlights, red taillights.

1. Black body, gray interior, jewel headlights, 12-spoke hubs (1972-1977).
2. White interior, smooth trunk lid, otherwise as type 1 (1977-1979).
3. White interior, smooth trunk lid, cast-in headlights, otherwise as type 1.
4. Black body, tan interior, smooth trunk lid, ? other details.
5. Black body, gray interior, cast-in headlights, 6-spoke hubs.

285-G MERRYWEATHER MARQUIS FIRE TENDER 177 mm 1970-1979
Fire truck with cast body, roof deck, unpainted left door and side hatch, rear panel, ladder hook and two-part extending ladder, spotlight and hose reel, and silver or unpainted base-bumper, 8-bolt plastic or 5-bolt sheet metal hubs, black tires, suspension, cream or black plastic interior, windows, red water tank filler cap and pump button, rubber hose with brass nozzle, jewel or cast-in headlights, blue or red dome light, silver body panels, grille and side decals.
1. Metallic dark red body and roof deck, sheet metal bells on roof, plastic 8-bolt front and (different pattern) rear hubs, jewel headlights, blue dome light, unpainted base, Fire Service labels.
2. Unpainted roof deck with cast-in bells, cast 5-bolt hubs, otherwise as type 1.
3. Bright red body, otherwise as type 1?
4. Bright red body, otherwise as type 2.
5. Bright red body, white-on-red Falck labels, silver painted base, red dome light, otherwise as type 2.
6. Bright red body, cast-in headlights, otherwise as type 2.

286-G FORD TRANSIT FIRE VAN 122 mm 1969-1975
Van with cast type 1 body, opening left and rear doors, sliding right door, base and unpainted or silver ladder, cast 6-spoke or concentric hubs, black tires, suspension, yellow plastic roof rack, cream interior, red and silver pump inside rear, yellow hose with metal nozzle, white antenna, silver grille and bumpers, jewel headlights, yellow taillights, labels.
1. Metallic dark red body, black base, concentric hubs, black bells, Fire Service labels.
2. Six-spoke hubs, unpainted bells, otherwise as type 1.
3. Six-spoke hubs, unpainted bells, metallic blue base, Falck labels, otherwise as type 1.
4. Nonmetallic bright red body, ? other details.

287-G FORD TRANSIT POLICE ACCIDENT UNIT 122 mm 1967-1974
Van with cast type 1 body, opening left and rear doors, sliding right door, roof rack and sign, and base, cast concentric hubs, black tires, suspension, gray plastic interior, windows, gray TV monitor on roof, inside rack with signs and cones, white antenna, driver figure, blue dome light, jewel headlights, red taillights, silver grille and bumpers, Police and Accident Unit labels.
1. Cream upper body, orange lower body, charcoal base, all labels blue and white (1967-1970).
2. White body, orange side panel labels with black Police lettering, black base (1971-1974).

288-G SUPERIOR CADILLAC AMBULANCE 152 mm 1974-1979
Ambulance with cast body, opening rear door, unpainted siren, roof light mounts, grille-headlights-front bumper, rear bumper, and painted base, Speedwheels with 4+4 or 12-spoke chromed hubs, cream plastic interior, windows, dome lights, removable stretcher with patient.
1. White upper body, red lower body, red dome and roof lights, black base, 4+4-spoke hubs, red-white-green window pattern, black Ambulance labels.
2. Red upper body, white lower body and roof, blue dome and roof lights, brown base, 12-spoke hubs, blue tinted windows, Falck labels.
3. Black body, white roof, Falck labels, ? other details.

289-G ROUTEMASTER BUS 121 mm 1964-1980
Doubledecker with cast body and hood-base, turned hubs or 5-bolt cast hubs with black tires or Speedwheels, cream plastic interior, windows, driver and conductor, silver grille and headlights, orange taillights, London Transport lower side decals or

labels, various upper side decals or labels. Earlier casting with three upper and two lower window bars (1964-1977):
1. Red body and base, turned hubs, Tern Shirts decals.
2. Red body and base, 5-bolt hubs, Tern Shirts decals.
3. Red body and base, turned hubs, Schweppes decals.
4. Red body and base, 5-bolt hubs, Schweppes decals.
5. Red body and base, turned hubs, left Schweppes decal, right Festival of London Stores label (1968).
6. Red body and base, turned hubs, Esso Tyres upper and London Transport lower labels.
7. Five-bolt hubs, otherwise as type 6.
8. Speedwheels, otherwise as type 6.
9. Gold body and base, ? hubs, Dinky Toys labels. Later casting without window bars, with Speedwheels, blue lower interior, adhesive labels (1977-1980):
10. Red body and base, Esso Tyres labels.
11. Red body and base, Jackson's the Tailors labels.
12. Red body and base, Visit Madame Tussaud's labels with cream background.
13. Dark blue background labels, otherwise as type 12.
14. Silver body and base, no conductor or driver, Woolworth Welcomes the World labels. Many promotional versions exist; shown in this book is one produced by the Model Car Collectors' Club of New Zealand.

290-G DOUBLE DECKER BUS 102 mm #29c_1954-1963
Doubledecker with cast body (basically as 29c) and chassis-hood, cast, turned or plastic hubs, black tires, originally with Leyland grille of three horizontal and many vertical lines, with or without box on front of roof, concave or convex taillights, with or without number 290 on base, upper deck always cream, black and red Dunlop decals.
1. Red lower deck, no number, concave taillights, roof box, cast hubs.
2. Green lower deck, otherwise as type 1.
3. Red lower deck, 290 on base, otherwise as type 1.
4. Green lower deck, 290 on base, otherwise as type 1.
5. Red lower deck, 290 on base, no roof box, otherwise as type 1.
6. Green lower deck, 290 on base, no roof box, otherwise as type 1.
7. Red lower deck, AEC grille with V at top center, 290 at base, no roof box, cast hubs, concave taillights.
8. Green lower deck, otherwise as type 7.
9. Red lower deck, convex taillights, otherwise as type 7.
10. Red lower deck, convex taillights, no number on base, otherwise as type 7.
11. Green lower deck, convex taillights, otherwise as type 7.
12. Green lower deck, convex taillights, no number on base, otherwise as type 7.
13. Red lower deck, AEC grille with V, roof box, convex taillights, no number on base, cast hubs.
14. Green lower body, otherwise as type 13.
15. Red lower deck, turned hubs, otherwise as type 13.
16. Green lower deck, turned hubs, otherwise as type 13.
17. Red lower deck, red plastic hubs, otherwise as type 13.
18. Green lower deck, green plastic hubs, otherwise as type 13.
19. Red lower deck, Exide decals (as on 291), ? other details.
20. Green lower deck, otherwise as type 19.

290-H SR N6 HOVERCRAFT 139 mm 1970-1976
Same casting and parts as 281, yellow wings, white engine cover, unpainted revolving screen, base with number, concentric hubs, black tires, white plastic door, yellow interior, blue propeller, dark blue skirt, white SR. N6 labels.
1. Metallic red body, charcoal base, yellow wings.
2. Metallic red body, black base, yellow wings.
3. Bright red body, black base, yellow-orange wings?

291-G DOUBLE DECKER BUS 102 mm 1959-1963
Same castings and parts as 290, Leyland grille (3 horizontal, many vertical lines), body with roof box and convex taillights, red cast, unpainted turned or red plastic hubs,

black tires, black and orange Exide Batteries decals.
1. Red body and cast hubs.
2. Red body, turned hubs.
3. Red body and plastic hubs.

291-H   ATLANTEAN CITY BUS   123 mm   1974-1978
Doubledecker with cast body, base-engine compartment, and unpainted attachment, Speedwheels, plastic interior, windows, silver headlights, white and blue "Kenning car, van and truck hire" labels.
1. Light red body, white base and interior.
2. Light red body, white base, blue interior.
3. Light red body, blue base and interior.

292-G   ATLANTEAN BUS   121 mm   1962-1966
Doubledecker with cast body and base-engine cover (not same as 291), black tires, plastic interior, windows, silver headlights, red taillights. Casting with no step under front doors, which extend to bottom of casting.
1. Red and cream body, Regent logo on upper red band, Corporation Transport and coat of arms on lower red panel, cream interior. Casting with step under front doors:
2. Red and cream body, details as type 1.
3. Red and cream body, yellow lower "Ribble" decal, ? interior, other details as type 1.
4. Red and cream body, no upper logo, yellow lower "Ribble" decal, red interior, other details as type 1.
(292 GREEN LINE BUS probably never issued)

293-G   ATLANTEAN BUS   121 mm   1964-1968
Same castings and parts as 292, turned hubs, black tires, red interior, BP upper logo, Corporation Transport lower logo, casting with step under doors, other details as 292.
1. Ivory and green body (logo on green), smooth roof.
2. Ribbed roof, otherwise as type 1.

293-H   SWISS POSTAL BUS   119 mm   1973-1978
Viceroy singledecker with cast body (same casting as 296), spoked chromed Speedwheels, black base and hubs, white plastic interior, clear or tinted windows, red stripe and black-on-orange PTT labels.
1. Yellow-orange body, cream roof, clear windows.
2. Blue tinted windows, otherwise as type 1.
3. Orange tinted windows, otherwise as type 1.

294-G   POLICE VEHICLES GIFT SET   1973-1980
Boxed set of 250 Police Mini-Cooper, 254 Police Land-Rover and:
1. 287 Ford Police Accident Unit (type 1 van, 1973-1974).
2. 272 Ford Police Accident Unit (type 2 van, 1974-1977).
3. 269 Ford Police Accident Unit (type 3 van, 1977-1980). Note: I assume type 3 set exists but have no proof.

295-G   STANDARD ATLAS KENEBRAKE   86 mm   1960-1964
Minibus with cast body, turned hubs, black tires, suspension, black sheet metal base, red plastic interior, windows, silver grille, bumpers and headlights, red taillights.
1. Pale blue lower, light gray upper base.
2. Pale blue entire body.

295-H   ATLANTEAN BUS   121 mm   1973-1976
Doubledecker with cast body, base-engine cover and unpainted attachment (same as 292 and 293), Speedwheels with spoked chromed hubs, white plastic interior, windows, silver headlights, black-on-yellow Yellow Pages logo on upper and lower sides plus both ends.
1. Yellow body and base, reversed lower front "Yellow Pages" lettering (i.e., mirror image).
2. Normal lower front lettering, otherwise as type 1.
3. Plastic upper body?

296-G   VICEROY 37 LUXURY COACH   119 mm   1972-1975
Cast body (=293), Speedwheels with spoked chromed hubs, black sheet metal base,

white or cream interior, tinted windows, no logo.
1. Metallic blue body, orange tinted windows.
2. Blue or untinted windows?

297-G   POLICE VEHICLES GIFT SET   1967-1973
Boxed set of 250 Police Mini-Cooper, 255 Ford Zodiac Police Car and 287 Ford Police Accident Unit (type 1 van).
1. White and orange 287.
2. All-white 287.

297-H   ATLANTEAN SILVER JUBILEE BUS   124 mm   1977
Same castings and parts as 292-293-295, Speedwheels with spoked chromed hubs, pale blue plastic interior, black-on-silver "The Queen's Silver Jubilee" upper labels, red and blue-on-silver "National" lower labels, white-on-black front and rear labels.
1. Silver body and base, labels as above.
2. Plastic upper body, otherwise as above?
3. Silver body and base, "Woolworth's welcomes the world" upper and "The Queen's Silver Jubilee" lower labels. Note: numerous promotional versions exist; this book shows "Join the M.B.F." and "S. P. Flowers Waste Products" models.

298-G   EMERGENCY SERVICES GIFT SET   1963-1966
Boxed set of figures and 258 Ford Fairlane Police Car, 263 Superior Ambulance, 276 Airport Fire Tender and 277 Superior Ambulance.
1. Standard colors.

299-G   POST OFFICE SERVICES SET   1958
Boxed set of 260 Royal Mail Van, 261 Telephone Van, 750 Telephone box, 011 Telegraph Messenger and 012 Postman.
1. Standard colors.

299-H   MOTORWAY SERVICES SET   1963-1967
Boxed set of 257 Rambler Fire Chief, 263 Superior Ambulance, 269 Jaguar Police Car and 434 Bedford Crash Truck.
1. Standard colors.

299-J   POLICE CRASH SQUAD SET   1979
Boxed set of 244 Plymouth Police Car, 732 Bell Police Helicopter and road signs.
1. Standard colors.

300-G   FARM TRACTOR   89 mm   #27a_1954-1971
Massey-Harris tractor with same castings and parts as 27a at first, red body, black sheet metal base and parts, cast wheels with yellow hubs later replaced by yellow hubs with black tires, cast brown driver replaced by blue plastic, yellow Massey-Harris decals, later replaced by Massey-Ferguson.
1. Cast wheels with yellow painted hubs, brown cast driver, Massey-Harris decals.
2. Cast wheels with yellow painted hubs, blue plastic driver, Massey-Ferguson decals.
3. Yellow 8-bolt hubs with black tires, blue plastic driver, Massey-Ferguson decals.

300-H   LONDON SCENE GIFT SET   1978-1980
Boxed set of 284 Austin Taxi and 289 Routemaster Bus.
1. Standard colors.

301-G   FIELD MARSHAL TRACTOR   76 mm   #27n_1954-1965
Tractor with same castings and parts as 27n at first, black stack and steering wheel, tan driver, black sheet metal base and parts, silver trim, cast wheels with painted hubs replaced by cast hubs and black tires.
1. Orange body, cast wheels with green painted hubs.
2. Yellow painted hubs, otherwise as type 1.
3. Orange body, unpainted cast hubs, black tires.
4. Red body, green cast hubs, black tires.
(301 M.A.S.H. SET never issued)
(301 MODERN MILITARY GIFT SET never issued)
(302 EMERGENCY SQUAD GIFT SET never issued)

303-G   COMMANDO SQUAD GIFT SET   1978-1980
Boxed set of 667 Armored Patrol Car, 687 Convoy Army Truck, and 745 Bell Army Helicopter.

1. Standard colors.

304-G   FIRE RESCUE GIFT SET   1978-1979
Boxed set of 195 Fire Chief's Range Rover, 282 Land-Rover Fire Appliance and 384 Convoy Fire Rescue Truck.
1. Standard colors.

305-G   DAVID BROWN TRACTOR   83 mm   1966-1975
Tractor with cast chassis, two-piece front axle mount and rear hubs, cast or plastic cab and front hubs, black tires, plastic hood, seat, driver, windows, fenders, rear hook, lift etc., working steering, David Brown and grille labels.
1. Red hood, fenders, mount, seat, hook and lift, black chassis and steering wheel, yellow cab and cast hubs, front of hood is a wide V-shape with side headlights, black and yellow "David Brown 950" labels.
2. Cream cab and seat, off-white hood, red chassis and hubs (cast rear, plastic front), pale yellow steering wheel, fenders, hook and lift, unpainted axle mount, white and black "Case-David Brown 995" labels, new hood with flat grille angled back toward bottom, no side headlights.
(307 "NEW AVENGERS" GIFT SET never issued)

308-G   LEYLAND 384 TRACTOR   86 mm   1971-1978
Tractor with cast body, unpainted base and cream rear hubs, cream plastic front hubs and stack, black tires, blue driver, sheet metal front axle mount and tow hook, silver grille, white and blue Leyland labels.
1. Metallic dark red body, unpainted metal steering wheel.
2. Orange body, unpainted metal steering wheel.
3. Dark blue body, black plastic steering wheel.

309-G   STAR TREK GIFT SET   1978
Boxed set of 357 Klingon Battle Cruiser and 358 Enterprise.
1. Standard colors.

310-G   FARM TRACTOR AND HAY RAKE   157 mm   #27ak_1954-1963
Models 300 and 324, formerly 27a and 27k.
1. Standard colors.

319-G   WEEKS TIPPING FARM TRAILER   105 mm   1961-1970
Open trailer with cast body, tailgate and chassis, cast supertoy or plastic hubs, black tires, black plastic hydraulic cylinder.
1. Red body, tailgate and chassis, yellow chassis.
2. Red plastic hubs, otherwise as type 1.
3. Yellow plastic hubs, otherwise as type 1.

320-G   HALESOWEN HARVEST TRAILER   133 mm   #27b_1954-1970
Open trailer with cast body including chassis, two removable racks, cast wheels or plastic hubs and black tires, small gray plastic front wheel, sheet metal tow hook.
1. Tan body, red chassis and racks, cast wheels with unpainted treads and yellow painted hubs. Identical to 27b.
2. All red body, yellow stakes, yellow plastic hubs, black tires.

321-G   MASSEY-HARRIS MANURE SPREADER   133 mm
#27c_1954-1971
Cast body and three silver rotors, cast wheels or yellow plastic hubs and black tires, spring belt, two pulleys, +/- yellow Massey-Harris logo. Same castings as 27c.
1. Red body, cast wheels with unpainted treads and yellow painted hubs, Massey Harris lettering.
2. Yellow plastic hubs, black tires, otherwise as type 1.
3. Yellow plastic hubs, black tires, no lettering, otherwise as type 1.
4. Red plastic hubs, black tires, no lettering, otherwise as type 1.

322-G   DISC HARROW   86 by 79 mm   #27h_1954-1973
Cast body and two sets of silver rollers, black sheet metal tow hook (if any) and mounts. Same castings as 27h.
1. Red and yellow frame with tow hook.
2. White and red frame, no hook.
3. White and blue frame, no hook.

323-G   TRIPLE GANG MOWER   111 mm   #27j_1954-1959

Cast frame, three subframes, three yellow blades and six green wheels, towing hitch at front and tow hook at rear of frame. Identical to 27j.

1. Red frame and subframes.

324-G HAY RAKE 76 mm #27k_1954-1971

Cast frame and two yellow spoked wheels, wire tines in red sheet metal mount, black sheet metal lever. Same castings as 27k.

1. Red frame, both 27k and 324 cast in.
2. Red frame, only 324 cast in.

325-G DAVID BROWN TRACTOR WITH DISC HARROW 152 mm 1967-1973

Set of 305 David Brown Tractor and 322 Disc Harrow.

1. Standard colors.

340-G LAND ROVER 92 mm #27d_1954-1971

Land Rover with cast open body, cast or plastic hubs, gray or black tires, spare wheel, black sheet metal windshield frame, steering wheel, front base and tow hook, tan cast or blue plastic driver. Same casting as 27d.

1. Light green body and cast hubs, tan interior and cast driver.
2. Orange body, red cast hubs, dark green interior, tan cast driver.
3. Red plastic hubs, blue plastic driver, otherwise as type 2.
4. Red body and plastic hubs, yellow interior, blue plastic driver.

341-G LAND ROVER TRAILER 78 mm #27m_1954-1971

Open trailer with cast body including tow bar with black sheet metal spring, cast or plastic hubs, gray (or black?) tires. Same casting as 27m.

1. Light green body and cast hubs.
2. Orange body, red cast hubs.
3. Orange body, red plastic hubs.
4. Red body?

342-G MOTOCART 111 mm #27g_1954-1960.

Open three-wheeled farm cart with cast chassis, tipping rear body, tan driver, black steering wheel and three wheels with unpainted treads and red painted hubs. Identical to 27g.

1. Light green chassis, dark tan tipping body.

342-H AUSTIN MINIMOKE 73 mm 1967-1975

Jeep-type vehicle with cast body and opening hood, turned or cast hubs with black tires or speedwheels, spare wheel on cast-in mount, gray-brown plastic top and dash, black sheet metal windshield frame, clear windshield, silver grille, engine and headlights, red taillights.

1. Metallic green body, turned hubs.
2. Metallic green body, speedwheels.
3. Metallic blue-green body, concentric cast hubs.

343-G DODGE FARM PRODUCE WAGON 108 mm #30n_1954-1964

Cast chassis-cab, rear body and hubs, black tires, sheet metal rear stakes matching rear body color, black front base and tow hook, silver grille, bumper and headlights. Same castings as 30n.

1. Dark rose-red chassis-cab, light blue rear body and hubs.
2. Green chassis-cab, yellow rear body and hubs.

344-G ESTATE CAR 105 mm #27f_1954-1961

Plymouth wagon with cast body and hubs, black tires, black sheet metal base with number 344 and big lettering, silver grille, bumper and headlights. Same casting as 27f.

1. Tan body, brown panels, cream hubs.
2. Gray body, red panels, ? hubs.

344-H LAND-ROVER 108 mm 1970-1977

Pickup truck with cast body, opening hood and doors, base-bumper, cast 5-bolt hubs with black tires and suspension or Speedwheels with 6-spoke hubs or 12-spoke chromed hubs, plastic interior, windows, black sheet metal tow hook, jewel or cast-in headlights, silver grille and engine.

1. Metallic dark blue body, white rear bed and base, 5-bolt cast hubs, jewel headlights, red cast-in taillights, yellow interior.
2. Metallic dark blue body, silver rear bed, black base, Speedwheels, jewel

headlights, no taillights, white interior.

3. Cast-in silver headlights, otherwise as type 2.
4. Red interior, cast-in silver headlights, Speedwheels with 6-spoke hubs, otherwise as type 2.

350-G TINY'S MINIMOKE 73 mm 1970-1973

Cast body and opening hood (=342), five-spoke cast hubs, black tires, white plastic top, dash and spare wheel cover, clear windshield and unpainted frame, giraffe driver, silver engine, grille, bumper and headlights, yellow and white stripe label on top.

1. Orange body.

351-G UFO INTERCEPTOR 198 mm 1971-1979

Cast body, gold louvers and jets, unpainted nose and trigger, orange landing skis, body parts and interior, blue windshield, pilot, red and white S.H.A.D.O. and red stripe labels, plastic missile with rubber nose.

1. Metallic olive green body, white missile with black nose.
2. Yellow missile with red nose, otherwise as type 1.

352-G ED STRAKER'S CAR 124 mm 1971-1975

Cast body, base and unpainted concentric hubs, black tires, plastic interior and windows, silver and sometimes black body panels.

1. Gold plated body, silver lights, vents and rear panels, unpainted base, blue interior.
2. Dark yellow body with silver lights and vents, black rear panels, black base, gray interior.
3. Red body, ? other details.
4. Yellow interior?

353-G SHADO 2 MOBILE 145 mm 1972-1980

Cast body, base (body color or pale green), unpainted missile launcher (unpainted, orange or green base) and radar screen, yellow plastic missiles with red or black noses, white interior, windows, 12 green or brown hubs, black treads, black grid at front of roof, white "Shado 2" labels. Base +/- two bars at rear.

1. Olive green body, pale green base with two bars at rear, unpainted launcher base, green hubs.
2. Metallic blue body, ? other details.

354-G PINK PANTHER CAR 175 mm 1972-1980

Plastic body, nose, windshield, black interior-base, flexible driver, +/- large black gyro-wheel and detachable rack rod, spoked Speedwheels.

1. Rose pink body, nose and driver, gyro-wheel.
2. Pale pink body, nose and driver, no gyro-wheel, "The Pink Panther" side labels, picture label on roof, model sold in bubblepack.

355-G LUNAR ROVING VEHICLE 114 mm 1972-1975

Open vehicle with cast body, base and steering fenders, unpainted steering rods, unpainted front and orange rear solar cells, unpainted 8-bolt hubs, black tires, white plastic steering handle, two seated astronaut figures.

1. White body, base and fenders.

357-G KLINGON BATTLE CRUISER 220 mm 1976-1979

Spacecraft with cast main body and parts, white plastic lower body and parts, labels on wings, white plastic discs supplied.

1. Metallic blue main body and cast parts.

358-G U.S.S. ENTERPRISE 234 mm 1976-1980

Spacecraft with cast and light cream cast body parts, unpainted firing lever, white plastic top, orange jets, red stripe and black lettering labels, white plastic discs and orange part supplied.

1. NCC-1701 registration.

359-G EAGLE TRANSPORTER 222 mm 1975-1979

Spacecraft with white cast frame and module, metallic olive green pods, unpainted engines, releasing lever and landing gear, black module base, red plastic cones, module doors, windows and landing gear and other parts.

1. Blue and white Alpha Moonbase labels.
2. Plastic frame?

360-G EAGLE FREIGHTER 222 mm 1975-1979

Cast freight module, pods, unpainted engines, releasing lever and landing gear, white cast or plastic frame, red plastic cones and parts, yellow waste cans, black module parts.

1. Red freight module, white pods and frame, "Danger—waste materials" lettering on waste cans.
2. White freight module and frame, metallic blue pods, no lettering on waste cans.
4. Metallic green pods, otherwise as type 2?

361-G ZYGON GALACTIC WAR CHARIOT 126 mm 1979-1980

Open vehicle with cast chassis with seats, body with missile launcher mount, six Speedwheels with 8-dot chromed hubs, red plastic jets, missile launcher, red missile, two red and black figures (two sizes).

1. Metallic olive green chassis, unpainted body, blue-black missile launcher, big figures that plug into seats.
2. Unpainted body and chassis, red missile launcher, otherwise as type 1.
3. Metallic blue body, white chassis, blue-black missile launcher, small figures without seat plugs; made in Italy.

362-G TRIDENT STAR FIGHTER 170 mm 1979-1980

Spacecraft with cast upper and lower body and fin, unpainted trigger, orange plastic parts, orange and yellow labels.

1. Black body and fin.

363-G ZYGON PATROLLER 210 mm 1979-1980

Spacecraft with cast upper and lower body, dark blue plastic engines, chrome bands, blue tinted cockpit canopy, black landing skis, red push buttons.

1. Red and white body; called Cosmic Interceptor, sold at Christmas 1979.
2. Silver upper and dark blue lower body (1980).

364-G NASA SPACE SHUTTLE 186 mm 1979

Spacecraft with cast body, wings, opening panels and black base, red plastic jets and wheels, three-piece white satellite (rockets and tank), American flag, black "United States" and window labels.

1. White body, wings, opening panels and satellite.

366-G SPACE SHUTTLE 186 mm 1979

Spacecraft identical to 364, no satellite.

1. White body, wings and opening panels.

367-G SPACE BATTLE CRUISER 204 mm 1979

Spacecraft with cast body, white plastic base and engines, white or black missiles, red jets, bands and push buttons, blue tinted opening canopy, seat and engine cover, red or blue pilot (same as smaller 361 type).

1. White body and missiles, red driver.
2. White body, black missiles, ? driver.
3. Blue driver, ? other details.
4. Dark blue body, called "Cosmic Cruiser", sold at Christmas, 1979.

368-G ZYGON MARAUDER 210 mm 1979

Spacecraft with cast body (=367), red plastic base, wing, nose, missiles and launchers, black tinted canopy, black interior.

1. White body.

370-G DRAGSTER SET 113 mm 1969-1976

Dragster with cast chassis and engine (=228), gold exhaust pipes, yellow rear body, yellow plastic front body, air intake and roll bar, small spoked front and big 5-spoke rear hubs, black tires, windshield, black driver, plastic and unpainted metal starter unit.

1. "Fireball", "Inch-pincher" and red-white stripe labels, light blue starter box.
2. Gray starter box, otherwise as type 1.

371-G U.S.S. ENTERPRISE 102 mm 1980

Small version of 358, cast body and engines, plastic body piece, black NCC-1701 registration label. Also sold as 801 and 803.

1. White body.

372-G KLINGON BATTLE CRUISER 100 mm 1980

Small version of 357, cast body and base, black-yellow-silver emblem labels. Also sold as 802 and 804.

1. Metallic dark blue body.

The New System of Catalog Numbers

CONVOY SERIES: these trucks were designed especially for Dinky Toys rather than being modeled after real vehicles. All have the same modernistic chassis-cab and Speedwheels with black or chromed 12-spoke hubs.

380-G CONVOY SKIP TRUCK 112 mm 1977-1980
Cast chassis-cab, Speedwheels, orange plastic bucket and arms, black base-bumper-grille, gray interior, clear windows and headlights.
1. Yellow chassis-cab.
2. Yellow-green chassis-cab, black hubs.
3. Metallic green chassis-cab.

380-G CONVOY SKIP TRUCK 112 mm 1977-1980
Cast chassis-cab, Speedwheels, orange plastic bucket and arms, black base-bumper-grille, gray interior, clear windows and headlights.
1. Yellow chassis-cab.
2. Yellow-green chassis-cab, black hubs.
3. Metallic green chassis-cab.

381-G GARDEN ROLLER 67 mm #105a_1954-1958
Cast handle and two roller halves; identical to 105a.
1. Green handle, red roller sides, unpainted surfaces.

381-H CONVOY FARM TRUCK 110 mm 1977-1980
Cast chassis-cab, Speedwheels, plastic rear stake body and opening tailgate, black base-bumper-grille, gray interior, clear windows and headlights.
1. Yellow chassis-cab, light brown rear body, black hubs.
2. Yellow chassis-cab and rear body?
3. Green chassis-cab, light brown rear body.

382-G WHEELBARROW 83 mm #105b_1954-1958
Cast body and unpainted wheel; identical to 105b.
1. Tan exterior, red interior.

382-H CONVOY DUMP TRUCK 118 mm 1978-1980
Cast chassis-cab, Speedwheels, plastic tipper, black base-bumper-grille, gray interior, clear windows and headlights.
1. Red chassis-cab, gray tipper, black hubs.
2. Red chassis-cab, black tipper, black hubs.
3. Orange chassis-cab, gray or red tipper?
4. Yellow chassis-cab, gray or red tipper?
5. Red chassis-cab and tipper?

383-G HAND TRUCK 127 mm #105c_1954-1958
Cast body, front axle mount, handle and yellow hubs, black tires, sheet metal tow hook; identical to 105c.
1. Green body and axle mount, yellow handle.
2. Blue body, axle mount and handle.

383-H CONVOY COVERED TRUCK 110 mm 1977-1980
Cast chassis-cab, Speedwheels, dark yellow plastic rear body and cover, black base-bumper-grille, white interior, clear windows and headlights and National Carriers and white-on-red medallion labels.
1. Light yellow chassis-cab, black hubs.
2. Hertz Rental logo: code two model by John Gay.

384-G GRASS CUTTER 60 mm #105e_1954-1958
Cast frame, red blades and green wheels; identical to 105e.
1. Yellow frame.

384-H CONVOY FIRE RESCUE TRUCK 126 mm 1977-1979
Cast chassis-cab, Speedwheels, red plastic rear body, white arms and platform, black base-bumper-grille, clear windows and headlights, yellow-on-red rescue labels.
1. Red chassis-cab, chrome hubs.
2. Los Angeles Fire Dept. logo: code two model by John Gay.

385-G SACK TRUCK 64 mm #107a_1954-1958
Cast frame, two black cast wheels; identical to 107a.
1. Blue frame.

385-H CONVOY ROYAL MAIL TRUCK 110 mm 1977-1979
Cast chassis-cab, Speedwheels, red plastic rear body and cover, black base-bumper-grille, gray interior, clear windows and headlights.
1. Red chassis-cab, black hubs.
2. Los Angeles Fire Dept. logo: code two model by John Gay.

386-G LAWN MOWER 140 mm #751_1954-1958
Cast frame parts and removable grass catcher, red blades, unpainted rollers and gears; identical to 751.
1. Green frame and outside of catcher, red inside of catcher.

(386 CONVOY AVIS RENTAL TRUCK never issued)
(387 CONVOY PICKFORDS TRUCK never issued)
(388 CONVOY COVERED VAN never issued)
(389 CONVOY CEMENT MIXER never issued)
(no# CONVOY TEXACO TANKER never issued)
(no# CONVOY WEETABIX VAN AND TRAILER never issued)

390-G CUSTOMIZED FORD TRANSIT VAN 133 mm 1978-1980
Van with cast type 3 body, opening side and rear doors, wide black tires, red plastic interior, chromed exhaust pipes, black base, windows, silver grille, bumper and headlights, colorful Vampire and flame labels.
1. Metallic dark blue body.

398-G FARM EQUIPMENT SET 1964-1965
Boxed set of 300 Tractor, 320 Harvest Trailer, 321 Spreader, 322 Harrow and 324 Hayrake.
1. Standard colors.

399-G FARM TRACTOR AND TRAILER 1969-1973
Boxed set of 300 Tractor and 428 4-Wheel Trailer.
1. Standard colors.

399-H CONVOY GIFT SET 1977-1979
Boxed set of 380 Skip Truck, 381 Farm Truck and 382 Dump Truck.
1. Standard colors.

400-G B.E.V. ELECTRIC TRUCK 86 mm #14a_1954-1960
Flat cart with cast body, tan driver, and hubs, black tires, black sheet metal base and tow hook, #14A cast into body. Identical to 14a.
1. Light blue body and hubs.
2. Light gray body and hubs.

401-G COVENTRY CLIMAX FORK LIFT 108 mm #14c_1954-1964
Cast body, tan driver, black steering wheel, green fork and hubs, gray tires, black sheet metal base and lift column, crank and line. Identical to 40c.
1. Orange body.
2. ? body, bale of paper: promotional for mill in Holland.

402-G BEDFORD T.K. COCA-COLA TRUCK 121 mm 1966-1969
Bottle truck with cast cab, rear body and black chassis, red plastic hubs, black tires, blue plastic interior, windows, load of cases, red and white Coca-Cola labels.
1. Red cab and rear body, ? grille, bumpers and headlights..
2. Red cab and rear body, white cab roof, grille, bumpers and headlights.

404-G CLIMAX CONVEYANCER FORK LIFT 97 by 85 mm 1967-1979
Cast body, fork, lift bars and orange base, yellow plastic hubs, black tires, yellow floor, blue driver, plastic seat, roll cage, top of lift, pallet, stack, operating crank, "Conveyancer" and other labels.
1. Red (or orange?) lower body and yellow upper body, black fork, seat, stack, crank, lift top etc., red pallet, "CG4" printed on body.
2. Orange entire body, CG4 labels, otherwise as type 1.
3. Orange entire body, CG4 labels, unpainted fork, otherwise as type 1.
4. Dark yellow body and lift, unpainted fork, brown seat, stack, lift top and crank, black pallet, black-on-yellow labels.

405-G UNIVERSAL JEEP 83 mm #25y_1954-1967
Jeep with cast body (=25y) and black steering wheel, cast or plastic hubs, black tires

and spare, black sheet metal windshield frame, base and tow hook.
1. Red body and cast hubs.
2. Green body, light green cast hubs.
3. Red body and plastic hubs.
4. Green body and plastic hubs.

406-G COMMER ARTICULATED TRUCK 171 mm 1964-1967
Semi-trailer with same castings and parts as 424, without plastic rear body parts. Never in catalog.
1. No other data.

407-G FORD TRANSIT VAN 122 mm 1966-1974
Van with cast type 1 body, opening left and rear doors, sliding right door, base and concentric hubs, black tires, suspension, red plastic interior, windows, jewel headlights, red taillights, silver grille and bumpers, logo decals or labels.
1. Pale blue body, white roof, charcoal base, black "Kenwood Domestic Appliances" decals.
2. Bright yellow body, light blue base, "Hertz Truck Rental" labels.
3. Bright yellow body, ? base, "Seaspeed BR" labels. (Rediffusion Colour TV version was never issued.)

408-G BIG BEDFORD LORRY 146 mm #522 _922 1956-1963
Open truck with cast chassis-cab, rear body and Supertoy hubs, gray tires, black sheet metal front base and tow hook, spare wheel, #522 under rear body, silver grille and headlights. Identical to previous versions.
1. Maroon chassis-cab, tan rear body and hubs.
2. Blue chassis-cab, light orange rear body, yellow hubs.

409-G BEDFORD ARTICULATED LORRY 165 mm #521 _921 _1956-1963
Semi-trailer truck with cast cab, semi and red hubs, black tires, black sheet metal cab base and tow hook, black and silver grille with headlights, black hitch.
1. Yellow-orange cab and semi, black fenders.

410-G BEDFORD END TIPPER 98 mm #25m _1954-1963
Dump truck with cast chassis-cab, tipper, opening tailgate and grille-bumper-headlights, cast or plastic hubs, black tires, black sheet metal base, tipping crank and spiral, +/- windows. Grille can be black and silver or (later) all silver.
1. Brown cab, yellow tipper and tailgate, ? cast hubs, no windows.
2. Dark yellow cab and cast hubs, blue tipper and tailgate, no windows.
3. Windows, otherwise as type 2.
4. windows, plastic hubs, silver grille, otherwise as type 2.
5. Red cab and cast hubs, pale yellow tipper and tailgate, no windows.
6. Windows, otherwise as type 5.
7. Windows, red plastic hubs, silver grille, otherwise as type 5.

410-H BEDFORD CF VAN 90 mm 1972-1979
Panel van with cast body, Speedwheels with chromed or black spoked hubs, unpainted sheet metal base, white plastic interior, windows, silver grille, bumper and headlights. Three castings: P = plain roof, R = ribbed roof, S = ribbed roof with square in center.
1. Red body, Royal Mail labels, chrome hubs, casting P?
2. Casting R, otherwise as type 1.
3. Black upper, red lower body, Simpsons logo, chrome hubs, casting R.
4. Bronze body, black roof, Belaco logo, chrome hubs, casting R.
5. Dark blue body, John Menzies logo, chrome hubs, casting R.
6. Dark yellow body, Danish Post Office logo, chrome hubs, casting R.
7. Casting S, otherwise as type 6.
8. White body, MJ Hire Service logo, chrome hubs, casting S.
9. Red and white body, Marley Tiles logo, chrome hubs, casting S.
10. White body, Modeller's World, chrome hubs, casting S.
11. Olive body, Parlophone logo, black hubs, casting S.
12. Cream body, Jimmy Carter logo, black hubs, casting S.
13. Light gray body, Opel logo, black hubs, casting S.

14. Red body, new Royal Mail logo, ? other details.

Minor variations of the above may well exist; other logo types are code 2 or 3; several will be shown in photos.

411-G   BEDFORD O SERIES TRUCK   102 mm   #25w_1954-1960
Cast chassis-cab, rear body, black and silver grille and light green hubs, black tires, black sheet metal base and tow hook, black bumper.
1. Light green cab and rear body.

412-G   AUSTIN WAGON   105 mm   #30j_1954-1960
Open truck with cast body, black grille with silver headlights, and hubs, black tires, black sheet metal base and tow hook. Identical to 30j.
1. Maroon body, red hubs.
2. Red body and hubs.
3. Light yellow body, green hubs.
4. Light yellow body, blue hubs.
5. Light medium blue body, yellow hubs.
6. Darker blue body, light blue hubs (413 minus cover).
7. Navy blue body, medium blue hubs.
8. Brown body, tan hubs.

412-H   BEDFORD CF AA VAN   90 mm   1971-1979
Panel van with cast body (=410) and roof sign, Speedwheels with spoked hubs, unpainted sheet metal base, white plastic interior, windows, silver grille, bumper and headlights, red dome light, black-on-yellow "AA Service" labels.
1. Dark yellow body and roof sign.
2. Light yellow body and roof sign.
3. Red body and sign, "Los Angeles County Fire Dept." labels: code two issue by John Gay.

413-G   AUSTIN COVERED WAGON   105 mm   #30s_1954-1960
Covered truck with cast body (=412), black grille with silver headlights, and hubs, black tires, sheet metal rear cover, black base and tow hook.
1. Red body, light gray cover and hubs.
2. Red body and hubs, tan cover.
3. Maroon body, light tan cover, red hubs.
4. Maroon body, cream cover, red hubs.
5. Maroon body, gray cover, red hubs.
6. Yellow body, tan cover, light green hubs.
7. Blue body, light blue cover and hubs.
8. Blue body, cream cover, yellow hubs.

414-G   DODGE REAR TIPPING WAGON   102 mm   #30m_1954-1964
Dump truck with cast chassis-cab, tipper, opening tailgate and hubs, black tires, black sheet metal front base, tipping lever, silver grille, bumper and headlights. Same castings as 30m.
1. Orange chassis-cab, light green tipper and hubs.
2. Light green chassis-cab and hubs, orange tipper?
3. Light blue chassis-cab and hubs, light gray tipper.
4. Light gray cab and hubs, light blue tipper?

415-G   MECHANICAL HORSE AND OPEN TRAILER   102 mm   #33w_1954-1959
Cast cab, trailer and black hubs, black tires, sheet metal hitch matching trailer color, silver grille and light. Identical to 33w.
1. Light blue body, cream trailer.

416-G   FORD TRANSIT MOTORWAY SERVICES VAN   129 mm   1975-1978
Van with cast type 2 body, opening left and rear doors, black base and 5-bolt hubs, black tires, suspension, red dome light, plastic interior, windows, jewel or cast-in headlights, silver grille and bumpers, plastic signs and cones, "Motorway Services" and stripe labels.
1. Light orange body, red interior, jewel headlights.

2. Yellow-orange body, cream interior, cast-in headlights.

417-G   LEYLAND COMET LORRY   144 mm   #531 _931 _1956-1959
Cast chassis-cab, rear body, gray tires, spare wheel, sheet metal rear stake body, black base and tow hook, silver grille bars, bumper and headlights. Identical to earlier versions.
1. Yellow chassis-cab, light green rear body and hubs.
2. Dark blue chassis-cab, yellow-orange rear body, red hubs.

417-H   FORD TRANSIT MOTORWAY SERVICES VAN   129 mm   1978-1980
Van with cast type 3 body, opening doors, brown base, 5-bolt cast hubs, black tires, suspension, red plastic interior and dome light, windows, silver grille, bumpers and headlights, red taillights, plastic signs and cones, labels as on 416.
1. Yellow-orange body.
2. AA logo, code 2 model by John Gay.

418-G   LEYLAND COMET WITH HINGED TAILBOARD   143 mm   #532 _932 _1956-1959
Open truck with cast chassis-cab, rear body, tailgate and Supertoy hubs, gray tires, spare wheel, black sheet metal base, silver grille bars, bumper and headlights.
1. Green chassis-cab, orange rear body and tailgate, light green hubs.
2. Dark blue chassis-cab, light blue rear body and tailgate, cream hubs.

419-G   LEYLAND COMET PORTLAND CEMENT TRUCK   143 mm   #533 _933 _1956-1959
Flat truck with cast chassis-cab, rear body and Supertoy hubs, gray tires, spare wheel, black sheet metal base, silver grille bars, bumpers and headlights, Portland Cement decals on doors, Ferrocrete and other lettering on rear body. Identical to earlier versions.
1. Yellow chassis-cab, rear body and hubs.

420-G   LEYLAND FORWARD CONTROL LORRY   108 mm   #25r_1954-1961
Open truck with cast body and hubs, black tires, black sheet metal front base and tow hook, silver grille, bumper and headlights, +/- 25R cast into bottom of body. With number, identical to 25r.
1. Red body, green hubs, number.
2. Orange body, ? hubs.
3. Light yellow body, light blue hubs, no number.
4. Light green body, light yellow hubs, number.
5. Gray body, ? hubs.
6. White body?

421-G   HINDLE SMART ELECTRIC LORRY   135 mm   #30w_1954-1959
Hindle Smart Helecs with cast cab, semi-trailer and maroon hubs, black tires, black chassis, black sheet metal cab base and trailer hitch, maroon tow hook, "British Railways" decal on cab, silver headlight. Identical to 30w.
1. Maroon cab and trailer.

422-G   FORDSON THAMES FLAT TRUCK   111 mm   #30r_1954-1960
Flat truck with cast body and hubs, black tires, black sheet metal base and tow hook, silver grille bars, bumper and headlights, +/- number 422 on bottom; without number, identical to 30r.
1. Red body and hubs, no number.
2. Red body and hubs, number.
3. Green body, light green hubs, no number.
4. Green body, light green hubs, number.

424-G   COMMER ARTICULATED TRUCK   171 mm   1963-1966
Semi-trailer with cast cab, hitch-fenders and semi-trailer, blue plastic hubs, black tires, spare wheel, black sheet metal cab base and tow hook, white plastic stakes, blue cover, windows, silver grille, bumper and headlights.
1. Light yellow cab, silver semi and hitch-fenders casting.
2. Gray cab, silver semi and hitch-fenders casting.

425-G   BEDFORD TK COAL TRUCK   121 mm   1964-1969
Flat truck with cast cab, rear body and silver chassis, red plastic hubs, black tires, light red plastic roof sign, blue interior, windows, black bumper, silver grille and headlights, red scale, black coal sacks, gold "Hall & Co." decal on roof sign, yellow and green decals on doors.
1. Red cab and rear body.

428-G   LARGE OPEN TRAILER   105 mm   #551 _951 _1956-1971
Open trailer with cast body and front axle mount, cast Supertoy or plain sheet metal hubs, black tires, sheet metal tow hook, wire tow bar. Identical to earlier versions with supertoy hubs.
1. Gray body, black axle mount, red Supertoy hubs (1956-1964).
2. Red body, white axle mount, sheet metal hubs (1968-1971).

429-G   FLAT TRAILER   69 mm   #25g_1954-1963
Cast flat body, front axle mount and hubs, black tires, black sheet metal tow hook, wire hitch, 25G cast on bottom. Identical to last 25g.
1. Red body and hubs.
2. Green body, light green hubs.

430-G   COMMER BREAKDOWN TRUCK   124 mm   #25x_1954-1964
Wrecker with cast chassis-cab and rear body, cast or plastic hubs, black tires, black sheet metal base, sheet metal boom matching rear body color, silver grille, bumper and headlights, crank, line and hook, +/- windows, white, black or blue "Dinky Service" logo. Identical to 25x without windows.
1. Tan chassis-cab, light green rear body, red cast hubs, no windows, white logo.
2. Black logo, otherwise as type 1.
3. Black logo, windows, otherwise as type 1.
4. Black logo, windows, red plastic hubs, otherwise as type 1.
5. Red chassis-cab, light gray rear body, blue cast hubs and logo, no windows.
6. Windows, otherwise as type 5.
7. Windows, blue plastic hubs, otherwise as type 5.

430-H   JOHNSON 2 TON DUMPER   106 mm   1976-1980
Light dumper with cast chassis, tipper and unpainted 8-bolt hubs, black tires, black plastic engine, seat and steering assembly, blue driver, white and black Johnson labels.
1. Yellow chassis, orange tipper.

431-G   GUY OTTER 4 TON LORRY   133 mm   #511 _911 _1956-1958
Open truck with cast chassis-cab with triangular front panels, rear body and Supertoy hubs, black tires, spare wheel, black sheet metal front base, dark blue tow hook, silver grille and headlights. Identical to later 511-911 casting.
1. Dark blue chassis-cab, light green rear body and hubs.

431-H   GUY WARRIOR 4 TON LORRY   136 mm   1958-1964
Cast chassis-cab with low hexagonal grille of horizontal lines, +/- windows, tan tow hook, other details as first 431.
1. Tan chassis-cab, green rear body, light green hubs, no windows.
2. Windows, otherwise as type 1.

432-G   GUY OTTER FLAT TRUCK   133 mm   #512 _912 _1956-1958
Flat truck with cast chassis-cab (=431 Otter), flat rear body and Supertoy hubs, black tires, spare wheel, black sheet metal front base, tow hook matching chassis-cab, silver grille and headlights. Identical to later 512-912.
1. Red chassis-cab, light blue rear body and hubs.
2. Light blue chassis-cab and hubs, red rear body.

432-H   GUY WARRIOR FLAT TRUCK   136 mm   1958-1964
Cast chassis-cab (=431 Warrior), +/- windows, tow hook matching chassis, other details as first 432.
1. Light green cab, red rear body and hubs, no windows.

432-J   FODEN TIPPER TRUCK   174 mm   1976-1979
Dump truck with cast cab, opening doors, tipper and chassis, yellow plastic tailgate, bumper and hubs, black tires, red interior, windows, black gas tank, tow hook,

hydraulic cylinder and stacks.
1. White cab, yellow tipper, red chassis.
2. White cab, yellow tipper, orange chassis.

433-G GUY OTTER FLAT TRUCK WITH TAILBOARD   133 mm
#513 _913 _1956-1958
Cast chassis-cab (= 431-432 Otter), flat rear body with tailboard, and Supertoy hubs, black tires, black sheet metal base, tow hook matching chassis, silver grille and headlights. Identical to later 513-913.
1. Dark blue chassis-cab, orange rear body, light blue hubs.

434-G BEDFORD TK CRASH TRUCK   122 mm 1964-1973
Wrecker with cast cab and rear body, plastic hubs, black or gray tires, red plastic interior, silver grille, bumper and headlights, red taillights, crank, line and hook.
1. White cab and body, green panels with cream "Top Rank Motorway Service" logo, black hubs, gray tires.
2. Black roof, red hubs, otherwise as type 1.
3. Red cab, white rear body, red "Auto Services" logo, ? other details.

435-G BEDFORD TK TIPPER   121 mm 1964-1971
Dump truck with cast cab, tipper and silver chassis, plastic hubs, black tires and hydraulic cylinder, hinged rear side panels matching tipper, cab interior, windows, silver grille, bumper and headlights.
1. Ivory cab, light blue roof and hubs, dark orange tipper, light tan interior (1964-1966).
2. Yellow cab, black roof, yellow tipper, ? hubs, ? interior.
3. Red hubs?

436-G FORD THAMES ATLAS COPCO COMPRESSOR   89 mm
1963-1969
Cast body and compressor housing, turned hubs, black tires, suspension, steering, black sheet metal base with number, dark yellow plastic opening panels of housing, silver compressor, white cab interior, windows, silver grille, bumpers and headlights, red taillights, blue and white Atlas Copco labels.
1. Dark yellow body and housing.

437-G MUIR HILL 2WL LOADER   121 mm 1962-1978
Cast body, chassis, arms and shovel, plastic or cast front hubs, cast rear hubs, black tires, unpainted sheet metal arms, black plastic hydraulic cylinders, driver, windows.
1. Red body, arms, plastic front and cast hubs, silver shovel, chassis and engine, casting with engine hood overhanging nose, nose with diamond and bars but no grille.
2. White shovel, otherwise as type 1.
3. Yellow body and shovel, orange arms, unpainted chassis, engine and cast hubs, new nose casting with grille, no overhang.
4. Yellow arms, otherwise as type 3.
5. Mustard yellow body, black arms, ? other details.

438-G FORD D800 TIPPER TRUCK   132 mm 1970-1977
Dump truck with cast cab, opening doors, tipper, tailgate and chassis, plastic or cast 5-bolt hubs, black tires, cream or white plastic interior, windows, black hydraulic cylinder, silver grille and bumper, jewel or cast-in headlights.
1. Metallic dark red cab, yellow tipper and plastic hubs, silver chassis, jewel headlights, cream interior.
2. Metallic light blue cab, otherwise as type 1.
3. Black chassis?
4. Peach cab, yellow tipper, silver chassis and cast-in headlights, white interior, unpainted cast hubs.
5. Yellow-orange tipper, otherwise as type 4.

439-G FORD D800 SNOW PLOW AND TIPPER   194 mm 1971-1977
Same castings and parts as 438 plus yellow snowplow, black plastic hydraulic cylinder and mount, unpainted sheet metal arms.
1. Metallic dark blue cab, cream interior, orange-tipper, silver chassis, jewel headlights.

---

headlights, white plastic hubs.
2. Cast-in silver headlights, otherwise as type 1.
3. Metallic dark blue cab, pale blue tipper, silver chassis and cast-in headlights, ? interior, ? hubs.
4. Metallic dark blue cab, gray tipper, silver chassis and cast-in headlights, ? interior, ? hubs.

440-G STUDEBAKER MOBILGAS TANKER   11 mm #30p_1954-1961
Tank truck with cast body and hubs, black tires, black sheet metal base, silver filler caps, grille, bumpers and headlights, blue and white Mobilgas decals.
1. Red body, blue-outlined white "Mobilgas" with separate letters.
2. Red body, blue "Mobilgas" on cream parallelogram background.

440-H FORD D800 TIPPER TRUCK   132 mm 1977-1978
Castings and parts as 438 except that cab doors do not open, silver cast-in headlights, white interior, black chassis, unpainted cast 5-bolt hubs, black tires.
1. Peach cab, yellow tipper.
2. Peach cab and tipper.

441-G STUDEBAKER CASTROL TANKER   111 mm #30pa_1954-1960
Same castings and parts as 440, red-on-cream or white Castrol logo decals.
1. Light green body and hubs.

442-G STUDEBAKER ESSO TANKER   111 mm #30pb_1954-1958
Same casting and parts as 440-441, Esso logo decals.
1. Red body and hubs, red-white-dark blue Esso decals.
2. Red body and hubs, red-cream-light blue Esso decals.

442-H LAND ROVER BREAKDOWN CRANE   121 mm 1974-1979
Land Rover with cast body, opening hood and doors, black base-bumper and boom, Speedwheels with 12-spoke chromed hubs, plastic interior, windows, blue roof sign, dome lights, white winch, line and hook, jewel headlights, black grille, unpainted or black tow hook.
1. White body, black interior, red dome lights, white-on-red "Motorway Rescue" labels on sides, white-on-blue "Rescue" on roof sign.
2. White body and interior, amber dome lghts, white-on-red Falck labels on sides and roof sign.
3. Red body, otherwise as type 2.

443-G STUDEBAKER NATIONAL BENZOLE TANKER   111 mm
1957-1958
Same casting and parts as 440-441-442, black "National Benzole Mixture" printed on tank.
1. Yellow body and hubs, orange and black emblem on sides and rear of tank.
2. Emblem only on rear, otherwise as type 1.

448-G CHEVROLET EL CAMINO AND TRAILERS   256 mm 1963-1967
Cast pickup truck body and silver trailer bodies, turned hubs, black tires, pickup has suspension and steering, black sheet metal pickup base with number, red plastic pickup interior and trailer bodies (one open, one closed), windows in pickup, silver grille, bumpers and headlights, red taillights, "Acme Trailer Hire" labels on closed trailer.
1. Pale turquoise upper, ivory lower body of pickup.

449-G CHEVROLET EL CAMINO PICKUP   111 mm 1961-1968
Pickup identical to that of 448, no trailers.
1. Pale turquoise upper, ivory lower body.
2. Cream upper, brown lower body; South African issue.

449-H FORD D800-JOHNSON ROAD SWEEPER   143 mm 1977-1979
Cast cab (doors do not open), tank, chassis, brush housing and unpainted 5-bolt hubs, black tires, white plastic interior, windows, black ducts etc., gray hose, two working brushes turned by spring belt from pulley on rear axle, painted bumper, grille and headlights.
1. Orange-red cab, metallic green tank, silver chassis, white grille, bumper and headlights.
2. Yellow-green cab and tank, black grille and bumper, silver headlights.

---

3. Colors as type 1, Johnston decals; promotional model.

450-G TROJAN 15CWT ESSO VAN   86 mm #31a_1954-1957
Box van with cast body and maroon hubs, black tires, black sheet metal base, silver grille, bumpers and headlights, red-white-blue Esso decal, white stripe. Identical to 31a.
1. Red body.

450-H BEDFORD TK CASTROL VAN   143 mm 1965-1970
Box van with cast cab, rear body and black chassis, red plastic hubs, black tires, white plastic overhead doors, red interior, windows, silver grille, bumpers, headlights and emblem, red taillights, white body panels with red "Castrol", white lettering below panels.
1. Metallic dark green cab and rear body.

451-G TROJAN 15CWT DUNLOP VAN   86 mm #31b_1954-1957
Same castings and parts as 450, black and yellow "Dunlop, the world's master tyre" decals. Identical to 31b.
1. Red body, maroon hubs.

451-H FORD D800 JOHNSTON ROAD SWEEPER   142 mm 1971-1976
Same castings and parts as 449-H but for earlier cab casting with opening doors.
1. Orange-red cab, metallic green tank, silver chassis, white grille, bumper and headlights.

452-G TROJAN 15CWT CHIVERS VAN   86 mm #31c_1954-1957
Same castings and parts as 450-451, yellow-black-red-white "Chivers Jellies" logo decals. Identical to 31c.
1. Green body, light green hubs.

453-G TROJAN 15CWT OXO VAN   86 mm #31d_1954
Same castings and parts as 450-451-452, silver and black "Beefy Oxo" decals. Identical to 31d.
1. Blue body and hubs.

454-G TROJAN 15CWT CYDRAX VAN   86 mm 1957-1959
Same castings and parts as 450-453, white "drink sweet sparkling, yellow and black "Cydrax" and apple design decals.
1. Light green body and hubs.

455-G TROJAN 15CWT BROOKE BOND TEA VAN   86 mm 1957-1961
Same castings and parts as 450-454, white and black "Brooke Bond Tea" decals.
1. Red body and hubs.

465-G MORRIS CAPSTAN VAN   99 mm 1957-1959
Van with cast body and hubs, black tires, black sheet metal base, silver grille, bumpers and headlights, blue "Have a Capstan" and cigarette design decals.
1. Pale blue body, navy blue front and side panels, medium blue hubs.

470-G AUSTIN A40 SHELL VAN   89 mm 1954-1956
Van with cast body and hubs, black tires, black sheet metal base, silver grille, bumpers and headlights, yellow and black Shell and Shell-BP lettering.
1. Light green front body, red rear body and hubs.

471-G AUSTIN A40 NESTLE'S VAN   89 mm 1955-1963
Same casting and parts as 470, gold "Nestle's" lettering.
1. Red body, yellow hubs.

472-G AUSTIN A40 RALEIGH VAN   89 mm 1957-1960
Same casting and parts as 470-471, gold and black "Raleigh Cycles" lettering.
1. Dark green body, yellow hubs.

NO# AUSTIN A40 OMNISPORT VAN   89 mm 1957?
Same casting and parts as 470-472, "Omnisport todo para el deporte" logo. Listed in A2Z as unconfirmed.
1. No other data.

475-G FORD MODEL T (1908)   79 mm 1964-1968
Oldtime car with cast body and chassis, light brown spoked hubs, black tires, brown plastic interior and steering wheel, two figures, gold grille-headlights and windshield frame, clear windshield, yellow and blue panels on body.

1. Blue body, black chassis.

476-G   MORRIS "BULLNOSE" (1913)   92 mm   1965-1970
Oldtime car with cast body, opening trunk and chassis, red spoked hubs, black tires, gray-brown plastic top, gold grille, headlights and windshield frame, clear windshield, red steering wheel and seat, driver, spare wheel.
1. Yellow body, dark blue chassis.

477-G   PARSLEY'S CAR   92 mm   1971-1972
Cast body and chassis (=476), black plastic opening trunk, yellow folded top, two-piece figure with swiveling head, other parts as 476.
1. Lime green body, black chassis.

480-G   BEDFORD CA KODAK VAN   83 mm   1954-1956
Van with cast body, black tires, black sheet metal base, silver grille, bumper and headlights, red and black "Kodak Cameras and Films" logo.
1. Yellow-orange body, red hubs.

481-G   BEDFORD CA OVALTINE VAN   83 mm   1955-1959
Same casting and parts as 480, "Ovaltine & Ovaltine Biscuits" logo.
1. Light blue body and hubs.

482-G   BEDFORD CA DINKY TOYS VAN   83 mm   1956-1958
Same casting and parts as 480 and 481, red "Dinky Toys" lettering.
1. Orange lower body and bumper, yellow upper body, hubs and grille.

485-G   SANTA SPECIAL MODEL T FORD   79 mm   1964-1968
Cast body and chassis (=475), yellow hubs and interior, Santa and tree figures, bag of gifts, Christmas design decals, otherwise as 475.
1. White body, red chassis.

486-G   DINKY BEATS MORRIS "BULLNOSE"   92 mm   1965-1969
Cast body, opening trunk and chassis (=476), red interior, yellow folded top, red hubs, three rock musician figures, various decals, otherwise as 476.
1. Pink body, turquoise wheels.

**490-G   ELECTRIC DAIRY VAN: EXPRESS DAIRY   86 mm
#30v_1954-1956**
Cast body, chassis and hubs, black tires, "Express Dairy" logo and silver light on nose. Identical to Express Dairy 30v.
1. Cream body, red chassis, hubs and logo.
2. Light gray body, light blue chassis and hubs, blue logo.

491-G   ELECTRIC DAIRY VAN: NCB   86 mm   #30v_1954-1960
Castings and parts as 490, NCB logo and silver light on nose. Identical to NCB 30v.
1. Cream body, red chassis, hubs and logo.
2. Light gray body, light blue chassis and hubs, blue logo.

492-G   LOUDSPEAKER VAN   83 mm   #34c_1954-1957
Cast body (= last type 28-280 vans), silver loudspeaker and light blue hubs, silver grille and bumper. Identical to 34c.
1. Dark blue body. (See 34c for other colors.)

492-H   ELECTION MINI-VAN   78 mm   1964-1966
Minivan with cast body, opening rear doors and black base, turned hubs, black tires, suspension, steering, red plastic interior, windws, gray equipment in rear, orange roof rack with loudspeakers and signboards, silver grille, bumpers and headlights, red taillights, green "Vote for Somebody" on white background.
1. White body.

500-E   CITROEN 2CV   89 mm   1974-1978
Updated French 500 casting, originally with round, later with rectangular headlights, other details as 500-H. Made in Spain.
1. Light gray body, round headlights (1974-1975).
2. Orange body, rectangular headlights (1976-1978).

500-F   TOURING CAR GIFT SET   1959
Boxed set of 24b-521 Peugeot 403, 24c-522 Citroen DS19, 24d-523 Plymouth Belvedere, 24e-524 Renault Dauphine and 24z-541 Simca Versailles.
1. Standard colors.

500-H   CITROEN 2CV 1966   89 mm   1967-1971
Car with cast body, opening hood and black base with number, gray turned hubs, black tires, suspension, plastic top partly open, interior, windows, jewel headlights, silver engine, grille and bumpers.
1. Light gray body, dark gray roof, red interior.
2. Dark blue body, blue roof, cream interior.

500   CITROEN 2CV, 1981: Solido-Dinky Cougar model.   See #1401.

501-F   AIRPLANE GIFT SET   1959-1962
Boxed set of 800 Mystere, 801 Vautour, 802 Sikorsky Helicopter and 803 Vickers Viscount.
1. Standard colors.

501-H   CITROEN DS19 POLICE CAR   112 mm   1967-1970
Cast body and black chassis with number 530, turned hubs, black tires, suspension, steering, gray plastic interior, windows, amber dome light, jewel headlights, silver bumpers, red taillights, white Police decals.
1. White roof and fenders, black-maroon body, black doors.

501   FIAT RITMO, 1981: Solido-Dinky Cougar model.   See 1403.

502-F   GARAGE   1959-1966
Plastic one-car garage. Also sold in England.
1. Light yellow.
2. Light blue.
3. Light gray (only in England).

502   BMW 530, 1981: Solido-Dinky Cougar model.   See 1404.

503-F   TOURING CAR GIFT SET   1963-1964
Boxed set of 521 Peugeot 403, 522 Citroen DS19, 543 Renault Floride, 544 Simca P60 and 545 De Soto Diplomat.
1. Standard colors.

503-H   PORSCHE CARRERA SIX   97 mm   1967-1971
Sports coupe with cast front body, front hood, opening rear body, and base with number, patterned hubs, black tires, plastic gullwing doors, black interior, clear windows and headlights, chrome engine, silver mirrors, black "Carrera 6" labels.
1. White front and rear body and doors, red front hood and base.

503   ALFA ROMEO GTV, 1981: Solido-Dinky Cougar model.   See 1405.

504   CITROEN VISA, 1981: Solido-Dinky Cougar model.   See 1402.

505-F   MASERATI 2000 SPORT   88 mm   #22a_1959-1961
Sports-racing car with cast body and white driver and steering wheel, turned hubs, black tires, black sheet metal base with number 22A, windshield, silver grille and headlights, orange taillights. Identical to 22a.
1. Red body.

505   PEUGEOT 504, 1981: Solido-Dinky Cougar model.   See 1406.

506-F   ASTON MARTIN DB3S   87 mm   1960-1961
Cast body (= 110), white driver and steering wheel, turned hubs, black tires, black sheet metal base with number, silver grille and headlights, red taillights, black racing number on white disc decal (12 through 17).
1. Green body.

506-H   FERRARI 275GTB   100 mm   1967-1972
GT car with cast body, opening hood, trunk and doors, and black base with number, spoked hubs, black tires, suspension, steering, black plastic interior, clear windows and headlights, chrome engine, bumpers and exhaust pipes, silver grille, jewel taillights.
1. Red body.
2. Orange-red body.
3. Yellow body.

506   ALFA ROMEO ALFASUD: exists only as Solido model, not as Dinky.

507-F   SIMCA 1500 BREAK   99 mm   1967-1971
Station wagon with cast body, opening doors and tailgate, and black base with number, turned hubs, black tires, suspension, red plastic interior, windows (rear window lowers), jewel headlights, silver grille and bumpers, red taillights.
1. White body.
2. Metallic medium gray body.
3. Metallic charcoal gray body.

507p-F   SIMCA 1500 POLICE   99 mm   1967?
Details as 507 plus dome light, antenna and Police decals. Few made.
1. White and blue-black body.

507   RENAULT 14: exists only as Solido model, not Dinky.

508-F   DAF   86 mm   1966-1971
Sedan with cast body, opening doors and black base, turned hubs, black tires, suspension, red plastic interior, windows, jewel headlights, silver bumpers and grille, red taillights.
1. Metallic light brown body.
2. Garnet red body.
3. Metallic dark gold body.

508   FORD FIESTA: exists only as Solido model, not Dinky.

509-F   FIAT 850   82 mm   1966-1971
Car with cast body, opening doors and black base, turned hubs, black tires, suspension, red plastic interior, windows, jewel head- and taillights, silver bumpers.
1. Yellow body.
2. Red body.
3. White body.

510-E   PEUGEOT 204 SEDAN   91 mm   1977-1979
Same castings and parts as French issue, silver engine, red interior and taillights, no suspension or steering.
1. Ivory body.
2. Reddish tan body.
3. White body.

510-F   TALBOT-LAGO RACING CAR   83 mm   #23h_1959-1960?
Grand Prix car with cast body and silver hubs, black tires, black sheet metal base with number 23H, silver grille and exhaust pipe, white driver, yellow number 5. Noticeably smaller than 230.
1. Blue body.

510-H   PEUGEOT 204 SEDAN   91 mm   1965-1971
Sedan with cast body, opening hood, and black base with number, turned hubs, black tires, suspension, steering, cream plastic interior, clear windows and headlights, black engine, silver grille and bumpers, taillights not painted separately.
1. Metallic maroon body, cream interior.

511-F   FERRARI RACING CAR   102 mm   #23j_1959-1963
Cast body (+/- patterned grille) and chromed hubs, black tires, black sheet metal base with number 23j, black grille opening, white driver, yellow racing number.
1. Red body, plain grille, number 1.
2. Red body, patterned grille, number 4.

511-H   PEUGEOT 204 CABRIOLET   87 mm   1968-1971
Convertible with cast body, opening hood and doors, and black base with number, turned hubs, black tires, suspension, black plastic interior and engine, windshield, silver bumpers, grille and headlights, silver bumpers.
1. Light blue body.
2. Red body.

512-F   LESKO KART   34 mm   1962-1966
Go-kart with cast body, plastic driver (red, yellow or light blue), black plastic wheels, wire steering wheel.
1. Blue body, silver engine.

513-F   OPEL ADMIRAL   114 mm   1966-1969
Sedan with cast body, opening hood and trunk, and black base with number, turned hubs, black tires, suspension, steering, cream plastic interior, windows, blue engine, silver grille, bumpers and headlights, orange taillights.
1. Metallic maroon body.

2. Metallic blue body.

Note: an Opel Diplomat prototype model was made using this model but was not put into production.

514-F ALFA ROMEO GIULIA TI   97 mm 1966-1971
Sports car with cast body and black base with number, turned hubs, black tires, suspension, steering, red plastic interior, windows, silver grille and bumpers, jewel headlights, red taillights.
1. Pale greenish-white body.
2. White body.
3. Pale silver gray body.
4. Pale tan body.
5. Metallic dark gray body (issued in Spain, 1968).

515-F FERRARI 250GT   109 mm 1963-1970
Sports coupe with cast body, opening hood and trunk, unpainted engine and silver base-bumpers with number, turned hubs, black tires, suspension, steering, cream plastic interior, clear windows and headlights, silver and red taillights.
1. Red body.
2. Metallic blue body.

516-F MERCEDES-BENZ 230SL   100 mm 1964-1970
Hardtop with cast body, opening hood, and silver base-bumpers with number, turned hubs, black tires, suspension, cream plastic top and interior, clear windows and headlights, green engine, red and silver taillights.
1. Metallic maroon body.
2. Metallic olive body.
3. Red body (sold in England, 1965-1966).

517-F RENAULT R8   94 mm 1962-1970
Sedan with cast body, turned hubs, black tires, suspension, steering, black sheet metal base with number, red plastic interior, windows, silver bumpers and headlights, red taillights.
1. Light yellow body.
2. Light blue body.
3. Blue body (made in Spain).
4. Cream body (made in Spain).

(517p RENAULT 8 POLICE CAR never issued)

518-E RENAULT 4L 1970   84 mm 1974-1978
Cast body with long grille including headlights, turned hubs, black tires, suspension?, black plastic base, tan interior, windows, silver grille, bumpers and headlights, red taillights. Modified French model made in Spain.
1. Dark blue body.
2. Light blue body.

518-F RENAULT 4L   84 mm 1962-1970
Cast body, turned hubs, black tires, suspension, steering, black sheet metal base with number, cream plastic interior, windows, silver grille, bumpers and headlights, silver and red taillights.
1. Brick red body.
2. Light blue body.
3. Light blue-gray body.
4. Dark maroon body.
5. Red body, Pompiers decals. Very few made.

518a-F RENAULT 4L AUTOROUTE SERVICE   84 mm 1970-1971
Same castings and parts as 518, gray interior, silver trim.
1. Yellow-orange body, Autoroute Service logo.

518p-F RENAULT 4L MAIL CAR   84 mm 1970-1971
Casting and details as 518a.
1. Yellow-orange body, blue postal emblem decals.

(519 FACEL VEGA FACELLIA (1961-62) never issued)

519-F SIMCA 1000   88 mm 1963-1971
Sedan with cast body, turned hubs, black tires, suspension, steering, black sheet metal base with number, cream plastic silver bumpers and headlights, +/- red taillights.
1. Dark red body including taillights.
2. Yellow body (small series).
3. Light blue body, red taillights.
4. Metallic silver gray body (small series).
5. Metallic dark blue body, white interior (made in Spain).
6. Turquoise body, red interior (made in South Africa).
7. Garnet red body, white interior (made in South Africa).

520-F CHRYSLER NEW YORKER   #24a_1959-1961
Convertible with cast body, cream steering wheel and chromed hubs, white tires, black sheet metal base with number 24A, plastic interior and windshield, silver grille, bumpers, headlights and trim, +/- red taillights. Identical to 24a.
1. Dark red body, ivory interior.
2. Yellow body, light green interior.
3. Metallic silver blue body, ivory interior.

520-H FIAT 600D   78 mm 1963-1970
Minicar with cast body, turned hubs, black tires, suspension, steering, black sheet metal base with number, red plastic interior, windows, silver bumper and headlights, red taillights. Also made in Spain.
1. Cream body (French or Spanish).
2. Red body, ? other details (French).

521-F PEUGEOT 403 SEDAN   104 mm #24b_1959-1961
Sedan with cast body, turned hubs, white tires, black sheet metal base with number 24B, windows, silver grille, bumpers and headlights, red taillights.
1. Pale yellow body.
2. Light gray body.

522-F CITROEN DS19   112 mm #24c_1959-1968
Sedan with cast body and chromed hubs, white tires, black sheet metal base with number 24C, windows, silver grille, bumpers and headlights, red taillights. Same castings and parts as 24c.
1. Dark orange body, cream roof.
2. Bright yellow body, blue-gray roof.

523-F PLYMOUTH BELVEDERE   110 mm #24d_1959-1961
Sedan with cast body and chromed hubs, white tires, black sheet metal base with number 24D, silver grille, bumpers, headlights and trim, red taillights, no windows. Identical to 24d.
1. Gray body, orange-red roof and lower sides.
2. Green body, black roof and lower sides.
3. Pale brownish-gray body, brown roof and lower sides.

523-H SIMCA 1500 SEDAN   99 mm 1963-1969
Sedan with cast body and opening trunk, turned hubs, black tires, suspension, steering, black sheet metal base with number, red plastic interior, windows, jewel head- and taillights, silver grille and bumper.
1. Light blue body.
2. Dark blue body.
3. Metallic gray body (two shades exist).

(523 SIMCA P60 DRIVING SCHOOL CAR (1962) never issued)

524-F RENAULT DAUPHINE   92 mm #24e_1959-1962
Sedan with cast body, turned hubs, black tires, black sheet metal base, silver bumpers, vents and headlights, red or orange taillights, windows. Identical to last 24e.
1. Red body, orange taillights.
2. Ivory body, red taillights.
3. Brick red body, orange taillights.
4. Turquoise body, red taillights.

524-H PANHARD 24CT COUPE   100 mm 1964-1969
Coupe with cast body, turned hubs, black tires, suspension, steering, black sheet metal

base with number, red plastic interior, clear windows (door windows lower) and headlights, silver bumpers, red taillights.
1. Metallic charcoal gray body.
2. Pale green body.

525-F PEUGEOT 403 U FAMILIALE   107 mm #24f_1959-1962
Station wagon with cast body, turned hubs, black tires, black sheet metal base with number 24F, silver grille, bumpers and headlights, red taillights, no windows. Identical to 24f.
1. Light blue body.

525-H PEUGEOT 404 BREAK   106 mm 1964-1970
Station wagon with cast body and opening hatch, turned hubs, black tires, suspension, steering, black sheet metal base with number, red plastic interior, windows, jewel headlights, silver grille and bumpers, red taillights.
1. Cream body.
2. Navy blue body.
3. Red body (fire department car, few made, 1964).

526-F MERCEDES-BENZ 190SL COUPE   98 mm #24h_1959-1963
Sports coupe with cast body, turned hubs, black or white tires, black sheet metal base with number 24H, windows, silver grille, and headlights, red taillights. Identical to last 24h.
1. Cream body, black roof.
2. Silver body, black roof.

527-F ALFA ROMEO 1900 COUPE   102 mm #24j_1959-1963
Sports coupe with cast body, turned hubs, black tires, black sheet metal base with number 24J, windows, silver grille, bumpers and headlights, red or orange taillights. Identical to 24j.
1. Red body.
2. Blue body.

528-F SIMCA VEDETTE CHAMBORD   110 mm #24k_1959-1961
Sedan with cast body, cast chromed or turned hubs, white tires, black sheet metal base with number 24K, windows, silver grille, bumpers and headlights, red taillights. Roof color also on lower sides and fin panels. Identical to 24k.
1. Cream body, red sides and roof, cast hubs.
2. Cream body, red sides and roof, turned hubs.
3. Light green body, dark green sides and roof, cast hubs.
4. Light green body, dark green sides and roof, turned hubs.

528-H PEUGEOT 404 CABRIOLET   104 mm 1966-1971
Convertible with cast body, opening hood and doors, and black base-bumpers with number, turned hubs, black tires, suspension, red plastic seats, windshield, woman driver, black folded top, green engine, jewel headlights, silver grille and bumpers, red taillights.
1. White body.
2. Light tan body.
3. Metallic blue body.

529-F VESPA 2CV   66 mm #24l_1959-1963
Minicar with cast body and chromed hubs, black tires, black sheet metal base with number 24L, windows, silver grille, bumpers and headlights, red taillights. Identical to 24l.
1. Blue body, gray roof panel.
2. Orange body, gray roof panel.

530-E CITROEN DS23   112 mm 1976-1978
Modified French #530 DS19 with narrower hood, bigger clear plastic headlights, silver engine, "DS23" and "Made in Spain" on base.
1. Metallic maroon body, black roof.

530-F VOLKSWAGEN KARMANN-GHIA   95 mm #24m_1959-1962
Coupe with cast body (two casting types), turned hubs, white tires, black sheet metal base, windows, silver bumpers and headlights.

The New System of Catalog Numbers

1. Red body, black roof, casting with wide blunt nose.
2. Red body, black roof, casting with narrow sharp nose.
3. Orange-red body, black roof, casting with narrow sharp nose.

530-H   CITROEN DS19 1963   112 mm   1964-1970
Sedan with cast body, opening hood and trunk, and black base with number, turned hubs, black tires, suspension, steering, spare wheel, cream plastic interior, windows, green engine, jewel headlights, silver bumpers, red taillights. Also sold in Spain and England.
1. Maroon body, cream roof.
2. Pale olive green body, white or light gray roof.

531-F   FIAT 1200 GRANDE VUE   91 mm   1959-1962
Sedan with cast body, cast chromed or turned hubs, black or white hubs, black base with number, windows, silver grille, bumpers and headlights, red taillights.
1. Cream body, metallic silver blue roof, cast hubs.
2. Cream body, metallic silver blue roof, turned hubs.
3. Metallic brown body, cream roof, cast hubs.
4. Metallic brown body, cream roof, turned hubs.

532-F   LINCOLN PREMIERE   117 mm   1959-1965
Limousine with cast body, cast chromed or turned hubs, white tires, black sheet metal base with number, windows, silver grille, bumpers and headlights, red taillights.
1. Pale blue body, silver roof, cast hubs.
2. Pale blue body, silver roof, turned hubs.
3. Medium blue body, silver roof, turned hubs.
4. Metallic lime green body, dark green roof, cast hubs.
5. Metallic lime green body, dark green roof, turned hubs.
6. Metallic gray body, garnet red roof, ? hubs.

533-F   PEUGEOT 203   100 mm   #24r_1959
Sedan with cast body and chromed hubs, white tires, black sheet metal base, no number, silver grille, bumpers and headlights, large rear window. Identical to later type 24r.
1. Dull blue body.
2. Light gray body.

533-H   MERCEDES-BENZ 300SE   116 mm   1963-1970
Sedan with cast body, turned hubs, black tires, suspension, steering, black sheet metal base with number, cream plastic interior, windows, silver grille, bumpers and headlights, red taillights.
1. Metallic blue body.
2. Metallic dark red body, orange taillights?
3. Metallic orange body.

534-F   SIMCA 8 SPORTS   95 mm   #24s_1959
Roadster with cast open body, cream steering wheel and chromed hubs, black or white tires, black sheet metal base, no number, red painted interior, silver grille, bumpers and lights, thick top bar of windshield frame (straight rear edge). Identical to later type 24s.
1. Bluish ivory body.
2. Black body.

534-H   BMW 1500   105 mm   1963-1968
Car with cast body, turned hubs, black tires, suspension, steering, black sheet metal base with number, white plastic interior, silver grille, bumpers and lights.
1. Red body.
2. Lime green body.

535-F   CITROEN 2CV   88 mm   #24t_1959-1963
Small car with cast body, cast or turned hubs, black tires, black sheet metal base, no number, silver grille, headlights and sometimes bumpers, three red or orange taillights. Identical to later type 24t.
1. Maroon body, dark gray roof panel, cream cast hubs, silver bumpers, orange taillights.
2. Maroon bumpers, pale blue-gray turned hubs, otherwise as type 1.

3. Light gray body, dark gray roof panel, cream cast hubs, silver bumpers, red taillights.
4. Dull blue body and bumpers, dark blue roof panel, pale blue-gray turned hubs, red taillights.

540-F   STUDEBAKER COMMANDER   109 mm   #24y_1959-1961
Coupe with cast body and chromed hubs, white tires, black sheet metal base with number 24Y, silver grille, bumpers and headlights, red taillights. Identical to 24y.
1. Ivory body, garnet red roof and side panels.
2. Dark orange body, cream roof and side panels.

540-H   OPEL KADETT   92 mm   1963-1970
Sedan with cast body, turned hubs, black tires, suspension, steering, black sheet metal base with number, cream plastic interior, windows, silver stripes, grille, bumpers and headlights.
1. Red body.
2. Light green body.
3. Light blue body.

541-F   SIMCA VERSAILLES   105 mm   #24z_1959-1960
Identical to 24z, not sold individually but included in a gift set. See 24z for details.

541-H   MERCEDES-BENZ COACH   112 mm   1963-1971
Light bus with cast body, turned hubs, black tires, suspension, black sheet metal base with number, gray plastic interior, windows, silver grille, bumpers, headlights and trim.
1. Dark red lower body, light cream upper body.

542-F   SIMCA ARIANE TAXI   105 mm   #24zt_1959-1962
Taxi with cast body (=24z), unpainted meter with red flag, white Taxi sign with red letters, cast or turned hubs, white tires, black sheet metal base with number 24ZT, windows, silver grille, bumpers and headlights, red taillights. Identical to 24zt.
1. Black body, red roof.

542-H   OPEL REKORD   105 mm   1964-1969
Sedan with cast body and opening doors, turned hubs, black tires, suspension, black sheet metal base with number, red plastic interior, windows, jewel headlights, silver grille and bumpers, red taillights.
1. Metallic silver tan body.
2. Metallic light blue body.

543-F   RENAULT FLORIDE   97 mm   1960-1963
Coupe with cast body, turned hubs, white tires, black sheet metal base with number, windows, silver bumpers, rear grille and headlights, red taillights.
1. Metallic silver green body.
2. Metallic gold body.
3. Metallic light green-gold body.
4. White body (pre-production or small series?).

544-F   SIMCA P60 ARONDE   98 mm   1959-1963
Sedan with cast body, cast chromed or turned hubs, white tires, black sheet metal base with number, windows, silver trim, grille, bumpers and headlights, red taillights.
1. Maroon body, cream roof, cast hubs.
2. Maroon body, cream roof, turned hubs.
3. Light gray body, dusty blue roof, cast hubs.
4. Light gray body, dusty blue roof, turned hubs.
5. Cream body, red roof, ? hubs.

545-F   DE SOTO DIPLOMAT   113 mm   1960-1963
Sedan with cast body, turned hubs, white tires, suspension, black sheet metal base with number, windows, silver trim, grille, bumpers and red and silver taillights.
1. Orange body, black roof.
2. Metallic dark green body, cream roof.
3. White and blue?

546-F   AUSTIN-HEALEY 100   89 mm   1960-1961
Cast body (=103), cream steering wheel, and driver in blue, turned hubs, black tires,

black sheet metal base with number, windshield, silver grille, bumpers and headlights, black taillights.
1. White body, red interior.

546-H   OPEL REKORD TAXI   104 mm   1963-1967
Taxi with cast body (=554), turned hubs, white tires, suspension, steering, black sheet metal base with number 554, red plastic interior, black Taxi sign with yellow lettering, windows, silver trim, grille, bumpers and headlights, red taillights.
1. Black body.

547-F   PANHARD PL17   107 mm   1960-1968
Sedan with cast body, turned hubs, black tires, suspension, steering, black sheet metal base with number, cream plastic interior, windows, silver trim, bumpers and headlights, red silver taillights. Casting with front door handles at front of doors:
1. Brick red body.
2. Pale grayish lilac body. Casting with front door handles at rear of doors:
3. Dark orange body.
4. Pale grayish lilac body. Casting with body updated, same as Junior #102:
5. Brick red body.
6. Pale blue body.
7. Pale grayish lilac body.

548-F   FIAT 1800 FAMILIALE   105 mm   1960-1963
Station wagon with cast body, turned hubs, white tires, suspension, steering, black sheet metal base with number, red plastic interior, windows, silver trim, grille, bumpers and headlights, red taillights.
1. Light yellow body, brown roof.
2. Light yellow body, black roof.
3. Light yellow body, dark green roof.
4. Pale blue-gray body, dark blue roof.
5. Pale blue-gray body, purplish-blue roof.
6. Pale blue-gray body, black roof.
7. Pale lilac body, black roof. Soutrh African reissue (1966):
8. Tan and yellow.
9. Dark blue and black.
10. Ivory body.
11. Green body.

549-F   BORGWARD ISABELLA TS   102 mm   1961-1965
Sports coupe with cast body, turned hubs, black tires, suspension, steering, black sheet metal base with number, red plastic interior, windows, silver trim, grille, bumpers and headlights, silver and red taillights.
1. Turquoise body.
2. Metallic silver gray body.

550-F   CHRYSLER SARATOGA   129 mm   1961-1966
Sedan with cast body, turned hubs, white tires, suspension, steering, black sheet metal base with number, red plastic interior, windows, silver grille, bumpers and headlights, red taillights.
1. Pale pink body with white trim (also sold in England).
2. Bright pink body, white trim.
3. Pale lilac body, black trim.

551-F   ROLLS-ROYCE SILVER WRAITH   116 mm   1959-1961
Limousine with cast body (=150), turned hubs, black tires, suspension, black sheet metal base with number, windows, chromed plastic grille, bumpers and headlights, red taillights.
1. Light gray upper, dark gray lower body.

551-H   FORD TAUNUS 17M POLIZEI   104 mm   1963?-1967
Cast body (=559), turned hubs, black tires, suspension, steering, black sheet metal base with number 559, gray plastic interior, windows, blue dome light, silver grille, bumpers and headlights, red taillights, yellow Polizei decals.
1. Dark green body, white fenders.

The New System of Catalog Numbers

552-F CHEVROLET CORVAIR   106 mm   1961-1967
Sedan with cast body, turned hubs, white tires, suspension, steering, black sheet metal base with number, cream interior, windows, silver trim, bumpers and headlights, red taillights.
1. Red body.
2. Light blue body.
3. Light blue-gray body. South African issues:
4. Metallic silver gray body.
5. Dark gray body.
6. Gray-green body.

553-F PEUGEOT 404   103 mm   1961-1967
Sedan with cast body, turned hubs, black tires, suspension, steering, black sheet metal base with number, red plastic interior, windows, silver trim, grille, bumpers and headlights, red taillights.
1. Pale yellow-ivory body, "404" cast on nose with round zero.
2. Pale yellow-ivory body, "404" with low wide zero.
3. Pale gray-green body, "404" with low wide zero.
4. White body, green interior, low wide zero? South African issues:
5. Off-white body.
6. Gray-green body.
7. Metallic charcoal gray body.

554-F OPEL REKORD   105 mm   1961-1966
Sedan with cast body, turned hubs, white tires, suspension, steering, black sheet metal base with number, pale blue plastic interior, windows, silver trim, grille, bumpers and headlights, red taillights.
1. Tannish yellow body, cream roof.
2. Light brown body, cream roof.
3. Turquoise body, cream roof. South African issues:
4. Metallic dark green body.
5. Light blue body.
6. Bright blue body.

555-F FORD THUNDERBIRD   122 mm   1961-1969
Convertible with cast body, turned hubs, white tires, suspension, steering, black sheet metal base with number, driver (two types: smaller with blue coat, black hair; larger with gray coat, brown hair), silver trim, grille, bumpers and headlights, red and silver taillights.
1. Maroon body, mustard yellow interior.
2. Maroon body, pale blue interior.
3. White body, red interior. South African issues:
4. Cream body, red interior.
5. Bright blue body, red interior.
6. Metallic blue body, red interior.

556-F CITROEN ID19 AMBULANCE   116 mm   1962-1970
Modified 539 station wagon with cast body and opening tailgate, turned hubs, black tires, suspension, steering, black sheet metal base with number, cream plastic interior and opening hatch, windshield, driver (two types: gray plastic interior includes gray stretcher, silver bumpers and headlights, red and silver taillights, blue "Ambulance Municipale" decals.
1. Light gray body, two words on logo decal equally long.
2. Light gray body, "Ambulance" slightly longer than "Municipale".

557-F CITROEN AMI-6   92 mm   1962-1970
Sedan with cast body and opening hood and trunk, turned hubs, black tires, suspension, steering, spare tire or detailed silver engine, black sheet metal base with number, red plastic interior, windows, wire front guard, silver grille, bumpers and headlights, red taillights.
1. Yellow-green body, white roof, spare tire.
2. Yellow-green body, white roof, engine.

3. Light blue body, white roof, spare tire.
4. Light blue body, white roof, engine.
5. Brighter blue body, white roof, engine.

558-F CITROEN 2CV 1961   88 mm   1962-1970
Minicar with cast body, gray turned hubs, black tires, suspension, black sheet metal base with number, red plastic interior, windows, silver grille, bumpers and headlights, red taillights.
1. Light yellow body, dark tan roof.
2. Light tan body, dark tan roof.
3. Light olive green body, dark green roof.

559-F FORD TAUNUS 17M   104 mm   1962-1969
Sedan with cast body, turned hubs, white tires, suspension, steering, black sheet metal base with number, red plastic interior, windows, silver grille, bumpers and headlights, red and silver taillights.
1. Ivory body.
2. Metallic gold body.

560-F PEUGEOT D3A VAN   90 mm #25bv 1959-1962
Van with cast body, cast or turned hubs, black tires, black sheet metal base with number 25B, silver grille, bumper and headlights, one red taillight, tampo-print or decal logo.
1. Dark green body, turned hubs, yellow "Postes" decals.
2. Turquoise body, "Cibie/" decals as on 561, ? other details (prototype or small series).
3. Gray body, no logo, ? hubs.

560-H CITROEN 2CV MAIL VAN   84 mm   1963-1970
Light box van with cast body and opening rear door, yellow turned hubs, black tires, black sheet metal base, no number, silver grille, bumper and headlights, light or dark blue decals on doors.
1. Dark yellow body, light blue decals.
2. Dark yellow body, dark blue decals.
3. Yellow and white body, "Philips" decals (small series).

561-F CITROEN 1200KG VAN   90 mm #25c 1959-1966
Van with cast body and sliding door, cast or turned hubs, black tires, black sheet metal base, with number 25C, silver grille, bumper and headlights, logo decals.
1. Ceam body and cast hubs, blue-cream-green Ch. Gervais decals (1959).
2. Dark turquoise body, yellow turned hubs, red-yellow-black "Cibie" decals (1960-1963).
3. White upper body, light blue lower body and turned hubs, blue and red "Glaces Gervais" decals (1963-1966).
4. Dark blue body, unpainted turned hubs, cream "Baroclem" decals (1964).

561-H RENAULT 4L MAIL CAR 84 mm 1968-1972 Van with cast body (=518), turned hubs, black tires, black sheet metal or plastic base, red interior, windows, silver grille, bumpers and headlights, red taillights, blue decals.
1. Yellow-orange body, sheet metal base (=518p).
2. Yellow-orange body, plastic base.

562-F CITROEN 2CV FIRE VAN   84 mm #25d 1959-1963
Cast body and opening rear door (=560-H), cast or turned red hubs, black tires, black sheet metal base with number 25D, silver grille, bumper and headlights, coat of arms decals on doors. Identical to 25d.
1. Red body and cast hubs.
2. Red body and turned hubs.

562h-F CITROEN 2CV WEGENWACHT VAN   84 mm   1965-1968
Same castings and parts as 562, unpainted turned hubs, black Wegenwacht decals on doors. Made for sale in The Netherlands.
1. Yellow body.

563-F RENAULT ESTAFETTE PICK-UP   96 mm   1960-1962
Covered pickup with cast body, gray turned hubs, black tires, spare wheel, black sheet

metal front base with number, green plastic rear cover, windows, light gray grille, bumpers and headlights, red taillights.
1. Orange body, green removable cover.

564-F RENAULT ESTAFETTE GLASS TRUCK   96 mm   1963-1965
Same castings and parts as 563, "563" and "pick up" on base, turned hubs match body color, taillights not painted separately, no rear cover, brown plastic rack with gold "Miroitier" lettering, glass and mirror on rack.
1. Orange-red body and hubs.

564-H CARAVELAIR ARMAGNAC 420 CARAVAN 130 mm 1969-1971
Trailer with cast body, turned hubs, black tires, cream plastic roof and hitch, tan interior-chassis with axle holders and number, windows.
1. White body with light blue lower side panels.

565-F RENAULT ESTAFETTE CAMPER   96 mm   1965-1971
Cast body, turned hubs, black tires, black sheet metal base with number, light blue plastic right and rear doors and hatch, cream plastic roof and rear interior, red front interior, windows, jewel headlights, silver grille and bumpers, red taillights, red and green flower pattern on rear seat.
1. Light blue body and doors.

566-F CITROEN 1200KG POLICE VAN   117 mm   1965-1970
Van with cast body, blue turned hubs, black tires, plastic sliding doors, clear and barred windows, battery-powered amber dome light, black plastic base with number and battery mount, red Police sign, white Police lettering, silver grille and headlights, red taillights.
1. Blue-black body, white roof and lower body panels.

567-F MERCEDES-BENZ UNIMOG WITH SNOWPLOW   145 mm 1967-1970
Truck with cast body, plow, hitch, yellow steering wheel, yellow turned hubs, black tires, spare tire, black sheet metal plow arms and front base, yellow windshield frame, dark brown plastic removable rear cover, black hydraulic cylinder.
1. Yellow body and attachment, yellow and black plow.

568-F BERLIET LADDER TRUCK   201 mm   1968-1970
Fire ladder truck with cast front and rear body, two-piece red ladder mount and red Supertoy hubs, black tires, black plastic base, gray interior, windows, unpainted two-piece extending ladder, two cranks, silver headlights and steps.
1. Red body, silver rear deck.

569-F BERLIET STRADAIR DUMP TRUCK   175 mm   1967-1971
Dumper with cast cab, opening hood, rear body, four opening side panels, dark green chassis and Supertoy hubs, black tires, red plastic cab interior, black engine and rear body frame (body tips to side on frame), clear windows and headlights, silver grille, red taillights, tipping lever.
1. Pale aqua green cab and rear body.

570-F PANHARD PARIS BUS   143 mm #29d 1959
Singledeck bus with cast body and hubs, black tires, black sheet metal base, silver trim, grid cast under roof. Identical to 29d.
1. Cream upper, dark green lower body.

570-H PEUGEOT J7 VAN   108 mm   1967-1971
Van with cast body, sliding and opening doors, and black base with number, turned hubs, black tires, plastic roof, windows, gray interior, black antenna, jewel headlights, silver grille, red taillights, red and black "Allo Fret" logo on white-background labels.
1. Dark blue body and roof.
2. Dark blue body, white roof.

570a-F PEUGEOT J7 AUTOROUTE SERVICE VAN 112 mm 1970-1971
Castings and parts as 570, ? other details.
1. Orange body.

570p-F PEUGEOT J7 FIRE VAN   108 mm   1972
Casting and parts as 570, amber dome light, red hubs, coat of arms on door.
1. Red body, without "Meccano" on base.

The New System of Catalog Numbers

2. Red body, "Meccano" on base.

571-F CHAUSSON BUS 154 mm #29f_1959-1960
Singledeck bus with cast body and hubs, white tires, black sheet metal base, silver trim, emblem cast on sides. Identical to 29f.
1. Red lower, cream upper body.
2. Navy blue lower, ivory upper body.

571-H SAVIEM VAN WITH HORSE AND SULKY 115 mm 1969-1971
Van with cast body, opening rear doors and ramp, blue turned hubs, black tires, white roof, tan plastic side panels, cream cab and rear interior, clear windows and headlights, red taillights, white and black horse, green sulky with driver and spoked wheels.
1. Blue body, white roof, tan side panels.

572-F BERLIET GBO DUMP TRUCK 188 mm 1970-1971
Heavy dumper with cast chassis and cab, yellow plastic tipper and hubs, black tires, bumper, stack and tipping mechanism, gray interior, windows, silver grille and lights.
1. Red chassis and cab, yellow tipper.

575-F PANHARD S.N.C.F. SEMI-TRAILER 165 mm #32ab_1959-1963
Semi with cast cab, semi-trailer, navy blue cast or turned hubs, black tires, spare wheel, navy blue sheet metal rear cover and tow hook, black cab base, silver grille, bumpers and headlights, yellow and blue lettering flanking S.N.C.F. shield. Identical to last type of 32ab.
1. Navy blue cab, semi and cover, and cast hubs.
2. Navy blue turned hubs, otherwise as type 1.

576-F PANHARD ESSO SEMI-TRAILER 179 mm #32c_1959-1963
Tanker semi with cast cab (=575) and tanker semi, cast or turned red hubs, black tires, spare wheel, unpainted sheet metal ladder and catwalk, black cab and tanker bases, latter with number 32C, silver grille, bumper and headlights, white stripes, red-white-blue Esso decals. Identical at first to last type of 32c.
1. Red cab, semi-trailer and cast hubs, smaller (medium) wings on logo than on original 32c model.
2. Even smaller wings on logo, red turned hubs, otherwise as type 1.

577-F SIMCA CARGO VAN: BAILLY 133 mm #33an_1959-1961
Van with cast chassis-cab, rear body, opening rear doors and hubs, black tires, spare wheel, black sheet metal front and rear body base, silver grille, bumper and headlights, red taillights, yellow-on-black Bailly logo. Identical to 33an.
1. Yellow chassis-cab, body, cast hubs, white rear roof.

577-H BERLIET GAK CATTLE TRUCK 134 mm 1965-1971
Livestock truck with cast cab, metallic brown chassis-interior of cab, yellow turned hubs, black tires, green plastic rear body and ramp with yellow panels, windows, two black and white cows, silver cab trim and lights, gray bumper and grille.
1. Green cab and rear body.

578-F SIMCA CARGO DUMP TRUCK 127 mm #33b_1959-1969
Dumper with cast chassis-cab, tipper, opening tailgate and green cast or turned hubs, black tires, spare wheel, black sheet metal front base, wire tipping lever, silver grille, bumper and headlights. Grooved rear bed (= last 33b).
1. Dark green cab, chassis and cast hubs, silver tipper and tailgate.
2. Green turned hubs, otherwise as type 1.

579-F SIMCA CARGO GLASS TRUCK 129 mm #33c_1959-1967
Flat truck with cast chassis-cab and rear body, cast or turned hubs, black tires, spare wheel, black sheet metal rack holding glass and mirror, black front base, silver grille, bumper and headlights, "Miroitier" decal on one side of rack, red "Saint-Gobain" on other side.
1. Yellow-orange chassis-cab, rack and cast hubs, bright green body (also sold in England).
2. Gray chassis-cab, rack and cast hubs, dark green flatbed.
3. Lighter gray chassis-cab and rack, dark green body, cream turned hubs.

580-F BERLIET DUMP TRUCK 128 mm #34a_1959-1970
Quarry dumper with cast chassis-cab and tipper, blue turned hubs, black tires, spare

wheel mount, black sheet metal front base with number 34, tipping mechanism and crank, black front fenders with red lights, silver grille, bumper and headlights. Identical to 34a.
1. Dark blue chassis-cab, orange tipper.

581-F BERLIET FLAT TRUCK WITH CONTAINER 125 mm #34b_1959-1965
Truck with cast chassis-cab (=580) and rear flatbed, container and sliding panel, cast or turned hubs, black tires, spare wheel, black sheet metal front base with number 34, light gray tow hook, black front fenders with red lights, silver grille, bumpers and headlights.
1. Maroon chassis-cab and cast hubs, light gray flatbed, dark gray container and panel, no logo.
2. Dark gray turned hubs, otherwise as type 1.

581n-F BERLIET BAILLY CONTAINER TRUCK 125 mm 34bn_1959-1965?
Same castings and parts as 581, with Bailly logo on container.
1. Maroon chassis-cab and cast hubs, light gray flatbed, dark gray container and panel.
2. Dark gray turned hubs, otherwise as type 1.

582-F CITROEN U23 WRECKER 125 mm #35a_1959.1971
Tow truck with cast body, red cast or turned hubs, black tires, spare wheel, black sheet metal boom and base, winch with line and hook, silver cab and headlights, yellow "Dinky Service" logo.
1. Dark red body and cast hubs.
2. Dark red body and turned hubs.

583-F BERLIET FIRE ENGINE 118 mm #32e_1959-1963
Fire truck with cast body, silver ladder and two red and cream hose reels, red cast or turned hubs, white tires, black sheet metal base with number 32, red and unpainted ladder racks, silver grille, bumper, headlights, catwalks and rear fittings, cream hose reel.
1. Red body and cast hubs.
2. Red body and turned hubs.

584-F BERLIET GAK COVERED TRUCK 136 mm 1961-1965
Truck with cast cab, rear body and brown chassis-interior of cab, cream turned hubs, black tires, spare wheel, removable green plastic rear cover, windows, silver cab trim and headlights, gray bumper and grille, yellow tow hook.
1. Yellow cab and rear body, green cover.

585-F BERLIET GAK DUMP TRUCK 127 mm 1961-1964
Dumper with cast cab, tipper, opening tailgate and gray chassis-interior of cab, gray turned hubs, black tires, spare wheel, red hydraulic cylinders, silver cab trim and headlights, tan grille and bumper, bed of tipper with wide or narrow grooved stripes.
1. Blue cab, orange tipper with wide stripes.
2. Blue cab, orange tipper with narrow stripes.

586-F CITROEN P55 MILK TRUCK 177 mm 1961-1965
Bottle truck with cast chassis-cab and rear body, blue turned hubs, black tires, spare wheel, black sheet metal cab base with number, thirty gray and white plastic milk cases, windows, white grille, silver headlights, red taillights.
1. White body, blue front fenders, bumper and hubs.

587-F CITROEN 1200KG PHILIPS VAN 122 mm 1964-1970
Van with cast body and two raising doors, red turned hubs, black tires, black sheet metal base with number, clear plastic frame on roof with red "Philips" lettering, white interior, windows, red and silver grille, red Philips logo on left, silver panels.
1. Dark yellow body.

588-F BERLIET GAK BREWERY TRUCK 127 mm 1964-1970
Flat truck with cast cab, red flatbed and removable stakes with yellow logo, brown chassis-interior of cab, cream turned hubs, black tires, spare wheel, load of brown plastic barrels and cream bottle cases, windows, silver cab trim and headlights, gray

grille and bumper, logo "Bieres-Limonades-Eaux Minerales".
1. Yellow cab, red rear body and stakes.
2. Red cab, ? other details, Kronenbourg logo.

589-F BERLIET GAK WRECKER 122 mm 1965-1969
Tow truck with cast body, cab and winch, turned hubs, black tires, windows, dome light, cream interior, windows, black hook with line, silver cab trim and headlights, gray grille and bumper, yellow taillights and "Depannage" logo.
1. Red body.

589a-F BERLIET GAK AUTOROUTE WRECKER 122 mm 1970-1971
Same castings and parts as 589, black rear panels and "Depannage Autoroutes" logo.
1. Orange body.

590-F CITY ROAD SIGNS #40_1959-1968
Six cast signs, identical to 40.
1. Silver bases and poles, red-white-blue signs.

591-F COUNTRY ROAD SIGNS #41_1959-1969
Six cast signs, identical to 41.
1. Silver bases and poles, red-white-blue signs.

592-F ESSO GAS PUMPS #49d_1959-1963
Cast Esso sign, two gas pumps, and gray base. Pumps riveted to base, sign removable. Identical to 49d.
1. Red-white-blue sign, red-white and blue-white pumps.

592-H ROAD SIGNS 1969-1971
Twelve city traffic signs.
1. Red-white-blue signs.

593-F ROAD SIGNS 1969-1971
Twelve highway traffic signs.
1. Red-white-blue signs.

594-F TRAFFIC LIGHT 100 by 90 mm 1969-1971
Plastic light and pole on gray base, red markings, battery mount.
1. Black light and pole.

595-F SALEV CRANE 156 mm #50_1959-1961
Mobile crane with cast body, chassis, blue driver, cream steering wheel, cast or turned hubs, black tires, red sheet metal crane boom and mount, two cranks, line and hook, black stripes, rivet head outside casting as last type 50.
1. Gray upper body, red lower body, crane and cast hubs, yellow chassis.
2. Red turned hubs, otherwise as type 1.

595-H TRAFFIC SIGNS 1969-1970
Twelve signs in 1969, twelve in 1970, included in boxes with models.
1. Unpainted cast bases, red-white-blue plastic signs.

596-F LMV STREET SWEEPER 124 mm 1960-1963
Sweeper with cast body and chassis, cream turned hubs, black tires, windows, adjustable brush in black plastic mount, silver grid and headlights, red lights and stop sign.
1. Cream body and hubs.

597-F COVENTRY CLIMAX FORK LIFT 108 mm 1959-1961
Same castings and parts as 14c/401.
1. Orange body, yellow fork.

600-G ARMORED CORPS PERSONNEL #150_1954-?
Four standing and two seated figures, identical to 150, renumbered for U.S. market.
1. Brown uniforms.

601-G AUSTIN PARA-MOKE 76 mm 1967-1978
Same casting and parts as 342 Mini-Moke on olive plastic pallet, with olive and green parachute and olive attachment. Moke has olive-tan plastic top, turned hubs with black tires and Speedwheels, +/- silver headlights.
1. Olive body, turned hubs.
2. Olive body, Speedwheels.

602-G ARMORED COMMAND CAR 160 mm 1976-1978

187

The New System of Catalog Numbers

Unreal vehicle with cast body, front panel and unpainted radar screen, eight Speedwheels, black plastic top, base-bumper and parts, gray interior, windshield, driver, olive fuel cans, silver headlights, olive and white star emblem label.

1. Dark green body.

603-G ARMY PRIVATE (seated)   1957-1971
Figure with khaki uniform, black beret, seat plug.

1. Diecast figure (1957-1965).
2. Plastic figure (1966-1971).

604-G ROYAL TANK CORPS PRIVATE (seated)   #150a_1954-?
Cast figure, identical to 150a, renumbered for U.S. market.

1. Black uniform and beret.

604-H LAND ROVER BOMB DISPOSAL UNIT   110 mm   1976-1978
Cast body (=344), opening hood and doors, and black base, no number, black Speedwheels, white plastic interior, olive top, blue dome light, windshield, sheet metal towing hook, red-on-white "Explosive Disposal" label on header, orange labels on fenders.

1. Olive body and top.

606-G ROYAL ARTILLERY PERSONNEL   #160_1954-?
Set of four figures, identical to 160, renumbered for U.S. market.

1. Khaki uniforms.

608-G ROYAL ARTILLERY GUNNER (seated)   #160b_1954-?
Cast figure, identical to 160b, renumbered for U.S. market.

1. Khaki uniform.

609-G 105MM HOWITZER WITH CREW   199 mm   1974-1978
Cast 5-piece gun and olive hubs, black plastic tires and nose of gun, wire trigger, three olive figures.

1. Olive gun and hubs.

612-G COMMANDO JEEP   108 mm   1973-1979
Jeep with cast body, dashboard, chasis and olive 5-bolt hubs, black plastic tires, guns, antenna and equipment, olive gas cans and steering wheel, driver in olive, tow hook, spare wheel, silver headlights.

1. Olive body, dashboard and chassis.
2. Camouflage finish?

(613 M.A.S.H. JEEP never issued)

615-G U.S. ARMY JEEP AND 105MM HOWITZER   295 mm   1968-1978
Set of #612 Jeep and #609 Howitzer minus gun crew figures and Jeep equipment, plus star and number labels on Jeep, light gray steering wheel, antenna, gas can and nose of howitzer.

1. Olive Jeep and howitzer.

616-G AEC TANK TRANSPORTER WITH TANK   318 mm   1976-1978
Set of #683 Tank, camouflage net, and transporter with cast cab, semi and parts, olive plastic hubs, black tires, white plastic interior, windows, jewel headlights, black grille, white-on-black labels.

1. Olive tank and transporter.

617-G VOLKSWAGEN KDF & 50MM ANTITANK GUN   274 mm   1968-1977
Cast KDF body, chassis, 5-part gun, and 5-bolt olive KDF hubs, black tires, spare wheel, gray plastic KDF top and interior, gun nose and wheels, black and white emblem labels on KDF, number label on gun.

1. Olive KDF and gun.

618-G AEC TRANSPORTER WITH SIKORSKY HELICOPTER   318 mm   1976-1980
Same semi-trailer transporter as in #616, with camouflage net, plus cast upper and lower helicopter body and opening door, black plastic rotors, winch control and small wheels, winch line and hook, Army labels.

1. Olive transporter and helicopter.

619-G BREN GUN CARRIER AND ANTITANK GUN   184 mm   1976-1978
Set of #622 Carrier and 625 Gun.

1. Olive carrier and gun.

620-G ARMY TRANSPORT WAGON   #151b _1954-1955?
Same model as 151b, with cast driver, renumbered for U.S. market.

1. Green body and top?

620-H BERLIET MISSILE LAUNCHER   150 mm   1970-1973
Cast body and 6-bolt olive hubs, black plastic tires and launcher, white and red missile, windows, olive sheet metal base and tow hook, silver front bumer, launching spring and trigger.

1. Olive body.

621-G THREE TON ARMY WAGON   114 mm   1954-1963
Bedford truck with cast chassis-cab, rear body and olive hubs, black tires and spare, olive sheet metal base, black base and tow hook, silver headlights, emblem decals, +/- driver, +/- windows, number on chassis.

1. Olive body and cover, no driver or windows.
2. Olive body and cover, driver, no windows.
3. Olive body and cover, driver, windows.

622-G TEN TON ARMY TRUCK   136 mm   1954-1963
Foden truck with cast chassis-cab, rear body and olive hubs, black tires, spare wheel, olive sheet metal rear cover, black base and tow hook, silver headlights, emblem decals, +/- driver, number on chassis.

1. Olive body and cover, no driver.
2. Olive body and cover, driver.

622-H BREN GUN CARRIER   125 mm   1975-1978
Vehicle with cast body, olive plastic hubs, black base, treads and parts, two brown soldier figures, labels.

1. Olive body.

623-G ARMY COVERED WAGON   105 mm   1954-1963
Bedford truck with cast body and olive hubs, black tires, spare wheel, olive sheet metal cover, black base and tow hook, silver headlights, emblem decals, +/- driver, number on bottom of body.

1. Olive body and cover, no driver.
2. Olive body and cover, driver.

624-G DAIMLER MILITARY AMBULANCE   #30hm_1954-1955?
Cast body (=30h/253) and olive hubs, black tires, black sheet metal base, red crosses on white squares, silver headlights. For US market.

1. Olive body, no number on base.
2. Olive body, number 253 on base.

625-G AUSTIN COVERED WAGON'   104 mm   #30sm_1954
Cast body, olive hubs, black tires, olive sheet metal rear cover, black base and tow hook, black and silver grille with headlights. Identical to 30sm. For US market.

1. Olive body and cover.

625-H SIX POUNDER ANTITANK GUN   159 mm   1975-1977
Cast 5-piece gun and olive hubs, black tires and nose of gun, wire trigger, plastic bullets.

1. Olive body.

626-G MILITARY AMBULANCE   111 mm   1956-1966
Cast body, opening rear doors and Supertoy hubs, black tires, black sheet metal base, red crosses on white circles, silver headlights, emblem decals, +/- driver, +/- windows, number on bottom of body.

1. Olive body, no driver or windows.
2. Olive body, driver, no windows.
3. Olive body, driver, windows.

(628-G STANDARD ATLAS ARMY BUS never issued)

640-G BEDFORD ARMY TRUCK   102 mm   #25wm_1954
Cast chassis-cab, rear body, grille with silver headlights, and olive hubs, black tires, black sheet metal base and tow hook. For U.S. market?

1. Olive body and chassis-cab.

641-G ONE TON ARMY TRUCK   79 mm   1954-1962

Lumber truck with cast body and olive hubs, black tires, olive sheet metal rear cover, black base with bumber, silver headlights, emblem decals, +/- driver, +/- windows.

1. Olive body and cover, no driver or windows.
2. Olive body and cover, driver, no windows.
3. Olive body and cover, driver, windows.

642-G RAF PRESSURE REFUELLER   140 mm   1957-1962
Tanker with cast body, tank and blue-gray Supertoy hubs, black tires, black sheet metal base and tow hook, roundel decal, number on bottom of body, +/- driver, +/- windows.

1. Blue-gray body and tank, no driver or windows.
2. Blue-gray body and tank, driver, no windows.
3. Blue-gray body and tank, driver, windows.

643-G 200 GALLON ARMY WATER TANKER   89 mm   1958-1964
Tank truck with cast body, tank and olive hubs, black tires, spare wheel, black sheet metal base, silver headlights, emblem decal, +/- driver, +/- windows, number on bottom of body.

1. Olive body and tank, no driver or windows.
2. Olive body and tank, driver, no windows.
3. Olive body and tank, driver, windows.

645-G SHELLS   1979-1978
Shells for #615, 617, 654 and 683.

1. Unpainted.

650-G LIGHT TANK   68 mm   #152a_1954-?
Identical to 152a, for U.S. market.

1. Green body?

651-G CENTURION TANK   135 mm   1954-1970
Tank with cast body, turning turret, olive gun and hubs, black treads, black sheet metal base with number, emblem decals.

1. Olive body and turret, rubber treads.
2. Olive body and turret, plastic treads.

654-G 155 MM MOBILE GUN   151 mm   1974-1979
Cast body, gun, shield and unpainted control wheel, olive plastic base and hubs, silver gray treads, black parts, wire trigger, white and olive labels.

1. Olive body, gun and shield.

656-G 88MM ANTI AIRCRAFT GUN   218 mm   1975-1979
Cast front and rear assemblies, shield, mount and gun, black chassis and tow bar, olive plastic hubs, black tires, jacks and gun collar, wire trigger, stripe and emblem labels, plastic bullets.

1. Olive gun, mount, shield, front and rear assemblies.

660 THORNEYCROFT MIGHTY ANTAR TANK TRANSPORTER   337 mm   1956-1964
Low loader with cast cab, chassis, semi-trailer, two ramps, and olive Supertoy hubs, black tires, silver headlights, emblem decals, +/- driver, +/- windows.

1. Olive cab and semi-trailer, no driver or windows.
2. Olive cab and semi-trailer, driver, no windows.
3. Olive cab and semi-trailer, driver, windows.

660-H 88MM MOBILE AA GUN WITH CREW   218 mm   1978-1980
Set of #656 Gun and three plastic soldier figures.

1. Olive and black gun.

661-G SCAMMELL RECOVERY TRACTOR   133 mm   1957-1966
Wrecker with cast body, rear deck and boom, and olive hubs, black tires, black sheet metal base, crank, ratchet, pulley, line and hook, silver headlights, emblem decals, +/- driver, +/- windows, number on bottom of body.

1. Olive body and cast hubs, no driver or windows.
2. Olive body and cast hubs, driver, no windows.
3. Olive body and cast hubs, driver, windows.
4. Olive body and plastic hubs, driver, windows.

662-G 88MM ANTI AIRCRAFT GUN WITH CREW   218 mm   1976-1977

The New System of Catalog Numbers

Non-mobile version of #656, with three plastic soldier figures.
1. Olive and black gun?

665-G HONEST JOHN MISSILE LAUNCHER   188 mm 1968-1976
Truck with cast chassis-cab, cast or plastic rear body, turning mount and raising launcher, plastic rear body, black sheet metal cab base, two black plastic hydraulic cylinders, windshield, silver headlights, emblem decals, +/- driver, wire trigger, white plastic missile with black rubber nose cone, sometimes with black checkered pattern.
1. Olive body and cast rear, driver?, cast hubs.
2. Olive body, plastic rear and hubs, driver.
3. No driver, otherwise as type 2.
4. No driver or silver headlights, new decals, otherwise as type 2.
5. Gray body, olive plastic rear and hubs, driver.

666-G MISSILE ERECTOR VEHICLE & CORPORAL MISSILE 242 mm 1959-1964
Truck with cast cab, hood, chassis, rear arms and mounts, trailer body, four jacks, unpainted gears and trailer missile mount, and olive hubs, black tires, spare tire, sheet metal parts and black trailer base, crank, white plastic missile with rubber nose cone, sheet metal inner cylinder, truck windows, driver, silver headlights, emblem and missile marking decals.
1. Olive truck and trailer.

667-G MISSILE SERVICING PLATFORM VEHICLE 197 mm 1960-1964
Truck with cast body, swiveling mount, jacks, and Supertoy hubs, black tires, black sheet metal cab base, olive upper and lower arms, olive plastic platform, wire rods, silver headlights, emblem decals.
1. Olive body, no windows.
2. Olive body, windows.

667-H ARMORED PATROL CAR   80 mm 1976-1979
Armored car with cast body, rotating turret and base, black plastic Speedwheels, spare wheel and antenna, "Armoured Car/Scout Car" on base.
1. Light olive body, turret and base.

668-G FODEN ARMY TRUCK   197 mm 1976-1979
Truck with cast cab, chassis, rear body and opening doors, light olive plastic rear cover, tailgate, tow hook and hubs, black plastic tires, interior and bumper, spare wheel, windows, emblem labels.
1. Light olive body, chassis and cover.

669-G U.S. ARMY UNIVERSAL JEEP   82 mm 1956-1958
Jeep with cast body (=405) and olive hubs, black steering wheel, black tires and spare, black sheet metal base and tow hook, olive windshield frame, silver headlights, white star emblems.
1. Olive body.

670-G DAIMLER ARMORED CAR   73 mm 1954-1970
Cast body, rotating turret and olive hubs, black tires, black sheet metal base with number, emblem decals.
1. Olive body and turret.

671-G RECONNAISSANCE CAR   89 mm #152b _1954
Cast body and olive hubs, black tires, black sheet metal base. Identical to 152b. For the U.S. market.
1. Olive body.

671-H MARK 1 CORVETTE   260 mm 1976-1979
Ship with cast hull, superstructure, bridge, tan deck and unpainted launcher, light gray plastic parts and lifeboats, plastic bullets, black-on-silver F17 labels, speedwheels.
1. Light gray hull, superstructure and bridge.

672-G ARMY JEEP   69 mm #153a _1954
Jeep with cast body, steering wheel and olive hubs, black tires and spare, olive sheet metal windshield frame, white star emblems. Identical to 153a, the smallest Dinky Toys Jeep. For the U.S. market.
1. Olive body.

672-H O.S.A. MISSILE BOAT   204 mm 1976-1979
Ship with cast hull, deck and superstructure, black mast, launchers and other parts, Speedwheels, plastic bullets, yellow triggers, black-on-gray number 175 labels.
1. Light gray hull, white deck and superstructure.

673-G DAIMLER SCOUT CAR   67 mm 1954-1962
Light armored car with cast upper and lower body, brown driver, and olive hubs, black tires, number on bottom, emblem decals.
1. Olive body.

673-H SUBMARINE CHASER   197 mm 1977-1978
Ship with cast hull, deck and superstructure, black plastic turret, antenna, mast and radar tripod, yellow firing controls.
1. Gray hull, light gray deck, white superstructure.

674-G AUSTIN CHAMP   70 mm 1954-1971
Jeep-type car with cast body and olive hubs, black tires and spare, olive sheet metal windshield frame, black plastic steering wheel, silver headlights, emblem decals.
1. Olive body, driver figure.
2. Olive body, no driver.
3. White body, U.N. livery, green hubs.
4. Plastic hubs?
5. Metal steering wheel?

674-G COAST GUARD AMPHIBIOUS MISSILE LAUNCHER 155 mm 1976-1978
Car-boat with cast body and unpainted spotlight, black plastic base and Speedwheels, red interior, olive driver, light blue mast with jets, yellow and blue launcher, windshield, blue and white "Coast Guard" and stripes, plastic bullets.
1. White body.

675-G FORD FORDOR ARMY STAFF CAR   102 mm #139am _1954-1957
Sedan with cast body (=170) and olive hubs, black tires, black sheet metal base with number 170, white star decals, silver headlights. Identical to 139am except for number on base.
1. Olive body.

675-H MOTOR PATROL BOAT   170 mm 1973-1977
Boat with cast hull, deck and superstructure, black guns, containers and trigger, orange masts, boats and missile rack, silver gray figure, red bullets, Speedwheels, black-on-silver number 153 labels.
1. Light gray hull and superstructure, cream deck.

676-G SARACEN ARMORED PERSONNAL CARRIER   83 mm 1955-1962
Armored car with cast body, chassis, rotating turret and olive Supertoy hubs, black tires, emblem decals, no number.
1. Olive body, chassis and turret.

676-H DAIMLER ARMORED CAR   73 mm 1972-1976
Cast body and rotating turret, black sheet metal base, no number, black Speedwheels and antenna.
1. Olive body, French decals (French issue, 1972).
2. Light olive body, English labels (English issue, 1973-1976).

677-G AEC ARMORED COMMAND VEHICLE   133 mm 1957-1962
Large armored car with cast body and olive Supertoy hubs, black tires, black sheet metal base with number, emblem decals.
1. Olive body.

677-H TASK FORCE SET   1972-1974
Boxed set of 680 Ferret, 681 DUKW and 682 Alvis.
1. Tan Ferret, blue-gray DUKW, light olive Alvis.
2. All three vehicles light olive.

678-G AIR-SEA RESCUE LAUNCH   170 mm 1976-1979
Boat with cast hull, deck and superstructure, orange plastic gun and parts, white mast, boat, rack and parts, blue windows, "RAF", "Rescue" and roundel labels. Same hull and deck castings as #675.
1. Black hull, light gray deck, yellow superstructure.

680-G FERRET SCOUT CAR   80 mm 1972-1979
Light armored car with cast body and base, black plastic Speedwheels and spare wheel.
1. Tan body.
2. Light olive body (in #677).

681-G DUKW AMPHIBIAN   127 mm 1972-1979
Cast body and chassis, small black Speedwheels.
1. Blue-gray body.
2. Light olive body (in #677).

682-G ALVIS STALWART LOAD CARRIER   103 mm 1972-1979
Cast body, black plastic chassis and Speedwheels, windows.
1. Light olive body.

683-G CHIEFTAIN TANK   217 mm 1972-1979
Cast body, rotating turret, raising two-piece gun and black turning turret top (raises gun), light olive plastic chassis and hubs, black or silver gray treads, black grille and parts, wire trigger, white-on-olive number label. Two base lettering types, one unknown to me.
1. Light olive body, turret and gun, silver gray treads.
2. Black treads, otherwise as type 1.
3. Camouflage body, turret and gun, black treads.

686-G 25 POUNDER FIELD GUN   89 mm 1957-1970
Gun with cast chassis, raising gun and olive hubs, black tires, number on bottom of chassis.
1. Olive chassis and gun.

687-G FIELD GUN TRAILER   56 mm 1957-1965
Two-wheel trailer with cast chassis and olive hubs, black sheet metal base (no number) and tow hook, black tires.
1. Olive body.

687-H CONVOY ARMY TRUCK   110 mm 1977-1980
Covered truck with cast chassis-cab (=380 series), olive plastic rear body and cover, black chassis-bumper-grille and Speedwheels, gray interior, clear windows and headlights, white-on-olive "Army" labels.
1. Light olive chassis-cab, body and cover.
2. Same colors, Harrods labels: code 2 model by John Gay.

688-G LIGHT ARTILLERY TRACTOR   79 mm 1957-1961
Morris tractor with cast body, olive hubs, black tires and spare, black sheet metal base (no number) and tow hook, driver figure, +/- windows, silver headlights, emblem decals.
1. Olive body and cast hubs, no windows.
2. Olive body and metal hubs, windows.
3. Olive body and plastic hubs, windows.

689-G MEDIUM ARTILLERY TRACTOR   140 mm 1957-1966
Covered Leyland truck with cast front body, rear body-chassis and Supertoy hubs, black tires, two spare wheels, olive sheet metal rear cover, black tow hook, +/- driver, emblem decals, number on chassis.
1. Olive body and cover, no driver.
2. Olive body and cover, driver.

690-G MOBILE ANTI-AIRCRAFT GUN   115 mm #161b _1954-?
Same castings and parts as 161b. For U.S. market.
1. Olive body.

690-H SCORPION TANK   120 mm 1974-1980
Tank with cast body, upper and lower rotating turret, olive plastic hubs, black treads and antennas, red-brown base, net, wire trigger, plastic bullets, number labels, sheet of decals.
1. Light olive body and turret.

691-G 18 POUNDER QUICK FIRING FIELD GUN   78 mm

The New System of Catalog Numbers

#162 _1954-?
Same castings and parts as 162. For U.S. market.
1. Olive body.

691-H   STRIKER ANTI-TANK VEHICLE   122 mm   1974-1980
Cast body and launcher, light olive plastic hubs, silver gray or black treads, black base, turret, antennas, mufflers, launcher interior and triggers and swiveling machine gun, number labels, plastic bullets.
1. Light olive body, silver gray treads.
2. Light olive body, black treads.

692-G   5.5 INCH MEDIUM GUN   ?? mm   1955-1962
Cast gun, mount and two-piece chassis, olive Supertoy hubs, black/tires, number on bottom.
1. Olive gun and chassis, one white-painted panel.

692-H   LEOPARD TANK   198 mm   1974-1979
Tank with cast body, rotating upper and lower turret, raising gun and black turning turret top (which raises gun), olive plastic hubs, black treads, base, antennas, machine gun and parts, black and white emblem labels, sheet of decals, plastic bullets.
1. Olive body and turret.

693-G   7.2 INCH HOWITZER   131 mm   1958-1967
Cast chassis, gun and olive hubs, black tires, olive cast or plastic control wheel (does not actually raise gun), one white painted panel, tire treads either square or tractor-type diagonal.
1. Olive gun and chassis, cast control wheel.
2. Olive gun and chassis, plastic control wheel.

694-G   HANOMAG 7,5 MM TANK DESTROYER   171 mm   1975-1980
Vehicle with cast body, chassis, mount and two-piece gun, and front hubs, olive rear hubs, black plastic tires, treads, base and parts, trigger wire, plastic bullets, number and emblem labels.
1. Grayish olive body.

695-G   HOWITZER AND TRACTOR   265 mm   1962-1966
Set of 689 Artillery Tractor and 693 Howitzer.
1. Olive tractor and howitzer.

696-G   LEOPARD ANTI-AIRCRAFT TANK   152 mm   1975-1979
Tank with cast body, upper and lower rotating turret, two raising guns, and radar screen, olive plastic hubs and parts, black treads, antennas and base, plastic bullets, sheet of decals.
1. Olive body, guns and turret.

697-G   25 POUNDER FIELD GUN SET   212 mm   1957-1971
Boxed set of 686 Field Gun, 687 Trailer and 688 Tractor.
1. Olive vehicles.

698-G   TANK TRANSPORTER AND TANK GIFT SET   1957-1965
Boxed set of 651 Centurion Tank and 660 Mighty Antar Transporter.

699-G   MILITARY VEHICLES SET   1955-1960
Boxed set of 621 Army Wagon, 641 One Ton Truck, 674 Austin Champ and 676 Saracen.
1. Standard colors.

699-H   LEOPARD RECOVERY TANK   147 mm   1975-1977
Tank/wrecker with cast body, plow blade, arm and unpainted hook and lever, olive sheet metal arms, black tow hook, olive plastic hubs, black treads, base, swiveling machine gun, antenna and parts, black and white emblem labels, sheet of decals.
1. Olive body, blade and arm.

700-G   SEAPLANE   70 by 102 mm   _#63b_1954-1957
Cast body and two floats, four red 2-blade propellers, black G-AVKW registration. Identical to last 63b without metal clip.
1. Silver body and floats.

700-H   DIAMOND JUBILEE R.A.F. SPITFIRE   140 by 172 mm   1979
Chromed version of #741, mounted on plinth, with medallion and post.

1. Chromed body.

702-G   DH COMET JET AIRLINER   145 by 185 mm   1954-1956   _#999
Cast upper body, lower body-wings and ten small unpainted wheels, blue trim and lettering (B.O.A.C. on fuselage, G-ALYV on fin), black G-ALYV on right wing, silver windows, 702 under one wing. Renumbered 999.
1. White fuselage, silver wings and stabilizers.
(703 HANDLEY PAGE HERALD never issued)
(703 AVRO VULCAN BOMBER see 707)

704-G   AVRO YORK AIRLINER   124 by 160 mm   _#70a_1954-1960
Cast fuselage, wings and two small wheels, four red 3-blade propellers, olive sheet metal base, black G-AGJC registration, blue cockpit windows. Identical to last 70a.
1. Silver fuselage and wings.

705-G   VICKERS VIKING AIRLINER   98 by 140 mm   _#70b_1954-1963
Cast upper fuselage, lower fuselage-wings, two red 4-blade propellers, pale blue windows, black G-AGOL registration. Identical to last 70b.
1. Silver fuselage and wings.

706-G   VICKERS VISCOUNT AIRLINER   130 by 150 mm   1956-1957
Cast upper fuselage, lower fuselage-wings and six small wheels, four red 4-blade propellers, blue nose, blue and gold tailfin, blue and silver window-stripe-"Air France" decals.
1. Silver fuselage and wings, white fuselage top.
(707 AVRO VULCAN BOMBER see 749)

708-G   VICKERS VISCOUNT AIRLINER   130 by 150 mm   1957-1965
Same castings and parts as 706, red G-AOJA registration, Union Jack on fin, red "B E A"-black window decals.
1. Silver lower fuselage and wings, white fuselage top and rear.
2. Light gray lower body and wings, red fuselage top and rear.
3. Black B E A logo, treaded wheels, otherwise as type 2?

710-G   BEECHCRAFT BONANZA   106 by 130 mm   1965-1976
Cast upper fuselage and lower fuselage-wings, white plastic removable engine hood, propeller and interior, red opening hatch, +/- brown luggage, windows, black wheels, black-red-white labels.
1. White upper fuselage, red lower fuselage and wings, treaded wheels, luggage, N8695M registration.
2. No luggage, otherwise as type 1.
3. No luggage, smooth wheels, otherwise as type 1.
4. Yellow upper fuselage, bronze lower fuselage and wings, smooth wheels, no luggage, N2835M registration.
5. White upper fuselage, blue lower fuselage, red wing parts and trim, smooth wheels, no luggage, N2835M registration.
6. N4480W registration, otherwise as type 5.

712-G   U.S. ARMY T42A   115 by 148 mm   1972-1977
Cast upper fuselage and lower fuselage-wings (= 715 Baron), white plastic interior, windows, black wing tanks, engine hood, 2-blade propellers and folding landing gear, U.S. Army labels with number 24506.
1. Olive fuselage and wings.

715-G   BRISTOL 173 HELICOPTER   127 mm   1956-1972
Cast body and four small wheels, two red 3-blade rotors, red stripes, silver and gold windows, black G-AUXR registration.
1. Aqua body.

715-H   BEECHCRAFT C65 BARON   115 by 148 mm   1968-1976
Cast upper body and lower fuselage-wings, yellow plastic propellers, removable engine hoods, yellow or white folding landing gear, red interior, windows, jewel nose light, yellow-black-white stripe and lettering labels, N555C registration, +/- number under wing.
1. Cream fuselage and wings, yellow wing tips, white landing gear.
2. Cream wing tips, yellow landing gear, otherwise as type 1.
3. Red fuselage and wings, yellow wing tips and landing gear.

4. No number 715 cast under wing, otherwise as type 3.

716-G   WESTLAND-SIKORSKY S51 HELICOPTER   67 mm   1957-1962
Cast body and three small wheels, red main and vertical rear rotors, silver nose windows, cream top and G-ATWX registration.
1. Red body.

717-G   BOEING 737 LUFTHANSA   150 by 150 mm   1970-1975
Cast upper fuselage and lower fuselage-wings, plastic engines, retractable black plastic/white metal landing gear with operating lever, blue fin, black nose, silver cockpit windows, yellow and blue emblem and blue-silver-black-white window-door-name labels.
1. White body, wings and engines.
2. White body and wings, blue engines.

718-G   HAWKER HURRICANE   11C ? by 188 mm   1972-1975
Cast and plastic pieces, ? other details, gunfire sound mechanism.
1. Gray and green camouflage above, gray below.

719-G   SUPERMARINE SPITFIRE MARK II   140 by 172 mm   1969-1976
Cast upper fuselage-wings and two lower fuselage pieces with black plastic wheels, black plastic propeller, yellow blade tips, black parts, clear canopy, red-blue roundels and red-white-blue flags. "Battle of Britain" or ordinary box.
1. Green-brown camouflage above, pale green below, decals.
2. Labels, otherwise as type 1.
3. No labels or decals, no rings cast into wings to locate them, otherwise as type 1.

721-G   JUNKERS JU87B STUKA DIVE BOMBER   150 by 188 mm   1969-1980
Cast upper fuselage-tail, lower body-wings, two wing bottom panels, two landing gear and black or unpainted bomb, black or yellow plastic propellers and wheels, clear canopy, yellow nose and rudder, black and white crosses on wings.
1. Olive upper fuselage and landing gear, light blue lower surfaces, black bomb and propeller, yellow blade tips, labels.
2. Unpainted bomb, decals, otherwise as type 1.
3. Unpainted bomb, decals, yellow propeller, otherwise as type 1.

722-G   HAWKER HARRIER   125 by 182 mm   1970-1980
Cast upper fuselage-wings, lower fuselage, and unpainted parts, black plastic retractable landing gear and nose, silver gray pilot, clear canopy, red-white-blue roundel and flag labels.
1. Metallic blue and olive upper fuselage and wings, white lower fuselage.

723-G   HS125 EXECUTIVE JET   134 by 132 mm   1970-1975
Cast upper and lower fuselage, wings and unpainted folding ramp and landing gear, clear windows, black nose cowling and wheels, orange and red stripe labels.
1. Silver? upper fuselage, yellow lower fuselage and wings, metallic blue engines.
2. White upper fuselage, metallic blue lower fuselage, wings and engines.

724-G   SIKORSKY SEA KING HELICOPTER   160 mm   1971-1979
Cast upper and lower body and opening side door, plastic windows, interior, door latch, rotors and black wheels, winch line with hook, plastic space capsule, opening hatch and interior.
1. White upper body and hatch, metallic blue lower body, red interior, blue rotors, white capsule and hatch, yellow interior.
2. Black helicopter interior, otherwise as type 1.
3. Black rotors and interior, otherwise as type 1.
4. Black rotors and interior, yellow capsule, otherwise as type 1.

725-G   ROYAL NAVY F4K PHANTOM II   192 by 132 mm   1972-1977
Cast upper fuselage, lower fuselage-wings, folding landing gear and unpainted launcher control, black plastic nose, jets and wheels, clear canopy, two figures, two white missiles, "Royal Navy", "153", roundels (two sizes) and other labels.
1. Blue body.

726-G   MESSERSCHMITT 109E   148 by 165 mm   1972-1976
Cast upper fuselage-wings, light blue lower fuselage and folding landing gear, black

plastic wheels, brown propeller and parts, olive cockpit, clear canopy, battery mount (operates propeller), black and white cross labels.
1. Tan and olive camouflage on upper fuselage and wings.
2. Gray and olive? camouflage on upper fuselage and wings, yellow nose.

727-G   U.S.AIR FORCE PHANTOM F4 MARK II   192 by 132 mm   1974?-1977
Cast upper fuselage, lower fuselage-wings, folding landing gear and unpainted launcher control, black plastic nose, jets and wheels, clear canopy, two figures, US roundel labels. Same casting and parts as #725.
1. Brown and olive camouflaged upper surfaces, gray lower wings, brown lower fuselage.
2. Gray and olive camouflage?

728-G   R.A.F. DOMINIE   134 by 132 mm   1972-1975
Cast upper fuselage, lower fuselage, wings, engines and unpainted landing gear and ramp, black plastic wheels, amber windows, roundel, flag and XG172 labels. Same casting as 723.
1. Metallic blue and olive upper surfaces, metallic blue lower surfaces and engines.

729-G   PANAVIA M.R.C.A. (TORNADO)   ? by 164 mm   1973-1976
Cast and plastic parts, retractable landing gear connected to swing-wing mechanism, details unavailable.
1. Dark green and gray camouflage upper surfaces, unknown lower surfaces.

730-G   TEMPEST II FIGHTER   53 by 64 mm   #70b_1954-1955
Single casting, red 4-blade propeller, roundels. Identical to last 70b.
1. Silver plane.

730-H   PHANTOM II F4K   192 by 132 mm   1973-1976
Cast upper fuselage, lower fuselage-wings, unpainted folding landing gear and launcher control, black plastic wheels, nose and jets, two figures, white missile, "Navy", "AC" and roundel labels.
1. Light gray upper, off-white lower surfaces.
2. Assembled from 730 upper and 733 lower castings, the latter in camouflage colors.
3. Chromed landing gear, ? other details.

731-G   TWIN ENGINED FIGHTER   51 by 76 mm   #70d_1954-1955
Single casting, two red 3-blade propellers. Identical to 70d.
1. Silver plane.

731-H   S.E.P.E.C.A.T JAGUAR   194 by 106 mm   1973-1976
Cast upper fuselage-wings, lower fuselage and unpainted folding landing gear and ejection control, black plastic wheels, nose and jets, orange pilot, clear opening canopy, sheet metal ejection seat, roundel and flag labels.
1. Metallic blue with olive camouflage on upper surfaces, light gray lower fuselage.

732-G   GLOSTER METEOR TWIN JET FIGHTER   64 by 67 mm   #70c_1954-1962
Single casting, roundel decals. Identical to 70c.
1. Silver plane.

732-H   BELL 47 POLICE HELICOPTER   164 mm   1972-1980
Cast cab-engine section, cream sheet metal lower tail, orange or red plastic upper tail and skids, black rotors, clear canopy, pilot figure, black Police labels, plastic sign and cones.
1. Blue cab-engine, orange upper tail and skids, blue-gray pilot.
2. Red upper tail and skids, otherwise as type 1.
3. Red Captain Scarlet pilot, otherwise as type 1.

733-G   SHOOTING STAR JET FIGHTER   56 by 61 mm   #70f_1954-1972
Cast body and wing tanks, U.S. star decals. Identical to last 70f.
1. Silver body.

733-H   BUNDESLUFTWAFFE F4K PHANTOM II   192 by 132 mm   1973-1979
Same castings and parts as 727, other data unavailable.
1. Gray and olive camouflage.

734-G   SUPERMARINE SWIFT FIGHTER   62 by 50 mm   1955-1962
Cast body and three chromed wheels, roundel and flag decals, silver canopy.
1. Gray and olive camouflage.

734-H   P47 THUNDERBOLT   ? by 190 mm   1975-1978
Cast and plastic parts, details unavailable, battery-powered propeller.
1. Silver fuselage with black stripe.

735-G   GLOSTER JAVELIN FIGHTER   92 by 83 mm   1956-1966
Cast upper fuselage, lower fuselage-wings and three chromed wheels, silver canopy, roundel and flag decals.
1. Gray plane with olive camouflage on upper surfaces.

736-G   HAWKER HUNTER FIGHTER   71 by 53 mm   1955-1963
Cast body and three chromed wheels, silver canopy, roundel and flag decals.
1. Gray plane with olive camouflage on upper surfaces.

736-H   BUNDESMARINE SEA KING HELICOPTER   160 mm   1973-1978
Cast upper and lower body and opening hatch, black plastic interior, rotors and wheels, windows, winch line and hook, number and cross labels. Same castings and parts as 724.
1. Light gray body, red engine cowling and stabilizer surface.

737-G   B.A.C. LIGHTNING FIGHTER   94 by 56 mm   1959-1968
Cast body and three chromed wheels, black plastic nose, roundel and flag decals.
1. Silver plane.

738-G   DH110 SEA VIXEN   86 by 80 mm   1960-1965
Cast upper fuselage-wings, lower body and three chromed wheels, black nose, silver canopy, Royal Navy and roundel decals.
1. Gray upper, white lower surfaces.

739-G   MITSUBISHI A6M5 ZERO-SEN   148 by 184 mm   1976-1977
Cast fuselage, lower body-wings and lower wing panel, and folding landing gear, black plastic wheels, red battery-powered propeller and antenna, clear canopy, red and white roundels and white-on-blac "61-131" labels.
1. Metallic turquoise upper, gray lower surfaces, black engine cowling.

741-G   SPITFIRE MARK II   140 by 172 mm   1976-1980
Same castings and parts as 719 but not motorized, blue and white roundels and red-white-blue flag labels, black plastic parts.
1. Tan and olive camouflaged upper, pale greenish-gray lower surfaces.

744-G   SEA KING ARMY HELICOPTER   160 mm   1976-1980
Same castings and parts as 724 and 736, black rotors and wheels, white-on-olive Army labels. Issued in set 618.
1. Olive body.

745-G   BELL 47 ARMY HELICOPTER   164 mm   1978-1980
Same castings and parts as 732, black rotors, white-on-olive Army labels. Issued in set 303.
1. Olive body.

749-G   AVRO VULCAN BOMBER   160 mm   1955-1956
Identical to #992: planned as 703, then 707, then 749; issued as 992 with number 749 cast on it. Cast in aluminum in small quantities.
1. Silver plane.

750-G   TELEPHONE CALL BOX   59 mm   #12c_1954-1960
Single casting, identical to 12c.
1. Red box, silver windows.

751-G   POLICE BOX   67 mm   #47a_1954-1960
Single casting, identical to 47a.
1. Dark blue box, silver windows.

751-H   MISSILES   1971-1976
Spares for #358 Enterprise.

751-J   SHUTTLECRAFT   1979-1980?
Spare for #364 Space Shuttle.

753-G   POLICE CONTROLLED CROSSING   152 mm   1962-1964
Road, signs, lamp standard, police box, policeman figure.

1. Gray road, ? other details.

754-G   PAVEMENT SET   1958-1962
Cardboard straight and curned road sections.
1. Gray and tan.

754-H   STARTER UNIT   1971
Starter for #370 Dragster.
1. Gray plastic box.

755-G   LAMP STANDARD (Single Arm)   146 mm   1960-1964
Cast base, plastic pole with orange light.
1. Light gray base, tan pole.

755-H   HARPOONS   1967-1978
Six harpoon missiles for #100 FAB-1.

756-G   LAMP STANDARD (Double Arm)   146 mm   1960-1964
Cast base, plastic pole with two orange lights.
1. Light gray base, tan pole.

756-H   ROCKETS   1967-1978
Spare missiles for #100, 104 and 353.

758-G   BOMB   1970-1978
Spare bomb for #721.

759-G   ROCKET   1972-1976
Spare rocket for #351.

760-G   PILLAR BOX   1954-1960
Cast mailbox with "EIIR" monogram cast in.
1. Red with black bottom.

760-H   ROCKET   1973-1978
Spare rocket for #725 and 730.

763-G, 764-G   POSTERS FOR ROAD HOARDINGS   1959-64, 1959-63
Advertising labels for #765 billboard.

765-G   ROAD HOARDING   106 mm   1959-1964
Plastic billboard and braces, white-on-black "David Allen & Sons" label on top, six advertising labels.
1. Green sign, tan braces.

766-G   BRITISH ROAD SIGNS: COUNTRY SET A   1959-1964
Six cast signs: bend to left, cattle crossing, crossroads, narrow bridge, railroad crossing gates, road junction.
1. White-black-red signs.

767-G   BRITISH ROAD SIGNS: COUNTRY SET B   1959-1964
Six cast signs: bend to right, grade crossing, humpback bridge, low bridge, steep hill, winding road.
1. White-black-red signs.

768-G   BRITISH ROAD SIGNS: TOWN SET A   1959-1964
Six cast signs: major road ahead, no entry (two), no right turn, school children, traffic circle.
1. White-black-red signs.

769-G   BRITISH ROAD SIGNS: TOWN SET B   1959-1964
Six cast signs: No waiting, road junction, school children, stop ahead, 30 mph/end 30 mph (two).
1. White-black-red-yellow signs.

770-G   ROAD SIGNS SET   #47_1954-1955
Set of twelve cast road signs, identical to #47.
1. White-black-red signs.

771-G   INTERNATIONAL ROAD SIGNS   1953-1963
Set of twelve cast signs.
1. White-black-red-blue-silver signs.

772-G   BRITISH ROAD SIGNS   1959-1963
Combined 766, 767, 768, 769 sets: 24 cast signs.
1. Signs and colors as before.

773-G   FOUR-WAY TRAFFIC LIGHT   64 mm   #47a_1954-1963

Cast four-sided light, identical to 47a.
1. Black and white pole and light box.

777-G   BELISHA BEACON   **51 mm   #47d_1954-1963**
Cast beacon light, identical to 47d.
1. Black-white-yellow.

778-G   ROAD REPAIR WARNING BOARDS   **1962-1967**
Six plastic signboards: two go-stop, one keep left, one road torn up, one danger, one no entry.
1. Red-white-gray-green.

780-G   PETROL PUMP SET   **#49_1954-1955**
Cast pumps, identical to #49.
1. Colors as before.

781-G   ESSO PETROL PUMPS   **114 mm   1955-1965**
Cast base and two pumps.
1. Tan base, Esso pumps.

782-G   SHELL PETROL STATION   **203 mm   1960-1970**
Plastic base and booth, four cast pumps, Shell sign, two figures.
1. Gray base, Shell pumps, ? other details.

783-G   BP PETROL STATION   **203 mm   1960-1965**
Plastic base and booth, four cast pumps, BP sign, two figures.
1. Gray base, yellow and white BP pumps, tan and green booth.

784-G   GOODS TRAIN SET   **1972-1975?**
Plastic locomotive, two freight cars.
1. Blue locomotive, one yellow and one red car.

785-G   SERVICE STATION   **337 by 185 mm   1960-1963**
Plastic station and building with sliding doors, ? other details.
1. Tan and red.

786-G   TIRE RACK WITH TIRES   **52 mm   1960-1967**
Cast rack with assorted tires, Dunlop decal.
1. Green rack.

787-G   LIGHTING KIT   **960-1964**
Light bulbs, sockets and wire for #785 or 954.

788-G   MARREL BUCKET   **68 mm   1960-1967**
Cast bucket with unpainted sheet metal arms, for #966.
1. Gray bucket.

790-G   GRANITE CHIPS   **1960-1962**
Bag of gray plastic chips.

791-G   COAL   **1960-1962**
Bag of black plastic chips.

792-G   PACKING CASES   **1960-1964**
Three tan plastic cases and lids, Hornby Dublo lettering.

793-G   PALLETS   **29 by 35 mm   1960-1964**
Plastic pallets for #404 or 930. Colors vary.

794-G   LOADING RAMP   **1955_#994**
Sheet metal ramp for #982 Car Carrier.
1. Blue ramp.

796-G   HEALEY SPORTS BOAT ON TRAILER   **108 mm   1960-1969**
Orange cast trailer, three gray or black smooth or treaded plastic wheels, boat with cream plastic hull, clear windshield, white steering wheel, plastic deck-interior.
1. Red deck.
2. Yellow deck.
3. Green deck.

797-G   HEALEY SPORTS BOAT   **94 mm   1960-1969**
Plastic boat as in #796, cream hull.
1. Red deck.
2. Yellow deck.
3. Green deck.

798-G   EXPRESS PASSENGER TRAIN   **301 mm   #16_1954-1959**

Cast engine-tender and two interlocking cars, red hubs, white tires, British Railways decals, black chassis and engine nose, cab and tender roof, silver windows.
1. Green engine, cream cars with maroon side panels.

800-F   MYSTERE IV-A FIGHTER   **68 by 59 mm   #60a_1959-1964**
Cast body, three black wheels, blue canopy, roundel and flag decals. Identical to 60a.
1. Silver plane.

800-H   RENAULT SINPAR 4X4   **83 mm   #815_1974**
Open car with cast body and olive turned hubs, black plastic tires, base, steering wheel, antenna and interior equipment, olive sheet metal folding frame with clear windshield, removable gray-green plastic top, suspension, silver headlights, red taillights, two soldier figures.
1. Olive body.

801-F   VAUTOUR FIGHTER   **92 by 80 mm   #60b_1959-1964**
Cast body, six black wheels, blue canopy, roundel and flag decals. Identical to 60b.
1. Silver plane.

801-G   U.S.S. ENTERPRISE   **102 mm   1980**
Identical to #371, small version of #358. British issue.
1. White body, black parts and lettering.

801-H   AMX 13T TANK   **108 mm   #817 _1973-1975**
Tank with cast body and turning turret, black sheet metal base, olive plastic hubs, gray treads. Reissue of #817.
1. Olive body, plastic antenna (1973-1974).
2. Olive body, no antenna (1975).

802-F   SIKORSKY S58 HELICOPTER   **75 mm   #60d_1959-1961**
Cast body, two black wheels, two black 4-blade rotors, larger one with yellow tips, blue and olive trim, yellow windows, black Sabena decals. Identical to 60d.
1. White upper, black lower body.

802-G   KLINGON BATTLE CRUISER   **100 mm   #372_1980**
Identical to #372, small version of #357. British issue.
1. Metallic blue body.

802-H   155 ABS HOWITZER   **146 mm   #819_1974**
Reissue of #819 with same castings, similar details.
1. Olive gun and chassis.

803-F   VICKERS VISCOUNT   **132 by 150 mm   #60e_1959-1961**
Cast upper fuselage and lower fuselage-wings, six metal wheels, four unpainted 4-blade propellers, blue nose cowling, F-BGNX registration, Air France, flag, emblem, window and trim decals. Identical to 60e.
1. Silver lower fuselage and wings, white upper fuselage.

803-G   U.S.S. ENTERPRISE   **102 mm   #371_1980**
Identical to 371 and 801. U.S. issue.
1. White body, black parts and lettering.

803-H   UNIC S.N.C.F. SEMI-TRAILER TRUCK   **255 mm   1967-1969**
Truck with cast cab, semi-trailer, removable tailgate and dark blue hubs, black tires and spare, cream plastic semi roof, light gray rear door, cab interior and trailer rests, black sheet metal cab base and hitch, silver grille, black bumper, red taillights on yellow panels, SNCF upper and "Pam Pam" lower labels.
1. Dark blue cab and semi.

804-F   NORD 2501 NORATLAS   **132 by 171 mm   1959-1963**
Cast upper fuselage-wings and lower fuselage, three metal wheels, two unpainted 4-blade propellers, blue cockpit windows, roundel and flag decals.
1. Silver plane.

804-G   KLINGON BATTLE CRUISER   **100 mm   #372_1980**
Identical to #372 and 802. U.S. issue.
1. Metallic blue body.

804-H   MERCEDES-BENZ UNIMOG TRUCK   **93 mm   #821_1973**
Reissue of #821 with same castings and details, new number on base.
1. Olive body.

805-F   UNIC MULTIBUCKET TRUCK   **132 mm   1966-1971**

Truck with cast cab, chassis-rear body, two light gray bucket arms, black control lever and black turned hubs, black tires and spare, dark gray plastic bucket, white Primagaz propane tank, black bucket hooks and hydraulic cylinders, black cab trim, silver grille, bumpers and headlights.
1. Red cab, light gray chassis and rear body.

806-F   BERLIET 6X6 ARMY WRECKER   **157 mm   #826_1973**
Reissue of #826, with same castings, similar details.
1. Olive body.

807-F   RENAULT ARMY AMBULANCE   **85 mm   #820_1973**
Reissue of #820 with same casting and opening rear door, olive turned hubs, black plastic tires and base with number (820 has metal base), windows, red cast-in crosses on white square panels, number and red cross labels.
1. Olive body.

808-F   GMC SAHARA WRECKER   **172 mm   1972-1974**
Tow truck with cast cab and chassis-hood, tan turned hubs, black tires and spare, tan plastic rear body, interior and hood, black cab top, crane boom, winch with line and hook, sheet metal windshield frame, black and silver headlights, red taillights.
1. Tan cab, chassis and body.
2. Olive cab, chassis and body.

809-F   GMC ARMY TROOP TRANSPORTER   **158 mm   1970-1974**
Covered truck with cast cab and chassis-hood, olive turned hubs, black tires and spare, black cab roof and winch with line and hook, olive plastic rear body, opening tailgate and cover, driver figure, black and silver headlights, red taillights, sheet metal windshield frame, white star decals.
1. Olive cab, chassis, hood and rear body.

810-F   COVERED 4-WHEEL TRAILER   **111 mm   #70_1959-1962**
Truck trailer with cast body and front axle mount, cast or turned hubs, black tires, green sheet metal cover and tow hook, wire tow bar.
1. Yellow body and cast hubs.
2. Yellow body and turned hubs.
3. Red body and cast hubs.
4. Red body and turned hubs.
Note: an Esso prototype exists, as do versions made privately of #32a parts, but none of these was ever issued by the factory.

810-H   DODGE 4X4 COMMAND CAR   **104 mm   1972-1974**
Covered car with cast body and chassis with number, olive turned hubs, black tires and spare, olive-gray plastic top, black box, driver figure, antenna, olive sheet metal windshield frame, silver headlights, black taillights.
1. Olive body and chassis.

811-F   CARAVAN TRAILER   **116 mm   1959-1963**
Trailer with cast body and silver hubs, black tires, small front wheel, black sheet metal base and tow bar, windows, white roof, red stripes.
1. Cream body, smooth central roof panel.
2. Cream body, ribbed central roof panel.

812-F   ONE-WHEEL TRAILER   **27 mm   1965-1969**
Plastic trailer with one wheel, identical to that included in #536.
1. Cream trailer.

813-F   AMX 155 SELF-PROPELLED GUN   **96 mm   1968-1971, 1974**
Cast body, two-piece gun, adjustable mount and olive front hubs, olive plastic hubs, gray treads, black parts and net, camouflage net.
1. Olive body and gun casting with wire brace.
2. Olive body and revised gun casting without brace.

814-F   PANHARD AML ARMORED CAR   **72 mm   1963-1971**
Cast body and turning turret, olive turned hubs, black tires, black sheet metal base, two black plastic antennas, silver lights, flag decal.
1. Olive body and turret.

815-F   PANHARD EBR TANK   **103 mm   #80a_1959-1963**
Cast body, turning turret, gun barrel and four wheels, olive turned hubs, black tires,

The New System of Catalog Numbers

black sheet metal base, silver headlights, red taillights, flag decals.
 1. Olive body, turret and wheels.

815-H RENAULT SINPAR MILITARY POLICE CAR 83 mm 1969-1970
Same casting and parts as #800, with triangular plastic antenna from front fenders to rear of top.
 1. Olive body, light gray antenna.
 2. Olive body, black antenna.

816-F HOTCHKISS-WILLYS JEEP 66 mm #80bp_1959-1963
Jeep with cast body, cast or turned olive hubs, black tires and spare, black sheet metal base, olive sheet metal windshield frame and steering wheel, plastic driver (olive or tan uniform, helmet or cap), silver headlights, red taillights.
 1. Olive body and cast hubs, slick tires, no tow hook.
 2. Olive body and turned hubs, treaded tires, olive tow hook, rear of casting revised.

816-H BERLIET GAZELLE ROCKET TRUCK 137 mm 1969-1971
Open version of #824 Berliet truck with cast body, turned hubs, black tires, windows, gray plastic launcher, white and red rocket, black lettering, white bumper.
 1. Olive body and hubs.

817-F AMX 15T TANK 108 mm #80c_1959-1970
Cast body, turning turret, gun barrel, and olive front and rear hubs, olive plastic inner hubs, treads, black sheet metal base, silver headlights, flag decals. Type 1 identical to 80c.
 1. Olive body and turret, black treads.
 2. Olive body and turret, gray treads and antenna.

818-F BERLIET 6X6 COVERED ARMY TRUCK 146 mm
#80d_1959-1970
Cast chassis-cab, rear body, and olive hubs, black tires and spares, olive sheet metal rear cover and tow hook, silver grille and headlights, flag decals.
 1. Olive body, black sheet metal base with number 80D.
 2. Olive body, olive sheet metal base, no number.

819-F ABS 155 HOWITZER 146 mm #80e_1959-1970
Cast barrel, swiveling mount, two-part chassis and wheel mounts, and olive hubs, black tires, wire parts. Identical to 80e.
 1. Olive gun barrel, mount and chassis.

820-F RENAULT ARMY AMBULANCE 85 mm #80f_1959-1970
Van with cast body and opening rear door, olive turned hubs, black tires, black sheet metal base, windows, red cast-in crosses on white square panels, silver headlights, flag decals. Identical to 80f. Reissued as #807 with plastic base.

821-F MERCEDES-BENZ COVERED UNIMOG 93 mm 1960-1970
Truck with cast body, olive turned hubs, black tires and spares, olive sheet metal windshield frame and tow hook, black sheet metal base, olive plastic cover, silver headlights, flag decals. Reissued as #804.
 1. Olive body and cover.

822-F M3 HALFTRACK 118 mm 1960-1971
Cast body and olive rear hubs, olive turned front hubs, black tires and tracks, black sheet metal base with number and mounts for black rollers, olive tow hook, silver winch, flag decals, +/- olive plastic mount with black machine gun.
 1. Olive body, no machine gun.
 2. Olive body, machine gun.

823-F FIELD KITCHEN TRAILER 65 mm 1962-1966
Trailer with cast body, olive turned hubs, black tires, spare wheel, olive plastic chimney, olive sheet metal base.
 1. Olive body.

823-H GMC ARMY TANK TRUCK 158 mm 1969-1970
Castings of #809 with plastic tank and cab cover, ? other details.
 1. Olive body and tank.

824-F BERLIET GAZELLE 6X6 ARMY TRUCK 134 mm 1963-1970
Cast body with number, olive turned hubs, black tires, spare wheel, olive rear

cover, windows, black sheet metal base, olive tow hook, silver headlights, red taillights, flag decal.
 1. Olive body.

825-F DUKW AMPHIBIAN 171 mm 1963-1971
Cast lower body with number, olive cast hubs, black tires, olive plastic upper body, black sheet metal axle clips, olive windshield frame and propeller, silver winch and headlights, red taillights, flag decal.
 1. Olive body, no driver.
 2. Olive body, driver.

826-F BERLIET ARMY WRECKER 171 mm 1965-1971
Cast chassis-cab, rear body, mount and two-piece telescopic crane boom, olive turned hubs, black tires, spare wheel operating winch with line and hook, black sheet metal base, windows, silver grille, winches and headlights, flag decals. Type 2 reissued as #806.
 1. Olive body, same chassis as #818.
 2. Olive body, new chassis (as #806).

827-F PANHARD EBR FL-10 TANK 103 mm 1964-1971
Cast body, turning turret and four wheels, four olive turned hubs, black tires, black sheet metal base with number, silver headlights, red taillights, flag decal.
 1. Olive body and turret.

828-F JEEP WITH SS10 MISSILES 67,69 mm 1964-1971
Same castings and parts as 816, olive plastic missile rack and driver.
 1. Olive body, no tow hook.
 2. Olive body, modified casting with tow hook.

829-F JEEP WITH 106SR GUN 67, 69 mm 1964-1971
Same castings and parts as 816 and 828, olive plastic gun mount and driver.
 1. Olive body, no tow hook.
 2. Olive body, modified casting with tow hook.

830-F RICHIER ROAD ROLLER 112 mm #90a_1959-1969
Cast body, chassis, roof, front mount, two-piece front roller and two side rollers (unpainted surfaces, red sides) and driver in blue, metal exhaust and roof pillars, black sheet metal base and tow hook, cream steering wheel, silver grilles, red trim. Identical to 90a.
 1. Yellow-orange body.

833-F TRANSFORMER		1962-1969

Plastic parts; for #898.
 1. Gray transformer.

834-F ACCESSORIES FOR PONTOON BRIDGE 1963-1970
Parts for #884.
 1. Olive parts.

835-F LARGE BLACK TIRES	1959-1971
836-F LARGE WHITE TIRES	1959-1971
837-F SMALL BLACK TIRES	1959-1971
838-F SMALL WHITE TIRES	1959-1971

Each set contains twelve tires.
 1. Slick tires (1959-1960).
 2. Treaded tires (1961-1971).

839-F RACING TIRES	1959-1963

 1. Twelve black treaded tires.

839-H RALLY DECALS	1971

 1. Two sets of decals for rally cars.

840-F ELASTIC FOR FIRE TRUCK	1959-1970

 1. ?

841-F AMX TANK TREADS	1959-1974

Twelve replacement treads.
 1. Black rubber (1959-1965).
 2. Gray plastic (1966-1974).

842-F BLACK VESPA TIRES	1959-1964

 1. Twelve small black tires for #529 Vespa.

843-F MILITARY TIRES	1962-1971
844-F PIPES	1959-1971

 1. Twelve black treaded tires.

 1. Six black plastic pipes for #893.

845-F VAUBAN BARRIERS	1959-1970

 1. Ten gray plastic barriers.

846-F OIL DRUMS	1959-1970

 1. Ten gray plastic oil drums.

847-F BARRELS	1959-1970

 1. Ten brown plastic barrels.

848-F TRUNKS	1959-1970

 1. Ten brown plastic trunks.

849-F PACKING CASES	1959-1970

 1. Ten cream plastic packing cases.

850-F CASES OF BOTTLES	1959-1970

 1. Ten plastic cases with bottles.

851-F ASSORTED FREIGHT	1959-1970

 1. Two each of 846, 147, 848, 849 and 850.

852-F HALFTRACK TREADS	1962-1971

 1. Black rubber replacement treads for #822.

853-F TIRES FOR GBO	1962-1964, 1967-1968

 1. Twelve black tires for #886 or 888.

854-F MILK CRATES	1962-1968

 1. Ten white plastic cases of bottles for #586.

855-F RENAULT R4 TIRES	1962-1970

 1. Twelve black tires for #518.

856-F MACHINE GUN	1963-1971

 1. Black plastic gun for #822 halftrack.

857-F RACING FRONT TIRES	1970-1971
858-F RACING REAR TIRES	1970-1971

 1. Wide tires for #1417 and 1422.

859-F LARGE DIAMETER TIRES	1970

 1. Black plastic tires for #1419 Ford.

860-F BATTERY (1.5 volt)	1963-?
861-F LIGHT BULBS (1.5 volt)	1964-?
862-F LIGHT BULB (1.5 volt)	1965-?
863-F MAZDA BATTERY	1964-?
864-F LIGHT BULB	1968-?

870-F OCEAN LINER "FRANCE" 263 mm 1962-1971
Ship with cast hull, white plastic superstructure, masts and lettering, red and black funnels, black two-wheel units, removable red bottom of hull with white propellers, in clear plastic box with blue bottom.
 1. Black hull, white superstructure.

881-F GMC CIRCUS TRUCK AND TRAILER 340 mm 1969-1971
Cast truck cab, truck and trailer chassis, yellow trailer body and hitch, maroon trailer front axle mount and turned hubs, black tires and spare, yellow plastic rear truck body, opening tailgate, trailer silding doors and opening cage doors, black cab roof, winch and tow hooks, three animals in green cages, amber roof glass, maroon sheet metal windshield frame and steering wheel, Pinder labels.
 1. Maroon cab and both chassis.

882-F PEUGEOT 404 AND CIRCUS CARAVAN 219 mm 1969-1971
Set of #536 Peugeot and #564 Caravan; car has white plastic roof rack with red-lettered sign, caravan has Pinder lettering.
 1. Red car with white stripe, yellow caravan with white roof and red chassis.

883-F AMX BRIDGELAYING TANK 96 mm 1964-1971
Cast body (=817), new superstructure and hubs, olive plastic folding bridge, bridgelaying apparatus (with metal rods) and inner hubs, black treads, black sheet

The New System of Catalog Numbers

metal base, silver headlights, flag decals.
1. Olive tank and bridge; base with number 817.
2. Olive tank and bridge; new base with number 883.

884-F BROCKWAY PONTOON BRIDGE TRUCK   175 mm   1961-1970
Truck with cast cab, chassis-rear body and arms, olive turned hubs, black tires and spare, black sheet metal rear springs and control bars, olive plastic bridge parts, windows, olive rubberized plastic pontoons, silver winch and headlights, red taillights, flag decals.
1. Olive body and bridge.

885-F BLAW-KNOX BULLDOZER   143 mm   1959-1961
French issue of British #961.
1. Orange body, gray blade.

885-H SAVIEM PIPE TRUCK   222 mm   1966-1971
Truck with cast body, red plastic cab, sliding doors, wheels and hooks, black tires, front base and racks, driver in blue, windows, jewel headlights, load of metal rods, magnets.
1. Light gray body, red cab.

886-F RICHIER ROAD GRADER   176 mm   1960-1965
Cast body, front axle mount, control mount, two-piece blade mount, gray blade, driver in blue, red plastic hubs and parts, black tires and painted parts, black sheet metal control levers, metal control rods, green engine.
1. Yellow body and mounts.

887-F MUIR HILL DUMP TRUCK   106 mm   1959-1961
French issue of British #962.
1. Cream body, red wheels.

887-H UNIC AIR FUEL TANKER: BP   306 mm   1963-1971
Tanker semi with cast cab and semi chassis, white plastic tank and hubs, black tires, spare, cab interior, battery holder and parts, green tank base, yellow tank top and caps, black sheet metal base, hitch and ladders, plastic and metal spigot, gray hose.
1. White-yellow-green cab, green semi chassis.

888-F BERLIET GBO SAHARIEN   171 mm   1966-1968
Truck with cast body and cab and unpainted winch mount, tan plastic hubs, black tires, black sheet metal base, windows, black exhaust stack, wire boom, winch crank, line and hook.
1. Tan body, white roof, steel metal spring under hole in rear deck.
2. No spring, otherwise as type 1.

888I-F BERLIET GBO "LANGUEDOCIENNE"   171 mm   196?
Promotional version of #888 with "Croix-Rouge" and "La Languedocienne" decals.
1. Tan body, white roof?

889-F COLES MOBILE CRANE   163 mm   1959
French issue of British #972.
1. Dark orange body, dark yellow cabin and crane.

889-H BERLIET PARIS BUS   224 mm   1965-1970
Cast body and black base with number, dark green turned hubs, black tires, suspension, steering, dark green plastic opening doors, light brown interior, windows, gray running boards, jewel headlights, red taillights, silver grille, black and white signs, Dunlop and destination labels.
1. Dark green lower body and roof, white upper body.

889u-F BERLIET URBAN BUS   224 mm   1965-1970
Castings and parts as 889 bus, different lettering and colors.
1. Red lower body, doors and hubs, dark cream upper body and roof.

890-F BERLIET TANK TRANSPORTER   315 mm   1959-1970
Flat semi with cast cab, semi-trailer and two folding ramps, cast and turned olive hubs, black tires and spare, black sheet metal base, windows, silver winch, grille and headlights, flag decals.
1. Olive cab and semi-trailer.

891-F SE 210 CARAVELLE   172 by 180 mm   #60f_1959-1968
Airliner with cast upper body, lower fuselage-wings, engines and opening stair ramp, ten small wheels, blue nose cowling, silver cockpit windows, F-BGNY

registration, Air France logo, flag, trim and window decals.
1. White upper fuselage, silver lower fuselage, wings, engines and tail. Regular issue.
2. Air Algerie logo: small series.
3. Swissair logo: small series.
4. Scandinavian Air System logo: small series.

892-F LOCKHEED CONSTELLATION   182 by 199 mm   #60c_1959-1962
Airliner with cast upper fuselage-tail and lower fuselage-wings, six small wheels, four 3-blade propellers, red cones, blue cockpit windows, F-BHBX registration, Air France logo, flag, trim and window decals.
1. Silver plane.

893-F UNIC PIPE TRUCK   225 mm   #39b_1959-1970
Truck with cast cab, chassis, white roof rack and semi-trailer, cast and turned tan hubs, black tires, two spares, black sheet metal hutch, and mount for unpainted rest wheel, black plastic pipes, windows, wire bars. Type 1 is identical to 39a.
1. Tan cab and semi, white roof rack, center bar of semi is pierced.
2. Bar is not pierced, othwerwise as type 1.

894-F UNIC-BOILLOT AUTO TRANSPORTER 325 mm   #39a_1959-1968
Car carrier with cast cab, chassis, upper and lower semi decks and sliding ramp, orange turned hubs, black tires, spare, black sheet metal semi base and hitch/rest, unpainted rest wheel, wire and sheet metal apparatus to move upper deck, blue "Dinky Toys Service Livraison" decals. Type 1 is identical to 39a.
1. Silver and orange cab, silver semi, no windows.
2. Windows, otherwise as type 1.

895-F UNIC MULTIBUCKET TRUCK   132 mm   #38a_1959-1965
Truck with cast cab, body-chassis, arms, gray bucket and black bar, cast and turned yellow hubs, black tires and spare, unpainted metal lever and parts, black plastic hydraulic cylinders. Identical to 38a.
1. Gray and yellow cab, yellow rear body, chassis and arms.

896-F WILLEME COVERED SEMI-TRAILER TRUCK   265 mm   #36b_1959-1971
Truck with cast cab, semi-trailer and opening doors, cast and turned orange hubs, black tires and spare, black sheet metal hitch, black cab base and orange tow hook, green plastic rear cover, small rest wheels, silver grille, bumpers and headlights.
1. Red cab, orange and red semi, straight bars on back of cab casting (=36b).
2. Curved inner surfaces of these bars, otherwise as type 1.
3. Less detailed semi casting, otherwise as type 2.

897-F WILLEME LUMBER TRUCK   225 mm   #36a_1959-1971
Truck with cast cab (=896) and semi-trailer, yellow turned hubs, black tires and spare, black sheet metal hitch and rest, unpainted metal rest wheel, wire bars, load of logs. Type 1 is identical to 36a.
1. Orange cab with straight rear bars, yellow semi with pierced center bar.
2. Curved rear cab bars, otherwise as type 1.
3. Semi center bar not pierced, curved rear cab bars, otherwise as type 1.

898-F BERLIET TRANSFORMER CARRIER   315 mm   1961-1965
Low loader with cast cab, semi-trailer and two folding ramps (=890), cast and turned yellow hubs, black tires, two spares, black sheet metal base and hitch, windows, gray plastic transformer (=833), silver winch, grille and headlights, yellow and black striped rear bumper.
1. Orange cab and semi.

899-F DELAHAYE FIRE TRUCK   120 mm   #32d_1959-1970
Ladder truck with cast body and two-piece ladder mount, red turned hubs, white tires, unpainted two-piece sheet metal aerial ladder, rack and windshield frame, black base, white steering wheel, silver running boards, deck, grille and headlights, two operating cranks. Identical to 32d.
1. Red body and ladder mount.

900-G BUILDING SITE GIFT SET   1964
Boxed set of 437 Loader, 960 Concrete Mixer, 961 Bulldozer, 962 Muir Hill Dumper and 965 Euclid Dumper.

1. Standard colors.

901-G FODEN 8 WHEEL TRUCK   188 mm   #501 _1955-1957
Open truck with cast chassis-cab, rear body and Supertoy hubs, gray or black tires, spare wheel, black sheet metal cab base, tow hook matching chassis, silver grille, bumper and headlights.
1. Orange chassis-cab, gray-brown body, green hubs.
2. Red? chassis-cab, gray-brown body, ? hubs.
3. Dark blue chassis-cab, light blue body, ? hubs.

902-G FODEN 8 WHEEL FLAT TRUCK   188 mm   #502 _1955-1960
Cast chassis-cab, flat rear body and Supertoy hubs, gray or black tires, spare wheel, black sheet metal cab base, tow hook matching chassis, silver grille, bumper and headlights. Identical to last 502.
1. Red chassis-cab and hubs, light green body.
2. Orange chassis-cab, light green body and hubs.

903-G FODEN 8 WHEEL FLAT TRUCK WITH TAILBOARD   188 mm   #503 _1955-1960
Cast chassis-cab, flat rear body with tailboard, and Supertoy hubs, gray or black tires, spare wheel, black sheet metal cab base, tow hook matching chassis, silver grille, bumper and headlights. Identical to second type 903.
1. Light blue chassis-cab and hubs, tan rear body.
2. Dark purplish-blue chassis-cab, orange rear body, light blue hubs.

(904 FODEN 8-WHEEL TANK TRUCK: never so numbered. See 941.)

905-G FODEN 8 WHEEL FLAT TRUCK WITH CHAINS   188 mm   #505 _1955-1964
Cast chassis-cab, flat rear body, six stakes, and Supertoy hubs, gray or black tires, spare wheel, chain around rear body, black sheet metal cab base, tow hook matching chassis, silver grille, bumpers and headlights. Identical to second type 505.
1. Red chassis-cab and hubs, light gray rear body.
2. Maroon chassis-cab and rear body, red hubs.
3. Green chassis-cab and rear body, light green hubs.

908-G THORNEYCROFT MIGHTY ANTAR WITH TRANSFORMER   337 mm   1962-1966 Low loader with cast cab, chassis, semi-trailer, red folding ramps & Supertoy hubs, black tires, spare wheel, gray plastic transformer (=833), windows, blue driver, silver grille & headlights, black & white stripe decals on ramps.
1. Dark yellow cab, light gray semi-trailer.

911-G GUY OTTER FOUR TON TRUCK   133 mm   #511 _1954-1956 /#431
Open truck with cast chassis-cab, open rear body and Supertoy hubs, details as last type 511.
1. Dark blue chassis-cab, light blue rear body and hubs.

912-G GUY OTTER FOUR TON FLAT TRUCK   133 mm   #512 _1954-1956 /#432
Flat truck with cast chassis-cab, flat rear body and Supertoy hubs, details as last type 512.
1. Dark blue chassis-cab, orange rear body, light blue hubs.

913-G GUY OTTER FLAT TRUCK WITH TAILBOARD   133 mm   #513 _1954-1956 /#433
Truck with cast chassis-cab, flat rear body with tailboard, and Supertoy hubs, details as last type 513.
1. Dark purplish-blue chassis-cab, orange rear body, light blue hubs.
2. Green chassis-cab, light green rear body and hubs.

914-G A.E.C. ARTICULATED TRUCK   210 mm   1967-1974
Semi-trailer truck with cast cab, chassis, semi, black folding rest and cab base, metal or plastic hubs, black tires and grille, green rear cover, red tailgate, white or blue interior, clear windows and headlights, silver bumper.
1. Red cab and plastic hubs, white semi, white British Road Services logo, white cab interior, painted grille.
2. White cab, unpainted metal hubs, white semi, ? logo, blue cab interior, grille label.

194

The New System of Catalog Numbers

915-G AEC ARTICULATED FLAT TRUCK   210 mm 1973-1975
Semi-trailer truck with cast cab, flat semi, black cab base, unpainted hubs and folding rest, black tires, plastic cab interior, windows, jewel headlights, silver grille and bumper, white-on-orange "Truck Hire Co. Liverpool" and stripe labels.
1. Dark orange cab, white semi, ivory interior, painted grille.
2. Black cab interior, grille label, otherwise as type 1.
3. White cab and semi, "Thames Board Mills" logo: promotional model.

917-G GUY OTTER VAN: SPRATTS   132 mm #514 _1955-1956
Van with cast chassis-cab, rear body, opening rear doors and red Supertoy hubs, black tires, spare wheel, black sheet metal bases, black and red Spratts logo, silver grille and headlights.
1. Red chassis-cab, cream rear body, square casting around license plate.
2. Triangular casting side panels, otherwise as type 1.

917-H MERCEDES-BENZ TRUCK AND TRAILER   397 mm 1968-1977
Covered truck and trailer with cast cab, opening doors, chassis, rear body, trailer body, chassis and front axle mount, unpainted black hubs, black tires, plastic truck and trailer covers, white tailgates and cab roof panel, red cab interior, silver and black grille, silver bumper, jewel headlights, red taillights.
1. Blue cab and chassis, yellow bodies, blue covers.
2. White covers, otherwise as type 1.
3. White covers and cab roof, otherwise as type 1.

918-G GUY OTTER VAN: EVER READY   132 mm 1955-1958
Same castings and parts as 917 van, white-orange-black-yellow "Ever Ready Batteries for Life" logo, white "Ever Ready" on front of rear body, cab casting with triangular panels beside license plate.
1. Blue chassis-cab and rear body, red hubs.

919-G GUY OTTER VAN: GOLDEN SHRED   132 mm 1957-1958
Same castings and parts as 917 and 918 vans, yellow and black "Robertson's Golden Shred" logo with colorful golliwog figure, cab casting with triangular panels beside license plate.
1. Red chassis-cab and rear body, yellow hubs.

920-G GUY WARRIOR VAN: HEINZ   137 mm 1959-1960
Van with cast chassis-cab, rear body, opening rear doors and yellow Supertoy hubs, black tires, spare wheel, black sheet metal bases, windows, silver grille, bumper and headlights, green "Heinz 57 Varieties" logo with ketchup bottle.
1. Red chassis-cab, dark yellow rear body.

921-G BEDFORD ARTICULATED TRUCK   165 mm #521 _1954-1955 _#409
Same castings and parts as 521 and 409.
1. Dark yellow cab and semi-trailer, black fenders and hitch.
2. Red cab, yellow semi-trailer, black fenders and hitch?

922-G BIG BEDFORD TRUCK   146 mm #522 _1954-1955 _#408
Same castings and parts as 522 and 408.
1. Maroon chassis-cab, tan rear body and hubs.
2. Dark blue chassis-cab, light orange rear body, dark yellow hubs.

923-G BEDFORD S VAN: HEINZ   146 mm 1955-1959
Van with cast chassis-cab, rear body, opening rear doors, and yellow Supertoy hubs, gray tires, spare wheel, black sheet metal bases, silver grille, bumper and headlights.
1. Red chassis-cab, yellow-orange rear body, turquoise and red "Heinz 57 Varieties" logo with bean can.
2. Dark green "Heinz 57 Varieties" logo with ketchup bottle, otherwise as type 1.

924-G AVELING BARFORD CENTAUR DUMP TRUCK   180 mm 1972-1977
Quarry dumper with cast cab, cab floor, tipper, silver chassis and unpainted tip release, red plastic hubs, black tires, white cab interior, windows, two black hydraulic cylinders with springs, black muffler, silver grille and headlights, black and white stripe label on front bumper, black "Aveling-Barford" labels.
1. Red cab, yellow tipper.

925-G LEYLAND DUMP TRUCK   192 mm 1965-1970
Dumper with cream cast cab and chassis and silver bumper, cast or plastic tipper, eight blue plastic hubs, black tires, white tailgate, light blue interior, clear windows and headlights, cream axle covers, silver grille, blue "Leyland" lettering, "Sand Ballast Gravel" and stripe labels.
1. Orange cast tipper.
2. Orange plastic tipper.
3. Red plastic tipper.
4. White plastic tipper.

930-G BEDFORD PALLET-JEKTA VAN   168 mm 1960-1964
Van with cast chassis-cab, rear body, two opening rear doors, silver Supertoy hubs, black tires, black sheet metal base, crank to operate rear floor sections, three orange plastic pallets, silver headlights, black-edged red "Meccano" and "Dinky Toys" logo.
1. Yellow upper, orange lower cab and rear body, orange chassis, no windows.
2. Windows, otherwise as type 1.

931-G LEYLAND COMET OPEN TRUCK   140 mm #531 _1954-1955 _#417
Same castings and parts as 531 and 417.
1. Dark blue chassis-cab, yellow-orange rear body, red hubs.

932-G LEYLAND COMET FLAT TRUCK WITH TAILBOARD   143 mm #532 _1954-1955 _#418
Same castings and parts as 532 and 418.
1. Green chassis-cab and hubs, orange rear body.

933-G LEYLAND COMET CEMENT TRUCK   143 mm #533 _1954-1955 _#419
Same castings and parts as 533 and 419.
1. Yellow chassis-cab, rear body and hubs.

934-G LEYLAND OCTOPUS OPEN TRUCK   194 mm 1956-1964
Eight-wheel truck with cast chassis-cab, open rear body, cast supertoy or plastic hubs, black tires, spare wheel, black sheet metal base, tow hook matching chassis color, silver grille and headlights.
1. Tan chassis-cab with green trim, green rear body, red cast hubs, no windows.
2. Dark blue chassis-cab with yellow trim, yellow rear body, red plastic hubs, no windows.
3. Windows, otherwise as type 2?

935-G LEYLAND OCTOPUS WITH CHAINS   194 mm 1964-1966
Flat truck with cast chassis-cab (=934), rear body and stakes, chain around rear body, black sheet metal base and tow hook, eight plastic hubs, black tires, spare wheel, red grille, silver headlights.
1. Green chassis-cab with ivory trim, ivory rear body, red hubs.
2. Blue chassis-cab with white trim, white? rear body, gray hubs.
3. Gray trim and rear body, otherwise as type 2.

936-G LEYLAND 8 WHEEL TEST CHASSIS   197 mm 1965-1969
Cast chassis and three "5 Tons" weights, red plastic cab, turning driveshaft and hubs, 12 black tires, clear axle covers, silver grille and headlights, "Another Leyland on Test" labels.
1. Silver chassis, yellow weights.
2. Silver and black chassis, yellow weights.
3. Silver chassis, gray weights.
4. Dark green chassis?, ? weights.

940-G MERCEDES-BENZ TRUCK   200 mm 1977-1979
Covered truck with cast cab, rear body and chassis, red interior and hubs, black tires and grille, light gray rear cover, white tailgate, windows, simplified #917 casting.
1. White cab and rear body, red chassis.
2. Dark green and white, "Cory" logo: Belgian promotional model.

941-G FODEN 8 WHEEL TANKER: MOBILGAS   188 mm #504 _1954-1957
Tanker with cast chassis-cab and red Supertoy hubs, black or gray tires, spare wheel, black sheet metal cab base, ladder and catwalk, red sheet metal tank components and tow hook, silver grille, bumper and headlights, red-white-blue Mobilgas emblems (also on rear of tank), blue-outlined white "Mobilgas" lettering.
1. Red chassis-cab, tank and filler caps, gray tires.
2. Red chassis-cab and tank, black filler caps and tires.

942-G FODEN 8 WHEEL TANKER: REGENT   188 mm 1955-1957
Same castings and parts as 941, blue-outlined cream "Regent" lettering, plus red-white-blue emblem on rear of tank.
1. Blue chassis-cab, red-white-blue tank.

943-G LEYLAND OCTOPUS TANKER: ESSO   194 mm 1957-1964
Tanker with cast chassis-cab (=934, 935), red sheet metal tank components and tow hook, black cast base, ladder, catwalk and filler caps, red plastic hubs, black tires, spare wheel, silver grille and headlights, cream stripe with blue "Esso Petroleum Company Ltd.", plus red-white-blue Esso emblem on rear of tank.
1. Red chassis-cab and tank.

944-G LEYLAND OCTOPUS TANKER: SHELL-B.P.   194 mm 1963-1969
Tanker with cast chassis-cab (=943), plastic hubs, black tires, spare wheel, white plastic tank on dark yellow base, black sheet metal cab base, tow hook matching chassis color, silver grille, bumper and headlights, red and yellow Shell and green-yellow-white B.P. labels.
1. White upper and dark yellow lower cab, light gray chassis, gray hubs, no windows.
2. Windows, otherwise as type 1.
3. Yellow hubs, ? other details.
4. White cab, black chassis, white tank with black stripe, white hubs, windows, Corn Products Ltd. logo: promotional model.

945-G A.E.C. ARTICULATED TANKER   266 mm 1966-1977
Tanker with cast cab, cab chassis, base, tank, tank chassis and trailer rest (+/-wheels), cast or plastic hubs, black tires, plastic tank top and filler caps, interior, windows, fuel tank and gray hose, silver grille and bumper, jewel or silver cast-in headlights.
1. White cab, tank, base, fillers and rest, red rest wheels and fuel tank, light gray hubs and cab interior, Esso emblems and red logo panels, plus "Put a Tiger in your Tank" design on rear.
2. No rear label, otherwise as type 1.
3. No rear label, light gray cab, otherwise as type 1.
4. Green cab, tank and tank chassis, black cab chassis, interior and base, brown fuel tank, light gray filler caps, unpainted cast hubs and rest including cast-in wheels, white Lucas Oil logo.

948-G McLEAN TRACTOR-TRAILER   195 mm 1961-1967
Semi with cast cab, cab chassis, semi chassis and rest wheels, red plastic hubs, black tires, light gray semi body and opening rear doors, windows, silver grille and headlights, red taillights, red-white-black "McLean Trucking Company" emblems and stripes.
1. Red cab, black semi chassis.

949-G WAYNE SCHOOL BUS   222 mm 1961-1966
Bus with cast body, black sheet metal base, red plastic interior and hubs, black tires, windows, silver emblem, bumper and headlights, red lights, black rear bumper and "School Bus" and other lettering.
1. Light orange body, black trim.
2. Light orange body, red trim.

(950 CAR TRANSPORTER SET never issued)
(Was to include 136, 138, 162, 168, 342 and 974: 1969)

950-G FODEN ARTICULATED TANKER   266 mm 1978-1980
Tanker semi with cast cab, cab chassis, opening doors, tank chassis, and unpainted trailer rest, white plastic tank and hubs, black tires, cab interior, pipes and fuel tank,

black or gray tank top and filler caps, windows, plastic hose, silver headlights. logo labels.

  1. Red cab and tank chassis, black tank top, black-red-blue Burmah emblems and black Burmah lettering labels.

  2. Gray tank top and filler caps, otherwise as type 1.

  3. Gray tank top and filler caps, Shell logo labels, otherwise as type 1.

951-G TRUCK TRAILER   **105 mm** **#551** _1954-1955 _#428
Same castings and parts as 551 and 428.

  1. Light gray body.

952-G BEDFORD VEGA MAJOR LUXURY COACH 245 mm 1964-1971
Bus with cast body, opening hatch, base and patterned hubs, black tires, suspension, steering, cream plastic interior, windows, working amber lights, battery mount in base, silver grille and bumpers, jewel or silver cast-in headlights, red taillights, trim labels.

  1. Light gray body and base, white interior, cast-in headlights, no sheet metal battery rack, "Lowland" lettering.

  2. Ivory body, light gray base, cream interior, cast-in headlights, silver and maroon trim labels with "Vega Major".

  3. Light blue interior, jewel headlights, otherwise as type 2.

  4. Cream body, chocolate brown trim, ? other details.

  5. Yellow base, 5-bolt hubs, ? other details.

953-G CONTINENTAL TOURING COACH   **222 mm 1963-1966**
Bus with cast body (=949), black sheet metal base, red plastic hubs, black tires, plastic interior, windows, silver emblem, bumpers, lights and trim, red lights, red-on-cream "Dinky Continental Tours" decals.

  1. Pale aqua body, white roof, tan interior.

  2. White interior, otherwise as type 1.

954-G FIRE STATION   **252 by 203 mm 1961-1964**
Plastic brick-pattern walls, red doors, cream roof, gray floor, red lettering.

  1. All plastic.

954-H BEDFORD VEGA MAJOR LUXURY COACH 245 mm 1972-1977
Reissue of 952 minus battery and working lights, with black cast base, unpainted 5-bolt hubs, bright blue interior, maroon and silver labels with "Vega Major" lettering.

  1. Ivory body.

955-G COMMER FIRE ENGINE   **140 mm #555** _1955-1969
Fire truck with cast body and two-piece silver ladder, cast Supertoy or plastic hubs, black tires, black sheet metal base, tow hook and ladder mount, two bells, gray hose reels, silver grille, bumpers, headlights and rear panels.

  1. Red body and cast hubs, no windows.

  2. Windows, otherwise as type 1.

  3. Red body and plastic hubs, windows.

956-G BEDFORD FIRE ESCAPE   **197 mm 1958-1969**
Ladder truck with body and two-piece ladder mount, red plastic hubs, black tires, black sheet metal base with number, two-piece unpainted aerial ladder, two bells, cranks, gears and lines to operate ladder, silver grille, bumper, headlights and rear deck, +/- black step on each side.

  1. Red body, no windows.

  2. Red body, windows.

956-H BERLIET FIRE ESCAPE   **200 mm 1969-1974**
Same castings and parts as #568, cream plastic interior, black plastic base with number, hubs with metal caps, silver stripe.

  1. Metallic maroon cab and ladder mount, silver rear body.

  2. Falck labels, otherwise as type 1.

957-G FIRE SERVICE GIFT SET   **1959-1966**
Boxed set of 257 Fire Chief's Car, 955 and 956 Fire Engines.

  1. Standard colors.

958-G GUY WARRIOR SNOW PLOW TRUCK   **197 mm 1961-1966**
Open truck with cast chassis-cab, rear body, tailgate, front rack and raising snowplow, yellow Supertoy hubs, black tires, spare wheel, black sheet metal cab base and plow

mount, black plastic hydraulic cylinder, windows, blue dome light.

  1. Yellow and black chassis-cab and plow, yellow rear body and tailgate.

  2. Silver plow, otherwise as type 1.

959-G FODEN DUMP TRUCK WITH PLOW   **166 mm 1962-1968**
Dumper with cast cab, tipper, chassis and plow, red plastic hubs, black tires, hydraulic cylinders and parts, blue driver, windows, silver grille, headlights and plow blade.

  1. Red cab, tipper and plow (except blade), silver chassis.

  2. Silver tipper, otherwise as type 1.

960-G ALBION CHIEFTAIN CONCRETE MIXER   **130 mm 1960-1968**
Truck with cast body, barrel and unpainted gears, wire mount, black plastic hubs, gray (or black?) tires, spare wheel, silver grille and headlights. Barrel turns as truck rolls.

  1. Orange body, gray barrel with blue trim on ring gear, no windows.

  2. Windows, otherwise as type 1.

  3. Windows, yellow barrel with blue trim, otherwise as type 1.

961-G BLAW KNOX BULLDOZER   **143 mm #561** _1955-1964
Tractor with cast body, blade, black arms, stacks and hubs, and tan driver, black sheet metal base, tow hook, blade mounts and control levers, black hydraulic cylinders, black or green rubber treads.

  1. Red body and blade.

  2. Yellow body, light gray blade.

  3. ? plastic body, green and orange blade?

961-H VEGA MAJOR COACH: PTT   **245 mm 1973-1977**
Same casting as 954, unpainted 5-bolt hubs, light blue plastic interior, red stripe and black-on-orange PTT labels.

  1. Light orange body, light yellow roof.

962-G MUIR HILL DUMP TRUCK   **106 mm #562** _1955-1965
Dumper with cast chassis-cab, tipper, tan driver, black swiveling seat and steering wheel, and wheels or hubs, black sheet metal base, front axle mount and tow hook, silver ornament and headlights.

  1. Yellow body and tipper, cast wheels with red hubs and unpainted treads.

  2. Red hubs, black rubber tires, otherwise as type 1.

963-G BLAW-KNOX HEAVY TRACTOR   **118 mm #563** _1955-1959
Tractor with cast body (=961), tan driver, black stacks and light green hubs, green (or black?) rubber treads, black sheet metal base, tow hook and control levers.

  1. Red body.

  2. Orange body.

  3. Yellow body.

963-H ROAD GRADER   **238 mm 1973-1975**
Cast front body, cab-engine, yellow base and swiveling front axle mount, pale blue lower frame, and unpainted swiveling blade and hubs, black tires and interior, orange painted engine hood.

  1. Orange front body, yellow cab-engine casting.

964-G ELEVATOR LOADER   **156 mm #564** _1952-1954
Cast frame, chute, hopper, rollers, gears, and light blue Supertoy hubs, gray tires, #964 cast on hopper, other details as #564.

  1. Yellow body, light blue chute and hopper.

  2. Blue body, yellow chute and hopper.

970-G JONES FLEETMASTER CANTILEVER CRANE   **174 mm 1967-1974**
Crane truck with cast Bedford cab, crane base, black chassis, two-piece hinged white crane boom, and unpainted hook and parts, hubs with metal caps, black tires, red plastic crank, winches and interior, windows, white sheet metal clip, silver grille, bumper, emblem and headlights, red taillights, "Jones" and stripe labels.

  1. Red cab and crane base.

  2. Red cab and crane base, white roof.

  3. Metallic red cab and crane base.

  4. Yellow cab and crane base.

971-G COLES MOBILE CRANE   **162 mm #571** _1955-1966

Cast body, black chassis, blue driver, and yellow Supertoy hubs, gray (or black?) tires, black sheet metal base, yellow boom, two cranks, line and hook, black-on-yellow "Coles" and black-and-white stripe decals.

  1. Dark yellow body.

972-G COLES 20-TON CRANE TRUCK   **245 mm 1955-1969**
Truck with cast body, crane base and boom, black sheet metal bases, yellow cast or plastic hubs, gray or black tires, driver in blue, silver grille, bumper and headlights, two cranks, lines and hook, black-on-yellow "Coles" decals.

  1. Orange body, yellow-orange crane base, boom and cast hubs, gray tires, no stripe decals.

  2. Plastic hubs, black tires, black and white stripe decals, otherwise as type 1.

973-G GOODS YARD CRANE   **102 by 178 mm #752** _1955-1959
Crane with cast base, swiveling mount and boom, two cranks, lines and hook, black lettering. Identical to #752.

  1. Dark yellow crane and mount, blue base.

973-H EATON YALE ARTICULATED TRACTOR SHOVEL   **178 mm 1971-1975**
Cast main and front body, yellow base, shovel and arm, orange ram mount, unpainted sheet metal bases, yellow plastic hubs, black tires, white plastic cab interior, windows, yellow painted engine hood, unpainted shovel interior, black-on-yellow Yale labels.

  1. Orange main and front body, window in cab roof.

  2. Yellow main and front body, closed cab roof, whole shovel unpainted.

974-G A.E.C. HOYNOR CAR TRANSPORTER   **322 mm 1969-1975**
Car carrier with cast cab, chassis, upper and lower semi decks and two folding ramps, unpainted parts, hubs with metal caps, black tires, white plastic interior, windows, two removable red plastic blocks, black hydraulic cylinders, jewel headlights, silver grille and bumper, "Silcock & Colling Ltd." and "SC" emblem labels.

  1. Metallic blue cab, yellow chassis and upper deck, orange lower deck and ramps.

975-G RUSTON BUCYRUS EXCAVATOR   **190 mm 1963-1967**
Power shovel with cast two-piece chassis, boom, shovel and opening shovel bottom, yellow plastic body, gray panel, controls and hubs, gray or black muffler, black treads, red and green pulleys, windows, silver catwalk, "Ruston-Bucyrus" labels.

  1. Red chassis, gray muffler, green boom and shovel, rubber treads.

  2. Plastic treads, otherwise as type 1.

  3. Black muffler, ? other details.

976-G MICHIGAN 180-111 TRACTOR DOZER   **147 mm 1967-1976**
Cast body, chassis, axle mount, bar, red blade and silver parts, red plastic seat, engine covers and hubs, black tires and hydraulic cylinders, silver and red lights, "Michigan" labels.

  1. Yellow body and chassis.

977-G SERVICING PLATFORM VEHICLE   **130 mm 1960-1964**
Truck with cast body, dark cream jacks, red swiveling mount and Supertoy hubs, black tires, spare wheel, black sheet metal cab base, red lower and upper arms, red plastic platform, windshield, silver taillights. Same castings and parts as #667.

  1. Dark cream body.

977-H SHOVEL DOZER   **151 mm 1973-1977**
Tractor with cast body, chassis, yellow arms, dark orange shovel with unpainted interior, black plastic interior, hubs, treads and hydraulic cylinders, dark orange painted silver grille and vents, light orange sheet metal chassis panels, red stripes.

  1. Yellow body and chassis.

978-G BEDFORD TK REFUSE WAGON   **152 mm 1964-1980**
Garbage truck with cast cab, chassis and tipping frame, pale gray plastic rear body and opening panels, red plastic or unpainted cast 6-bolt hubs, black tires, red plastic interior, +/- white plastic roof rack, two garbage cans and lids, windows, silver grille, bumper and headlights, red "Refuse Wagon" and black-and-yellow stripe and emblem labels.

The New System of Catalog Numbers

1. Green cab, white roof rack, charcoal chassis, red hubs.
2. Metallic green cab, otherwise as type 1.
3. Lime green cab, with cast-in roof rack, black chassis, cast hubs.
4. Lime green cab with cast-in roof rack, black chassis, cast hubs.
5. Pale yellow-green cab with cast-in roof rack, dark brown chassis, cast hubs.

979-G MAUDSLEY RACE HORSE TRANSPORTER 175 mm 1961-1964
Horse van with cast body, light gray chassis and two opening ramps, and yellow Supertoy hubs, black tires, two gray plastic horses, silver grille and headlights, "Newmarket Race Horse Transport Service Ltd." and horsehead decals.
1. Light gray body, yellow side ramps.

980-G MAUDSLEY HORSE BOX 175 mm 1955-1961?
Same castings and parts as #979, red hubs, yellow "Express Horse Van" and "Hire Service" lettering. For the U.S. market.
1. Maroon body, chassis and ramps.

980-H COLES HYDRA CRANE 210 mm 1972-1979
Crane truck with cast cab, black chassis, telescopic 3-piece boom and mount matching cab color, unpainted jacks, controls, hook and hubs, black tires, spare, black hydraulic cylinders, windows, silver grille and bumper, black and white "Coles" labels.
1. Dark yellow cab, boom and mount.
2. Orange cab, boom and mount.

**981-G MAUDSLEY HORSE BOX: BRITISH RAILWAYS 175 mm
#581 _1955-1961**
Same castings and parts as #979 and 980, red hubs, red-and-yellow British Railways emblem and "Express Horse Box Hire Service" lettering.
1. Maroon body, base and ramps.

982-G PULLMORE CAR TRANSPORTER 248 mm #582 _1954-1963
Car carrier with cast cab, hitch, semi body, chassis and opening ramp, blue ridged and Supertoy hubs, black tires, spare wheel, black and silver grille-headlights, black bumper, blue "Dinky Toys Delivery Service" lettering, sheet metal #794 ramp included with model. Minor casting variations not listed here.
1. Light blue cab and semi, no windows.
2. Light blue cab, tan semi, no windows.
3. Blue cab, light blue semi, no windows.
4. Blue cab, light blue semi, windows.
5. Blue cab, tan semi, ? other details.

983-G CAR CARRIER AND TRAILER 474 mm 1958-1963
Combination of 984 Car Carrier and 985 Trailer.
1. Red bodies, light gray decks and hubs.

984-G CAR CARRIER 244 mm 1958-1963
Cast cab, chassis, body sides, opening ramp with light gray roadbed, light gray upper and lower decks, deck extension on cab roof, and Supertoy hubs, black tires, crank, gears and parts to operate upper deck, silver grille, bumper and headlights, yellow "Dinky Auto Service" lettering.
1. Red cab, chassis, semi sides and ramp exterior.

984-H ATLAS DIGGER 242 mm 1974-1979
Cast body, silver lower body, orange chassis, yellow or unpainted shovel, and yellow parts, cast or plastic boom arms, plastic hydraulic cylinders, red interior and exhaust pipe, black hubs and treads, windows, black-on-yellow "AB 1702" labels.
1. Dark yellow body, cast arms and shovel, ? cylinders.
2. Dark yellow body, unpainted shovel, silver gray cylinders, black plastic arms.
3. Dark yellow body, unpainted shovel, black plastic arms, yellow cylinders.

985-G CAR TRANSPORTER TRAILER 230 mm 1958-1963
Cast body, lower deck, opening ramp, black front axle mount, and light gray Supertoy hubs, black tires, unpainted sheet metal tow bar, yellow "Dinky Auto Service" lettering.
1. Red body, light gray lower deck and roadbeds of upper deck and ramp.

**986-G THORNEYCROFT MIGHTY ANTAR LOW LOADER 305 mm
1956-1964**

Semi with cast cab, chassis, semi and light gray Supertoy hubs, black tires, golden brown plastic ship's propeller on dark brown pallet, windows, black bed section and grille, silver headlights, red "Scimitar" label on propeller.
1. Red cab, light gray semi.

987-G ABC-TV MOBILE CONTROL ROOM 151 1962-1969
Van with cast body (=967), light gray mobile camera and Supertoy or plastic hubs, black tires, black sheet metal base, cameraman figure, clear and white windows, yellow cable, silver roof, grille, bumper and headlights, red taillights, red-yellow-blue emblems, white "A.B.C. Television" and other lettering.
1. Light blue upper body, light gray lower body and supertoy hubs, dark red stripe.
2. Light gray plastic hubs, otherwise as type 1.

988-G ABC-TV TRANSMITTER VAN 243 mm 1962-1969
Van with cast body (=968), unpainted cast base of silver gray plastic dish on roof, light gray Supertoy or plastic hubs, black sheet metal base, clear and white windows, silver roof, grille, bumpers and headlights, red taillights, red-yellow-blue emblems, white "ABC-TV" lettering.
1. Light blue upper body, light gray lower body and Supertoy hubs, dark red stripe.
2. Light gray plastic hubs, otherwise as type 1.

989-G CAR TRANSPORTER 243 mm 1963-1965
Same castings and parts as #984, red plastic hubs, red "Auto Transporters" decals.
1. Yellow cab, light gray sides, metallic blue upper deck and extension, yellow and metallic blue chassis and ramp.
2. Brown ramp, otherwise as type 1?

990-G CAR TRANSPORTER SET 1956-1958
Boxed set of 982 Car Transporter and 154, 156, 161 and 162 cars.
1. Standard colors.

**991-G A.E.C. MONARCH THOMPSON TANKER 153 mm #591
_1955-1958**
Tanker with cast body and yellow Supertoy hubs, gray tires, black sheet metal base, silver grille and headlights, yellow "Shell Chemicals" lettering, red and yellow Shell emblem. Identical to #591 except for lettering: 591 has "Shell Chemicals Limited" with thinner letters.
1. Red body, dark yellow tank.

992-G AVRO VULCAN BOMBER 160 mm 1955-1956
Cast aluminum body, roundel and stripe decals. Planned as #703, then 707, finally 749, has #749 cast under wings, #992 on box. Few were made.
1. Silver plane.

994-G LOADING RAMP 233 mm #794 _1955-1964
Sheet metal ramp for use with #982 Car Transporter; identical to #794.
1. Light blue ramp, dark blue lettering.

997-G CARAVELLE SE210 AIRLINER 172 by 180 mm 1962-1965
Airliner with cast upper fuselage, lower fuselage-wings, and engines, small black cast or plastic wheels, blue "F-BGNY" and trim, silver cockpit windows, "Air France", flag, window and trim decals.
1. Silver plane with white upper fuselage, metal wheels.
2. Plastic wheels, otherwise as type 1.

998-G BRISTOL BRITANNIA AIRLINER 181 by 225 mm 1959-1965
Airliner with cast upper fuselage, lower fuselage-wings, and small wheels, four red 4-blade propellers, blue nose cowling, "C-FCZA", "Canadian Pacific" and "421", red stripes, silver windows.
1. Silver plane, white upper fuselage and fin, red or blue decals.
2. Metallic gray body, red decals.
3. Plastic wheels?

**999-G DE HAVILLAND COMET AIRLINER 145 by 185 mm
#702 _1956-1965**
Airliner with cast upper fuselage-tail, lower fuselage-wings and small wheels, black "G-ALYX", blue "B.O.A.C." and trim, silver windows. Identical to #702 except for registration: 702 is G-ALYV.

1. Silver lower fuselage and wings, white upper fuselage and tail.
2. Metallic gray lower fuselage and wings, otherwise as type 1.

1001-G STATION STAFF 1952-1953 _#051
HO scale set of six figures; same figures as #001.
1. Blue uniforms.

1003-G PASSENGERS 1952-1953 _#053
HO scale set of six figures; same figures as #003.
1. Varying colors.

1400-F PEUGEOT 404 TAXI 103 mm 1967-1971
Taxi with cast body, cast hubs, black tires, suspension, steering, red plastic opening roof hatch, white taxi sign with red letters, tan interior, windows, black sheet metal base with number, jewel headlights, silver grille, bumpers and trim, red taillights, red-gold-black emblem decals.
1. Black body, red roof and pillars.

1401-F ALFA ROMEO 1600 RALLY 97 mm 1967-1970
Rally car with cast body and black base with number, turned hubs, black tires, suspension, steering, tan plastic interior, windows (door windows open), jewel head- and taillights, silver grille and bumpers, number 8, rally and yellow stripe decals. Same casting and as #514.
1. Red body, yellow stripes.

1401-H CITROEN 2CV-6 80 mm 1981
Small sedan with cast body, eight-spoke Speedwheels, open or closed plastic roof, light gray base, bumpers and grille, interior, windows. Made by Solido. Also numbered 500.
1. Red body, orange interior, tan closed roof.
2. Red-orange body, orange interior, tan opening roof.
3. Green body, light gray interior and opening roof.
4. Gray closed roof, otherwise as type 3.

1402-F FORD GALAXIE 125 mm 1967-1971
Sedan with cast body, opening hood, trunk and four doors, and black base with number, metal hubs with chromed hubcaps, black tires, suspension, steering, red or ivory plastic interior, windows, chromed engine, grille, bumpers and headlights, red and chrome taillights.
1. Light brown body, red interior.
2. Light brown body, ivory interior?
3. Dark purple body, ivory interior.

1402-H CITROEN VISA 80 mm 1981
Sedan with cast body, Speedwheels with chromed 8-spoke hubs, off-white or light gray plastic interior and base with number, grille and bumper, clear or green tinted windows and headlights. Made by Solido. Also numbered 504.
1. Metallic dark red body, light gray base and interior.
2. Metallic dark green body, off-white base and interior.
3. Metallic blue-green body, off-white base and interior.
4. Metallic garnet red body, off-white base and interior.

1403-F MATRA M530 96 mm 1967-1971
Sports coupe with cast body, opening hood and doors, raising lights and lever, removable roof panels, and base with number, turned hubs, black tires, red plastic interior, windows, black grille, silver bumpers and headlights, red taillights.
1. White body and base, red interior.
2. Orange-red body and base, ivory interior

1403-H FIAT RITMO (or STRADA) 93 mm 1981
Sedan with cast body, eight-spoke Speedwheels, plastic interior, base with grille and bumpers, windows, tinted headlights. Made by Solido. Also numbered 501.
1. Metallic copper-orange body, tan base and interior.
2. Metallic blue body, yellow base and interior.
3. Metallic tan body, tan base and interior.

1404-F CITROEN ID19 TV CAMERA CAR 115 mm 1968-1969
Station wagon with cast body and opening tailgate, turned hubs, black tires,

suspension, steering, black sheet metal base, tan plastic interior, light gray opening hatch, red roof rack, gray roof-mounted camera with white operator and wire antenna, gray equipment in back of car, silver grille, bumpers and headlights, red taillights and side panels with white and black "Radio Télé Luxembourg" or initial decals.
1. Light gray body, full name decals.
2. Black RTL initials, white "Luxembourg", otherwise as type 1.
3. Initials as type 2 but T is checkered, otherwise as types 1 and 2.

1404-H   BMW 530   112 mm   1981
Sedan with cast body, eight-spoke Speedwheels, gray plastic base and interior, tinted windows, black and silver grille, silver headlights. Made by Solido. Also numbered 502.
1. Metallic green body.
2. Metallic purple body.

1405-F   OPEL REKORD 1900 COUPE   107 mm   1968-1970
Coupe with cast body, opening hood and doors, silver patterned hubs, black tires, suspension, red plastic interior, windows, black base with number, chromed engine, grille, bumpers and headlights, red taillights.
1. Metallic silver blue body.
2. Black roof, as Opel Commodore: prototype only.

1405-H   ALFA ROMEO GTV COUPE   100 mm   1981
Coupe with cast body, Speedwheels with 8-spoke chromed hubs, tan plastic interior and base with number, yellow tinted windows, black grille, silver headlights, green and white four-leaf clover decal. Made by Solido. Also numbered 503.
1. Bright red body.
2. Dull red body.
3. Yellow body.

1406-F   RENAULT R4 SINPAR MICHEL TANGUY   87 mm   1968-1971
Open car with cast body, olive turned hubs, black tires, suspension, unpainted metal cone on grille, olive sheet metal windshield frame with clear windshield, black plastic interior, camera and base with number, silver lights, red-white-blue-cream trim, two figures in light blue.
1. Olive body.

1406-H   PEUGEOT 504TI   110 mm   1981
Sedan with cast body, eight-spoke Speedwheels, plastic base, interior, and grille, windows, chromed bumpers and lights, tinted headlights. Made by Solido. Also numbered 505.
1. Greenish-gold body, black interior, light brown base.
2. Metallic blue body, light blue interior and base.
3. Metallic dark blue body, light blue interior and base.
4. Yellow-gold body, light brown interior and base.

1407-E   SIMCA 1100   92 mm   1974-1978
Reissue of French 1407, "Made in Spain" on base.
1. Metallic olive green body.

1407-F   SIMCA 1100   92 mm   1968-1972
Sedan with cast body, opening hood and hatch, turned hubs, black tires, suspension, tan plastic interior, dark olive engine, windows, black base with number, silver grille, bumpers and headlights, red taillights.
1. Metallic silver gray body.

1408-F   HONDA S800 COUPE   78 mm   1969-1970
Sports coupe with cast body and opening hood, turned hubs, black tires, suspension, black plastic base with number, red interior, windows, silver engine, grille, bumpers and headlights, red taillights.
1. Bright yellow body.
2. Greenish-gold body: only a few made.

(1409 SIMCA 1800 prototype only, never issued)

1409-F   CHRYSLER 180   104 mm   1970-1971
Sedan with cast body, opening front doors, and black base with number, patterned silver hubs, black tires, suspension, tan plastic interior, clear windows and headlights,

black grille, silver bumpers, red taillights, "Chrysler 180" on raised panel on base.
1. Metallic blue body.

1410-F   MOSKVITCH   95 mm   1968-1971
Sedan with cast body and opening hood, turned hubs, black tires, suspension, steering, cream plastic interior, windows, black base with number, dark olive engine, silver grille, bumpers and headlights, orange taillights.
1. Maroon body.

1411-F   ALPINE A310   95 mm   1968-1971
Sports coupe with cast body, silver gray plastic hubs, black tires, cream interior, opening rear hatch, windows, black base with number, silver engine.
1. Red body.

1412-F   JEEP WRECKER   84 mm   1968-1971
Jeep with cast body, yellow and black bumpers, and red steering lever, yellow turned hubs, black tires, spare wheel, red sheet metal windshield frame, orange plastic boom, black brace, hook and jewel spotlight, silver headlights.
1. Red body.

1413-E   CITROEN DYANE   91 mm   1977-1978
Reissue of French 1413, no luggage, "Made in Spain" on base.
1. Ivory body.

1413-F   CITROEN DYANE   91 mm   1968-1971
Small car with cast body, opening hood and hatch, turned hubs, black tires, spare wheel, suspension, red plastic interior, windows, ivory roof, black base with number, silver engine, grille, bumpers and headlights, three pieces of plastic luggage, "Made in France" on base.
1. Ivory body.

1414-F   RENAULT R8 GORDINI   93 mm   1968-1970
Sedan with cast body, turned hubs, black tires, suspension, steering, black sheet metal base with number, black plastic interior, driver in yellow, windows, four jewel headlights, silver bumpers, red taillights, white stripe decals.
1. Blue body.
2. R8S version, golden yellow body, +/- driver: small series.
3. Mustard yellow body, otherwise as type 2: small series.

1415-E   PEUGEOT 504   105 mm   1974-1975
Reissue of French 1415, black interior, "Made in Spain" on base.
1. Pale yellow body.

1415-F   PEUGEOT 504   105 mm   1969-1971
Sedan with cast body, opening hood, trunk and four doors, and black base with number, turned hubs with chromed caps, black tires, suspension, steering, cream plastic interior, chromed engine, grille, bumpers and lights, "Made in France" on base.
1. Light blue body.
2. Dark blue-green body: only a few made.

1416-E   RENAULT R6   90 mm   1974-1976
Reissue of French 1416, new headlight design, "Made in Spain" on base.
1. Red body.
2. Yellow body.
3. Yellow body, postal emblems: small series.

1416-F   RENAULT R6   90 mm   1969-1971
Sedan with cast body, opening hood and front doors, turned hubs, black tires, suspension, cream plastic interior, windows, black base with number, dark olive engine, silver grille, bumpers and headlights, "Made in France" on base.
1. Red body.

1416p-F   RENAULT R6 FIRE CHIEF   90 mm   1970
Same castings and parts as 1416, with decals. Small series.

1417-F   MATRA FORMULA 1   95 mm   1969-1971
Grand Prix car with cast body, unpainted engine-gearbox and upper front suspension, 6-star cast hubs, wide black tires, plastic driver, windshield, chromed front and rear

suspension and exhaust pipes, black-on-white number 17 labels, number on bottom of car.
1. Blue body with white nose.

1419-F   FORD THUNDERBIRD   121 mm   1969-1971
Sedan with cast body, gray plastic hubs, black tires, suspension, cream plastic interior, windows, black base with battery mount and cover, chromed switch, grille and bumpers, working red taillights.
1. Metallic lime green body.
2. Metallic lime green body with black roof.
3. Metallic red body with black roof: prototype only.
4. Metallic silver gray body with black roof: prototype only.

1420-F   OPEL COMMODORE GS   107 mm   1970-1971
Hardtop with cast body, opening doors and black hood, turned hubs with chromed hubs, black tires, suspension, black plastic interior and base with number and "Opel Rekord", windows, chromed engine, vent window frames, grille, bumpers and headlights.
1. Red body, black roof and hood.

1421-F   OPEL 1900 GT   96 mm   1969-1971
Coupe with cast body, opening doors and hood, and black base with number, gray plastic hubs with chromed hubcaps, black tires, suspension, red plastic interior, windows, chromed engine, luggage rack and bumpers, jewel headlights, red taillights.
1. Dark blue body.

1422-F   FERRARI FORMULA 1   94 mm   1969-1971
Grand Prix car with cast body, engine-gearbox and upper front suspension, silver 6-star hubs, wide black tires, white plastic wing and driver, windshield, chromed front and rear suspension and exhaust pipes, black roll bar, white number 26 decals.
1. Red body.

1423-F   PEUGEOT 504 CABRIOLET   101 mm   1969-1971
Convertible with cast body, turned hubs, black tires, black plastic interior, grille and base with number, clear windshield and headlights, silver bumpers, red taillights.
1. Dark blue body.

1424-E   RENAULT R12TL   101 mm   1977-1978
Reissue of French 1424 without opening doors, "Made in Spain" on base.
1. Yellow, black interior and grille.

1424-F   RENAULT R12   101 mm   1969-1970
Sedan with cast body and opening front doors, turned hubs, black tires, suspension, red plastic interior, windows, black base with number and "Made in France", silver grille, bumpers and headlights, red taillights.
1. Tan body.

1424g-E   RENAULT R12 GORDINI   101 mm   1974-1978
Reissue of French 1424g, "Made in Spain" on base.
1. Blue body (slightly darker than French issue).

1424g-F   RENAULT R12 GORDINI   101 mm   1971
Same castings and parts as 1424, number 1424G on base, white stripe decals, black interior and grille, opening doors, "Made in France" on base.
1. Blue body.

1425-F   MATRA 630   105 mm   1969-1971
Sports car with cast body, removable front hood, opening rear, turned hubs, chromed hubs, black tires, black plastic interior, windows, red cables, chromed engine, radiator, windshield wiper and filler cap, clear headlights, red taillights, black-on-white number 5 decals.
1. Blue body, six-star hubs.
2. Blue body, solid spoked hubs (as used on #1426).

1426-F   ALFA ROMEO CARABO BERTONE   97 mm   1969-1971
Car with cast body, patterned chromed hubs, cream plastic interior, black rear panels and base with number, green tinted windows, orange nose stripe.
1. Metallic lime green body.

(1427 SIMCA 1500 POLICE CAR never issued)

The New System of Catalog Numbers

1428-E PEUGEOT 304   96 mm   1974-1978
Reissue of French 1428, white interior, "Made in Spain" on base.
1. Metallic green body.

1428-F PEUGEOT 304   96 mm   1969-1971
Sedan with cast body, turned hubs, black tires, suspension, red plastic interior, windows, black base with number and "Made in France", yellow tinted headlights, silver grille and bumpers, red taillights.
1. Off-white body.

1429-F PEUGEOT 404 POLICE CAR   106 mm   1970-1971
Station wagon with cast body and opening hatch, turned hubs, black tires, suspension, steering, gray plastic interior and rear seat adjuster, amber dome light, windows, antenna, black base, jewel headlights, silver grille and bumpers, red taillights, white and black "Police" decals.
1. White body, black doors, upper hatch and window posts.

1430-F FIAT-ABARTH 2000 PININFARINA   91 mm   1970-1971
Sports car with cast body, roof, opening rear and base, spoked chromed hubs, black tires, cream plastic interior, windows, chromed engine, black rear panels, white emblems and stripes.
1. Orange-red body and base.
(1431 PORSCHE 917 never issued)

1432-F FERRARI 312P   99 mm   1970-1971
Sports-racing car with cast body, air intake and base with number, chromed 5-star hubs, black tires, black interior, clear windshield and headlights, chromed mirror, black-on-white number 60 decals.
1. Red body and base.

1433-F SURTEES TS5   95 mm   1971-1974
Grand Prix car with cast body, base with number, unpainted engine-gearbox and upper front suspension, chromed five-star hubs, wide black tires, chromed plastic lower suspension, upper engine, cooler and mirrors, white front wings and driver, blue seat-dash-roll bar, windshield, black-on-white number 14 decals.
1. Red body.

1435-F CITROEN PRESIDENTIELLE   151 mm   1970-1971
Limousine with cast body, chassis with number, opening rear doors and trunk, and front axle cover, turned hubs, black tires, suspension, cream plastic interior, clear windows and headlights, driver, chromed hood ornament and bumpers, red taillights, paper French flag on staff.
1. Metallic dark gray body and chassis, metallic silver gray roof.

1450-E SIMCA 1100 POLICE CAR   92 mm   1977-1978
Sedan with cast body, opening hood and hatch, turned hubs, black tires, suspension, tan plastic interior, windows, blue dome light, black base with number and "Made in Spain", silver grille, bumpers and headlights, red taillights, dark green engine, white-on-black "Police" labels.
1. White body, black doors, window frames, hood and hatch.

1451-E RENAULT 17TS   100 mm   1977-1978
Sedan with cast body, opening doors, hood and hatch, and black base with number and "Made in Spain", turned hubs, black tires, brown plastic interior, windows, chromed engine and vents, gray and black grille, bumpers and headlights, red taillights.
1. Yellow-tan body.

1452-E PEUGEOT 504   105 mm   1977-1978
Sedan with cast body, opening hood and trunk, and black base with number and "Made in Spain", turned hubs, black tires, suspension, black plastic interior, windows, chromed engine, grille, bumpers and lights.
1. Metallic brown body.

1453-E RENAULT R6   90 mm   1977-1978
Sedan with cast body and opening front doors, turned hubs, black tires, suspension, yellow plastic interior, windows, black base with number and "Made in Spain", silver grille, bumpers and headlights, red taillights.
1. Dusty blue body.

1454-E MATRA SIMCA BAGHEERA   93 mm   1978
Coupe with cast body, opening doors and black base with number and "Made in Spain", turned hubs, black tires, black plastic interior and grille, windows, silver headlights, red taillights.
1. Light green body.

1455-E CITROEN CX PALLAS   102 mm   1978
Sedan with cast body, opening front doors, and black base with number and "Made in Spain", turned hubs, black tires, black plastic interior, hatch panel and grille, clear windows and headlights, silver bumpers, red taillights.
1. Metallic dark blue body.

1539-E VW SCIROCCO   87 mm   1980
Sedan with cast body, opening doors and black base with number and "Made in Spain", black plastic grille and wheels with silver hubs, brown interior, windows, silver bumpers and headlights, red taillights.
1. Metallic green body.

1540-E RENAULT R4   90 mm   1980
Small car with cast body, opening doors, and black base with number and "Made in Spain", black plastic grille and wheels with silver hubs, cream interior, windows, gray bumpers, silver headlights, red taillights.
1. Metallic green body.

1541-E FORD FIESTA   81 mm   1981
Sedan with cast body, opening doors and black base with number and "Made in Spain", black plastic wheels with silver hubs, cream interior, windows, silver bumpers and headlights, red taillights.
1. Metallic blue body.

1542-F CHRYSLER 1308   93 mm   1981
Sedan with cast body, opening doors, and silver base-bumpers with number and "Made in Spain", black plastic grille and wheels with silver hubs, cream interior, windows, silver headlights, red taillights.
1. Metallic dark blue-green body.

1543-E OPEL ASCONA   96 mm   1980
Sedan with cast body, opening doors and black base with number and "Made in Spain", black plastic grille and wheels with silver hubs, brown interior, silver bumpers and headlights, red taillights.
1. Orange body.

2162-G FORD CAPRI SALOON   175 mm   1973-1976
Sedan, 1/25 scale, with opening doors, hood and trunk. ? other details.
1. Metallic blue body, black roof.

2214-G FORD CAPRI RALLY CAR   175 mm   1974-1976
Same castings and parts as #2162.
1. Red body, black roof and hood, number 12 and other decals.

2253-G FORD CAPRI POLICE CAR   175 mm   1974-1976
Same castings and parts as #2162 and 2214.
1. White body, blue dome light, Police sign and accessories.

Dinky Toys Action Kits

First introduced in 1971, these offered numerous Dinky Toys in kit form. Some were available as late as 1978. I have no firsthand knowledge of the kits and will simply list them and equate them with the readymade models to which they correspond:

1000 Rolls-Royce Phantom V =152	1971-1977	1017 Routemaster Bus =289	1973-1977	1037 Chieftain Tank =683	1974-1978
1002 Volvo P1800S =116	1971-1976	1018 Atlantean Bus =295	1973-1977	1038 Scorpion Tank =690	1975-1978
1003 Volkswagen 1300 =129	1971-1976	1023 AEC Single Decker Bus =283	1972-1978	1039 Leopard Recovery Tank =699	not issued
1004 Ford Panda Police Car =270	1971-1976	1025 Ford Transit Van =407	1971-1976	1040 Sea King Helicopter =724	1973-1978
1005 Peugeot 504 Cabriolet *	not issued	1027 Lunar Rover =355	1972-1976	1041 Hawker Hurricane =718	1973-1976
1006 Ford Escort Mexico =168	1973-1977	1029 Ford Tipper =438	1971-1976	1042 Spitfire Mark II =719	1973-1976
1007 Jensen FF =188	1971-1976	1030 Land Rover Breakdown =442	1974-1977	1043 S.E.P.E.C.A.T Jaguar =731	1973-1976
1008 Mercedes-Benz 600 =128	1973-1978	1032 Army Land Rover =344	1975-1978	1044 Messerschmitt 109E =726	1973-1976
1009 Lotus Formula 1 =225	1971-1976	1033 U.S. Army Jeep =615	1971-1976	1045 Panavia M.R.C.A. =729	1975-1976
1012 Ferrari 312/B2 =226	1973-1976	1034 105mm Mobile Gun =654	1974-1978	1050 Motor Patrol Boat =675	1975-1978
1013 Matra MS30 =200	not issued	1035 Striker Antitank Veh. =691	1975-1977	* Readymade model never issued, nor was kit.	
1014 Beach Buggy =227	1975-1977	1036 Leopard Tank =692	1975-1977		

Hong Kong Dinky Toys

In 1968, not long after the production of six 1/42 scale Dinky Toys car models in Hong Kong, a new series of small-scale models came onto the market, most of them also made in Hong Kong. Some were made in goodly quantities and marketed both in Britain and America, often in two different colors; others were made in small quantities, and most collectors (including this writer) have never seen them. Unfortunately, some of these models have been particularly prone to metal fatigue. Two racing car models were made by Best Box (now Efsi) of The Netherlands, while six pieces of heavy equipment were originally made by Mercury of Italy, then by Mercury of Canada, and Gibbs of the United States, before being produced for Dinky by Universal of Hong Kong. The Universal products, which were marketed by the Kresge (K-Mart) chain in the U.S.A., will be shown in the photo section along with the Hong Kong Dinky Toys, as will the two Best Box racing cars.

10-H FORD CORSAIR   68 mm 1968-?
Sedan with cast body, opening hood and trunk, and unpainted base-grille-headlights, solid unpainted metal hubs, black tires, red plastic interior, windows, silver engine block.
1. Yellow body.
2. Metallic dark gold body.

11-H JAGUAR E-TYPE 2=2   68 mm 1968-?
Sports coupe with cast body, opening hood, and black base, spoked metal hubs, black tires, white interior, windows, silver engine block, headlights and bumpers.
1. Red body.
2. Metallic maroon body.

12-H CORVETTE STING RAY   68 mm 1968-?
Sports coupe with cast body, opening hood, and unpainted base, metal hubs (solid, solid semi-spoked or pierced spoked), black tires, white plastic interior, windows, silver engine block, red taillights.
1. Medium blue body.
2. Metallic dark blue body.

13-H FERRARI 250LM   62 mm 1968-?
Sports coupe with cast body, opening rear, and black base, metal hubs (two or more types), black tires, pale blue plastic interior, silver engine block, grille and headlights, orange taillights.
1. Red body.
2. Metallic maroon body.

14-H CHEVROLET CHEVY II   71 mm 1968-?
Sedan with cast body, opening hood and trunk, and unpainted base-grille-lights-bumpers, metal hubs, black tires, white plastic interior, windows, orange taillights.

1. Yellow body.
2. Metallic maroon body.

15-H ROLLS-ROYCE SILVER SHADOW   ? mm 1968?
No data.
1. Blue body.

16-H FORD MUSTANG   72 mm 1968-?
Sports coupe with cast body, opening hood and trunk, and black base, metal hubs, black tires, red or white interior, windows, chromed grille and bumpers, silver engine and headlights, red taillights.
1. White body, red interior.
2. Ivory body, red interior.
3. Metallic dark blue body, white interior.

17-H ASTON MARTIN DB6   ? mm 1968?
No data.
1. White body.

18-H MERCEDES-BENZ 230SL   67 mm 1968-?
Coupe with cast body, opening hood and trunk, and unpainted base-grille-bumpers-headlights, metal hubs (two or more types), black tires, silver engine block, red taillights.
1. Gloss white body and black hardtop.
2. Matt white body and black hardtop.

19-H MGB ROADSTER   60 mm 1968-?
Sports car with cast body, opening hood and trunk, and unpainted base-grille-bumpers, metal hubs, black tires, black interior, windshield, silver engine, red taillights.
1. Pale blue body.
2. Red body.

3. Turquoise body.
4. Metallic green body.

20-H CADILLAC COUPE DE VILLE   84 mm 1968-?
Coupe with cast body, opening hood and trunk, and unpainted base-grille-bumpers-lights, solid metal hubs, black tires, red plastic interior, windows, black engine, red taillights.
1. White body.
2. Metallic silver body.
3. Metallic gold body.

21-H FIAT 2300 STATION WAGON   71 mm 1968-?
Wagon with cast body, opening hood and hatch, and unpainted base-grille-bumpers-lights, red plastic interior, windows, silver engine block, red taillights.
1. Blue body.
2. Yellow body, white roof.

22-H OLDSMOBILE TORONADO   84 mm 1968-?
Sedan with cast body, opening hood ansd trunk, and unpainted base-grille-bumpers, metal hubs, black tires, red plastic interior, silver engine block.
1. Metallic silver blue body.

23-H ROVER 2000   ? mm year?
No data.

24-H FERRARI SUPERFAST   ? mm year?
No data.
1. Red body.

25-H FORD ZEPHYR 6   ? mm year?
No data.

26-H MERCEDES-BENZ 250SE   ? mm year?

No data.
1. Bronze body.

27-H BUICK RIVIERA   ? mm year?
No data.

28-H FERRARI FORMULA 1   ? mm year?
No data.

29-H FORD FORMULA 1   ? mm year?
No data.

30-H VOLVO P-1800   ? mm year?
No data.

31-H VW 1600TL FASTBACK   ? mm 1968?
No data.
1. Metallic green body.

32-H VAUXHALL CRESTA   ? mm 1968?
No data.
1. Dark green body.

33-H JAGUAR MARK X   ? mm 1968?
No data.

60-H COOPER FORMULA 1   66 mm 1968-?
Grand Prix car with cast body, unpainted V12 engine and base with chassis and gearbox, 5-spoke metal hubs, black tires, white plastic driver, windshield, number 10. Made by Best Box.
1. Blue body with two white stripes.

61-H LOTUS FORMULA 1   66 mm 1968-?
Grand Prix car with cast body, unpainted H16 engine and base with chassis and gearbox, 5-spoke metal hubs, black tires, white plastic driver, windshield, number 4. Made by Best Box.
1. Green body with yellow stripe.

94-H INTERNATIONAL BULLDOZER   58 mm 1968-?
Tractor with cast body, blade, and base with towhook, yellow plastic hubs, black treads, silver engine and parts, black grilles.
1. Dark yellow body, blade and base.

95-H INTERNATIONAL SKID SHOVEL   83 mm 1968-?
Tractor with cast body (=94), arms, shovel back, and base with tow hook, yellow plastic hubs, black treads, yellow sheet metal shovel, silver engine and parts, black grilles.
1. Dark yellow body, arms, shovel and base.

96-H PAYLOADER SHOVEL   66 mm 1968-?
Shovel with cast body, arms, shovel and muffler, red plastic hubs, black tires, silver and red grille, no base.
1. White body, arms, shovel and muffler.

97-H EUCLID R-40 DUMP TRUCK   81 mm 1968-?
Quarry dumper with cast chassis-cab and tipper, yellow plastic hubs, black tires, silver grille, no base.
1. Light yellow chassis-cab and tipper.

98-H MICHIGAN SCRAPER   101 mm 1968-?
Scraper with cast cab and trailer, yellow plastic hubs, black tires, silver grille and parts, black seat and dash, no base.
1. Yellow cab and trailer.

99-H CATERPILLAR GRADER   98 mm 1968-?
Grader with cast body, blade, and rear axle mounts, orange plastic hubs, silver engine

and grille, black steering wheel.
1. Orange body, blade and mounts.

The following models were made for Airfix (then owner of Dinky Toys) by Universal of Hong Kong, presently the owner of Matchbox and Dinky. They have also been sold in the U.S.A. under the Kidco name. All of their bases are lettered "Dinky Toys" and "Made in Hong Kong".

101-H CORVETTE 1956   66 mm 1980
Sports coupe with cast body and opening hood, unpainted engine, fast wheels, windows, chromed plastic base, grille and bumpers.
1. White body, red stripes.

103-H CHEVETTE HATCHBACK   71 mm 1980
Hatchback with cast body and opening hatch, fast wheels, light brown interior, windows, chromed plastic base, grille and bumpers, trim labels.
1. Yellow body.

104-H HONDA ACCORD   70 mm 1980
Hatchback with cast body and opening hatch, fast wheels, light brown interior, windows, chromed plastic base-grille-bumpers, trim labels.
1. Light purple body.

105-H TOYOTA CELICA   70 mm 1980
Hatchback with cast body and opening hatch, fast wheels, light brown interior, windows, chromed plastic base-grille-bumpers, #3 and trim labels.
1. Dull red body.

106-H DATSUN 280Z   73 mm 1980
Hatchback with cast body and opening hatch, fast wheels, light brown interior, windows, black plastic base-grille-bumpers, black trim.
1. Dark orange body.

107-H BMW TURBO   68 mm 1980
M1 coupe with cast body, fast wheels, windows, black plastic base-grille-bumper, trim label.
1. Light orange body.

108-H ALFA ROMEO   68 mm 1980
Sports coupe with cast body, fast wheels, windows, black plastic base, trim labels.
1. Magenta body.

110-H CHEVY STEPSIDE PICKUP   69 mm 1980
Pickup with cast body, fast wheels, light brown racks, windows, chromed base-grille-bumpers, trim labels.
1. Blue body.

111-H CHEVY CAMPER PICKUP   72 mm 1980
Camper with cast body (=110), fast wheels, brown plastic camper with tan and brown labels, windows, black plastic base-grille-bumpers.
1. Yellow body.

113-H CHEVY 4X4 PICKUP   68 mm 1980
Pickup with cast body (=110, 111), fast wheels, black plastic rear cover, windows, chromed base-grille-bumpers, trim and "4X4" labels.
1. Red body.

114-H PONTIAC FIREBIRD   71 mm 1980
Coupe with cast body, fast wheels, tan plastic interior, windows, chromed base-grille-bumpers, yellow Firebird emblem label.
1. Black body.

115-H CHEVROLET CAMARO   72 mm 1980
Coupe with cast body and opening hood, unpainted engine, fast wheels, tan plastic

interior, windows, black base-grille-bumpers, yellow stripes, "Z28" and trim labels.
1. Red body.

116-H CORVETTE 1963   72 mm 1980
Coupe with cast body and opening hood, unpainted engine, fast wheels, windows, chromed base-bumpers, red and yellow trim.
1. Dark blue body.

117-H CORVETTE 1971   69 mm 1980
Coupe with cast body and opening hood, unpainted engine, fast wheels, windows, black base and grille, black trim.
1. Yellow body.

119-H FORD VAN   73 mm 1980
Van with cast body, fast wheels, chromed plastic roof panel, tan interior, windows, black base-bumpers, silver grille and headlights, stripe labels.
1. Blue body.

120-H JEEP RENEGADE   68 MM 1980
Wagon with cast body, fast wheels, spare wheel, tan plastic interior, windows, chromed base-grille-bumpers, black roof panel and green trim labels.
1. Yellow body.

121-H CHEVY ESTATE VAN   67 mm 1980
Shell camper with cast body, fast wheels, tan plastic interior, windows, chromed base-grille-bumpers, trim labels.
1. Red body.

122-H SUN VAN   72 mm 1980
Van with cast body, fast wheels, windows, black base-grille-bumpers, "Sun Van" and design labels.
1. Dark orange body.

123-H YAMAHA 250MX   77 mm 1980
Motorcycle with cast and plastic body parts, cast spoked hubs, black tires, number 7 and trim labels.
1. Blue and black plastic and unpainted cast parts.

124-H HONDA MT250   82 mm 1980
Motorcycle with cast and plastic body parts, cast spoked hubs, black tires, "Honda" labels.
1. Orange and black plastic and unpainted cast parts.

125-H KAWASAKI F11 250   80 mm 1980
Motorcycle with cast and plastic body parts, cast spoked hubs, black tires, "Kawasaki" labels.
1. Red and black plastic and unpainted cast parts.

126-H SUZUKI TM400   77 mm 1980
Motorcycle with cast and plastic body parts, cast spoked hubs, black tires, "Suzuki", "CCI" and trim labels.
1. Yellow and black plastic and unpainted cast parts.

129-H FORD THUNDERBIRD   72 mm 1980
Convertible with cast body and opening trunk-spare wheel, fast wheels, white plastic interior, windshield, chromed base-grille-bumpers.
1. Red body.

130-H CXHEVROLET 1957 CONVERTIBLE   71 mm 1980
Convertible with cast body and opening trunk, fast wheels, white plastic interior, windshield, chromed base-grille-bumpers.
1. Dark blue body, white trim.

Late in 1987, shortly after acquiring the Dinky Toys name, Universal used that name on the bubblepacks of six Matchbox cars made in Macau. The models were painted in nonstandard Matchbox colors, but still bore the Matchbox name on their bases. Since they were never given Dinky numbers, we can only list them by their Matchbox numbers.

7 VW GOLF	72 mm 1987	44 CITROEN 15CV	77 mm 1987	60 TOYOTA SUPRA	78 mm 1987
Black body plus trim, number 9.		Dark green body.		White body plus trim, black hatch and wing.	
9 FIAT ABARTH	76 mm 1987	51 PONTIAC FIREBIRD	77 mm 1987	69 CORVETTE 1984	77 mm 1987
White body plus trim.		Light blue body plus trim, number 18.		Red upper, light gray lower body, plus trim.	

Models Inspired by Dinky Toys

Models closely resembling Dinky Toys have appeared at various times. In prewar days, the British firm of Johillco produced at least one such model, much resembling the Dinky 23a MG racer. In more modern times, Japan's Marusan firm made a small series of models based on Dinky Toys:

8501   PANHARD SEMI-TRAILER   160 mm
Cast cab and open semi, based on the French Dinky 32a but without a sheet metal rear cover, known to exist in light green and in orange.

8502   ROYAL MAIL VAN   79 mm
Cast body, clearly based on Dinky 260 and, like it, painted red.

8503   DAIMLER AMBULANCE   96 mm
Cast body, clearly based on 253 and painted white with red crosses.

8504   FORD MILK TRUCK   88 mm
Cast chassis-cab and rear body, based on the French Ford 25o Nestle truck, with blue chassis-cab and cream rear body with "Nestle" cast in.

8505   OBSERVATION COACH   113 mm
Cast body, based on Dinky 280 and painted light blue with dark blue trim.

8506   EUCLID DUMP TRUCK   ? mm
Cast chassis-cab and tipper, looking like Dinky 965 from the back but, as far as I can tell from a photo, not from the front. Color unknown.

8507   AUSTIN SERVICE CAR   88 mm
Cast body, based on the Dinky 470 van, in blue with "Service Car" decals.

Another firm inspired by Dinky was Lemeco of Sweden, whose 1950 series of diecast models included:

ML44 FRAZER NASH-BMW
ML47 WILLYS JEEP
ML58 FORD SEDAN
ML71 AUSTIN DEVON

Of these, I have only the Austin; resembling Dinky 152, it measures 86 mm and is painted dark cream with red hubs.

In more modern times, the Metosul firm of Portugal produced an Atlantean doubledeck bus, presumably using dies purchased from Dinky. It exists in numerous color and logo variations, two of which will be shown in a photo in this book.

Many Dinky Toys have been "chopped" into models never made by Dinky, and one example will be shown, an American-made

Models Inspired by Dinky Toys

Jurgens model of an ambulance made from a Dinky 131 Cadillac convertible body. Many white metal kit models also bear a resemblance to the Dinky Toys of old. One series, known as "Dinky Style", offers a range of interesting models in the style of prewar and early postwar Dinky Toys, but of vehicles not actually made by Dinky.

Around 1970, the firm of S. Kumar & Co., of Calcutta, India, bought a number of dies from Dinky Toys and produced them in India under the name of Nicky Toys. In some cases the lettering on the models and boxes was changed to give the new name, in others it was not. Since the models are made from actual Dinky Toys dies and, in almost all cases, bear their original Dinky numbers, we shall simply list them here, along with the colors I know them to exist in. There are surely other color variations for at least some of the Nicky Toys. But even if they were painted the same colors as the original Dinky Toys, which they are generally not, their quality in general and wheels in particular would mark them as non-original products.

050 VW 1500 POLICE CAR (144), blue and white.
051 MERCEDES-BENZ 220SE POLICE CAR (186), black with tan roof.
#? MERCEDES-BENZ 220SE TAXI (186), color unknown.
054 STANDARD HERALD (134), green.
113 MGB SPORTS CAR, metallic red.
115 PLYMOUTH FURY CONVERTIBLE, color unknown.
120 JAGUAR E-TYPE, green.
134 TRIUMPH VITESSE, metallic green.
137 PLYMOUTH FURY HARDTOP, red with black top.
142 JAGUAR MARK X, cream.
144 VOLKSWAGEN 1500, color unknown.

146 DAIMLER V8 (casting = 195), color unknown.
170 LINCOLN CONTINENTAL, silver with black top.
186 MERCEDES-BENZ 220SE, red; green.
194 BENTLEY S, yellow.
195 JAGUAR 3.4, red.
#? JAGUAR 3.4 POLICE CAR, red and white.
238 JAGUAR D-TYPE, olive.
239 VANWALL, blue.
295 STANDARD MINIBUS, blue.
295 STANDARD AMBULANCE, white.
405 UNIVERSAL JEEP (civilian), red; blue.

405 UNIVERSAL JEEP (military), khaki.
626 MILITARY AMBULANCE, green.
660 MIGHTY ANTAR TANK TRANSPORTER, green.
693 7.2 HOWITZER, olive.
708 VICKERS VISCOUNT, color unknown.
735 GLOSTER JAVELIN, silver; camouflage.
738 SEA VIXEN, silver, RAF and Indian versions.
949 WAYNE SCHOOL BUS, color unknown.
953 CONTINENTAL BUS, color unknown.
962 MUIR HILL DUMPER, green.
999 DH COMET, silver or gray, with white and blue, BOAC logo.

PRICE GUIDE

This revised price guide was done by members of the DINKY TOY CLUB of AMERICA, specifically the founder, Jerry Fralick (MEM #1). This guide is an attempt to make listed prices more realistic to the collectible market in today's economy. The pictures are the same of those that were used in the earlier price guides. This revised price guide is more usable in that page numbers have been added to the index. A page number(s) refers to the picture location of the referenced toy.

As in past price guides, a price range is given. The range represents the difference in toys that are collectible, but may be without boxes, or a "common" piece at the low end of the price scale to a higher price that one might find for a toy MINT and with a box. Keep in mind, it is possible for a collector to pay more for one toy than another of the same description. Some color or logo types are worth more. Scarce color or two tone combinations can sometimes command higher prices. Play worn or toys that may be in need of restoration would be less than the low price range figure. This guide does not present a value for toys that have been restored. Models that have both old and new system numbers have been priced the same.

Finally, multiple sources were used in updating the values. Market values were compared from various auction results, both here in the United States as well as in England. Additionally, the values were compared to prices shown at national toy shows, and dealer's and collector's sales lists. If you have any comments regarding this new price guide, you can write to me c/o Schiffer Publishing or to the DINKY TOY CLUB of AMERICA @ P.O. Box 11, Highland, Maryland, 20777, or check out the DTCA webpage at www.dinkytoy.org.

Old Numbering System		Price	Pg.
1-F	Station Staff, 1934	$350-450	11
1-G	Station Staff, 1931	$350-450	11
1-R	Farmyard Equipment Set, 1952	$1500-2000	11
1-R	Military Set, 1955	$600-800	-
2-F	Railroad Passengers, 1934	$275-300	-
2-G	Farm Animals, 1932	$1000-1200	11
2-R	Commerical Vehicles, 1952	$2500-3000	-
3-F	Animals, 1934	$750-1000	-
3-G	Passengers, 1932	$250-300	11
3-R	Passenger Cars, 1952	$2500-3000	-
4-F	Railroad Employees, 1934	$500-600	-
4-G	Engineering Staff, 1932	$350-400	11
4-R	Racing Cars, 1953	$350-400	-
5-F	Passengers, 1934	$600-800	-
5-G	Train & Hotel Staff, 1932	$350-450	11
5-R	Military Vehicles, 1953	$400-450	-
6-F	Shepherd Set, 1934	$550-650	-
6-G	Shepherd Set, 1934	$250-350	11
10-F	Assorted Figures, 1934	$250-275	-
12-G	Postal Set, 1938	$800-1200	-
12a-G	GPO Pillar Box, 1935	$75-100	11
12b-G	Air Mail Box, 1935	$75-100	-
12c-G	Phone Booth, 1936	$75-100	11
12d-G	Telegraph Messenger, 1938	$75-100	11
12e-G	Postman, 1938	$100-125	11
13-G	Hall's Distemper, 1931	$450-600	11
13a-G	Cook's Man, 1952	$90-100	11
14a-F	Triporteur, 1935	$350-450	9
14a-G	BEV Electric Truck, 1948	$75-100	20
14c-G	Fork Lift, 1949	$75-100	21
15-G	Railway Signals, 1937	$175-225	-
15a-G	Single Arm Signal, 1937	$50-65	-
15b-G	Double Arm Signal, 1937	$50-65	-
15c-G	Junction Signal, 1937	$50-65	-
16-21	British Trains, 1934 ff	$350-450	-
16-21	French Trains, 1935 ff	$450-550	-
16-21	Railroad cars, 1934 ff	$150-250	-
22-G	Modelled Miniatures, 1933	$2800-3200	-
22a-F	Sports Roadster, 1933	$500-600	-
22a-G	Sports Car, 1933	$500-600	-
22a-R	Maserati 2000, 1958	$150-175	45
22b-F	Sports Coupe, 1934	$500-600	-
22b-G	Sports Coupe, 1933	$500-600	-

28/2-G	Delivery Vans, 1934	$9500+	12	30w-G	Electric Articulated Lorry, 1953	$150-175	32
28/3-G	Delivery Vans, 1936	$9500+	12	31-G	Holland Coachcraft Van, 1935	$500-800	-
28a/y-G	Delivery vans, each	$1500+	-	31a-G	Trojan Esso Van, 1951	$175-200	32
29a-G	Motor Bus, 1934	$800+	-	31b-G	Trojan Dunlop Van, 1952	$175-200	32
29b-G	Streamline Bus, 1935	$200-225	12	31c-G	Trojan Chivers Van, 1953	$175-200	32
29b-G	Streamline Bus, no rear window	$175-200	12	31d-G	Trojan Oxo Van, 1953	$200-250	32
29c-G	Double Decker Bus, 1938	$175-200	12,24	32-G	Airflow Saloon, 1935	$300-350	
29d-F	Paris Bus, 1948	$250-275	14	32a-F	Panhard Covered Semi, 1952	$325-350	-
29d-R	Somua Paris Bus, 1952	$200-225	24	32ab-F	Panhard SNCF Semi, 1952	$325-350	32
29ds-F	Paris Bus, 1939	$225-250	-	32aj-F	Panhard Kodak Semi, 1952	$350-375	32
29e-F	Isobloc Coach, 1950	$275-300	24	32c-F	Panhard Esso Tanker, 1954	$325-350	32
29e-G	Single Deck Bus, 1948	$135-150	24	32d-F	Delahaye Fire Truck, 1955	$325-375	37
29f-F	Chausson Bus, 1956	$225-250	42	32e-F	Berliet Fire Engine, 1957	$350-375	37
29f-G	Observation Coach, 1950	$100-125	24	33-G	Mech. Horse & Trailers w/logo	$225-250	-
29g-G	Luxury Coach, 1951	$100-125	24	33a-F	Simca Cargo Van, 1955	$225-250	42
29h-G	Duple Roadmaster, 1952	$100-125	34	33a-G	Mechanical Horse, 1935	$225-250	15
30-G	Car Set, 1935	$5000+	-	33an-F	Simca Bailly Van, 1956	$225-250	42
30a-G	Chrysler Airflow, 1935	$375-400	14	33b-F	Simca Dump Truck, 1955	$200-225	42
30b-G	Rolls-Royce, 1935	$150-175	14	33b-G	Flat Trailer, 1935	$90-100	15
30c-G	Daimler, 1935	$150-175	14	33c-F	Simca Glass Truck, 1955	$225-250	42
30d-G	Vauxhall, 1935	$150-175	14	33c-G	Open Trailer, 1935	$90-100	15
30e-F	Breakdown Truck, 1936	$150-175	14	33d-G	Box Trailer, 1935	$90-100	15
30e-G	Breakdown Truck, 1935	$125-135	14	33e-G	Refuse Trailer, 1935	$90-100	15
30f-G	Ambulance, 1935	$175-200	14	33f-G	Petrol Tank Trailer, 1935	$100-125	15
30g-G	Caravan, 1936	$150-175	14	33r-G	Mechanical Horse & Trailer, 1935	$300-400	-
30h-G	Daimler Ambulance, 1950	$125-135	25	33w-G	Mech. Horse & Open Trailer, 1947	$100-125	15
30hm-G	Daimler Army Ambulance, 1952	$175-200	38	34a-F	Berliet Dump Truck, 1955	$175-200	42
30j-G	Austin Wagon, 1950	$125-150	27	34a-G	Air Mail Car, 1935	$300-350	15
30m-G	Rear Tipping Wagon, 1950	$125-150	27	34b-F	Berliet Container Truck, 1956	$250-275	42
30n-G	Farm Produce Wagon, 1950	$125-150	27	34b-G	Royal Mail Van, 1938	$300-350	15
30p-G	Petrol Tanker, 1950	$175-200	29	34bn-F	Berliet Bailly Truck, 1959	$275-300	-
30pa-G	Castrol Tanker, 1952	$150-175	-	34c-G	Loudspeaker Van, 1948	$100-125	28
30pb-G	Esso Tanker, 1952	$150-175	-	35-G	Small Cars Set, 1936	$600-700	-
30r-G	Ford Flat Truck, 1951	$100-125	29	35a-F	Sima 5, 1939	$450-500	15
30s-G	Austin Covered Wagon, 1950	$150-175	27	35a-G	Saloon Car, 1936	$150-175	15
30sm-G	Austin Military Truck, 1952	$225-250	38	35a-R	Citroen Wrecker, 1955	$275-300	42
30v-G	Electric Dairy Van, 1949	$125-150	29	35b-G	Racer, 1936	$100-125	15

Code	Description	Price	Ref
35c-G	MG Sports Car, 1936	$125-150	15
35d-G	Austin 7 Car, 1938	$125-150	15
36-G	Motor Cars Set, 1937	$10,000+	-
36a-F	Willeme Logger Semi, 1956	$275-300	46
36a-G	Armstrong-Siddeley, 1937	$150-175	16,17
36b-F	Willeme Covered Semi, 1958	$300-325	46
36b-G	Bentley, 1937	$150-175	16,17
36c-G	Humber, 1937	$150-175	16
36d-G	Rover, 1937	$150-175	16,17
36e-G	British Salmson 2-Seat, 1937	$800-1000	16
36f-G	British Salmson 4-Seat, 1937	$800-1000	16
36g-G	Taxi, 1937	$150-175	16
37a-G	Civilian Motorcyclist, 1938	$100-125	16
37b-G	Police Motorcyclist, 1938	$100-125	16
37c-G	Despatch Rider, 1938	$100-125	16
38a-F	Unic Multibucket, 1957	$250-275	50
38a-G	Frazer Nash-BMW, 1940	$100-125	17
38b-G	Sunbeam-Talbot, 1940	$125-150	17
38c-G	Lagonda, 1940	$125-150	17
38d-G	Alvis, 1940	$125-150	17
38e-G	Armstrong-Siddeley, 1946	$125-150	17
38f-G	Jaguar, 1946	$125-150	17
39-G	U.S.A. Saloon Cars, 1939	$2800+	-
39a-F	Unic Auto Transporter, 1957	$300-350	50
39a-FG	Packard Super 8, 1939	$135-150	18
39b-F	Unic Pipe Truck, 1959	$290-325	54
39b-G	Oldsmobile 6, 1939	$150-200	18
39c-G	Lincoln Zephyr, 1939	$150-200	18
39d-G	Buick Viceroy, 1939	$150-200	18
39e-G	Chrysler Royal, 1939	$150-200	19
39f-FG	Studebaker State Commander, 1939	$150-200	18
40-F	City Traffic Signs, 1953	$150-175	-
40a-G	Riley Saloon, 1947	$125-150	22
40b-G	Triumph 1800, 1948	$125-150	22
40d-G	Austin Devon, 1949	$125-150	22
40e-G	Standard Vanguard, 1948	$125-150	22
40f-G	Hillman Minx, 1951	$125-150	30
40g-G	Morris Oxford, 1950	$125-150	30
40h-G	Austin Taxi, 1951	$125-150	-
40j-G	Austin Somerset, 1953	$125-150	40
41-F	Road Traffic Signs, 1953	$200-225	-
42-G	Police Set, 1936	$1200+	-
42a-G	Police Box, 1936	$100-125	20
42b-G	Police 'cycle Patrol, 1936	$90-100	16
42c-G	Policeman, 1936	$80-100	-
42d-G	Policeman, 1936	$80-100	-
43-G	R.A.C. Set, 1935	$1500+	-
43-a	R.A.C. Box, 1935	$200-225	-
43b-G	R.A.C. 'cycle Patrol, 1935	$100-125	16
43c-G	R.A.C. Guide, 1935	$60-75	-
43d-G	R.A.C. Guide, 1935	$60-75	-
44-G	A.A. Set, 1935	$1500+	-
44a-G	A.A. Box, 1935	$175-200	126
44b-G	A.A. Motorcycle Patrol, 1935	$100-125	16
44c-G	A.A. Guide, 1935	$100-125	-
44d-G	A.A. Guide, 1935	$100-125	-
45-G	Garage, 1935	$500-600	-
46-G	Pavement Set, 1937	$200-225	-
46a-G	Pavement Set, 1948	$150-200	-
47-G	Road Signs, 1935	$150-175	-
47a/c-G	Traffic Signals, 1935, each	$35-40	25
47d-G	Belisha Beacon, 1935	$50-75	-
47e/t-G	Road Signs, 1935, each	$25-30	-
48-G	Petrol Station, 1935	$250-300	-
49-F	Petrol Pumps, 1935	$275-300	11
49-G	Petrol Pumps, 1935	$150-175	11
49a/d-F	Petrol Pumps, 1935, each	$75-100	11
49a/e-G	Petrol Pumps, 1935, each	$55-75	11
49d	Esso Gas Pumps, 1959	$125-135	39
49e-G	Pratts Oil Bin, 1935	$75-100	11
50-F	Salev Crane, 1957	$300-350	39
50-G	British Navy Ships, 1934	$300-325	-
50a/k-G	Individual Ships, 1934	$75-100	-
51-G	Famous Liners, 1934	$300-350	-

51a-G	United States Liner, 1936	$90-110	-
51b/g-G	British Liners, each	$90-110	-
52-G	Queen Mary, 1934	$175-190	126
52c/d-F	Normandie, 1937	$175-190	126
53a/b-F	Dunkerque, 1937	$175-190	-
60-F	Airplanes, 1934	$2000+	-
60-G	Aeroplanes Set, 1934	$1500+	-
60-R	Airplane Set, 1957	$800+	-
60/68	Individual aircraft, prewar	$300-400	108, 114, 116,117
60y	Fuel Tender, 1938	$275-300	19
63-G	Maia composite, 1939	$250-300	-
63a-G	Maia Flying Boat, 1939	$250-300	-
63b-G	Mercury Seaplane, 1939	$100-125	111
70-F	Covered Trailer, 1957	$175-200	42
70a-G	Avro York, 1946	$150-175	114
70b-G	Tempest II, 1946	$125-150	118
70c-G	Vickers Viking, 1947	$125-150	115
70d-G	Twin Engine Fighter, 1946	$125-150	118
70e-G	Gloster Meteor, 1946	$125-150	118
70f-G	Shooting Star, 1947	$125-150	118
80a-F	Panhard EBR, 1958	$200-225	43
80b-F	Hotchkiss Jeep, 1958	$175-200	43
80c-F	AMX 13, 1958	$175-200	43
80d-F	Berliet Army Truck, 1958	$200-225	43
80e-F	155 Howitzer, 1958	$150-175	43
80f-F	Renault Army Ambulance, 1959	$175-200	43
90-F	Richier Roller, 1958	$250-275	46
100/104	Doll House & Furniture, 1936	$3000+	-
105a-G	Garden Roller, 1948	$50-60	22
105b-G	Wheelbarrow, 1949	$50-60	22
105c-G	Hand Truck, 1949	$50-60	22
105e-G	Grass Cutter, 1949	$50-60	22
107a-G	Sack Truck, 1949	$50-60	22
139a-G	Ford Fordor, 1949	$150-175	25
139am-G	Ford Staff Car, 1950	$225-250	38
139b-G	Hudson Commodore, 1949	$175-210	25

140a-G	Austin Atlantic, 1951	$150-175	31
140b-G	Rover 75, 1951	$150-175	30
150-G	Royal Tank Corps, 1938	$450-500	-
150a/e-G	Military figures, each	$60-75	-
151-G	Medium Tank Unit, 1938	$450-500	-
151a-G	Medium Tank, 1937	$150-175	19
151b-G	Covered Wagon, 1938	$125-150	19
151c-G	Field Kitchen, 1938	$75-100	19
151d-G	Water Tank Trailer, 1938	$75-100	19
152-G	Light Tank Unit, 1938	$550-650	-
152a-G	Light Tank, 1938	$150-175	19
152b-G	Reconnaissance Car, 1938	$150-175	19
152c-G	Austin Staff Car, 1938	$100-125	19
153a-G	Jeep, 1946	$125-135	19
156-G	Mechanized Army, 1939	$3000+	-
160-G	Artillery Personnel, 1939	$225-250	-
160a/d-G	Artillery figures, each	$35-50	-
161-G	Anti-Aircraft Set, 1939	$850+	-
161a-G	Searchlight Truck, 1939	$335-360	19
161b-G	Anti-Aircraft Gun, 1939	$150-175	19
162-G	Field Gun Unit, 1939	$250-300	-
162a-G	Light Dragon Tractor, 1939	$150-175	19
162b-G	Ammunition Trailer, 1939	$75-100	19
162c-G	18 Pounder Gun, 1939	$75-100	19
280-G	Delivery Vans, 1937	$1500+	12
280-R	Delivery Van, 1948	$225-250	-
280a/f-G	Delivery vans, each	$600-750	-
501-G	Foden Open Truck, 1947	$350-450	20
502-G	Foden Flat Truck, 1947	$350-450	20
503-G	Foden with Tailboard, 1947	$350-450	20
504-G	Foden Tanker, 1948	$350-450	20
505-G	Foden with Chains, 1948	$350-450	-
501/5-G	Fodens, type 2 grille, each	$350-450	33
511-G	Guy Open Truck, 1947	$275-300	21
512-G	Guy Flat Truck, 1947	$275-300	21
513-G	Guy with Tailboard, 1947	$300-325	21
511/3-G	Guys, type 2	$375-400	-

514-G	Guy Slumberland Van, 1949	$550-675	28
514-G	Guy Lyons Van, 1951	$850-950	-
514-G	Guy Weetabix Van, 1952	$1200-1500	28
514-G	Guy Spratts Van, 1953	$450-525	28
521-G	Bedford Articulated, 1948	$175-225	21
522-G	Big Bedford, 1952	$225-250	32
531-G	Leyland Comet, 1949	$225-250	28
532-G	Leyland with Tailboard, 1952	$200-225	28
533-G	Leyland Portland Cement, 1953	$225-250	28
551-G	Truck Trailer, 1948	$65-75	21
555-G	Commer Fire Engine, 1952	$175-200	37
561-G	Blaw-Knox Bulldozer, 1949	$150-175	23
562-G	Muir-Hill Dumper, 1948	$125-150	23
563-G	Blaw-Know Tractor, 1948	$135-160	23
564-G	Elevator Loader, 1952	$125-135	39
571-G	Coles Mobile Crane, 1949	$150-175	28
581-G	Horse Box, 1953	$500-600	36
582-G	Car Transporter, 1953	$250-275	36
591-G	AEC Shell Tanker, 1952	$225-275	32
701-G	Shetland Flying Boat, 1947	$475-575	-
751-G	Lawn Mower, 1949	$75-90	22
752-G	Goods Yard Crane, 1953	$125-135	39

New Numbering System

001-G	Station Staff, 1954	$175-200	-
001-R	Buick Riviera, 1965	$175-200	71
001-R	Blazing Inferno, 1979	$50-75	-
002-G	Farmyard Animals, 1954	$350-400	-
002-R	Corvair Monza, 1965	$225-250	71
002-R	Space War Station, 1979	$100-125	-
003-G	Passengers, 1954	$175-225	-
003-R	Chevrolet Impala, 1965	$175-200	71
004-G	Engineering Staff, 1954	$250-300	-
004-R	Oldsmobile 88, 1965	$175-200	71
005-G	Train & Hotel Staff, 1954	$200-225	-
005-R	Ford Thunderbird, 1965	$175-200	71
006-G	Shepherd Set, 1954	$275-350	-
006-R	Rambler Classic, 1965	$150-175	71
007-G	Petrol Attendants, 1960	$75-90	-
008-G	Fire Personnel, 1961	$75-90	126
009-G	Service Station Personnel, 1962	$75-90	-
010-G	Road Maintenance Personnel, 1962	$75-90	-
011-G	Telegraph Messenger, 1954	$50-60	-
012-G	Postman, 1954	$50-60	-
013-G	Cook's Man, 1954	$50-60	-
041-G	Civilian Motorcyclist, 1954	$75-100	-
042-G	Police Motorcycle, 1954	$75-100	-
043-G	Police Cycle & Sidecar, 1954	$75-100	-
045-G	AA Cycle & Sidecar, 1954?	$75-100	-
050-G	Railway Staff, 1961	$50-60	-
051-G	Station Staff, 1954	$50-60	-
052-G	Railway Passengers, 1961	$50-60	-
053-G	Passengers, 1954	$50-60	126
054-G	Station Personnel, 1961	$50-60	-
061-G	Ford Prefect, 1958	$50-60	47
062-G	Singer Roadster, 1958	$125-150	47
063-G	Commer Van, 1958	$125-150	47
064-G	Austin Lorry, 1957	$125-150	47
065-G	Morris Pickup, 1957	$125-150	47

066-G	Bedford Flat Truck, 1957	$125-150	47
067-G	Austin Taxi, 1959	$125-150	47
068-G	Royal Mail Van, 1959	$125-150	47
069-G	Massey-Ferguson Tractor, 1959	$125-150	47
070-G	AEC Mercury Tanker, 1959	$135-175	47
071-G	VW Delivery Van, 1960	$135-175	47
072-G	Bedford Artic Truck, 1959	$135-150	47
073-G	Land Rover & Trailer, 1960	$150-175	47
076-G	Lansing Bagnall/Trailer, 1960	$150-175	47
078-G	Lansing Bagnall/Tractor, 1960	$150-175	-
100-F	Renault 4L, 1962	$150-160	63
100-G	Frazer Nash-BMW, 1954	$125-150	-
100-R	Lady Penelope, 1966	$225-300	75
101F-	Peugeot 404, 1962	$175-200	63
101-G	Sunbeam Talbot, 1954	$150-175	17
101-R	Sunbeam Alpine, 1957	$225-250	45
101-R	Thunderbirds, 1967	$200-250	75
102-F	Panhard PL17, 1963	$175-225	63
102-G	Lagonda, 1954	$150-175	17
102-R	MG Midget, 1957	$200-225	45
102-R	Joe's Car, 1969	$150-200	83
103-F	Renault R8, 1963	$225-250	63
103-G	Alvis Tourer, 1954	$150-175	17
103-R	Austin-Healey, 1957	$225-250	45
103-R	Spectrum Patrol Car, 1968	$175-200	75
104-F	Simca 1000, 1964	$150-175	63
104-G	Armstrong-Siddeley, 1954	$150-175	17
104-R	Aston Martin, 1957	$200-225	45
104-R	Spectrum Pursuit, 1968	$250-300	75
105-F	Citroen 2CV, 1964	$200-225	63
105-G	Jaguar SS, 1954	$125-150	17
105-R	Triumph TR2, 1957	$200-225	45
105-R	Maximum Security, 1968	$150-175	75
106-F	Opel Kadett, 1965	$150-175	63
106-G	Austin Atlantic, 1954	$150-175	31
106-R	The Prisoner Minimoke, 1968	$300-350	75
106-R	Thunderbirds, 1974	$150-225	75
107-G	Sunbeam Alpine, 1955	$200-225	40
107-R	Magic Mini, 1967	$300-325	75
108-G	MG Midget, 1955	$200-225	40
108-R	Sam's Car, 1969	$150-200	75
109-G	Austin-Healey, 1955	$200-225	40
109-R	Gabriel's Model T, 1969	$125-150	83
110-G	Aston Martin, 1956	$200-225	40
110-R	Aston Martin DB5, 1966	$150-175	71
111-G	Triumph TR2, 1956	$200-225	40
111-R	Cinderella's Coach, 1976	$75-100	75
112-G	Austin-Healey Sprite, 1961	$125-150	59
112-R	Purdey's Triumph, 1978	$85-110	94
113-G	MGB Sports, 1962	$125-135	59
114-G	Triumph Spitfire, 1963	$125-135	65
115-G	Plymouth Fury, 1965	$150-175	65
115-R	U.B. Taxi, 1978	$50-75	99
116-G	Volvo P1800S, 1966	$125-150	71
117-G	Four Berth Caravan, 1963	$100-125	64
118-G	Glider Set, 1967	$75-125	64
120-G	Jaguar E-Type, 1967	$125-150	59
120-R	Happy Cab, 1978	$75-100	99
121-G	Goodwood Racing Set, 1963	$1500+	-
122-G	Touring Cars Set, 1963	$1500+	
122-R	Volvo Estate Car, 1977	$75-100	99
123-G	Mayfair Set, 1963	$1800+	
123-R	Austin Princess, 1977	$75-100	49
123p-G	Princess Police Car, 1979?	$125-150	101
124-G	Holiday Set, 1964	$600-800	-
124-R	Rolls-Royce Phantom V, 1977	$125-150	94
125-G	Fun Ahoy Set, 1964	$250-300	-
126-G	Motor Show Set, 1967	$1500+	-
127-G	Rolls-Royce Silver Cloud, 1964	$125-150	70
128-G	Mercedes-Benz 600, 1964	$125-150	70
129-G	MG Midget, 1955	$750-900	45
129-R	Volkswagen 1300, 1965	$100-125	-
130-G	Ford Consul Cortina, 1963	$100-125	65
131-G	Cadillac Eldorado, 1956	$150-175	41

131-R	Jaguar E-Type, 1968	$100-125	76
132-G	Packard Convertible, 1955	$150-175	40
132-R	Ford GT40, 1967	$100-125	76
133-G	Cunningham, 1955	$125-150	40
133-R	Ford Cortina, 1965	$75-125	65
134-G	Triumph Vitesse, 1963	$75-125	64
135-G	Triumph 2000, 1963	$75-125	64
136-G	Vauxhall Viva, 1964	$75-125	70
137-G	Plymouth Fury, 1963	$100-125	65
138-G	Hillman Imp, 1963	$75-125	63
139-G	Ford Cortina, 1963	$75-125	65
140-G	Morris 1100, 1963	$75-125	65
141-G	Vauxhall Estate Car, 1963	$75-125	65
142-G	Jaguar X, 1962	$75-125	59
143-G	Ford Capri, 1962	$75-125	59
144-G	Volkswagen 1500, 1963	$75-125	64
145-G	Singer Vogue, 1962	$75-125	59
146-G	Daimler 2.5 Litre, 1963	$125-150	64
147-G	Cadillac 62, 1962	$125-150	62
148-G	Ford Fairlane, 1962	$125-150	62
149-G	Sports Car Set, 1958	$1500+	-
149-R	Citroen Dyane, 1971	$75-100	84
150-G	Rolls-Royce Silver Wraith, 1959	$125-150	55
151-G	Triumph Renown, 1954	$150-175	22
151-R	Vauxhall Victor, 1966	$125-150	71
152-G	Austin Devon, 1954	$150-175	22
152-R	Rolls-Royce Phantom, 1965	$125-150	72
153-G	Standard Vanguard, 1954	$150-175	22
153-R	Aston Martin DB6, 1966	$150-160	73
154-G	Hillman Minx, 1954	$150-175	30
154-G	Ford Taunus 17M, 1966	$125-150	72
155-G	Ford Anglia, 1961	$125-150	58
156-G	Rover 75, 1954	$150-175	30
156-R	Saab 96, 1966	$125-150	72
157-G	Jaguar XK120, 1954	$200-225	35
157-R	BMW 2000 Tilux, 1968	$125-150	76
158-G	Riley Saloon, 1954	$150-175	22
158-R	Rolls-Royce Silver Shadow, 1967	$150-175	76
159-G	Morris Oxford, 1954	$150-175	30
159-R	Ford Cortina, 1967	$100-125	76
160-G	Austin A30, 1958	$150-175	49
160-R	Mercedes 250SE, 1968	$125-150	76
161-G	Austin Somerset, 1954	$150-175	40
161-R	Ford Mustang, 1965	$125-150	71
162-G	Ford Zephyr, 1956	$150-175	-
162-R	Triumph 1300, 1967	$125-150	72
163-G	Bristol 450, 1956	$125-150	-
163-R	VW 1600TL, 1966	$100-125	72
164-G	Vauxhall Cresta, 1957	$150-175	48
164-R	Ford Zodiac, 1966	$125-150	72
165-G	Humber Hawk, 1959	$175-200	73
165-R	Ford Capri, 1969	$125-150	79
166-G	Sunbeam Rapier, 1958	$150-175	49
166-R	Renault R16, 1967	$100-125	76
167-G	AC Aceca, 1958	$175-200	48
168-G	Singer Gazelle, 1959	$150-175	53
168-R	Ford Escort, 1968	$100-125	76
169-G	Studebaker Golden Hawk, 1958	$175-200	48
169-R	Ford Corsair, 1967	$100-125	76
170-G	Ford Fordor, 1954	$150-175	25
170-R	Lincoln Continental, 1964	$150-175	73
171-G	Hudson Commodore, 1954	$175-200	25
171-R	Austin 1800, 1965	$100-125	71
172-G	Studebaker Land Cruiser, 1954	$175-200	35
172-R	Fiat 2300 Wagon, 1965	$100-125	71
173-G	Nash Rambler, 1958	$125-150	48
173-R	Pontiac Parisienne, 1968	$100-125	76
174-G	Hudson Hornet, 1958	$175-200	48
174-R	Mercury Cougar, 1969	$100-125	79
175-G	Hillman Minx, 1958	$125-150	49
175-R	Cadillac Eldorado, 1969	$100-125	79
176-G	Austin A105, 1958	$150-175	49
176-R	NSU RO-80, 1969	$100-125	79
177-G	Opel Kapitän, 1961	$100-125	59

178-G	Plymouth Plaza, 1959	$150-175	52	203-G	Custom Range Rover, 1979	$75-100	97
178-R	Mini Clubman, 1975	$75-100	94	204-G	Ferrari 312P, 1971	$75-100	84
179-G	Studebaker President, 1958	$175-200	48	205-G	Talbot-Lago, 1962	$100-125	-
179-R	Opel Commodore, 1971	$75-100	84	205-R	Lotus Cortina Rally, 1968	$75-100	78
180-G	Packard Clipper, 1958	$175-200	49	206-G	Maserati, 1962	$150-175	-
180-R	Rover 3500, 1979	$75-100	99	206-R	Custom Sting Ray, 1977	$100-125	94
181-G	Volkswagen, 1956	$150-175	41	207-G	Alfa Romeo, 1962	$150-175	-
182-G	Porsche 356A, 1958	$200-225	45	207-R	Triumph Rally, 1977	$100-125	94
183-G	Fiat 600, 1958	$100-125	49	208-G	Cooper-Bristol, 1962	$175-200	-
183-R	Morris Mini, 1966	$100-125	72	208-R	VW-Porsche 914, 1971	$75-100	84
184-G	Volvo Amazon, 1961	$125-150	58	209-G	Ferrari, 1962	$150-175	-
185-G	Alfa Romeo 1900, 1961	$150-175	58	210-G	Vanwall, 1962	$150-175	-
186-G	Mercedes-Benz 220SE, 1961	$150-175	59	210-R	Alfa Romeo 33, 1971	$75-100	79
187-G	VW Karmann-Ghia, 1959	$175-200	52	211-G	Triumph TR7, 1975	$75-100	94
187-R	De Tomaso Mangusta, 1968	$100-125	79	212-G	Ford Cortina Rally, 1967	$75-100	73
188-G	Four Berth Caravan, 1961	$100-125	59	213-G	Ford Capri Rally, 1971	$75-100	84
188-R	Jensen FF, 1968	$125-150	76	214-G	Hillman Imp Rally, 1966	$75-100	71
189-G	Triumph Herald, 1959	$125-150	53	215-G	Ford GT, 1966	$75-100	73
189-R	Lamborghini Marzal, 1968	$125-150	79	216-G	Ferrari Dino, 1967	$75-100	78
190-G	Caravan, 1956	$100-125	44	217-G	Alfa Romeo OSI, 1968	$75-100	78
190-R	Monteverdi 375L, 1970	$125-150	79	218-G	Lotus Europa, 1970	$75-100	84
191-G	Dodge Royal, 1959	$175-200	52	219-G	Jaguar Big Cat, 1977	$75-100	99
192-G	De Soto Fireflite, 1958	$175-200	49	220-G	Racing Car, 1954	$75-100	-
192-R	Range Rover, 1970	$90-110	85	220-R	Ferrari P5, 1970	$75-100	84
193-G	Rambler Cross Country, 1961	$125-150	58	221-G	Speed of the Wind, 1954	$110-115	-
194-G	Bentley S2, 1961	$125-150	58	221-R	Corvette Sting Ray, 1969	$100-125	79
195-G	Jaguar Mark II, 1960	$125-150	55	222-G	Streamlined Racing Car, 1954	$125-135	-
195-R	Fire Ranger Rover, 1971	$100-125	85	222-R	Hesketh 308E, 1978	$75-100	85
196-G	Holden Special, 1963	$100-125	64	223-G	McLaren Can-Am, 1970	$75-100	84
197-G	Mini-Traveller, 1961	$125-135	59	224-G	Mercedes-Benz C111, 1970	$75-100	84
198-G	Rolls-Royce Phantom, 1962	$125-150	62	225-G	Lotus Formula I, 1970	$75-100	85
199-G	Austin Countryman, 1961	$100-125	-	226-G	Ferrari 312B, 1972	$75-100	85
200-G	Midget Racer, 1954	$150-175	15	227-G	Beach Buggy, 1974	$75-100	94
200-R	Matra 630, 1971	$100-125	84	228-G	Super Sprinter, 1970	$75-100	83
201-G	Racing Car Set, 1965	$700+	-	299-G	Motorway Services Set, 1970	$1100+	-
201-R	Plymouth Stock Car, 1979	$75-100	99	230-G	Talbot-Lago, 1954	$100-125	34
202-R	Custom Land Rover, 1979	$75-100	97	231-G	Maserati, 1954	$100-125	34

232-G	Alfa Romeo, 1954	$100-125	34
233-G	Cooper-Bristol, 1954	$100-125	34
234-G	Ferrari, 1954	$125-150	34
235-G	H.W.M., 1954	$125-150	34
236-G	Connaught, 1956	$125-150	44
237-G	Mercedes-Benz, 1957	$125-150	45
237-R	Dinky Way Set, 1978	$150-175	103
238-G	Jaguar D-Type, 1957	$125-150	45
239-G	Vanwall, 1958	$135-175	48
240-G	Cooper Racer, 1963	$100-125	65
240-R	Dinky Way Set, 1978	$200-250	-
241-G	Lotus Racer, 1963	$75-100	65
241-R	Jubilee Taxi, 1977	$75-100	99
242-G	Ferrari Racer, 1963	$100-125	65
243-G	B.R.M. Racer, 1964	$100-125	65
243-R	Volvo Police Car, 1978	$75-100	101
244-G	Plymouth Police Car, 1977	$75-100	91
245-G	Superfast Set, 1968	$250-275	-
246-G	International GT Set, 1968	$250-275	-
249-G	Racing Car Set, 1955	$1100+	-
250-G	Fire Engine, 1954	$150-175	12
250-R	Mini-Cooper Police, 1968	$100-125	
251-G	Road Roller, 1954	$95-115	23
251-R	Pontiac Police Car, 1971	$100-125	84
252-G	Bedford Refuse Wagon, 1954	$150-175	20
252-R	RCMP Police Car, 1969	$100-125	81
253-G	Daimler Ambulance, 1954	$125-150	25
254-G	Austin Taxi, 1954	$150-175	44
254-R	Range Rover Police, 1972	$75-100	86
255-G	Tunnel Land-Rover, 1955	$100-125	37
255-R	Ford Zodiac Police, 1967	$75-100	80
255-R	Mini Clubman Police, 1977	$75-100	94
256-G	Humber Hawk Police, 1960	$150-175	53
257-R	Rambler Fire Chief, 1961	$125-150	58
258-G	De Soto Police Car, 1960	$150-175	55
258-G	Dodge Police Car, 1961	$150-175	55
258-G	Ford Police Car, 1962	$150-175	55
258-G	Cadillac Police Car, 1967	$150-175	55
259-G	Fire Engine, 1962	$125-150	57
260-G	Royal Mail Van, 1955	$150-175	37
260-R	Bundespost Volkswagen, 1971	$200-225	-
261-G	Telephone Van, 1956	$135-150	42
261-R	Ford Taunus Police, 1967	$250-300	-
262-G	Volkswagen PTT, 195_	$850+	44
262-R	Volkswagen PTT, 1966	$225-300	72
263-G	Superior Ambulance, 1962	$125-150	60
263-R	Airport Rescue, 1978	$75-100	98
264-G	RCMP Patrol Car, 1962	$150-175	64
264-R	Rover 3500 Police, 1979	$75-100	101
265-G	Plymouth Taxi, 1960	$150-175	55
266-G	Plymouth Taxi, 1965	$150-175	55
266-R	ERF Fire Tender, 1976	$100-125	98
267-G	Superior Ambulance, 1967	$100-125	60,80
267-R	Paramedic Truck, 1979	$100-125	96
268-G	Renault Minicab, 1962	$125-150	60
268-R	Range Rover Ambulance, 1974	$75-100	90
269-G	Jaguar Police Car, 1962	$125-150	60
269-R	Ford Transit Police, 1978	$75-100	97
270-G	AA Motorcycle Patrol, 1959	$75-100	-
270-R	Ford Panda Police, 1969	$75-100	80
271-G	Touring Secours Cycle, 1959	$250-275	35
271-R	Ford Transit Fire Van, 1975	$75-100	91
272-G	ANWB Cycle, 1959	$300-325	35
272-R	Ford Transit Police, 1975	$75-100	91
273-G	RAC Mini-Minor Van, 1966	$150-175	69
274-G	AA Mini-Minor Van, 1965	$125-150	69
274p-G	Mason's Paint Van, 1970	$250-275	69
274-R	Ford Transit Ambulance, 1978	$75-100	97
275-G	Brinks Armored Car, 1964	$75-100	67
276-G	Airport Fire Tender, 1962	$100-125	60
276-R	Ford Transit Ambulance, 1976	$75-100	91
277-G	Superior Ambulance, 1962	$125-150	-
277-R	Police Land-Rover, 1979	$75-100	101
278-G	Vauxhall Ambulance, 1964	$95-110	69

No.	Name	Price	Page
278-R	Plymouth Yellow Cab, 1978	$75-100	99
279-G	Diesel Roller, 1965	$75-100	69
280-G	Observation Coach, 1954	$135-150	24
280-R	Mobile Bank, 1966	$125-135	69
281-G	Luxury Coach, 1954	$125-150	24
281-R	Fiat Camera Car, 1967	$150-175	73
281-R	Army Hovercraft, 1973	$75-100	83
282-G	Duple Roadmaster, 1954	$125-150	34
282-R	Austin Taxi, 1966	$75-100	73
282-R	Fire Land-Rover, 1974	$75-100	90
283-G	BOAC Coach, 1956	$100-125	42
283-R	Single Deck Bus, 1971	$75-100	86
284-G	Austin Taxi, 1972	$75-100	85,96
285-G	Merryweather Fire Tender, 1970	$100-120	81
286-G	Ford Transit Fire Van, 1969	$75-100	81
287-G	Ford Accident Unit, 1967	$75-100	80
288-G	Superior Ambulance, 1974	$100-125	86
289-G	Routemaster Bus, 1964	$100-125	68,69,101
290-G	Double Decker Bus, 1954	$125-150	60
290-R	Hovercraft, 1970	$75-100	81
291-G	Double Decker Bus, 1959	$125-150	60
291-R	Atlantean Bus, 1974	$75-100	90
292-G	Atlantean Bus, 1962	$95-115	60
293-G	Atlantean Bus, 1964	$95-115	60
293-R	Swiss Post Bus, 1973	$75-100	90
294-G	Police Vehicles Set, 1973	$125-150	106
295-G	Standard Atlas, 1960	$75-100	57
295-R	Atlantean Bus, 1973	$75-100	90
296-G	Viceroy Coach, 1972	$75-100	86
297-G	Police Vehicles Set, 1967	$125-150	-
297-R	Silver Jubilee Bus, 1977	$75-100	101
298-G	Emergency Services, 1963	$800+	-
299-G	Post Office Set, 1958	$500+	-
299-R	Motorway Set, 1963	$1000+	-
299-R	Crash Squad Set, 1979	$100-125	106
300-G	Farm Tractor, 1954	$100-125	23
300-R	London Scene Set, 1978	$75-100	96
301-G	Field Marshal Tractor, 1954	$125-150	23
303-G	Commando Squad Set, 1978	$150-175	107
304-G	Fire Rescue Set, 1978	$125-150	107
305-G	David Brown Tractor, 1966	$75-100	74
308-G	Leyland Tractor, 1971	$75-100	86
309-G	Star Trek Set, 1978	$150-175	-
310-G	Tractor & Hay Rake, 1954	$150-175	-
319-G	Tipping Trailer, 1961	$75-100	57
320-G	Harvest Trailer, 1954	$75-100	23
321-G	Manure Spreader, 1954	$75-100	23
322-G	Disc Harrow, 1954	$75-100	23
323-G	Triple Gang Mower, 1954	$75-125	23
324-G	Hay Rake, 1954	$75-100	23
325-G	Brown Tractor & Harrow, 1967	$125-135	-
340-G	Land-Rover, 1954	$100-125	23
341-G	Land-Rover Trailer, 1954	$50-75	23
342-G	Motocart, 1954	$125-150	23
342-R	Austin Minimoke, 1967	$75-100	74
343-G	Dodge Farm Truck, 1954	$125-150	27
344-G	Estate Car, 1954	$100-125	24
344-R	Land-Rover, 1970	$75-100	81
350-G	Tiny's Minimoke, 1970	$150-175	83
351-G	Shado Interceptor, 1971	$125-150	82
352-G	Ed Straker's Car, 1971	$150-175	83
353-G	Shado 2 Mobile, 1972	$200-250	82
354-G	Pink Panther, 1972	$175-200	83
355-G	Lunar Rover, 1972	$125-150	83
357-G	Klingon Cruiser, 1976	$125-150	102
358-G	USS Enterprise, 1976	$125-150	102
359-G	Eagle Transporter, 1975	$200-250	105
360-G	Eagle Freighter, 1975	$175-200	105
361-G	Zygon Chariot, 1979	$150-175	105
362-G	Trident Star Fighter, 1979	$175-200	105
363-G	Zygon Patroller, 1979	$175-200	102
364-G	Space Shuttle, 1979	$150-175	105
366-G	Space Shuttle, 1979	$175-200	105
367-G	Battle Cruiser, 1979	$150-175	102

368-G	Zygon Marauder, 1979	$150-175	102	416-G	Ford Motorway Van, 1975	$75-100	91
370-G	Dragster Set, 1969	$125-150	83	417-G	Leyland Comet, 1956	$225-250	28
371-G	USS Enterprise, 1980	$125-150	-	417-R	Ford Motorway Van, 1978	$75-100	97
372-G	Klingon Cruiser, 1980	$125-150	-	418-G	Leyland with Tailboard, 1956	$225-250	28
380-G	Convoy Skip Truck, 1977	$75-100	97	419-G	Leyland Cement Truck, 1956	$275-325	28
381-G	Garden Roller, 1954	$50-75	22	420-G	Leyland FC Lorry, 1954	$125-150	27
381-R	Convoy Farm Truck, 1977	$75-100	97	421-G	Hingle Smart, 1954	$125-150	32
382-G	Wheelbarrow, 1954	$50-75	22	422-G	Thames Flat Truck, 1954	$125-150	29
382-R	Convoy Dump Truck, 1978	$75-100	97	424-G	Commer Articulated, 1963	$150-175	66
383-G	Hand Truck, 1954	$50-75	22	425-G	Bedford Coal Truck, 1964	$175-200	66
383-R	Convoy Covered Truck, 1977	$75-100	97	428-G	Open Trailer, 1956	$75-100	96
384-G	Grass Cutter, 1954	$75-100	22	429-G	Flat Trailer, 1954	$75-100	-
384-R	Convoy Fire Truck, 1977	$75-100	97	430-G	Commer Breakdown, 1954	$150-175	29
385-G	Sack Truck, 1954	$50-75	22	430-R	Johnson Dumper, 1976	$75-100	97
385-R	Convoy Mail Truck, 1977	$75-100	97	431-G	Guy Open Truck, 1956	$450-500	54
386-G	Lawn Mower, 1954	$75-90	22	431-R	Guy Warrior, 1958	$350-400	-
390-G	Custom Ford Van, 1978	$75-100	98	432-G	Guy Flat Truck, 1956	$450-500	54
398-G	Farm Equipment, 1964	$1200+	-	432-R	Guy Warrior, 1958	$350-400	-
399-G	Tractor & Trailer, 1969	$200-225	-	432-R	Foden Tipper, 1976	$75-100	91
399-R	Convoy Set, 1977	$75-100	-	433-G	Guy with Tailboard, 1956	$400-450	-
400-G	BEV Electric Truck, 1954	$75-100	-	434-G	Bedford Crash Truck, 1964	$125-150	66
401-G	Fork Lift, 1954	$75-100	21	435-G	Bedford Tipper, 1964	$125-150	66
402-G	Coca-Cola Truck, 1966	$200-250	69	436-G	Ford Compressor, 1963	$100-125	66
404-G	Climax Fork Lift, 1967	$75-100	82	437-G	Muir Hill Loader, 1962	$100-125	66
405-G	Universal Jeep, 1954	$75-125	31	438-G	Ford Tipper, 1970	$75-100	91
406-G	Commer Artic. Truck, 1964	$150-175	-	439-G	Ford Snowplow-Tipper, 1971	$100-125	91
407-G	Ford Transit Van, 1966	$75-100	74	440-G	Studebaker Mobil Tanker, 1954	$125-150	29
408-G	Big Bedford Lorry, 1956	$225-250	32	440-R	Ford Tipper, 1977	$75-100	91
409-G	Bedford Articulated, 1956	$175-225	21	441-G	Stude. Castrol Tanker, 1954	$150-175	29
410-G	Bedford End Tipper, 1954	$125-150	20	442-G	Stude. Esso Tanker, 1954	$125-150	29
410-R	Bedford CF Van, 1972	$75-100	88,89	442-R	Land-Rover Breakdown, 1974	$75-100	90
411-G	Bedford O Truck, 1954	$125-150	21	443-G	Stude. Benzole Tanker, 1957	$150-175	29
412-G	Austin Wagon, 1954	$125-150	27	448-G	El Camino & Trailers, 1963	$150-175	57
412-R	Bedford AA Van, 1971	$75-100	90	449-G	El Camino Pickup, 1961	$100-125	-
413-G	Austin Covered Wagon, 1954	$125-150	27	449-R	Johnson Sweeper, 1977	$75-100	86
414-G	Dodge Rear Tipper, 1954	$125-150	27	450-G	Trojan Esso Van, 1954	$175-200	32
415-G	Mechanical Horse, 1954	$125-150	-	450-R	Bedford Castrol Van, 1965	$200-250	74

451-G	Trojan Dunlop Van, 1954	$175-200	32
451-R	Johnson Sweeper, 1971	$75-100	86
452-G	Trojan Chivers Van, 1954	$200-225	32
453-G	Trojan Oxo Van, 1954	$250-300	32
454-G	Trojan Cydrax Van, 1957	$175-200	32
455-G	Trojan Brooke Bond Van, 1957	$175-200	32
465-G	Morris Capstan Van, 1957	$225-250	32
470-G	Austin Shell Van, 1954	$175-200	37
471-G	Austin Nestle Van, 1955	$175-200	37
472-G	Austin Raleigh Van, 1955	$175-200	37
475-G	Model T Ford, 1964	$125-150	68
476-G	Morris Bullnose, 1965	$125-150	68
477-G	Parsley's Car, 1971	$125-150	68
480-G	Bedford Kodak Van, 1954	$175-200	37
481-G	Bedford Ovaltine Van, 1955	$175-200	37
482-G	Bedford Dinky Van, 1956	$175-200	37
485-G	Santa Model T Ford, 1964	$175-200	68
486-G	Dinky Beats Morris, 1965	$125-150	68
490-G	Express Dairy Van, 1954	$150-175	29
491-G	NCB Dairy Van, 1954	$150-175	29
492-G	Loudspeaker Van, 1954	$125-150	28
492-R	Election Minivan, 1964	$150-175	66
500-F	Citroen 2CV, 1974	$125-150	-
500-S	Touring Car Set, 1959	$1000+	-
500-R	Citroen 2CV, 1967	$125-150	76,95
501-F	Airplane Set, 1959	$1200+	-
501-R	Citroen DS19 Police, 1967	$125-150	73
502-F	Garage, 1959	$125-150	-
503-F	Touring Car Set, 1963	$1200+	-
503-R	Porsche Carrera 6, 1967	$125-150	77
505-F	Maserati 2000, 1959	$150-175	45
506-F	Astone Martin, 1960	$150-175	45
506-R	Ferrari 275GTB, 1967	$125-150	73
507-F	Simca 1500 Break, 1967	$125-150	72
508-F	DAF, 1966	$125-150	72
509-F	Fiat 850, 1966	$125-150	72
510-F	Peugeot 204, 1977	$125-150	-

510-S	Talbot-Lago, 1959	$175-200	-
510-R	Peugeot 204, 1965	$150-175	95
511-F	Ferrari Racer, 1959	$125-150	34
511-R	Peugeot 204 Cabrio, 1968	$150-175	77
512-F	Lesko Kart, 1962	$175-200	62
513-F	Opel Admiral, 1966	$125-150	72
514-F	Alfa Romeo Giulia, 1966	$125-150	73
515-F	Ferrari 250GT, 1963	$125-150	63
516-F	Mercedes-Benz 230SL, 1964	$125-150	70
517-F	Renault R8, 1962	$125-150	63
518-S	Renault 4L, 1974	$100-125	94
518-F	Renault 4L, 1962	$125-150	63
518a-F	Renault Autoroute, 1970	$125-150	-
518p-F	Renault Mail Car, 1970	$125-150	-
519-F	Simca 1000, 1963	$125-150	63
520-F	Chrysler New Yorker, 1959	$225-250	41
520-R	Fiat 600D, 1963	$75-100	63
521-F	Peugeot 403, 1959	$150-200	44
522-F	Citroen DS19, 1959	$175-225	44
523-F	Plymouth Belvedere, 1959	$175-250	48
523-R	Simca 1500, 1963	$100-125	63
524-F	Renault Dauphine, 1959	$125-150	47
524-R	Panhard 24CT, 1964	$125-150	70
525-F	Peugeot 403U, 1959	$175-200	48
525-R	Peugeot 404 Break, 1964	$125-150	70
526-F	Mercedes-Benz 190SL, 1959	$150-175	49
527-F	Alfa Romeo 1900, 1959	$125-150	52
528-F	Simca Chambord, 1959	$125-150	52
528-R	Peugeot 404 Cabrio, 1966	$175-200	72
529-F	Vespa 2CV, 1959	$150-175	52
530-S	Citroen DS23, 1976	$75-100	94
530-F	VW Karmann-Ghia, 1959	$175-200	-
530-R	Citroen DS19, 1964	$125-150	70
531-F	Fiat 1200, 1959	$100-125	52
532-F	Lincoln Premiere, 1959	$200-225	62
533-F	Peugeot 203, 1959	$175-200	-
533-R	Mercedes-Benz 300SE, 1963	$100-125	64

534-F	Simca 8 Cabrio, 1959	$150-175	-
534-R	BMW 1500, 1963	$150-175	64
535-F	Citroen 2CV, 1959	$175-200	31
538-F	Renault 16TX	$125-150	94
538-F	Buick Roadmaster, 1954	$250-300	35
539-F	Citroen ID19	$175-200	64
540-F	Studebaker Commander, 1959	$200-225	41
540-R	Opel Kadett, 1963	$125-150	63
541-F	Simca Versailles, 1959	$150-175	-
541-R	Mercedes-Benz Coach, 1963	$125-150	66
542-F	Simca Ariane Taxi, 1959	$150-175	-
542-R	Opel Rekord, 1964	$150-175	70
543-F	Renault Floride, 1960	$125-150	53
544-F	Simca Aronde, 1959	$125-150	52
545-F	De Soto Diplomat, 1960	$150-175	53
546-F	Austin-Healey, 1960	$175-200	45
546-R	Opel Rekord Taxi, 1963	$175-200	64
547-F	Panhard PL17, 1960	$150-175	53
548-F	Fiat 1800 Familiare, 1960	$150-175	53
549-F	Borgward Isabella, 1961	$150-175	58
550-F	Chrysler Saratoga, 1961	$275-300	55
551-F	Rolls-Royce, 1959	$200-225	55
551-R	Ford Taunus Polizei, 1963	$175-200	70
552-F	Chevrolet Corvair, 1961	$175-200	58
553-F	Peugeot 404, 1961	$200-225	59
554-F	Opel Rekord, 1961	$175-200	59
555-F	Ford Thunderbird, 1961	$200-225	58
556-F	Citroen Ambulance, 1962	$225-250	62
557-F	Citroen Ami-6, 1962	$175-200	62
558-F	Citroen 2CV, 1962	$175-200	62
559-F	Ford Taunus 17M, 1962	$175-200	62
560-F	Peugeot Mail Van, 1959	$175-200	61
560-F	Peugeot Van, no logo	$150-175	-
560-R	Citroen Main Van, 1963	$125-150	-
561-F	Citroen Gervais Van, 1959	$200-225	-
561-F	Citroen Cibie Van, 1960	$200-225	-
561-F	Citroen Baroclem Van, 1964	$225-250	-
561-R	Renault 4L Mail Car, 1968	$125-150	77
562-F	Citroen 2CV Fire Van, 1959	$225-250	53
562h-F	Citroen Wegenwacht, 1965	$150-175	61
563-F	Estafette Pickup, 1960	$150-175	54
564-F	Estafette Glass Truck, 1963	$175-200	66
564-R	Armagnac Caravan, 1969	$100-125	81
565-F	Estafette Camper, 1965	$125-150	73
566-F	Citroen Police Van, 1965	$150-175	81
567-F	Unimog Snowplow, 1967	$175-200	74
568-F	Berliet Ladder Truck, 1968	$175-200	80
569-F	Berliet Dump Truck, 1967	$175-200	74
570-F	Panhard Paris Bus, 1959	$250-275	24
570-R	Peugeot J7 Van, 1967	$150-175	74
570a-F	Autoroute Van, 1970	$150-175	-
570p-F	Peugeot Fire Van, 1972	$150-175	81
571-F	Chausson Bus, 1959	$250-275	42
571-R	Saviem Horse Van, 1969	$350-400	82
572-F	Berliet Dump Truck, 1970	$175-200	81
575-F	Panhard SNCF Semi, 1959	$300-325	32
576-F	Panhard Esso Tanker, 1959	$300-325	32
577-F	Simca Bailly Van, 1959	$250-275	
577-R	Berliet Cattle Truck, 1965	$175-200	69
578-F	Simca Dump Truck, 1959	$200-225	42
579-F	Simca Glass Truck, 1959	$225-250	42
580-F	Berliet Dump Truck, 1959	$200-225	42
581-F	Berliet Container Truck, 1959	$175-200	42
581a-F	Bailly Container Truck, 1959	$200-225	-
582-F	Citroen Wrecker, 1959	$250-325	42
583-F	Berliet Fire Engine, 1959	$350-400	37
584-F	Berliet Covered Truck, 1961	$175-200	57
585-F	Berliet Dump Truck, 1961	$200-225	57
586-F	Citroen Milk Truck, 1961	$500-600	57
587-F	Citroen Philips Van, 1964	$600-700	69
588-F	Berliet Brewery Truck, 1964	$400-500	69
589-F	Berliet Wrecker, 1965	$225-250	69
589a-F	Autoroute Wrecker, 1970	$225-250	69
590-F	City Road Signs, 1959	$175-200	-

591-F	Country Road Signs, 1959	$175-200	-
592-F	Esso Gas Pumps, 1959	$200-225	39
592-R	Road Signs, 1969	$150-175	127
593-F	Road Signs, 1969	$200-225	127
594-F	Traffic Light, 1969	$75-100	82
595-F	Salev Crane, 1959	$300-350	39
595-R	Traffic Signs, 1969	$125-150	126
596-F	Street Sweeper, 1960	$225-250	54
597-F	Fork Lift, 1959	$150-175	-
600-G	Armored Corps Figures, 1954	$200-250	-
601-G	Austin Para-Moke, 1967	$175-200	74
602-G	Command Car, 1976	$100-125	93
603-G	Seated Private, 1957	$50-75	-
604-G	Tank Corps Private, 1954	$50-75	-
604-R	Bomb Disposal Unit, 1976	$100-125	93
606-G	Artillery Personnel, 1954	$175-200	-
608-G	Artillery Gunner, 1954	$50-75	-
609-G	Howitzer with Crew, 1974	$50-75	87
612-G	Commando Jeep, 1973	$50-75	87
615-G	Jeep & Howitzer, 1968	$75-100	80
616-G	AEC Tank Transporter, 1976	$125-150	100
617-G	VW KDF & Antitank Gun, 1968	$150-175	80
618-G	Helicopter Transporter, 1976	$125-150	100
619-G	Bren Gun Carrier & Gun, 1976	$100-125	92
620-G	Army Truck, 1954	$150-175	-
620-R	Missile Launcher, 1970	$125-150	87
621-G	3-Ton Army Truck, 1954	$150-175	38
622-G	10-Ton Army Truck, 1954	$150-175	38
622-R	Bren Gun Carrier, 1975	$75-100	92
623-G	Covered Army Truck, 1954	$150-175	38
624-G	Daimler Ambulance, 1954	$150-175	38
625-G	Austin Truck, 1954	$250-300	-
625-R	Antitank Gun, 1975	$75-100	87
626-G	Military Ambulance, 1956	$125-150	38
640-G	Bedford Army Truck, 1954	$250-300	-
641-G	1-Ton Army Truck, 1954	$125-150	38
642-G	RAF Refueller, 1957	$150-175	43
643-G	Army Water Tankers, 1958	$150-175	38
650-G	Light Tank, 1954	$175-200	-
651-G	Centurion Tank, 1954	$150-175	38
654-G	155 MM Gun, 1974	$75-100	87
656-G	Anti-Aircraft Gun, 1975	$75-100	92
660-G	Tank Transporter, 1956	$150-175	38
660-R	Mobile AA Gun & Crew, 1978	$75-100	-
661-G	Scammell Wrecker, 1957	$200-225	43
662-G	88 MM AA Gun & Crew, 1976	$75-100	-
665-G	Honest John Launcher, 1968	$225-250	51
666-G	Missile Erector, 1959	$350-400	51
667-G	Servicing Platform, 1960	$300-325	54
667-R	Armored Patrol Car, 1976	$75-100	92
668-G	Foden Army Truck, 1976	$75-100	92
669-G	US Army Jeep, 1956	$150-175	38
670-G	Daimler Armored Car, 1954	$150-175	38
671-G	Reconnaissance Car, 1954	$150-175	-
671-R	Mark 1 Corvette, 1976	$75-100	93
672-G	Army Jeep, 1954	$125-150	-
672-R	OSA Missile Boat, 1976	$100-125	93
673-G	Daimler Scout Car, 1954	$125-150	38
673-R	Submarine Chaser, 1977	$125-150	93
674-G	Austin Champ, 1954	$125-150	38
674-R	Coast Guard Amphibian, 1976	$125-150	93
675-G	Ford Staff Car, 1954	$200-250	38
675-R	Motor Patrol Boat, 1973	$100-125	93
676-G	Saracen, 1955	$250-300	-
676-R	Daimler Armored Car, 1972	$125-150	38,87
677-G	Command Vehicle, 1957	$125-150	43
677-R	Task Force Set, 1972	$125-150	104
678-G	Rescue Launch, 1976	$125-150	93
680-G	Ferret Scout Car, 1972	$75-100	87
681-G	DUKW Amphibian, 1972	$125-150	87
682-G	Alvis Stalwart, 1972	$125-150	87
683-G	Chieftain Tank, 1972	$125-150	87
686-G	Field Gun, 1957	$100-125	43
687-G	Field Gun Trailer, 1957	$100-125	43

687-R	Convoy Truck, 1977	$75-100	97	726-G	Messerschmitt 109E, 1972	$150-175	121
688-G	Light Artillery Tractor, 1957	$100-125	43	727-G	USAF Phantom, 1974	$250-300	124
689-G	Medium Artillery Tractor, 1957	$100-125	43	728-G	RAF Dominie, 1972	$175-200	122
690-G	Anti-Aircraft Gun, 1954	$125-150	-	729-G	Panavia MRCA, 1973	$125-150	-
690-R	Scorpion Tank, 1974	$125-150	92	730-G	Tempest II, 1954	$115-135	118
691-G	Field Gun, 1954	$125-150	-	730-R	Navy Phantom, 1973	$110-125	124
691-R	Striker, 1974	$125-150	92	731-G	Twin Engine Fighter, 1954	$115-135	118
692-G	Medium Gun, 1955	$125-150	43	731-R	SEPECAT Jaguar, 1973	$110-125	123
692-R	Leopard Tank, 1974	$125-150	-	732-G	Gloster Meteor, 1954	$115-135	118
693-G	Howitzer, 1958	$125-150	43	732-R	Bell Police Copter, 1972	$125-150	101
694-G	Tank Destroyer, 1975	$100-125	92	733-G	Shooting Star, 1954	$100-125	118
695-G	Howitzer & Tractor, 1962	$200-225	-	733-R	Luftwaffe Phantom, 1973	$175-200	-
696-G	Leopard AA Tank, 1975	$125-150	92	734-G	Supermarine Swift, 1955	$100-125	118
697-G	Field Gun Set, 1957	$175-200	-	734-R	F47 Thunderbolt, 1975	$125-150	-
698-G	Tank & Transporter, 1957	$250-300	-	735-G	Gloster Javelin, 1956	$100-125	118
699-G	Military Vehicles, 1955	$600-700	-	736-G	Hawker Hunter, 1955	$125-150	118
699-R	Leopard Recovery Tank, 1975	$125-150	92	736-R	Sea King Helicopter, 1973	$100-125	100
700-G	Seaplane, 1954	$125-150	111	737-G	RAC Lightning, 1959	$100-125	118
700-R	RAF Spitfire, 1979	$125-150	-	738-G	Sea Vixen, 1960	$100-125	118
702-G	DH Comet, 1954	$200-225	115	739-G	Mitsubishi Zero, 1976	$125-150	122
704-G	Avro York, 1954	$135-175	114	741-G	Spitfire II, 1976	$125-150	121
705-G	Vickers Viking, 1954	$125-150	115	744-G	Sea King Helicopter, 1976	$100-125	100
706-G	Vickers Viscount, 1956	$125-150	116	745-G	Bell Helicopter, 1978	$100-125	100
708-G	Vickers Viscount, 1957	$150-175	116	749-G	Avro Vulcan, 1955	$3000+	-
710-G	Beechcraft Bonanza, 1965	$125-150	120	750-G	Telephone Box, 1954	$50-75	-
712-G	US Army T42a, 1972	$75-100	120	751-G	Police Box, 1954	$50-75	-
715-G	Bristol Helicopter, 1956	$125-150	117	753-G	Controlled Crossing, 1962	$75-100	-
715-R	Beechcraft Baron, 1968	$100-125	120	754-G	Pavement Set, 1958	$75-100	-
716-G	Sikorsky Helicopter, 1957	$125-150	117	755-G	Lamp Standard, 1960	$50-75	126
717-G	Boeing 747 Lufthansa, 1970	$150-200	119	756-G	Lamp Standard, 1960	$50-75	126
718-G	Hawker Hurricane, 1972	$150-200	-	760-G	Pillar Box, 1954	$50-75	11
719-G	Supermarine Spitfire, 1969	$150-200	121	765-G	Road Hoarding, 1959	$175-200	127
721-G	Junkers Stuka, 1969	$150-200	121	766-G	Road Signs, Country A, 1959	$125-150	-
722-G	Hawker Harrier, 1970	$150-175	123	767-G	Road Signs, Country B, 1959	$125-150	-
723-G	HS125 Executive Jet, 1970	$150-175	122	768-G	Road Signs, Town A, 1959	$125-150	126
724-G	Sea King Helicopter, 1971	$125-150	100	769-G	Road Signs, Town B, 1959	$125-150	126
725-G	Royal Navy Phantom, 1972	$150-175	124	770-G	Road Signs Set, 1954	$150-175	-

Number	Name	Price	Qty	Number	Name	Price	Qty
771-G	International Road Signs, 1953	$150-175	127	810-R	Dodge Command Car, 1972	$200-225	87
772-G	British Road Signs, 1959	$175-200	-	811-F	Caravan Trailer, 1959	$125-150	55
773-G	4-Way Traffic Light, 1954	$75-100	-	812-F	One Wheel Trailer, 1965	$100-125	72
777-G	Belisha Beacon, 1954	$50-75	-	813-F	AMX 155 SP Gun, 1968	$100-125	80
778-G	Road Repair Warning, 1962	$125-150	-	814-F	Panhard AML, 1963	$175-200	61
780-G	Petrol Pump Set, 1954	$150-175	-	815-F	Panhard EBR Tank, 1959	$200-225	43
781-G	Esso Pumps, 1955	$125-150	-	815-R	Sinpar MP Car, 1969	$100-125	-
782-G	Shell Petrol Station, 1960	$150-175	-	816-F	Hotchkiss Jeep, 1959	$175-200	43
783-G	BP Petrol Station, 1960	$150-175	-	816-R	Berliet Rocket Truck, 1969	$200-225	-
784-G	Goods Train, 1972	$100-125	-	817-F	AMX Tank, 1959	$175-200	43
785-G	Service Station, 1960	$225-275	56	818-F	Berliet Army Truck, 1959	$200-225	43
786-G	Tire Rack, 1960	$100-125	54	819-F	ABS Howitzer, 1959	$125-150	43
788-G	Marrel Bucket, 1960	$100-125	-	820-F	Renault Army Ambulance, 1959	$175-200	43
794-G	Loading Ramp, 1955	$35-50	36	821-F	MB Covered Unimog, 1960	$175-200	61
796-G	Healey Boat & Trailer, 1960	$135-150	55	822-F	M3 Halftrack, 1960	$200-225	61
797-G	Healey Sports Boat, 1960	$75-100	55	823-F	Field Kitchen, 1962	$200-225	61
798-G	Express Train, 1954	$200-225	126	823-R	GMC Tank Truck, 1969	$200-225	-
800-F	Mystere Fighter, 1959	$150-175	118	824-F	Berliet Gazelle, 1963	$200-225	61
800-R	Renault Sinpar, 1974	$125-150	87	825-F	DUKW Amphibian, 1963	$200-225	61
801-F	Vautour Fighter, 1959	$150-175	118	826-F	Berliet Wrecker, 1965	$200-225	61
801-G	USS Enterprise, 1980	$75-100	-	827-F	Panhard EBR Tank, 1964	$150-175	61
801-R	AMX Tank, 1973	$75-100	87	828-F	Jeep with Missiles, 1964	$150-175	61
802-F	Sikorsky Helicopter, 1959	$175-200	117	829-F	Jeep with Gun, 1964	$150-175	61
802-G	Klingon Cruiser, 1980	$75-100	-	830-F	Richier Roller, 1959	$250-300	46
802-R	155 Howitzer, 1974	$75-110	-	870-F	Ocean Liner "France", 1962	$300-350	93
803-F	Vickers Viscount, 1959	$175-200	-	881-F	Circus Truck & Trailer, 1969	$1200+	-
803-G	USS Enterprise, 1980	$75-100	102	882-F	Peugeot & Caravan, 1969	$700+	-
803-R	Unic SNCF Semi, 1967	$200-225	69	883-F	Bridgelaying Tank, 1964	$500-600	61
804-F	Noratlas, 1959	$200-250	115	884-F	Pontoon Bridge Truck, 1961	$600-700	56
804-G	Klingon Cruiser, 1980	$75-100	102	885-F	Blaw-Knox Bulldozer, 1959	$250-300	-
804-R	MB Unimog Truck, 1973	$150-175	-	885-R	Saviem Pipe Truck, 1966	$350-375	67
805-F	Unic Multibucket, 1966	$175-200	74	886-F	Richier Road Grader, 1960	$250-300	56
806-F	Berliet Army Wrecker, 1973	$200-225	-	887-F	Muir Hill Dump Truck, 1959	$225-250	-
807-F	Renault Army Ambulance, 1973	$150-175	87	887-R	Unic BP Tanker, 1963	$325-350	66
808-F	GMC Sahara Wrecker, 1972	$275-300	87	888-F	Berliet Saharien, 1966	$350-375	56
809-F	GMC Troop Transport, 1970	$275-300	81	888-F	Berliet Languedocienne	$400-450	-
810-F	Covered Trailer, 1959	$125-150	42	889-F	Coles Mobile Crane, 1959	$275-300	-

889-R	Berliet Paris Bus, 1965	$225-250	-		934-G	Leyland Octopus Open, 1956	$500-600	46
889u-F	Berliet Urban Bus, 1965	$225-250	73		935-G	Octopus with Chains, 1964	$800-900	46
890-F	Tank Transporter, 1959	$250-275	61		936-G	Leyland Test Chassis, 1965	$175-200	66
891-F	Caravelle Airliner, 1959	$300-350	116		940-G	Mercedes-Benz Truck, 1977	$125-150	98
892-F	Lockheed Constellation, 1959	$350-400	119		941-G	Foden Mobilgas Tanker, 1954	$375-400	33
893-F	Unic Pipe Truck, 1959	$375-400	54		942-G	Foden Regent Tanker, 1955	$400-450	36
894-F	Unic Auto Transporter, 1959	$325-350	50		943-G	Leyland Esso Tanker, 1957	$375-400	46
895-F	Unic Multibucket, 1959	$200-225	50		944-G	Leyland Shell-BP Tanker, 1963	$500-600	46
896-F	Willeme Covered Semi, 1959	$275-300	46		945-G	AEC Esso Tanker, 1966	$150-175	74
897-F	Willeme Lumber Truck, 1959	$325-350	46		945-G	AEC Lucas Tanker, 1977	$200-225	98
898-F	Berliet Transf. Carrier, 1961	$375-400	56		948-G	McLean Semi, 1961	$350-375	57
899-F	Delahaye Ladder Truck, 1959	$375-400	37		949-G	Wayne School Bus, 1961	$350-375	60
900-G	Building Site Set, 1964	$1200+	-		950-G	Foden Artic, Tanker, 1978	$150-175	98
901-F	Foden 8 Wheel Truck, 1955	$350-400	33		951-G	Truck Trailer, 1954	$75-100	21
902-G	Foden Flat Truck, 1955	$350-400	33		952-G	Bedford Vega Coach, 1964	$150-175	68
903-G	Foden with Tailboard, 1955	$500-600	33		953-G	Continental Coach, 1963	$400-450	60
905-G	Foden with Chains, 1955	$400-425	33		954-G	Fire Station, 1961	$350-400	-
908-G	Mighty Antar, 1962	$350-375	56		954-R	Bedford Vega Coach, 1972	$125-150	68
911-G	Guy Open Truck, 1954	$400-450	-		955-G	Commer Fire Engine, 1955	$150-175	37
912-G	Guy Flat Truck, 1954	$400-450	-		956-G	Bedford Fire Escape, 1958	$150-175	50
913-G	Guy with Tailboard, 1954	$500-600	-		956-R	Berliet Fire Escape, 1969	$200-225	80
914-G	AEC Coverd Truck, 1967	$150-175	67		957-G	Fire Service Set, 1959	$475-500	-
915-G	AEC Flat Truck, 1973	$125-150	89		958-G	Guy Snowplow Truck, 1961	$275-300	57
917-G	Guy Spratts Van, 1954	$500-600	28		959-G	Foden Dumper/Plow, 1962	$250-275	57
917-R	MB Truck & Trailer, 1968	$300-350	96		960-G	Albion Concrete Mixer, 1960	$150-175	54
918-G	Guy Ever Ready Van, 1955	$550-600	28		961-G	Blaw-Knox Bulldozer, 1955	$125-150	23
919-G	Guy Golden Shred Van, 1957	$1200+	28		961-R	Vega PTT Coach, 1973	$300-325	68
920-G	Guy Heinz Van, 1959	$1700+	36		962-G	Muir Hill Dumper, 1955	$125-150	23
921-G	Bedford Articulated, 1954	$200-225	21		963-G	Blaw-Knox Tractor, 1955	$125-150	23
922-G	Big Bedford, 1954	$250-300	-		963-R	Road Grader, 1973	$100-125	98
923-G	Bedford Heinz Van, 1955	$600+	36		964-G	Elevator Loader, 1952	$125-150	39
924-G	Aveling Barford Dumper, 1972	$125-150	89		965-G	Euclid Dumper, 1955/56	$150-175	39
925-G	Leyland Dumper, 1965	$200-225	67		966-G	Marrel MultiBucket Unit, 1960	$125-150	-
930-G	Bedford Jetka Van, 1960	$300-350	54		967-G	BBC TV Mobile Cont. Rm, 1958	$300-325	51
931-G	Leyland Open Truck, 1954	$200-250	-		967-G	Muir-Hill Loader-Trench/1973	$100-125	89
932-G	Leyland with Tailboard, 1954	$200-250	-		968-G	BBC TV Roving Eye Veh., 1959	$300-325	51
933-G	Leyland Cement Truck, 1954	$250-275	-		969-G	BBC TV Ext. Mast Veh., 1959	$300-325	51

970-G	Jones Crane, 1967	$100-125	67
971-G	Coles Crane, 1955	$150-175	28
972-G	Coles Crane Truck, 1955	$150-175	39
973-G	Goods Yard Crane, 1955	$150-175	-
973-R	Eaton Tractor Shovel, 1971	$100-125	86
974-G	AEC Car Transporter, 1969	$125-150	82
975-G	Bucyrus Excavator, 1963	$450-500	67
976-G	Michigan Dozer, 1967	$200-250	96
977-G	Servicing Platform, 1960	$250-300	54
977-R	Shovel Dozer, 1973	$150-175	90
978-G	Bedford Refuse Wagon, 1964	$150-175	67
979-G	Race Horse Van, 1961	$500-600	36
980-G	Horse Box, 1955	$325-350	36
980-R	Coles Hydra Crane, 1972	$150-200	89
981-G	BR Horse Box, 1955	$275-300	36
982-G	Pullmore Car Transport, 1954	$250-300	36
983-G	Car Carrier & Trailer, 1958	$550-600	-
984-G	Car Carrier, 1958	$425-450	50
984-R	Atlas Digger, 1974	$150-175	90
985-G	Car Carrier Trailer, 1958	$150-175	50
986-G	Mighty Antar Loader, 1956	$400-450	54
987-G	ABC TV Control Room, 1962	$400-450	51
988-G	ABC TV Transmitter, 1962	$400-450	51
989-G	Car Transporter, 1963	$1500+	50
990-G	Car Transporter Set, 1956	$2000+	-
991-G	AEC Shell Tanker, 1955	$250-300	-
992-G	Avrp Vulcan Bomber, 1955	$3000+	-
994-G	Loading Ramp, 1955	$50-75	36
997-G	Caravelle Airliner, 1962	$300-350	116
998-G	Bristol Brittania, 1959	$300-350	119
999-G	De Havilland Comet, 1956	$325-350	115
1001-G	Station Staff, 1952	$150-200	-
1003-G	Passengers, 1952	$150-200	-
1400-F	Peugeot 404 Taxi, 1967	$125-150	77
1401-F	Alfa Romeo 1600, 1967	$125-150	77
1401-R	Citroen 2CV-6, 1981	$100-125	-
1402-F	Ford Galaxie, 1967	$150-175	77

1402-R	Citroen Visa, 1981	$75-100	94
1403-F	Matra M530, 1967	$75-100	77
1403-R	Fiat Ritmo/Strada, 1981	$75-100	-
1404-F	Citroen TV Car, 1968	$200-225	77
1404-R	BMW 530, 1981	$100-125	94
1405-F	Opel Rekord Coupe, 1968	$75-100	77
1405-R	Alfa Romeo GTV, 1981	$80-90	94
1406-F	Renault Sinpar, 1968	$75-100	80
1406-R	Peugeot 504TI, 1981	$75-100	-
1407-S	Simca 1100, 1974	$75-1090	77,95
1407-F	Simca 1100, 1968	$100-125	77,95
1408-F	Honda Coupe, 1969	$150-175	77
1409-F	Chrysler 180, 1970	$100-125	78
1410-F	Moskvitch, 1968	$100-125	77
1411-F	Alpine A310, 1968	$100-125	78
1412-F	Jeep Wrecker, 1968	$125-150	78
1413-S	Citroen Dyane, 1977	$75-100	77,78
1413-F	Citroen Dyane, 1968	$100-125	77,78
1414-F	Renault R8 Gordini, 1968	$100-125	77
1415-S	Peugeot 504, 1974	$75-100	77,95
1415-F	Peugeot 504, 1969	$100-125	77,95
1416-S	Renault R6, 1974	$75-100	77
1416-F	Renault R6, 1969	$100-125	77
1417-F	Matra Formula I, 1969	$100-125	78
1419-F	Ford Thunderbird, 1969	$150-175	77
1420-F	Opel Commodore, 1970	$100-125	78
1421-F	Opel 1900 GT, 1969	$100-125	78
1422-F	Ferrari Formula I, 1969	$125-150	78
1423-F	Peugeot 504 Cabrio, 1969	$200-225	78
1424-S	Renault R12TL, 1977	$75-100	-
1424-F	Renault R12, 1969	$100-125	78,95
1424g-S	Renault R12 Gordini, 1974	$75-100	78
1424g-F	Renault R12 Gordini, 1971	$100-125	78
1425-F	Matra 630, 1969	$125-150	79
1426-F	Alfa Romeo Carabo, 1969	$100-125	78
1428-S	Peugeot 304, 1974	$75-100	78
1428-F	Peugeot 304, 1969	$150-175	78

1429-F	Peugeot 404 Police, 1970	$150-175	77
1430-F	Fiat Abarth 2000, 1970	$75-100	84
1432-F	Ferraro 312P, 1970	$75-100	84
1433-F	Surtees TS5, 1971	$75-100	78
1435-F	Citroen Presidentielle, 1970	$500-600	101
1450-S	Simca 1100 Police, 1977	$100-125	95
1451-S	Renault 17TS, 1977	$100-125	95
1452-S	Peugeot 504, 1977	$175-200	95
1453-S	Renault R6, 1977	$100-125	95
1454-S	Matra Bagheera, 1978	$75-100	95
1455-S	Citroen Pallas, 1978	$75-100	95
1539-S	VW Scirocco, 1980	$75-100	95
1540-S	Renault R4, 1980	$75-100	95
1541-S	Ford Fiesta, 1981	$75-100	95
1542-S	Chrysler 1308, 1981	$75-100	95
1543-S	Opel Ascona, 1980	$75-100	95
2162-G	Ford Capri, 1973	$75-100	-
2214-G	Ford Capri Rally, 1974	$75-100	-
2253-G	Ford Capri Police, 1974	$75-100	-
1000-1050	Kits, 1971-1975	$100-125	-

Hong Kong Dinky Toys (130-133)

12-H	Hong Kong Collector Case	$500+	-
10-33-H	Hong Kong cars, 1968, each	$40-50	130,131
94-99-H	Heavy Equipment, 1968, each	$40-50	132
101-130-H	Hong Kong models, 1980, each	$40-50	133

Dinky Toys Made in Holland (60-61)

| 57,60-61-H | Racing Cars, 1968, each | $150-175 | 130,131 |